RICHARDSO

MONITOR OF FREE-MASONRY;

BEING A

PRACTICAL GUIDE TO THE CEREMONIES

IN

ALL THE DEGREES

CONFERRED IN

MASONIC LODGES, CHAPTERS, ENCAMPMENTS, &c.

EXPLAINING THE

SIGNS, TOKENS AND GRIPS,

AND GIVING ALL THE

WORDS, PASS-WORDS, SACRED WORDS, OATHS,

AND

HIEROGLYPHICS USED BY MASONS.

THE INEFFABLE AND HISTORICAL DEGREES

ARE ALSO GIVEN IN FULL.

BY JABEZ RICHARDSON, A. M.

NEW YORK:

PUBLISHED BY LAWRENCE FITZGERALD,

No. 18 ANN STREET.

INDEX TO CONTENTS.

ENTERED ACCORDING TO ACT OF CONGRESS in the year 1860 by
BENJAMIN H. DAY, in the Clerk's Office of the United States District
Court for the Southern District of New York.

AUTHOR'S PREFACE.

MORE than thirty-five years have passed since WILLIAM MORGAN wrote his famous book revealing the mysteries of modern Free Masonry, and giving to the outside world a particular description of the ceremonies observed in the Lodges of the first six or seven degrees. The bare rumor that such a book was to be published created much astonishment and indignation among the Masonic fraternity of Western New York, and particularly those who had associated with Morgan in the meetings of the Craft. They soon ascertained the rumor to be true, and that Col. David C. Miller, the publisher of a newspaper in Batavia, was in fact then engaged in printing the book. Great efforts were immediately made by a large number of Free Masons to stop its publication—·first by arresting Morgan for debt—then by a complaint against him for larceny, during the prosecution of which his apartments were searched—and lastly by kidnapping the unfortunate man, taking him forcibly from the jail at Canandaigua, where he was confined on some pretence, carrying him in a close carriage to Fort Niagara, (then unoccupied,) and there murdering him in cold blood. These events occurred in September, 1826, but the Masonic brethren did not succeed in suppressing the book written by Morgan. Part of it had already been put to press by Col. Miller, and the remainder of the manuscript was so effectually concealed by the wife of the murdered man that it was not discovered by the Masons who searched his premises. This and other outrages, among which was the firing of Miller's printing office, alarmed the citizens of the whole western section of the State. Several arrests of supposed kidnappers took place, and the persons arrested were brought to trial. Col. Edward Sawyer, and Nicholas G. Chesebro, (both of Canandaigua,) Loton Lawson, John Sheldon, and Eli Bruce, Sheriff of Niagara County, were each found guilty of participation in the abduction of Morgan, and were sentenced to various terms of imprisonment. But still the murderers remained undetected.

Meantime the whole book had been published, and its contents had made public the somewhat ferocious oaths of the Free Masons. An immense excitement was created all over the country, which lasted many years. Free Masonry became unpopular, and numerous worthy and distinguished persons, including a great number of ministers of the Gospel, withdrew from the Society. Lodges and Chapters were disbanded, while their officers and members publicly renounced all future connection with the Masonic Order. Indeed, so great was the prejudice against Masons, caused by that inherent love of justice peculiar to American citizens, that a powerful political party was formed in the State of New York which threatened at one time to overcome or absorb all other party organizations. The murderers of Morgan (although known) were never prosecuted, and this fact kept alive the anti-Masonic excitement until the party almost became National, for it extended throughout the New England and Middle States, and killed off a score or two of prominent public men. But there must be an end to all things; and in the fulness of time the prejudice against Free Masonry died away. Then it was discovered that the Masons who kidnapped William Morgan were, after all, simply ruffians, and not by any means representatives of the main body of the Masonic fraternity.

And why should Masons, more than any other respectable class, be suspected of aiding the perpetration of a murder, or any other crime against society? Because, says the uninitiated reader, they bind their members by fearful and sanguinary oaths, and keep everything connected with their Lodges in such profound secrecy. This is a very natural conclusion for the unthinking multitude, but will scarcely pass current among those who possess any degree of reflection, and comprehend the promptings which govern the actions of men. These last would naturally inquire why should mankind as Masons differ from mankind as husbands, fathers, devoted friends or indeed as civilized beings?

Since the issue of Morgan's book, no other entirely original work has been published on the subject, though several more elaborate volumes have appeared, in which the writers have attempted to give in detail some of the higher degrees. But all have failed to make their revelations fully intelligible, either because they did not understand the subject, or else were careless or incompetent.

In the following pages I have endeavored to give exact descriptions of the Masonic ceremonies as they are (or should be) performed in the Lodges, Chapters, &c., of each degree. The information is intended, not only for the public at large who have a curiosity to fathom the wonderful secrets of Free Masonry, but for newly formed Masonic Societies, who desire a printed guide to facilitate their work.

Comparatively few persons among the multitudes who join the Masonic Lodges, extend their knowledge of the Craft beyond the Royal Arch Degree; and to such as have not been advanced, this work will be read with much interest. By the aid of it they may become familiar with the higher degrees of modern Masonry—with the Ineffable Degrees—and with those curious and enthusiastic Historical and Philosophical Degrees which are so mixed up with Jewish history and Christian Knight-errantry as to puzzle the matter-of-fact student of the present day.

And now a few words with Masonic friends as to my object in retiring from the Society and publishing this book. I am no enemy of Masonry; and I think that if it were possible to keep unworthy men out of our Lodges, it would be an unexceptionable institution. Considering that this has not been, and probably cannot be done, I am content to leave it. And as I have always looked upon our secret ceremonies and oaths as but the relics of a past age, and continued merely to preserve the ostensible antiquity of the institution rather than to bind our consciences, I do not hesitate to make them public.

The Society of Free Masons was formed at an early age of the world, when there were no laws to protect the weak against the strong. The oaths and obligations were then undoubtedly binding, not only for the protection of the members, but for the preservation of the very imperfect arts and sciences of that period. To suppose these oaths mean anything now is simply absurd. Mankind outside a Masonic Lodge does not care a straw what takes place within that secret conclave, except as a matter of curiosity. It is partly to gratify this spirit of inquisitiveness that I have written this book, and partly to give information to Free Masons themselves. More than half the persons who join Masonic Lodges do not understand anything of the principles of the Order. They go through certain ceremonies, pay their fees, and then forget it all in a short time. By having an authentic detail of the proceedings to read over at their leisure, they may become Masons in reality.

JABEZ RICHARDSON.

RICHARDSON'S

MONITOR OF FREE-MASONRY

FIRST DEGREE.

A LODGE OF ENTERED APPRENTICES.

IN opening a Lodge of Entered Apprentices, it is necessary that at least six Apprentices should be present, and one Past Master. They can only act under a charter or warrant from the Grand Lodge. The room in which they assemble should represent the ground floor of King Solomon's Temple. The fixtures of the room, and the seats of the officers are as in Engraving on page 6.

On taking his seat to open the Lodge, the Master gives one rap with his gavel, and says: "Brethren, I am about to open a Lodge of Entered Apprentices, for the dispatch of business, and I will thank you for your attention and assistance."

Master to the Junior Warden—Brother Junior, are they all Entered Apprentice Masons in the South?

Junior Warden—They are, Worshipful.

Master to the Senior Warden—Brother Senior, are they all Entered Apprentice Masons in the West?

Senior Warden—They are, Worshipful.

The Master then declares, "They are, also, in the East," and at the same time he gives one rap with his gavel, which calls up the Junior Deacon, who, as he rises, gives a sign by opening his left hand and placing the open fingers of the right hand on the palm of it. The Master then says:

Brother Junior Deacon, the first care of congregated Masons?

Junior Deacon—To see the Lodge tyled, Worshipful.

Master—Perform your duty, and inform the Tyler that we are about to open a Lodge of Entered Apprentices for the dispatch of business, and direct him to tyle accordingly.

The Junior Deacon then goes to the door of the Lodge and stations the Tyler outside of it with a drawn sword in his hand, at the same time whispering the words of the Master that he is about to open a Lodge, &c. He then closes the door, and gives three distinct knocks on the inside, which are answered by three knocks of the Tyler on the outside. The Junior Deacon then again gives one knock, (which is answered by a knock from the Tyler,) when he returns to his station and says: "The door is tyled, Worshipful," at the same time giving the due-guard, (explained hereafter,) which is never omitted when the Master is addressed.

Master—By whom is it tyled?

Junior Deacon—By a brother of this degree without the door, armed with the proper implements of his office.

Master—His duty there?

Junior Deacon—To keep off all cowans and cave-dropers; to see that none pass or re-pass except such as are duly qualified, and have permission from the Master. [Permission of the Chair, is sometimes said.]

Master—Let us now be clothed, brethren. [Here the members present put on their aprons and jewels, and resume their seats.]

The Worshipful Master then gives one rap with his gavel and addresses the Junior Deacon as follows:

Master—Brother Junior Deacon, your place in the Lodge?

Junior Deacon—At the right hand of the Senior Warden in the West.

Master—Your business there, Brother Junior?

Junior Deacon—To wait on the Worshipful Master and Wardens, act as their proxy in the active duties of the Lodge, and take charge of the door.

Master—The Senior Deacon's place in the Lodge?

Junior Deacon—At the right hand of the Worshipful Master in the east. [The Master, while asking the last question, gives two raps, which calls up all the subordinate officers.]

Master (to Senior Deacon)—Your duty there, Brother Senior?

Senior Deacon—To wait on the Worshipful Master and Wardens, act as their proxy in the active duties of the Lodge, attend to the preparation and introduction of candidates, and welcome and clothe all visiting brethren, [i. e. furnish them with an apron.]

Master (to Senior Deacon)—The Secretary's place in the Lodge, brother Senior?

Senior Deacon—At the left hand of the Worshipful Master in the east.

Master (to Secretary)—Your duty there, Brother Secretary?

Secretary—The better to observe the Worshipful Master's will and pleasure, record the proceedings of the Lodge; transmit a copy of the same to the Grand Lodge, if required; receive all moneys and money bills from the hands of the brethren, pay them over to the Treasurer, and take receipts for the same.

Master (to Secretary)—The Treasurer's place in the Lodge?

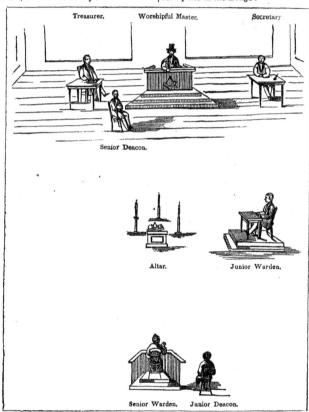

LODGE OF ENTERED APPRENTICES, FELLOW CRAFTS, OR MASTER MASONS.

Secretary—At the right hand of the Worshipful Master.

Master (to Treasurer)—Your duty there, Brother Treasurer?

Treasurer—Duly to observe the Worshipful Master's will and pleasure; receive all moneys and money bills from the hands of the Secretary; keep a just and true account of the same; pay them out by order of the Worshipful Master and consent of the brethren.

Master (to Treasurer)—The Junior Warden's place in the Lodge, Brother Treasurer?

Treasurer—In the south, Worshipful.

Master (to Junior Warden)—Your business there, Brother Junior?

Junior Warden—As the sun in the south at high meridian is the beauty and glory of the day, so stands the Junior Warden in the south, the better to observe the time; call the crafts from labor to refreshment; superintend them during the hours thereof; see that none convert the hours of refreshment into that of intemperance or excess; and call them on again in due season, that the Worshipful Master may have honor, and they profit and pleasure thereby.

Master (to Junior Warden)—The Senior Warden's place in the Lodge?

Junior Warden—In the west, Worshipful.

Master (to Senior Warden)—Your duty there, Brother Senior?

Senior Warden—As the sun sets in the west to close the day, so stands the Senior Warden in the west, to assist the Worshipful Master in opening his Lodge; take care of the jewels and implements; see that none be lost; pay the craft their wages, if any be due; and see that none go away dissatisfied.

Master (to Senior Warden)—The Master's place in the Lodge?

Sen. Warden—In the east, Worshipful.

Master—His duty there?

Senior Warden—As the sun rises in the east to open and adorn the day, so presides the Worshipful Master in the east to open and adorn his Lodge; set his crafts to work with good and wholesome instruction; or cause the same to be done.

Master (giving three raps with his gavel)—In like manner, so do I, strictly forbidding all profane language, or any disorderly conduct whereby peace and harmony may be interrupted. It is my will and pleasure that a Lodge of Entered Apprentice Masons be opened in this place for the dispatch of business. Brother Senior Warden, please communicate the same to the Junior Warden, that the brethren may have timely notice thereof.

The Senior Warden then delivers the Master's order to the Junior Warden, who gives three raps with his gavel, and says: "Brethren, it is our Worshipful Master's order that a Lodge of Entered Apprentice Masons be opened in this place for the dispatch of business. You will take due notice thereof, and govern yourselves accordingly."

Master—Attend to the signs, brethren.

Right Angles, or, the Sign of Distress.   Horizontals, or, Due-Guard.

The signs of this degree are now given by the Master and brethren, viz.: right-angles, horizontals, and perpendiculars. The right-angles are shown by holding open the left hand and crossing the palm of it with the open palm of the right hand at right-angles—the hands to be held out about twelve inches from the body. This is called the first sign of a Mason. It is the sign of distress in this degree. To draw a horizontal, raise your open right hand and arm to your neck, and holding the palm downwards, and the thumb partly under the hand, but parallel with the fingers, draw the hand from the left to the right shoulder by a quick motion. While you are doing this let the left hand drop perpendicularly by your side, the palm backward. This to show the perpendicular sign. The horizontal is called the due-guard.

The Master, the Senior Warden and the Junior Warden now, each of them, gives one rap with the gavel, when the Master says: "I now declare this Lodge of Entered Apprentice Masons duly opened for the dispatch of business." The Master then reads from a book the following: Behold how good and how pleasant it is for brethren to dwell together in unity! It is like the precious ointment upon the head that ran down upon the beard, even Aaron's beard, that went down to the skirts of his garments; as the dew of Hermon, and as the dew that descended upon the mountain of Zion, for there the Lord commanded the blessing, evermore. Amen. So mote it be.

After the opening prayer, or exercise, the Worshipful Master gives one rap with his gavel, when all the members take seats.

Master—Brother Senior Warden, have you anything for the good of our Craft?

Senior Warden—Nothing. Worshipful.

The same question is then put to the Junior Warden as to the south, with the same reply, when the Worshipful Master asks if any brother present has anything to lay before the Lodge. Some brother replies by proposing that the minutes of the last meeting be read.

Master—Brother Secretary, you will read the minutes.

The Secretary reads the name of the Lodge, time and manner of opening, names of officers present, and all the proceedings which took place, among which may have been proposed a new candidate for fellowship. If this is the case, the Master thus addresses the Lodge:

Master—Brethren, what is your pleasure on this proposition; how shall we dispose of it?

A Brother—I move the candidate be balloted for.

Master—If no objection is made, I shall now send round the balls, and we will proceed to ballot for John Smith to become a Mason and a member of this Lodge. Brother Senior Deacon, will you distribute them?

The Lodge now proceeds to ballot. One black ball will reject a candidate. The boxes may be passed three times, should a black ball appear. The Deacons are the proper persons to pass them; one of the boxes has black and white beans or balls in it, the other is empty; the one with the balls in it goes before, and furnishes each member with a black and a white ball; the empty box follows and receives them. There are two holes in the top of this box, with a small tube in each, one of which is black, and the other white, with a partition in the box. The members put both their balls into this box as their feelings may dictate. No one knows which is voted.

The Senior Deacon brings the box containing the ballots to the Worshipful Master, who, after looking into it, orders him to carry it to the Senior Warden, who looks at it and sends it to his Junior.

Master—How stands the ballots in the west, Brother Senior?

Senior Warden—Clear, Worshipful.

The same question is put to the Junior as to the south, who gives the same reply, when the Master declares the ballot to be clear, and that the candidate is duly elected a member of this Lodge. If one or more black balls appear among the white ones, it is announced that the candidate is rejected.

If the candidate be outside the Lodge, and ready for initiation, the Senior Deacon goes out to prepare him, while the usual business proceeds. It is conducted much the same as any Society business, if we except forms and ceremonies, such as saluting the Chair, &c.

The Master says: Does any brother present know of a brother in distress, or in difficulty?

In reply to this question, sick brothers are reported to the Lodge, as well as all cases where the charities of the Lodge are supposed to be needed, whether for a brother Mason, or for a deceased brother's family. The regular routine of business being over, the initiation of the new candidate proceeds.

INITIATING A NEW MEMBER.

The candidate (if present) having been conducted into a small preparation room adjoining the Lodge, he is there asked the following questions, and gives the following answers:

Senior Deacon to Candidate—Do you sincerely declare, upon your honor before these gentlemen, that, unbiassed by friends, uninfluenced by unworthy motives, you freely and voluntarily offer yourself a candidate for the mysteries of Masonry?

Candidate—I do.

Senior Deacon—Do you sincerely declare, upon your honor before these gentlemen, that you are prompted to solicit the privileges of Masonry by a favorable opinion conceived of the institution, a free desire of knowledge, and a sincere wish of being serviceable to your fellow creatures?

Candidate—I do.

Senior Deacon—Do you sincerely declare, upon your honor before these gentlemen, that you will cheerfully conform to all the ancient established usages and customs of the fraternity?

Candidate—I do.

The Senior Deacon now resigns the candidate to the Junior Deacon, or Conductor, and returns inside the Lodge, reporting to the Master that all is ready.

Master—Brethren, at the request of Mr. John Smith, he has been proposed and accepted in regular form as a member of this Lodge. I therefore recommend him as a proper candidate for the mysteries of Free Masonry, and worthy to partake of all the privileges of the fraternity.

While the Master is thus speaking inside the Lodge, the candidate is divested of his clothing, (shirt excepted,) and is made to put on a pair of red flannel drawers. He is then blindfolded, his left foot made bare, his right foot in a slipper, his left breast and arm naked, and a rope, called a cable-tow, put round his neck and left arm, (the rope is not put round the arm in some Lodges,) in which posture the candidate is conducted by the Junior Deacon to the door, where he is caused to give, or the Junior Deacon gives, three distinct knocks, which are answered by three from within ; the Junior Deacon gives one more, which is also answered by one from within. The door is then partly opened.

Senior Deacon—Who comes there ? Who comes there ? Who comes there ?

Junior Deacon—A poor blind candidate who has long been desirous of having and receiving a part of the rites and benefits of this worshipful Lodge, dedicated (some say erected) to God and held forth to the holy order of St. Johns, as all true fellows and brothers have done who have gone this way before him.

Senior Deacon—Is it of his own free will and accord he makes this request? Is he duly and truly prepared? worthy and well qualified ? and properly avouched for?

Junior Deacon—He possesses all these requisites.

Senior Deacon—By what further rights does he expect to receive this benefit ?

Junior Deacon—By being a man, free born, of lawful age, and under the tongue of good report.

The Senior Deacon then says—Since this is the case, you will wait till the Worshipful Master in the east is made acquainted with his request, and his answer returned.

The Senior Deacon repairs to the Master, when the same questions are asked and answers returned as at the door; after which, the Master says—Since he comes endowed with all these necessary qualifications, let him enter this worshipful Lodge in the name of the Lord, and take heed on what he enters.

The candidate then enters, the Senior Deacon at the same time pressing his naked left breast with the point of the compass.

Senior Deacon (to the candidate)—Did you feel anything ?

Candidate—I did.

Senior Deacon—What was it ?

Candidate—A torture.

The Senior Deacon then says—As this is a torture to your flesh, so may it ever be to your mind and conscience, if ever you should attempt to reveal the secrets of Masonry unlawfully.

The candidate is then conducted to the center of the Lodge, where he kneels, and the Senior Deacon kneels with him. The Master now gives three raps with his gavel, when all the brethren rise, and the Deacon pronounces the following prayer :

"Vouchsafe thine aid, Almighty Father of the universe, to this our present convention ; and grant that this candidate for Masonry may dedicate and devote his life to thy service, and become a true and faithful brother among us! Induc him with a competency of Thy divine wisdom, that by the secrets of our art he may be the better enabled to display the beauties of holiness, to the honor of Thy holy name. So mote it be. Amen !"

Master (putting his hand on the head of candidate)—In whom do you put your trust ?

Candidate—In God.

Master (taking him by the right hand) —Your trust being in God, your faith is well founded. Follow your leader and fear no danger.

The Senior Deacon then conducts the candidate three times regularly round the Lodge, and halts by the Junior Warden in the south, where the same questions are asked and answers returned as at the door. As the candidate and Conductor are passing round the room, the Master reads the following passage of Scripture, and takes the same time to read it, that they do to go round the Lodge room three times.

"Behold how good and how pleasant it is for brethren to dwell together in unity ! It is like the precious ointment upon the head, that ran down upon the beard, even Aaron's beard, that went down to the skirts of his garment : as the dew of Hermon, and as the dew that descended upon the mountains of Zion ;

10 RICHARDSON'S MONITOR OF FREE-MASONRY.

for there the Lord commanded the blessing, even life for ever more."

The candidate is then conducted to the Senior Warden in the west, where the same questions are asked and answers returned as before ; from thence he is conducted to the Worshipful Master in the east, who demands of him from whence he came, and whither he is traveling ?

Candidate answers—From the west, and traveling to the east.

Master—Why do you leave the west and travel to the east ?

Candidate—In search of light.

Master then says—Since the candidate is traveling in search of light, you will please conduct him back to the west from whence he came, and put him in the care of the Senior Warden, who will teach him how to approach the east, the place of light, by advancing upon one upright regular step, to the first step, his feet forming the right angle of an oblong square, his body erect at the altar before the Master, and place him in a proper position to take upon him the solemn oath or obligation of an Entered Apprentice Mason.

The Senior Warden receives the candidate, and leads him back to within about two paces of the altar in the center of the Lodge, there instructing him what to do, viz. : the candidate steps off one step with his left foot, and draws the heel of his right foot into the hollow thereof, making his two feet stand at right angles. He then steps off with his right foot. and kneels upon his left knee, in doing which the knees must each form a square. He places his left hand, with the palm up, under the Holy Bible, with square and compass upon it, that lays upon the altar, and his right hand on top of them. This is the position in which a candidate is placed when he takes upon him the oath or obligation of an Entered Apprentice Mason.

As soon as the candidate is placed in this position, the Worshipful Master approaches him, and says—Mr. Smith, you are now placed in a proper position to take upon you the solemn oath or obligation of an Entered Apprentice Mason, which I assure you is neither to affect your religion or your politics. If you are willing to take it, repeat your name and say after me :—" I, John Smith, of my own free will and accord, in presence of Almighty God, and this worshipful Lodge of Free and Accepted Masons, dedicated to God and held forth to the holy order of St. Johns, do hereby and hereon most solemnly and sincerely promise and swear, that I will always hail, ever conceal, and never reveal any part or parts, art or arts, point or points of the secrets, arts and mysteries of ancient Free Masonry, which I have received, am about to receive, or may hereafter be instructed in, to any person or persons in the known world, except it be a true and lawful brother Mason, or within the body of a just and lawfully constituted Lodge of such, and not unto him, nor unto them whom I shall hear so to be, but unto him and them only whom I shall find so to be, after strict trial and due examination or lawful information. Furthermore do I promise and swear, that I will not write, print, stamp, stain, hew, cut, carve, indent, paint, or engrave it on anything moveable or immoveable, under the whole canopy of heaven, whereby, or whereon the least letter, figure, character, mark, stain, shadow, or resemblance of the same may become legible or intelligible to myself or any other person in the known world, whereby the secrets of Masonry may be unlawfully obtained through my unworthiness. To all which I do most solemnly and sincerely promise and swear, without the least equivocation, mental reservation, or self evasion of mind in me whatever ; binding myself under no less penalty than to have my throat cut across, my tongue torn out by the roots, and my body buried in the rough sands of the sea at low water mark, where the tide ebbs and flows twice in twenty-four hours ; so help me God, and keep me steadfast in the due performance of the same."

Master—In token of your sincerity kiss the book. [Candidate kisses it.]

Master—Brother, to you the secrets of Masonry are about to be unveiled, and a brighter sun never shone luster on your eyes ; while prostrate before this sacred altar, do you not shudder at every crime ? have you not confidence in every virtue ? May these thoughts ever inspire you with the most noble sentiments ; may you ever feel that elevation of soul that shall scorn a dishonest act. Brother, what do you most desire ?

Candidate—Light.

Master (to brethren)—Brethren, stretch forth your hands and assist in bringing this new made brother from darkness to light.

The members having formed a circle round the candidate, the Master says— " And God said, let there be light, and there was light." At the same time, all the brethren clap their hands and stamp on the floor with their right foot as heavy as possible, the bandage dropping from the candidate's eyes at the same instant. This great and sudden transition from perfect darkness to a bright lighted room after the candidate has been so long blinded, and full of fearful apprehensions, often produces the most curious effects on him.

After the candidate is brought to light, the Master addresses him as follows :

Brother, on being brought to light, you first discover three great lights in Masonry by the assistance of three lesser ones ; they are thus explained : the three great lights in Masonry are the Holy Bible, Square and Compass. The Holy Bible is given to us as a rule and guide for our faith and practice ; the Square, to square our actions, and the Compass to keep us in due bounds with all mankind, but more especially with the brethren. The three lesser lights are three burning tapers, or candles placed on candlesticks, standing in a triangular group ; they represent the Sun, Moon, and Master of the Lodge, and are thus explained : As the sun rules the day and the moon governs the night, so ought the Worshipful Master with equal regularity to rule and govern his Lodge, or cause the same to be done.

The Worshipful Master now steps back a few paces, when the Senior Deacon addresses the candidate :

Senior Deacon—Brother, our Worshipful Master approaches you from the east under the step, sign and due-guard of an Entered Apprentice Mason ; observe his manner of giving them, and imitate him as near as you can, keeping your position. [Step off with left foot, and bring heel of right foot into the hollow thereof, to form a square. This is the first step in Masonry. Then give sign and dueguard, or right-angles and horizontals, as before explained.]

Master (advancing)—Brother, I now present you my right hand, in token of friendship and brotherly love. With it you will receive the true grip of an Entered Apprentice Mason. The name of

the grip is Boaz, and the Senior Deacon will instruct you in the precise manner it

is to be given, for it cannot be given truly except as he will explain to you.

Master—What is that ?

Candidate (instructed by Senior Deacon)—A grip.

Master—What grip ?

Candidate—The grip of an Entered Apprentice Mason.

Master—Has it a name ?

Candidate—It has.

Master—Will you give it to me ?

Candidate—I did not so receive it, neither can I so impart it.

Master—What will you do with it ?

Candidate—Letter it, or halve it.

Master—Halve it, and begin.

Candidate—You begin.

Master—Begin you.

Candidate—B-o

Master—A-z

Candidate—BOAZ.

Master—Right, Brother Boaz, I greet you. [Boaz is the name of the left hand pillar of the porch of King Solomon's Temple.] Arise, and salute the Junior and Senior Wardens as such, and convince them that you have been regularly initiated as an Entered Apprentice Mason, and have got the sign, grip and word.

The Master returns to his seat while the Wardens are examining the candidate, and gets a lamb-skin or white apron, presents it to the candidate, saying :

Master—Brother, I now present you with a lamb-skin or white apron ; it is an emblem of innocence, and the badge of a Mason ; it has been worn by kings, princes, and potentates of the earth, who have never been ashamed to wear it ; it is more honorable than the diadems of kings, or pearls of princesses, when worthily worn. It is more ancient than the Golden Fleece or Roman Eagle ; more honorable than the Star and Garter ; or any other order that can be conferred upon you at this, or any other time, except it be in the body of a just and fully constituted Lodge ; you will carry it to the Senior Warden in the West, who will teach you how to wear it as an Entered Apprentice Mason.

The candidate is conducted to the Senior Warden, who ties the apron on and turns up the flap instead of letting it fall down in front of the top of the apron. This is the way Entered Apprentice Masons wear, or ought to wear, their aprons until they are advanced. He is then conducted back to the Master, who again addresses him.

Master—Brother, as you are dressed, it is necessary you should have tools to work with ; I will now present you with the working tools of an Entered Apprentice Mason, which are the twenty-four inch guage and common gavel; they are thus explained: the twenty-four inch guage is an instrument made use of by operative masons to measure and lay out their work, but we as Free and Accepted Masons, make use of it for the more noble and glorious purpose of dividing our time. The twenty-four inches on the guage are emblematical of the twenty-four hours in the day, which we are taught to divide into three equal parts, whereby we find eight hours for the service of God, and a worthy distressed brother; eight hours for our usual vocations; and eight for refreshment and sleep. The common gavel is an instrument made use of by operative masons to break off the corners of rough stones, the better to fit them for the builder's use; but we, as Free and Accepted Masons, use it for the more noble and glorious purpose of divesting our hearts and consciences of all the vices and superfluities of life, thereby fitting our minds as living and lively stones, for that spiritual building, that house not made with hands, eternal in the Heavens. I also present you with a new name. It is CAUTION. It teaches you, as you are barely instructed in the rudiments of Masonry, that you should be cautious over all your words and actions, particularly when before the enemies of Masonry. I shall next present you with three precious jewels, which are a LISTENING EAR, a SILENT TONGUE, and a FAITHFUL HEART. A listening ear teaches you to listen to the instructions of the Worshipful Master; but more especially that you should listen to the cries of a worthy distressed brother. A silent tongue teaches you to be silent while in the Lodge, that the peace and harmony thereof may not be disturbed, but more especially, that you should be silent before the enemies of Masonry, that the craft may not be brought into disrepute by your imprudence. A faithful heart teaches you to be faithful to the instructions of the Worshipful Master at all times, but more especially, that you should be faithful and keep and conceal the secrets of Masonry, and those of a brother when given to you in charge as such, that they may remain as secure and inviolable in your breast as in his own before he confided them to you. I further present you with check words two; their names are TRUTH and UNION, and are thus explained: Truth is a divine attribute, and the foundation of every virtue. To be good and true, is the first lesson we are taught in Masonry. On this theme we contemplate, and by its dictates endeavor to regulate our conduct; hence, while influenced by this principle, hypocrisy and deceit are unknown among us; sincerity and plain dealing distinguish us, and the heart and tongue join in promoting each other's welfare, and rejoicing in each other's prosperity. Union, is that kind of friendship which ought to appear conspicuous in every Mason's conduct. It is so closely allied to the divine attribute, Truth, that he who enjoys the one, is seldom destitute of the other. Should interest, honor, prejudice, or human depravity, ever induce you to violate any part of the sacred trust we now repose in you, let these two important words, at the earliest insinuation, teach you to put on the check-line of truth, which will infallibly direct you to pursue that straight and narrow path which ends in the full enjoyment of the Grand Lodge above; where we shall all meet as Masons and members in the same family, in peace, harmony, and love; where all discord on account of politics, religion, or private opinion shall be unknown, and banished from within our walls.

Brother, it has been a custom from time immemorial to demand, or ask from a newly made brother something of a metallic kind, not so much on account of its intrinsic value, but that it may be deposited in the archives of the Lodge, as a memorial that you was herein made a Mason; a small trifle will be sufficient; anything of a metallic kind will do; if you have no money, anything of a metallic nature will be sufficient; even a button will do.

Candidate (who has no clothing but his red drawers)—I have nothing.

Master—Search yourself carefully.

Candidate searches, but nothing is found.

Master—Perhaps you can borrow a trifle.

Candidate tries to borrow, but no one will lend to him.

Master—Brother, let this ever be a striking lesson to you, and teach you, if you should ever see a friend, but more especially a brother, in a like pennyless situation, to contribute as liberally to his relief as his situation may require, and your abilities will admit, without material injury to yourself or family.

Master (to Senior Deacon)—Brother Senior, you will conduct him back from whence he came, and invest him of what he has been divested, and let him return for further instruction.

The candidate is now taken to the reception room, where he resumes his clothing, and when he returns into the Lodge, he is placed in the north-east corner as the youngest Apprentice, and is told by the Master that he there stands a correct upright Mason, and must ever conduct himself as such. The Master likewise delivers to him a charge, wherein he is cautioned never to reveal the secret do'ngs inside a Lodge of Free Masons, and never to recommend an unworthy person as a candidate for the honors that have then and there been conferred upon him.

The initiation of a candidate usually (though not necessarily) closes the business of a Lodge.

Master—If any brother has further business for this Lodge, he will present it now ; if not, the Secretary will read the minutes. [After the reading of the minutes, the Worshipful Master proceeds to close, and in doing so he is bound by his oath to give the whole or some part of the following.]

CLOSING LECTURE—FIRST SECTION.

Master (to Senior Warden)—From whence came you as an Entered Apprentice, Brother Senior ?

Senior Warden—From a Lodge of the most holy St. Johns, of Jerusalem.

Master—What came you here to do ?

Senior Warden—To improve myself in Masonry, and to learn to subdue my passions.

Master—Are you, then, a Mason ?

Senior Warden—I am so accepted among the brothers and fellows of the Craft.

Master—How do you prove to yourself that you are a Mason ?

Senior Warden—By being often tried, and never denied ; and I am ready and willing to be tried again.

Master—How shall I know you to be a Mason ?

Senior Warden—By signs, tokens, and the perfect points of entrance.

Master—What are signs ?

Senior Warden—Right angles, horizontals, and perpendiculars.

Master—Give me the sign ?

Senior Warden opens and holds out his left hand, and then lays the open right hand across it, as in the first figure on page 7.

Master—To what does it allude ?

Senior Warden—Right angles allude to the manner in which my hands were placed when I received the oath and obligation of an Entered Apprentice Mason, my left hand supporting the Holy Bible, square and compasses ; my right hand resting thereon. Horizontals and perpendiculars, [second figure on page 7.] allude to the penalty of the obligation, when I swore I would have my throat cut across from ear to ear, my tongue torn out by the roots, and my body buried in the rough sands of the sea, a cable's length from shore, at low water mark, where the tide ebbs and flows twice in twenty-four hours.

Master—Thank you, brother. What are tokens ?

Senior Warden—Certain friendly grips, whereby one brother can tell another in the dark as well as in the light.

[The Worshipful Master continues to question the Senior Warden as to the grips of an Entered Apprentice in nearly the same manner as a new candidate is questioned on his initiation, (see page 11,) and the replies are the same.]

Master—Where was you first prepared to be made a Mason ?

Senior Warden—In a room adjacent to the body of a just and lawfully constituted Lodge.

Master—How was you prepared ?

Senior Warden—I was divested of all metallic substances ; neither naked nor clothed, barefoot nor shod ; hood-winked ; with a cable-tow about my neck ; in which situation I was led to the door of the Lodge by one whom I afterwards found to be a brother.

Master—How did you know this to be a door, you being hood-winked ?

Senior Warden—By first meeting resistance, and afterwards gaining admittance.

Master—How gained you admission ?

Senior Warden—By three distinct knocks without, which were answered by three from within.

[The Master continues his inquiries as to the manner that the Senior Warden was initiated into the Lodge. The Warden answers each question by telling, in precise words, what was said and done to him on his initiation. Both the questions and answers are exactly those given on pages 9 to 11, where a candidate is going through his initiation, except that they are here spoken of in the past tense—the Warden replying that he did so and so on his first entrance into the Lodge, &c.]

Master—After your initiation into the mysteries of our Craft, what tools were you presented with ?

Senior Warden—The working tools of an Entered Apprentice Mason.

Master—What were they ?

Senior Warden—The twenty-four inch guage and common gavel.

Master—How were they explained?

Senior Warden—The twenty-four inch guage is an instrument made use of by operative masons to measure and lay out their work; but we, as Free and Accepted Masons, are taught to make use of it for the more noble and glorious purpose of dividing our time. The twenty-four inches on the guage are emblematical of the twenty-four hours of the day, which we are taught to divide into three equal parts; whereby we find eight hours for the service of God and a distressed worthy brother, eight for our usual vocation, and eight for refreshment and sleep. The common gavel is an instrument made use of by operative masons to break off the corners of rough stones, the better to fit them for the builder's use, but we, as Free and Accepted Masons, are taught to make use of it for the more noble and glorious purpose of divesting our hearts and consciences of all the vices and superfluities of life; thereby fitting our minds, as living stones, for that spiritual building, that house not made with hands, eternal in the Heavens.

Master—What was you next presented with?

Senior Warden—A new name.

Master—What was that?

Senior Warden—CAUTION.

Master—What does it teach?

Senior Warden—It teaches me, as I was barely instructed in the rudiments of Masonry, that I should be cautious over all my words and actions, especially when before its enemies.

Master—What was you next presented with?

Sen. Warden—Three precious jewels.

Master—What were they?

Senior Warden—A listening ear, a silent tongue, and a faithful heart.

Master—What do they teach?

Senior Warden—A listening ear teaches me to listen to the instructions of the Worshipful Master, but more especially to the cries of a worthy distressed brother. A silent tongue teaches me to be silent in the Lodge, that the peace and harmony thereof may not be disturbed; but more especially before the enemies of Masonry. A faithful heart, that I should be faithful, and keep and conceal the secrets of Masonry, and those of a brother, when delivered to me in charge, as such; that they may remain as secure and inviolable in my breast as in his own before they were communicated to me.

Master—What was next given to you?

Senior Warden—The Grand Master's check-word.

Master—What was that?

Senior Warden—TRUTH.

Master—How explained?

Senior Warden—Truth is a divine attribute, and the foundation of every virtue. To be good and true, are the first lessons we are taught in Masonry. On this theme we contemplate, and by its dictates endeavor to regulate our conduct; hence, while influenced by this principle, hypocrisy and deceit are unknown amongst us. Sincerity and plain-dealing distinguish us; and the heart and tongue join in promoting each other's welfare, and rejoicing in each other's prosperity.

Master—After your full initiation into the Lodge, what followed?

Senior Warden—I was conducted to the north-east corner thereof, and there caused to stand upright like a man, my feet forming a square; and I then received a solemn injunction, ever to walk and act uprightly before God and man—to submit conscientiously and truly to the Government of the country, and both in my private relations and outward demeanor to be particularly careful to avoid censure or reproach—never to reveal the secret doings inside a Lodge—and never to recommend an unworthy person as a candidate for the honors of our Craft.

SECOND SECTION.

Master—Brother, you have satisfied me as respects your initiation, but there remain many things yet unexplained: therefore I should like to know the REASON why you was divested of all metallic substance?

Senior Warden—Because Masonry regards no man on account of his worldly wealth or honors; it is therefore the internal and not the external qualifications that recommend a man to Masons.

Master—A second reason?

Senior Warden—There was neither the sound of an ax, hammer, or any other metal tool, heard at the building of King Solomon's temple.

Master—How could so stupendous a fabric be erected without the sound of ax, hammer, or any other metal tool?

Senior Warden—All the stones were hewed, squared, and numbered in the quarries where they were raised, all the timbers felled and prepared in the forests of Lebanon, and carried down to Joppa on floats, and taken from thence up to Jerusalem, and set up with wooden malls, prepared for that purpose: which, when completed, every part thereof fitted with that exact nicety, that it had more the resemblance of the handiworkmanship of the Supreme Architect of the universe, than of human hands.

Master—Why was you neither naked nor clothed?

Senior Warden—As I was an object of distress at that time, it was to remind me, if ever I saw a friend, more especially a brother in a like distressed situation, that I should contribute as liberally to his relief as his situation required, and my abilities would permit, without material injury to myself or family.

Master—Why was you neither barefoot nor shod?

Senior Warden—It was an ancient Israelitish custom adopted among Masons: and we read in the book of Ruth concerning their mode and manner of redeeming, and changing "for to confirm all things, a man plucked off his shoe and gave it to his neighbor, and this was testimony in Israel." This then, therefore, we do in confirmation of a token, and as a pledge of our fidelity; thereby signifying that we will renounce our own will in all things, and become obedient to the laws of our ancient institution.

Master—Why was you hood-winked?

Senior Warden—That my heart might be taught to conceal, before my eyes beheld the beauties of Masonry.

Master—A second reason?

Senior Warden—As I was in darkness at that time, it was to remind me that I should keep the whole world so respecting Masonry.

Master—Why had you a cable-tow about your neck?

Senior Warden—For two reasons. First, had I not submitted to the manner and mode of my initiation, that I might have been led out of the Lodge without seeing the form and beauties thereof. Secondly, had I recanted before being obligated, and made my escape, the people in the streets would have thought me either a crazy or a mad man; and some worthy Mason knowing my situation would have led me immediately back to the Lodge.

Master—Why did you give three distinct knocks at the door?

Senior Warden—To alarm the Lodge, and let the Worshipful Master, Wardens, and brethren know that a poor blind candidate prayed admission.

Master—What do these three distinct knocks allude to?

Senior Warden—A certain passage in Scripture wherein it says, "Ask and it shall be given, seek and ye shall find, knock and it shall be opened unto you."

Master—How did you apply this to your then case in Masonry?

Senior Warden—I asked the recommendations of a friend to become a Mason, I sought admission through his recommendations, and knocked, and the door of Masonry opened unto me.

Master—Why was you caused to enter on the point of some sharp instrument, pressing your naked left breast?

Senior Warden—As this was a torture to my flesh, so might the recollection of it ever be to my heart and conscience if ever I attempted to reveal the secrets of Masonry unlawfully.

Master—Why was you conducted to the center of the Lodge, and there caused to kneel for the benefit of a prayer?

Senior Warden—Before entering on this, or any other great and important undertaking, it is highly necessary to implore a blessing from Deity.

Master—Why was you asked in whom you put your trust?

Senior Warden—Agreeable to the laws of our ancient institution, no atheist could be made a Mason; it was therefore necessary that I should profess a belief in Deity; otherwise, no oath or obligation could bind me.

Master—Why did the Worshipful Master take you by the right hand, and bid you rise, follow your leader, and fear no danger?

Senior Warden—As I was in darkness at that time and could neither foresee nor avoid danger, it was to remind me that I was in the hands of an affectionate friend, in whose fidelity I might with safety confide.

Master—Why was you conducted three times regularly round the Lodge?

Senior Warden—That the Worshipful Master, Wardens, and brethren might see that I was duly and truly prepared.

Master—Why did you meet with those several obstructions on the way?

Senior Warden—This and every other Lodge is, or ought to be, a true representation of King Solomon's temple, which, when completed, had guards stationed at the east, west and south gates.

Master—Why had they guards stationed at those several gates?

Senior Warden—To prevent any from passing or repassing that was not duly qualified.

Master—Why did you kneel on your left knee, and not on your right, or both?

Senior Warden—The left side has ever been considered the weakest part of the body, it was therefore to remind me that the part I was now taking upon me was the weakest part of Masonry, it being that only of an Entered Apprentice.

Master—Why was your right hand placed on the Holy Bible, square and compass, and not your left, or both?

Senior Warden—The right hand has e'er been considered the seat of fidelity, and our ancient brethren worshiped a deity under the name of FIDES; which has been sometimes represented by two right hands joined together; at others, by two human figures holding each other by the right hand; the right hand, therefore, we use in this great and important undertaking, to signify in the strongest manner possible the sincerity of our intentions in the business we are engaged.

Master—Why did the Worshipful Master present you with a lamb-skin, or white apron?

Senior Warden—The lamb-skin has, in all ages, been deemed an emblem of innocence; he, therefore, who wears the lamb-skin, as a badge of a Mason, is thereby continually reminded of that purity of life and rectitude of conduct which is so essentially necessary to our gaining admission into the Celestial Lodge above, where the Supreme Architect of the Universe presides.

Master—Why did the Master make a demand of you, of something of a metallic nature?

Senior Warden—As I was in a poor and pennyless situation at that time, it was to remind me if ever I saw a friend, but more especially a brother, in the like poor and pennyless situation, that I should contribute as liberally to his relief as my abilities would admit and his situation required, without injuring myself or family.

Master—Why was you conducted to the north-east corner of the Lodge, and there caused to stand upright like a man, your feet forming a square, receiving at the same time a solemn charge ever to walk and act uprightly before God and man?

Senior Warden—The first stone in every Masonic edifice is, or ought to be, placed at the north-east corner, that being the place where an Entered Apprentice Mason receives his first instructions to build his future Masonic edifice upon.

THIRD SECTION.

Master—We have been saying a good deal about a Lodge. I want to know what constitutes a Lodge?

Senior Warden—A certain number of Free and Accepted Masons, duly as-sembled in a room, or place, with the Holy Bible, square and compass, and other Masonic implements, with a charter from the Grand Lodge empowering them to work.

Master—Where did our ancient brethren meet, before Lodges were erected?

Senior Warden—On the highest hills, and in the lowest vales.

Master—Why on the highest hills, and in the lowest vales?

Senior Warden—The better to guard against cowans and enemies, either ascending or descending, that the brethren might have timely notice of their approach to prevent being surprised.

Master—What is the form of your Lodge?

Senior Warden—An oblong square.

Master—How long?

Senior Warden—From east to west.

Master—How wide?

Senior Warden—Between north and south.

Master—How high?

Senior Warden—From the surface of the earth to the highest heaven.

Master—How deep?

Senior Warden—From the surface to the center.

Master—What supports your Lodge?

Senior Warden—Three large columns or pillars.

Master—What are their names?

Senior Warden—Wisdom, Strength, and Beauty.

Master—Why so?

Senior Warden—Because it is necessary there should be wisdom to contrive, strength to support, and beauty to adorn all great and important undertakings; but more especially this of ours.

Master—Has your Lodge any covering?

Senior Warden—It has; a clouded canopy, or starry-decked heaven, where all good Masons hope to arrive.

Master—How do they hope to arrive there?

Senior Warden—By the assistance of Jacob's ladder.

Master—How many principal round has it got?

Senior Warden—Three.

Master—What are their names?

Senior Warden—Faith, Hope, and Charity.

Master—What do they teach?

Senior Warden—Faith in God, hope in immortality, and charity to all mankind.

Master—Has your Lodge any furniture?

Senior Warden—It has; the Holy Bible, square, and compasses.

Master—To whom are they dedicated?

Senior Warden—The Bible to God, the square to the Master, and the compasses to the Craft.

Master—How explained?

Senior Warden—The Bible to God, it being the inestimable gift of God to man, for his instruction, to guide him through the rugged paths of life; the square to the Master, it being the proper emblem of his office; the compasses to the Craft, by a due attention to which, we are taught to limit our desires, curb our ambition, subdue our irregular appetites, and keep our passions and prejudices in due bounds with all mankind, but more especially with the brethren.

Master—Has your Lodge any ornaments?

Senior Warden—It has; the Mosaic, or chequered pavement; the indented tassel, that beautiful tasselated border which surrounds it; with the blazing star in the center.

Master—What do they represent?

Senior Warden—The Mosaic, or chequered pavement, represents this world, which, though chequered over with good and evil, yet brethren may walk together thereon and not stumble—the indented tassel, with the blazing star in the center, the manifold blessings and comforts with which we are surrounded in this life, but more especially those which we hope to enjoy hereafter—the blazing star, that prudence which ought to appear conspicuous in the conduct of every Mason, but more especially commemorative of the star which appeared in the east, to guide the wise men of Bethlehem, to proclaim the birth and presence of the Son of God.

Master—Has your Lodge any lights?

Senior Warden—It has three.

Master—How are they situated?

Senior Warden—East, west, and south.

Master—Has it none in the north?

Senior Warden—It has not.

Master—Why so?

Senior Warden—Because this and every other Lodge is, or ought to be, a true representation of King Solomon's temple, which was situated north of the ecliptic; the sun and moon, therefore, darting their rays from the south, no light was to be expected from the north; we, therefore, Masonically, term the north a place of darkness.

Master—Has your lodge any jewels?

Senior Warden—It has six; three movable, and three immovable.

Master—What are those three jewels that you call movable?

2

Senior Warden—The square, level, and plumb.

Master—What do they teach?

Senior Warden—The square, mortality; the level, equality; and the plumb, rectitude of life and conduct.

Master—What are the three immovable jewels?

Senior Warden—The rough ashlar, the perfect ashlar, and the trestle-board.

Master—What are they?

Senior Warden—The rough ashlar is a stone in its rough and natural state, the perfect ashlar is also a stone, made ready by the working tools of the Fellow Craft, to be adjusted in the building; and the trestle-board is for the master workman to draw his plans and designs upon.

Master—What do they represent?

Senior Warden—The rough ashlar represents man in his rude and imperfect state by nature; the perfect ashlar also represents man in the state of perfection, to which we all hope to arrive, by means of a virtuous life and education, our own endeavors and the blessing of God. In erecting our temporal building, we pursue the plans and designs laid down by the master workman on his trestle-board; but in erecting our spiritual building, we pursue the plans and designs laid down by the Supreme Geometrician of the Universe, in the book of Nature, which we, Masonically, term our spiritual trestle-board.

Master—Whom did you serve?

Senior Warden—My master.

Master—How long?

Senior Warden—Six days.

Master—What did you serve him with?

Senior Warden—Freedom, fervency, and zeal.

Master—What do they present?

Senior Warden—Chalk, charcoal, and clay.

Master—Why so?

Senior Warden—There is nothing freer than chalk, the slightest touch of which leaves a trace behind; nothing more fervent than charcoal, for when properly heated, it will cause the most obdurate metals to yield; nothing more zealous than clay, or earth, to bring forth.

Master—How is your Lodge situated?

Senior Warden—Due east and west.

Master—Why so?

Senior Warden—Because the sun rises in the east, and sets in the west.

Master—A second reason?

Senior Warden—Because the gospel was first preached in the east, and is spreading to the west.

Master—A third reason?

Senior Warden—The liberal arts and sciences began in the east, and are extending to the west.

Master—A fourth reason?

Senior Warden—Because all churches and chapels are, or should be so situated.

Master—Why are all churches and hapels so situated?

Senior Warden—Because King Solomon's temple was so situated.

Master—Why was King Solomon's temple so situated?

Senior Warden—Because Moses, after conducting the children of Israel through the Red Sea, by divine command, erected a tabernacle to God, and placed it due east and west, which was to commemorate, to the latest posterity, that miraculous east wind that wrought their mighty deliverance; and this was an exact model of Solomon's temple. Since that time, every well regulated and governed Lodge is, or ought to be so situated.

Master—To whom did our ancient brethren dedicate their Lodges?

Senior Warden—To King Solomon.

Master—Why so?

Senior Warden—Because King Solomon was our most ancient Grand Master.

Master—To whom do modern Masons dedicate their Lodges?

Senior Warden—To St. John the Baptist and St. John the Evangelist.

Master—Why so?

Senior Warden—Because they were the two most eminent Christian patrons of Masonry; and since their time, in every well regulated and governed Lodge, there has been a certain point within the circle, which circle is bounded on the east and west by two perpendicular parallel lines, representing the anniversary of St. John the Baptist, and St. John the Evangelist, who were perfect parallels, as well in Masonry as Christianity; on the vertex of which rests the book of the Holy Scriptures, supporting Jacob's ladder, which is said to reach the watery clouds; and in passing round this circle, we naturally touch on both these perpendicular parallel lines, as well as the book of the Holy Scriptures, and while a Mason keeps himself thus circumscribed, he cannot materially err.

This ends the Lecture. The Worshipful Master now gives one rap with his gavel, which brings the Junior Deacon on his feet, and says—Brother Junior, the last, as well as the first care of congregated Masons?

Junior Deacon—To see the Lodge 'yled, Worshipful.

Master—Attend to that part of your duty, and inform the Tyler that we are about to close this Lodge of Entered Apprentice Masons.

Junior Deacon steps to the door and informs the Tyler that the Lodge is about to be closed, and directs him to tyle accordingly; he then returns to his seat and says—We are tyled, Worshipful.

Master—How tyled?

Junior Deacon—With secresy and brotherly love; also a brother of this degree without the door, with a drawn sword in his hand.

The same questions as at the opening are now asked by the Master as to the respective positions and duties of the several officers of the Lodge, and the same replies given. He then reads the following closing charge from the Masonic Text Book:

Brethren, as we are about to quit this place and mix again with the world, I would warn you not to forget the duties which you have heard so frequently inculcated, and so forcibly recommended in this Lodge. Be dilligent, prudent, temperate and discreet; and remember that around this altar you have promised to befriend and relieve every worthy brother who shall need your assistance. Be ye, then, all of one mind; live in peace; and may the God of love and peace delight to dwell with and bless you.

Master (rising)—It is my will and pleasure that this Lodge of Entered Apprentice Masons be now closed, and stand closed till our next regular communication, unless convened by some sudden emergency; in which case, due and timely notice will be given. Brother Senior Warden, you will communicate the same to the Junior Warden in the south, that the brethren present may have due and timely notice, &c. [The Senior Warden informs the Junior Warden, and he the brethren, as above.]

Master—May the blessing of Heaven rest upon us, and all regular Masons, may brotherly love prevail, and every moral and social virtue cement us. So mote it be. Amen.

Here the signs are given. [See p. 7]

Master—How do Masons meet, Brother Senior?

Senior Warden—On the level, Worshipful.

Master—How do Masons part, Brother Junior?

Junior Warden—On the square, Worshipful.

Master—So let us meet, and so let us part, in the name of the Lord.

SECOND DEGREE.

A Lodge of Fellow Craft Masons.

The ceremonies in opening, closing, and conducting the business of a Lodge in this degree, are precisely the same as those in an Entered Apprentice's Lodge, except that there is a difference in the signs, and in some minor details, which will be explained in due course. Five officers can open a Lodge in this degree, viz.: Master, two Wardens, and two Deacons; but it is customary to have a Secretary and Treasurer in addition. On assembling at the Lodge the Worshipful Master puts on his hat (which, indeed, is the custom in each degree,) and rising, says:

Master—Brethren, I am about to open a Lodge of Fellow Craft Masons, in this place, for the dispatch of business, and I will thank you for your assistance. Every person present who is not of this degree will please to retire.

Master sits down, gives one rap with the gavel, and says: Brother Senior Warden, you will receive the pass-word in the west, and send it up to the east.

The Senior and Junior Deacons thereupon go to the Senior Warden and whisper the pass-word of this degree in his ear. [It is SHIBBOLETH! In late years, since all the doings and pass-words inside the Lodge have been made public, the Lodges have peculiar modes of their own to pronounce them.]

Senior Warden to Deacons—The word is right in the west; you will receive it from the brethren, and carry it up to the east.

The two Deacons then go round among the brethren and receive the word by holding one ear close to the mouth of each person who imparts it, and it is spoken in the lowest possible whisper. Any Fellow Craft Mason present who cannot pronounce it right is ordered out into the other room, and must there be examined to see what is the matter. After receiving it from all the members present, the Deacons go to the Worshipful Master and whisper it in his ear.

Master—The pass-word is correctly given, and I will now proceed to open a Lodge of Fellow Craft Masons. Brother Secretary, you will read the minutes of our last meeting.

The Secretary reads the minutes, and the business of the Lodge proceeds as in the Entered Apprentice's Degree. Should there be a candidate for advancement, the Worshipful Master directs the Deacons to instruct him. The candidate is taken into the preparation room by the Junior Deacon, and prepared in the manner following: All his clothing taken off,

except his shirt; furnished with a pair of drawers; his right breast bare; his left foot in a slipper; the right foot bare; a cable-tow twice round his neck; semi-hood-winked, or the right eye blinded, in which situation he is conducted to the door of the Lodge, where he gives two knocks, when the Senior Warden rises and says:

Senior Warden, to Master—Worshipful, while we are peaceably at work on the Second Degree of Masonry, under the influence of Faith, Hope and Charity, the door of our Lodge is alarmed.

Master, to Senior Deacon—Brother Senior, attend to the cause of that alarm, and see who comes there.

The Senior Deacon goes to the door and gives two raps on the inside in answer to those outside. Candidate (or

Junior Deacon for him) then gives a single rap, and then partly opens the door.

Senior Deacon—Who comes here ? Who comes here ?

Junior Deacon—A worthy brother, who has been regularly initiated as an Entered Apprentice Mason, served a proper time as such, and now wishes for further light in Masonry, by being passed to the degree of Fellow Craft.

Senior Deacon, to candidate—Is it of your own free will and accord you make this request ?

Candidate—It is.

Senior Deacon to Junior Deacon—Is he duly and truly prepared ?

Junior Deacon—He is.

Senior Deacon—Is he worthy and well qualified ?

Junior Deacon—He is.

Senior Deacon—Has he made suitable proficiency in the preceding degree ?

Junior Deacon—He has.

Senior Deacon—By what further right does he expect to obtain this benefit, and gain admission to our Lodge ?

Junior Deacon—By the benefit of a pass-word.

Senior Deacon—Has he a pass-word ?

Junior Deacon—He has not, but I have it for him.

Senior Deacon—Advance, and give it to me.

The Junior Deacon steps forward and whispers SHIBBOLETH in the ear of his Senior.

Senior Deacon—The pass is right ; and since this is the case, you will wait until the Worshipful Master in the east is made acquainted with your request, and his answer returned.

The Senior Deacon now goes to the Master and gives two raps, as at the door, which are answered by two from the Master ; when the same questions are asked, and answers returned, as at the door.

Master to Senior Deacon—Since he comes indued with all these necessary qualifications, let him enter this Worshipful Lodge in the name of the Lord, and take heed on what he enters.

The door is now opened and the candidate enters, conducted by the Junior Deacon.

Senior Deacon to candidate—Brother, when you entered this Lodge the first time, you entered on the point of the Compass pressing your naked left breast, which was then explained to you. You now enter it on the angle of the Square pressing your naked right breast, which

is to teach you to act upon the square with all mankind, but more especially with a brother Mason.

The candidate is then conducted twice regularly round the Lodge, and while he is thus walking the Worshipful Master reads from the seventh chapter of Amos, verses 7 and 8 : Thus he showed me, and behold the Lord stood upon a wall made by a plumb line, with a plumb line in his hand. And the Lord said unto me, Amos, what seest thou ? And I said, a plumb line. Then the Lord said, behold I will set a plumb line in the midst of my people Israel ; I will not again pass by them any more.

By the time the reading is ended, the candidate has made his second revolution around the Lodge, and he now halts before the Junior Warden in the south, where he gives two raps, and is answered by two, when the same questions are asked and answers returned as at the door. From thence he is conducted to the Senior Warden in the west, where the same questions are asked, and answers returned as before. He is then conducted to the Worshipful Master in the east, where the same questions are asked, and answers returned.

Master to Senior Deacon — From whence came you, and whither are you traveling ?

Senior Deacon—From the west, and traveling to the east.

Master—Why do you leave the west and journey towards the east ?

Senior Deacon—We are in search of more light in Masonry.

Master—Since this is the case, you will please conduct the candidate back to the west, from whence he came, and put him in the care of the Senior Warden, who will teach him how to approach the east, the place of light, by advancing upon two upright regular steps to the second step ; [the heel of the left foot is placed in the hollow of the right foot, in this degree] ; his feet forming the right angle of an oblong square, and his body erect at the altar before the Worshipful Master ; and cause him to kneel, in due form, to take the solemn oath or obligation of a Fellow Craft Mason.

The Senior Warden receives and instructs the candidate, directing him to step off with his left foot, and then with his right, and then bring the heel of the left foot in the hollow of the right. He then kneels on his right knee before the altar, making his left knee form a square. His left arm, as far as the elbow, should be held in a horizontal position, and the rest of the arm in a vertical position, forming another square—his arm supported by the square, held under his elbow.

Master leaves his seat, approaches the kneeling candidate, and says—Brother, you are now placed in a proper position to take on you the solemn oath, or obligation, of a Fellow Craft Mason, which I assure you, like your former obligation, will not interfere with your duty to your country or your Maker. If you are willing to take it, repeat your name, and say after me :—I, John Smith,' of my own free will and accord, in the presence of Almighty God, and this Worshipful Lodge of Fellow Craft Masons, erected to God, and dedicated to the holy order of St. Johns, do hereby and hereon most solemnly and sincerely promise and swear, in addition to my former obligation, that I will not give the secrets of the degree of a Fellow Craft Mason to any one of an inferior degree, nor to any other being' in the known world, except it be to a true and lawful brother, or brethren Fellow Craft Masons, or within the body of a just and lawfully constituted Lodge of such ; and not unto him nor unto them whom I shall hear so to be, but unto him and unto them only whom I shall find so to be, after strict trial and due examination, or lawful information. Furthermore, do I promise and swear, that I will not knowingly wrong this Lodge, nor a brother of this degree, to the value of two cents, myself, nor suffer it to be done by others, if in my power to prevent it. Furthermore, do I promise and swear, that I will support the Constitution of the Grand Lodge of the United States, and of the Grand Lodge of this State, under which this Lodge is held, and conform to all the bye-laws, rules, and regulations of this, or any other Lodge, of which I may, at any time hereafter, become a member. Furthermore, do I promise and swear, that I will obey all regular signs and summonses given, handed, sent, or thrown to me by the hand of a brother Fellow Craft Mason, or from the body of a just and lawfully constituted Lodge of such ; provided it be within the length of my cable-tow, or a square and angle of my work. Furthermore, do I promise and swear, that I will be aiding and assisting all poor and indigent brethren Fellow Crafts, their widows and orphans, wheresoever dispersed round the globe, they applying to me as such, and I finding them worthy, as far as in my power, without injuring myself or family. To all of which, I do most solemnly and sincerely promise and swear, without any hesitation, mental reservation, or self-evasion of mind in me whatever, binding myself under no less penalty than to have my left breast torn open, my heart and vitals taken from thence, thrown over my left shoulder, and carried to the valley of Jehosaphat, there to become a prey to the wild beasts of the field, and vultures of the air, should I wilfully violate, or transgress any part of this, my solemn oath or obligation, of a Fellow Craft Mason. So help me God, and keep me steadfast in the due performance of the same.

Master—Detach your hands and kiss the book twice.

Candidate kisses the Bible on the altar as directed, when the Senior Deacon moves the bandage which has blinded candidate's right eye, so that it covers both his eyes, leaving him entirely hoodwinked.

Master (laying his hand on candidate's head)—Brother, in your present situation, what do you most desire ?

Candidate—More light.

Master—Brethren, form on the square, stretch forth your hands, and assist in bringing this new-made brother to more light. [A short pause, and he continues.] And God said, Let there be light, and there was light.

At this moment the Senior Deacon suddenly strips off the bandage from the candidate's eyes, while the brethren present clap their hands and stamp on the floor, giving the grand shock, as in the Entered Apprentice's degree.

Master to candidate—Brother, on being brought to light, what do you discover in this degree different from what you saw as an Entered Apprentice ?

Candidate intimates that he sees nothing different.

Master—There is this difference : You behold on the altar one point of the compass elevated above the square, whereas in the former degree both points were underneath. This signifies to you that you have received more light in Masonry ; and as one point is yet hid beneath the square, so are you in darkness, as it regards one material point in Masonry. [The Master steps off from the candidate three or four steps, and continues.]   Brother, you now discover me as Master of this Lodge, approaching you from the east, under the sign and due-guard of a Fellow Craft Mason ; do as I do, as near as you can, keeping your position.

This sign is given by taking hold of the left breast, with the right hand, as though you intended to tear out a piece of it, then draw your hand, with the fingers partly clench-ed, from the left to the right side, with some quickness, and drop it down by your side.— The due-guard is giv-en by raising the left arm until that part of it between the elbow and shoulder is per-fectly horizontal, then raising the rest of the arm in a vertical posi-tion, so that that part of the arm below the elbow, and that part above it, forms a square. The two are always given together, and are called the sign and due-guard of a Fellow Craft. Master—Brother, I now present you with my right hand, in token of brother-ly love and confidence, and with it the pass-grip and word of a Fellow Craft Mason.

Sign and Due-guard of a Fellow-Craft.

The pass-grip is given by taking each other by the right hand, as though going to shake hands, and each putting his thumb between the fore and second fin-ger, where they join the hands, and pressing the thumb between the joints.

This is the regular pass-grip of a Fellow Craft Mason, and the name of it is SHIB-BOLETH. Its origin is explained here-after. In some Lodges the word is given in syllables, but usually it is pronounced entire.

The real grip of a Fellow Craft Mason is given by putting the thumb on the joint of the second finger where it joins the hand, and then each one should crook his thumb so he can stick the nail into the joint of the other. The name of the grip is JACHIN.

After the Worshipful Master has given the candidate these grips in due form, he says—Arise, brother Jachin, from a square to a perpendicular; go and salute the Ju-nior and Senior Wardens, and convince them that you have been regularly pass-ed to the degree of Fellow Craft. [The candidate goes and salutes the Wardens with the Fellow Craft sign.]

After saluting the Wardens he is con-ducted back to the Worshipful Master in the east, who thus addresses him: Bro-ther, I now have the honor of presenting you with a lamb-skin apron, as before, which I hope you will continue to wear with honor to yourself, and satisfaction to the brethren; you will please carry it to the Senior Warden in the West, who will teach you how to wear it as a Fel-low Craft Mason.

The candidate goes to the Senior War-den, who ties on his apron, and turns up one corner of the lower end, tucking it under the apron string.

Senior Warden—At the building of King Solomon's Temple, the workmen were distinguished by the manner in which they wore their aprons. Fellow Crafts wore theirs in the manner I have here arranged.

The candidate is again conducted by the Senior Deacon back to the Worship-ful Master in the east.

Master—Brother, as you are dressed, it is necessary you should have tools to work with: I will, therefore, present you with the tools of a Fellow Craft Ma-son. They are the plumb, square and level. The plumb is an instrument made use of by operative Masons to raise per-pendiculars; the square, to square their work; and the level, to lay horizontals: but we, as Free and Accepted Masons, are taught to use them for more noble and glorious purposes. The plumb teaches us to walk uprightly, in our se-veral stations, before God and man; squaring our actions by the square of virtue; and remembering that we are traveling on the level of time to that "undiscovered country, from whose bourne no traveler returns." I further present you with three precious jewels; their names are Faith, Hope, and Cha-rity; they teach us to have faith in God, hope in immortality, and charity to all mankind. The greatest of these three is Charity; for Faith may be lost in sight, Hope often ends in fruition, but Charity extends beyond the grave, through boundless realms of eternity.

The Senior Deacon now conducts the candidate back to the preparation room, where he puts on his clothes. While he is doing this the Lodge is prepared for his reception with floor cloth, columns, &c. When he is dressed, he returns, and as he enters the door of the Lodge, the Senior Deacon says: "We are now to return to the middle chamber of King Solomon's Temple." After they get inside, he continues:

Senior Deacon—Brother, we have now worked in speculative Masonry, but our forefathers wrought both in speculative and operative Masonry. They worked at the building of King Solomon's Temple, and many other masonic edifices; they wrought six days; they did not work on the seventh, because in six days God created the heavens and the earth, and rested on the seventh day. The seventh, therefore, our ancient brethren consecrated as a day of rest; thereby enjoying more frequent opportunities to contemplate the glorious works of creation, and to adore their great Creator. [Senior Deacon now steps forward a few steps.] Brother, the first thing that attracts our attention, are two large columns, or pillars, one on the left hand, and the other on the right; the name of the one on the left hand is Boaz, and denotes strength; the name of the one on the right hand is Jachin, and denotes establishment; they collectively allude to a passage in Scripture, wherein God has declared in his word, "In strength shall this house be established." These columns are eighteen cubits high, twelve in circumference, and four in diameter; they are adorned with two large chapiters, one on each, and these chapiters are ornamented with net work, lily work, and pomegranates; they denote Unity, Peace, and Plenty. The net work, from its connection, denotes union; the lily work, from its whiteness, purity and peace; and the pomegranate, from the exuberance of its seed, denotes plenty. They also have two large globes, or balls, one on each; these globes, or balls, contain, on their convex surfaces, all the maps and charts of the celestial and terrestrial bodies; they are said to be thus extensive, to denote the universality of Masonry, and that a Mason's charity ought to be equally extensive. Their composition is molten, or cast brass; they were cast on the banks of the river Jordan, in the clay-ground between Succoth and Zaradatha, where King Solomon ordered these and all other holy vessels to be cast. They were cast hollow; and were four inches, or a hand's breadth thick; they were cast hollow, the better to withstand inundations and conflagrations; they were the archives of Masonry, and contained the constitution, rolls, and records. [The Senior Deacon having explained the columns, he passes between them, advances a step or two, observing as he advances:] Brother, we will pursue our travels; the next thing that we come to, is a long, winding stair-case, with three, five, seven steps, or more. The three first allude to the three principal supports in Masonry, viz.: Wisdom, Strength, and Beauty; the five steps allude to the five orders in architecture, and the five human senses. The five orders in architecture are, the Tuscan, Doric, Ionic, Corinthian, and Composite; the five human senses are hearing, seeing, feeling, smelling, and tasting; the three first of which, have ever been highly essential among Masons: hearing, to hear the word; seeing, to see the sign; and feeling, to feel the grip, whereby one Mason may know another in the dark as well as in the light. The seven steps allude to the seven sabbatical years; seven years of famine; seven years in building the temple; seven golden candlesticks; seven wonders of the world; seven planets; but, more especially, the seven liberal arts and sciences, which are grammar, rhetoric, logic, arithmetic, geometry, music, and astronomy; for this, and many other reasons, the number seven has ever been held in high estimation among Masons. [Advancing a few steps further, the Senior Deacon continues:] Brother, the next thing we come to is the outer door of the middle chamber of King Solomon's Temple, which is partly open, but closely tyled by the Junior Warden.

Junior Warden [acting as Tyler]—Who comes here? who comes here?

Senior Deacon—A Fellow Craft Mason.

Junior Warden—How do you expect to gain admission?

Senior Deacon—By a pass, and a token of a pass.

Junior Warden—Give them.

The candidate, prompted by the Senior Deacon, gives the sign of a Fellow Craft, before explained, and the pass, SHIBBOLETH.

Junior Warden—What does it denote?

Senior Deacon—Plenty.

Junior Warden—How is it represented?

Senior Deacon—By a sheaf of wheat suspended near a water-ford.

Junior Warden—Why was this pass instituted?

Senior Deacon—In consequence of a

quarrel which had long existed between Jephthah, Judge of Israel, and the Ephraimites ; the latter of which had long been a stubborn, rebellious people, whom Jephthah had endeavored to subdue by lenient measures, but to no effect. The Ephraimites being highly incensed against Jephthah, for not being called to fight and share in the rich spoils o the Ammonitish war, assembled a mighty army, and passed over the river Jordan to give Jephthah battle ; but he, being apprised of their approach, called together the men of Israel, and gave them battle, and put them to flight ; and to make his victory more complete, he ordered guards to be placed at the different passes on the banks of the river Jordan, and commanded, if the Ephraimites passed that way, that they should pronounce the word SHIBBOLETH ; but they, being of a different tribe, pronounced it SIBBOLETH ; which trifling defect proved them spies, and cost them their lives : and there fell that day, at the different passes on the banks of the river Jordan, forty and two thousand. This word was also used by our ancient brethren to distinguish a friend from a foe, and has since been adopted as a proper password, to be given before entering any well regulated and governed Lodge of Fellow Craft Masons. [This and many other tokens, or grips, are frequently given by stranger Masons, when first introduced to each other. If given to a Mason, he will immediately return it. They can be given in company unobserved, when shaking hands.]

Junior Warden—Since this is the case, you will pass on to the Senior Warden in the west for further examination.

As they proceed towards the Senior Warden, the Senior Deacon says to candidate—Brother, the next thing we come to, is the inner door of the middle chamber of King Solomon's Temple, which we find partly open, but more closely tyled by the Senior Warden.

Senior Warden [acting as Tyler to the supposed chamber]—Who comes here ? who comes here ?

Senior Deacon—A Fellow Craft Mason.

Senior Warden—How do you expect to gain admission ?

Senior Deacon—By the grip and word.

Senior Warden—Give them.

Candidate takes Senior Warden by the Fellow Craft grip, [see page 22,] and says JACHIN.

Senior Warden—They are right ; you can pass on.

The Senior Deacon conducts the candidate towards the Worshipful Master in the east, who says :

Master—Who comes here ? who comes here ?

Senior Deacon—A Fellow Craft Mason.

Master, to the candidate—Brother, you have been admitted into the middle chamber of King Solomon's Temple, for the sake of the letter G. It denotes Deity, before whom we all ought to bow with reverence, worship, and adoration. It also denotes geometry, the fifth science ; it being that on which this degree was principally founded. By geometry, we may curiously trace Nature through her various windings to her most concealed recesses. By it we may discover the power, the wisdom, and the goodness of the Grand Artificer of the Universe, and view with delight the proportions which connect this vast machine.

This ends the advancement to the second degree, after which the Worshipful Master delivers to the new brother the following charge :

Master—Brother, being advanced to the second degree of Masonry, we congratulate you on your preferment. The internal, and not the external, qualifications of a man are what Masonry regards. As you increase in knowledge, you will improve in social intercourse. It is unnecessary to recapitulate the duties which, as a Mason, you are bound to discharge ; or enlarge on the necessity of a strict adherence to them, as your own experience must have established their value. Our laws and regulations you are strenuously to support ; and be always ready to assist in seeing them duly executed. You are not to palliate or aggravate the offences of your brethren ; but in the decision of every trespass against our rules, you are to judge with candor, admonish with friendship, and reprehend with justice. The study of the liberal arts, that valuable branch of education, which tends so effectually to polish and adorn the mind, is earnestly recommended to your consideration ; especially the science of geometry, which is established as the basis of our art. Geometry, or Masonry, originally synonymous terms, being of a divine moral nature, is enriched with the most useful knowledge ; while it proves the wonderful properties of Nature, it demonstrates the more important truths of morality. Your past behaviour and regular deportment, have merited the honor which we have now conferred ; and, in your new character, it is expected that you will conform to the principles of the

Order, by steadily persevering in the practice of every commendable virtue. Such is the nature of your engagements as a Fellow Craft, and to these duties you are bound by the most sacred ties.

CLOSING LECTURE—FIRST SECTION.

In many of the Lodges this first section is omitted in closing, but it is nevertheless a part of the ceremony.

Master, to Senior Warden—Are you a Fellow Craft Mason?

Senior Warden—I am; try me.

Master—By what will you be tried?

Senior Warden—By the Square.

Master—Why by the Square?

Senior Warden—Because it is an emblem of virtue.

Master—What is a Square?

Senior Warden—An angle extending to ninety degrees, or the fourth part of a circle.

Master—Where was you prepared to be made a Fellow Craft Mason?

Senior Warden—In a room adjacent to the body of a just and lawfully constituted Lodge of such, duly assembled in a room, or place, representing the middle chamber of King Solomon's Temple.

Master—How was you prepared?

Senior Warden—By being divested of all metals: neither naked nor clothed; barefooted nor shod; hood-winked; with a cable-tow twice round my neck; in which situation I was conducted to the door of the Lodge, where I gave two distinct knocks.

Master—What did those two distinct knocks allude to?

Senior Warden—The second degree in Masonry; it being that on which I was about to enter.

[The Master continues his inquiries as to the manner in which a candidate is advanced to the Fellow Craft degree. The Senior Warden answers by telling what occurred during such advancement. These questions and answers are but a repetition of those given on pages 20 to 22, during the initiation or advancement alluded to.]

SECOND SECTION.

Master—Have you ever worked as a Fellow Craft Mason?

Senior Warden—I have, in speculative; but our forefathers wrought both in speculative and operative Masonry.

Master—Where did they work?

Senior Warden—At the building of King Solomon's Temple, and many other Masonic edifices.

Master—How long did they work?

Senior Warden—Six days.

Master—Did they work on the seventh?

Senior Warden—They did not.

Master—Why so?

Senior Warden—Because in six days God created the heavens and the earth, and rested on the seventh day; the seventh day, therefore, our ancient brethren consecrated as a day of rest from their labors; thereby enjoying more frequent opportunities to contemplate the glorious works of creation, and adore their great Creator.

Master—Did you ever return to the sanctum sanctorum, or holy of holies, of King Solomon's Temple?

Senior Warden—I did.

Master—By what way?

Senior Warden—Through a long porch, or alley.

Master—Did anything particular strike your attention on your return?

Senior Warden—There did, viz.: two large columns, or pillars, one on the left hand, and the other on the right.

Master—What was the name of the one on the left hand?

Senior Warden—BOAZ, which denotes strength.

Master—What was the name of the one on the right hand?

Senior Warden—JACHIN, denoting establishment.

Master—What do they collectively allude to?

Senior Warden—A passage in Scripture, wherein God has declared in his word, "In strength shall this house be established."

Master—What were their dimensions?

Senior Warden—Eighteen cubits in height, twelve in circumference, and four in diameter.

Master—Were they adorned with any thing?

Senior Warden—They were; with two large chapiters, one on each.

Master—Were they ornamented with any thing?

Senior Warden—They were; with wreaths of net work, lily work, and pomegranates.

Master—What do they denote?

Senior Warden—Unity, Peace, and Plenty.

Master—Why so?

Senior Warden—Net work, from its connection, denotes union; lily work, from its whiteness and purity, denotes peace, and pomegranates, from the exuberance of its seed, denotes plenty.

Master—Were those columns adorned with any thing further?

Senior Warden—They were, viz : two large globes, or balls, one on each.

Master—Did they contain any thing?

Senior Warden—They did, viz. : all the maps and charts of the celestial and terrestrial bodies.

Master—Why are they said to be so extensive?

Senior Warden—To denote the universality of Masonry, and that a Mason's charity ought to be equally extensive.

Master—What was their composition?

Senior Warden—Molten, or cast brass.

Master—Who cast them?

Senior Warden—Our Grand Master, Hiram Abiff.

Master—Where were they cast?

Senior Warden—On the banks of the river Jordan, in the clay ground between Succoth and Zaradatha, where King Solomon ordered these, and all other holy vessels to be cast.

Master—Were they cast solid or hollow?

Senior Warden—Hollow.

Master—What was their thickness?

Senior Warden—Four inches, or a hand's breadth.

Master—Why were they cast hollow?

Senior Warden—The better to withstand inundations or conflagrations; they were the archives of Masonry, and contained the constitution, rolls and records.

Master—What did you next come to?

Senior Warden—A long, winding stair case, with three, five, seven steps, or more.

Master—What does the three steps allude to?

Senior Warden—The three principal supports in Masonry, namely : Wisdom, Strength, and Beauty.

Master—What do the five steps allude to?

Senior Warden—The five orders in architecture, and the five human senses.

Master—What are the five orders in architecture?

Senior Warden—The Tuscan, Doric, Ionic, Corinthian, and Composite.

Master—What are the five human senses?

Senior Warden—Hearing, seeing, feeling, smelling, and tasting; the first three of which have ever been deemed highly essential among Masons ; hearing, to hear the word; seeing, to see the sign; and feeling, to feel the grip, whereby one Mason may know another in the dark as well as in the light.

Master—What does the seven steps allude to?

Senior Warden—The seven sabbatical years; seven years of famine; seven years in building the temple; seven golden candlesticks; seven wonders of the world; seven planets; but more especially the seven liberal arts and sciences ; which are, grammar, rhetoric, logic, arithmetic, geometry, music, and astronomy. For these, and many other reasons, the number seven has ever been held in high estimation among Masons.

Master—What did you next come to?

Senior Warden—The outer door of the middle chamber of King Solomon's Temple, which I found party open, but closely tyled by the Junior Warden.

Master—How did you gain admission?

Senior Warden—By a pass, and token of a pass.

Master—What was the name of the pass?

Senior Warden—SHIBBOLETH.

Master—What does it denote?

Senior Warden—Plenty.

Master—Why so?

Senior Warden—From an ear of corn being placed at the water-ford.

Master—Why was this pass instituted?

Senior Warden—In consequence of a quarrel which had long existed between Jephthah, Judge of Israel, and the Ephraimites. [The rest of this answer is precisely the same as the answer of the Senior Deacon to the same question on page 24.]

Master—What did you next discover?

Senior Warden—The inner door of the middle chamber of King Solomon's Temple.

Master—How did you gain admission?

Senior Warden—By the grip and word.

Master—How did the Senior Warden dispose of you?

Senior Warden—He ordered me to be conducted to the Worshipful Master in the east, who informed me that I had been admitted into the middle chamber of King Solomon's Temple for the sake of the letter G.

Master—Does it denote any thing?

Senior Warden—It does ; DEITY—before whom we should all bow with reverence, worship, and adoration. It also denotes geometry, the fifth science ; it being that on which this degree was principally founded.

This ends the Lecture, and the Lodge is now closed with a similar admonition from the Master, and precisely the same ceremonies as those observed in closing a Lodge of Entered Apprentices, described on page 18, except that the signs given are of course those of a Fellow Craft (page 22) instead of the others.

THIRD DEGREE.

OPENING A LODGE OF MASTER MASONS.

The ceremonies of opening and conducting the business of a Lodge in this degree are the same as those of a Lodge of Entered Apprentices, already described. The arrangement of the Lodge is similar, and the same officers do duty. The traditional account of the death, several burials, and resurrections of Hiram Abiff, the widow's son, as here developed, is very interesting. We read in the Bible that Hiram Abiff was one of the head workmen employed at the building of King Solomon's Temple, and other ancient writings inform us that he was an arbiter between King Solomon and Hiram, King of Tyre; but his tragical death is nowhere recorded except in the archives of Free Masonry.

The Master Mason's Lodge is represented as the *sanctum sanctorum,* or holy of holies, of King Solomon's Temple, and on great occasions is, of course, ornamented different from those of preceding degrees.

A candidate for advancement to the Master Mason's degree is prepared by the Junior and Senior Deacons, who strip him naked, and furnish him with a pair of drawers reaching just above his hips, both legs of them being rolled above the knees. His shirt is then put over his head, and slipped down around his body, and is partly covered by his drawers—the sleeves and collar hang dangling behind, over the waistband of his drawers. A rope, or cable-tow, is put three times round his body, and he has a bandage over his eyes.

When all is ready the Senior Deacon returns inside the Lodge, and resumes his seat by the Worshipful Master. The Junior Deacon meantime conducts the candidate to the door of the Lodge, where he gives three distinct knocks.

Senior Warden (rising and addressing the Master)—Worshipful, while we are peaceably at work on the third degree of Masonry, under the influence of humanity, brotherly love, and affection, the door of our Lodge appears to be alarmed.

Master to Senior Deacon—Brother Senior, inquire the cause of the alarm.

The Senior Deacon steps to the door and answers the three knocks that have been given, by three more; (the knocks are much louder than those given on any occasion other than that of the admission of candidates in the several degrees:) one knock is then given without, and answered by one from within, when the door is partly opened.

Senior Deacon—Who comes there? who comes there? who comes there?

Junior Deacon—A worthy brother, who has been regularly initiated as an Entered Apprentice Mason, passed to the degree of a Fellow Craft, and now wishes for further light in Masonry, by being raised to the sublime degree of a Master Mason.

Senior Deacon—Is it of his own free will and accord he makes this request?

Candidate answers—It is.

Senior Deacon (to Junior)—Is he worthy and well qualified?

Junior Deacon—He is.

Senior Deacon—Has he made suitable proficiency in the preceding degrees?

Junior Deacon—He has.

Senior Deacon—By what further right does he expect to obtain this benefit?

Junior Deacon—By the benefit of a pass-word.

Senior Deacon—Has he a pass-word?

Junior Deacon—He has not, but I have it for him.

Senior Deacon—Give it me.

The Junior Deacon whispers in the ear of the Senior Deacon—TUBAL-CAIN.

Senior Deacon—The pass is right. You will wait until the Worshipful Master in the east be made acquainted with his request, and his answer returned.

The Senior Deacon goes to the Master, gives three knocks, and the same questions and answers pass between them relative to the candidate as were given and answered by the Senior and Junior Deacons at the door.

Master—Since he comes indued with all these necessary qualifications, let him en'er this worshipful Lodge in the name of the Lord, and take heed on what he enters.

The Senior Deacon returns to the door and repeats what the Master has said, when the candidate enters, and as he goes through the door the Senior Deacon stands in front holding a pair of compasses in both hands. He presses the points of the compasses against the naked right and left breasts of the candidate, saying: Brother, when you first entered this Lodge, you was received on the point of the compass pressing your naked left breast, which was then explained to you; when you entered it the second time, you was received on the angle of the square, which was also explained to you; on entering it now, you are received on the two extreme points of the compass pressing your naked right and left breasts, which are thus explained: As the most vital parts of man are contained between the two breasts, so are the most valuable tenets of Masonry contained between the two extreme points of the compass, which are, Virtue, Morality, and Brotherly Love.

The Senior Deacon then conducts the candidate three times regularly round the Lodge. The Junior Warden is the first of the three principal officers that the candidate passes, traveling with the sun, when he starts round the Lodge; and as he passes the Junior Warden, Senior Warden, and Master, the first time going round they each give one rap; the second time each gives two raps, and the third time, three raps. During the time the candidate is traveling round the room, the Master reads the following passage of Scripture, the traveling and the reading terminating at the same time : Remember now thy Creator in the days of thy youth, while the evil days come not, nor the years draw nigh, when thou shalt say, I have no pleasure in them : while the sun, or the moon, or the stars be not darkened, nor the clouds return after the rain : in the day when the keepers of the house shall tremble, and the strong men shall bow themselves, and the grinders cease, because they are few ; and those that look out of the windows be darkened, and the doors shall be shut in the streets ; when the sound of the grinding is low, and he shall rise up at the voice of the bird, and all the daughters of music shall be brought low. Also when they shall be afraid of that which is high, and fears shall be in the way, and the almond-tree shall flourish, and the grass-hoppers shall be a burden, and desire shall fail : because man goeth to his long home, and the mourners go about the streets : or ever the silver cord be loosed, or the golden bowl be broken at the fountain, or the wheel at the cistern. Then shall the dust return to the earth as it was ; and the spirit shall return unto God, who gave it.

The candidate now stops in front of the seat of the Junior Warden in the south. The Warden asks him the same questions that were asked at the door by the Senior Deacon when he entered the Lodge, and the same answers are given. He then goes to the Senior Warden in the west, where the same questions are asked, and answers given. He is then conducted to the Worshipful Master in the east, who, after asking the same questions again, and receiving the same answers, inquires whence he came and whither he is journeying.

Candidate—From the west, and traveling to the east.

Master—Why do you leave the west, and travel to the east?

Candidate—In search of more light.

Master to Senior Deacon—You will please conduct the candidate back to the west, from whence he came, and put him in the care of the Senior Warden, who will instruct him how to approach the east, by advancing upon three regular steps, to the third step in Masonry, his feet forming a square, his body erect, and cause him to kneel at the altar, in due form, to take upon himself the solemn oath or obligation of Master Mason.

The candidate being conducted towards the Senior Warden, that officer steps forward and places him in position, facing him towards the altar, and directing him to step off, first with his left foot, and second, with the right; each time forming a square with his feet, as in the Fellow Craft movement. The third step is with the left foot, bringing up the right, and placing the heels together in the position of a soldier. The candidate then kneels on both naked knees, and raises both hands and arms, in the manner of giving the grand hailing sign of distress, and holds them in this position until he is directed to place them on the Holy Bible, square and compass.

Master, to candidate—Brother, you are now placed in a proper position to take upon you the solemn oath and obligation of a Master Mason, which I assure you as a man, as a Mason, and as Master of this Lodge, will not interfere with the duty you owe to your God or your country. If you are willing to take this oath, repeat your name, and say after me—

I, John Smith, of my own free will and accord, in the presence of Almighty God, and this worshipful Lodge of Master Masons, erected to God and dedicated to the holy St. Johns, do hereby and hereon, [candidate now brings both hands down on the Holy Bible, square and compass, which lay on the altar,] most solemnly and sincerely promise and swear, in addition to my former obligations, that I will not give the secrets of a Master Mason to any one of an inferior degree, nor to any being in the known world, except it be to a true and lawful brother Master Mason, or within the body of a just and lawfully constituted Lodge of such; and not unto him or them whom I shall hear so to be, but unto him and them only whom I shall find so to be, after strict trial, due examination, or lawful information received. Furthermore, do I promise and swear, that I will not speak the Master Mason's word, which I shall hereafter receive, in any other manner except in that in which I shall receive it, which will be on the five points of fellowship, and at low breath. Furthermore do I promise and swear,

that I will not give the grand hailing sign of distress of this degree, except I am in real distress, or for the benefit of the craft, when at work; and should I see that sign given, or hear the words accompanying it, I will fly to the relief of the person so giving it, should there be a greater probability of saving his life than losing my own. Furthermore do I promise and swear, that I will not wrong this Lodge, nor a brother of this degree, to the value of one cent, knowingly, myself, nor suffer it to be done by others, if in my power to prevent it. Furthermore do I promise and swear, that I will not be at the initiating, passing, or raising a candidate at one communication, without a dispensation from the Grand Lodge, for that purpose. Furthermore do I promise and swear, that I will not be at the initiating, passing, or raising a candidate in a clandestine Lodge, nor converse upon the secrets of Free Masonry with a clandestine made Mason, or one that has been expelled or suspended, while he is under that sentence. Furthermore do I promise and swear, that I will not be at the initiating, passing, or raising of an old man in dotage, a young man in non-age, an atheist, irreligious libertine, madman, hermaphrodite, woman, or a fool. Furthermore do I promise and swear, that I will not speak evil of a brother Master Mason, neither behind his back nor before his face, but will apprise him of all approaching danger. Furthermore do I promise and swear, that I will not violate the chastity of a Master Mason's wife, mother, sister, or daughter, nor suffer it to be done by others, if in my power to prevent it, I knowing them to be such. Furthermore do I promise and swear, that I will support the constitution of the Grand Lodge of this State, under which this Lodge is held, and conform to all the by-laws, rules and regulations of this, or any other Lodge of which I may hereafter become a member. Furthermore do I promise and swear, that I will obey all due signs and summonses handed, sent, or thrown to me from a brother Master Mason, or from the body of a just and lawfully constituted Lodge of Master Masons, if within the length of my cable-tow. Furthermore do I promise and swear, that a Master Mason's secrets, given to me in charge as such, shall remain as secure and inviolable in my breast, as in his, before communicated, murder and treason only excepted: and they left to my only election. Furthermore do I promise and swear, that I will go on a Master Mason's errand, even barefoot, and bareheaded, to save his life or relieve his necessities. Furthermore do I promise and swear, that I will remember a brother Master Mason, when on my knees at my devotions. Furthermore do I promise and swear, that I will be aiding and assisting all poor and indigent Master Masons, their widows and orphans, wheresoever dispersed round the globe, (they making application to me as such, and I finding them worthy,) as far as is in my power, without injury to myself or family. Furthermore do I promise and swear, that if any part of this my solemn oath or obligation be omitted at this time, that I will hold myself amenable thereto, whenever informed. To all which I do most solemnly and sincerely promise and swear, with a fixed and steady purpose of mind in me to keep and perform the same, binding myself under no less penalty than to have my body severed in two in the midst, and divided to the North and South, my bowels burnt to ashes in the center, and the ashes scattered before the four winds of heaven, that there might not the least tract or trace of remembrance remain among men or Masons of so vile and perjured a wretch as I should be, were I ever to prove wilfully guilty of violating any part of this my solemn oath or obligation of a Master Mason; so help me God, and keep me steadfast in the due performance of the same.

Master, to candidate—What do you now most desire?

Candidate—Light.

Master—Brethren, please to stretch forth your hands and assist in bringing this new-made brother to more light in Masonry. "And God said, Let there be light, and there was light."

[The candidate has the bandage dropped from his eyes in the same manner as in preceding degrees, with three stamps on the floor, and three clapping of hands.]

Master, to candidate—On being brought to light, you first discover, as before, three great lights in Masonry, by the assistance of three lesser, with this difference, both points of the compass are elevated above the square, which denotes to you that you are about to receive all the light that can be conferred on you in a Mason's Lodge.

The Master steps back a few steps, and then advances again.

Master — Brother, you now discover me as Master of this Lodge, approaching you from the east, under the sign, step, and due-guard of a Master Mason.

The sign is the hailing sign of distress given on page 29. The words accompanying it are, "Is there no help for the widow's son?" As the last words are uttered, you let fall your hands in a manner to indicate solemnity. The due-guard

is given by putting the open right hand to the left side of the bowels, the palm of the hand flat, and downwards; then draw it quickly from the left to the right, and let it fall by your side.

After thus instructing the new candidate, the Master approaches him, and taking him by the hand, says :— Brother, in token of a continuation of true brotherly love and esteem, I present you with my right hand, and with it you will receive the pass-grip and word of a Master Mason. Take me as I take you.

The pass-grip is given by pressing the thumb between the joints of the second and third fingers where they join the hand, and the word is TUBAL-CAIN.

As the Master gives the grip, the following dialogue ensues, the Senior Deacon answering for the candidate:

Master—What is that?

Senior Deacon—The pass-grip of a Master Mason.

Master—Has it a name?

Senior Deacon—It has.

Master—Will you give it me?

Senior Deacon—I did not so receive it, neither can I so impart it.

Master—How will you dispose of it?

Senior Deacon—Letter, or syllable it.

Master—Syllable it, and begin.

Senior Deacon—No, you begin.

Master—No, begin you.

Senior Deacon—TU

Master—BAL-

Senior Deacon—CAIN.

Master – TUBAL

Senior Deacon—TUBAL-CAIN.

Master—Right, brother Tubal-Cain, I greet you ; arise from a square to a perpendicular, go and salute the Junior and Senior Wardens, and satisfy them that you are an obligated Master Mason, and are in possession of the true pass-grip and word.

While the two Wardens are examining the candidate, the Master returns to his place in the east, and gets an apron, with which he returns, when the Senior Warden speaks for himself and Junior.

Senior Warden—Worshipful, we are satisfied that brother John Smith is an obligated Master Mason.

Master, to candidate—Brother, I now have the honor to present you with a lamb-skin, or white apron, as before, which I hope you will wear with credit to yourself, and satisfaction and advantage to the brethren. You will please carry it to the Senior Warden in the west, who will teach you how to wear it as a Master Mason.

The candidate goes again to the Senior Warden, who ties on the apron, and lets the flap fall down before, in its natural and common situation. He then returns to the Master.

Master—Brother, I perceive you are clothed ; and it is of course necessary you should have tools to work with. I will now present you with the working tools of a Master Mason, which are all the implements of Masonry indiscriminately, but more especially the trowel. The trowel is an instrument made use of by operative masons to spread the cement, which unites a building into one common mass ; but we as Free and Accepted Masons are taught to make use of it for the more noble and glorious purpose of spreading the cement of brotherly love and affection, that cement which unites us into one sacred band, or society of friends and brothers, among whom no contention should ever exist, but that noble contention, or emulation, of who can best work or best agree. I also present you with three precious jewels ; their names are Humanity, Friendship, and Brotherly Love.

The Master then reads from a Masonic text-book the charge to a new candidate in this degree, and directs the Senior Deacon to conduct him back to the preparation room, where he will resume his usual clothing.

As soon as the candidate has gone out, the Lodge is called from labor to refreshment in the following manner, viz. :

Master to Senior Warden— Brother Senior, it is my order that this Lodge be called from labor to refreshment, and to be on again at the sound of the gavel.

The Senior Warden repeats this order to his Junior, and the Junior Warden notifies the brethren that the Lodge is called from labor to refreshment, and he thereupon gives three raps, when all the brethren leave their seats. This is done in order that when the candidate returns into the Lodge, he may think that all is over, and that he has received the whole degree. When he comes in, then, he finds some of the brethren drinking, some laughing and talking, and others (as he thinks) preparing to go home. Many of the members come forward, on his appearance, and salute him—one gives the pass-grip, another the due-guard, and a third asks him how he likes the degree, &c. Meantime the Master goes to his seat in the east unobserved, and gives one rap with his gavel. Instantly the brethren all resume their seats, leaving the candidate alone in the middle of the floor, and he finds himself somewhat embarrassed until the Master beckons to him to come towards the east. Taking up a book, the Master says :

Master—Brother, you no doubt think yourself a perfect Master Mason, and that you are entitled to all our privileges. Is it not so ?

Candidate usually answers that it is.

Master—It then becomes my duty to undeceive you, and to inform you that you are not a Master Mason, neither do I know that you ever will be one, until I can ascertain how you withstand the amazing trials and dangers that await you. You must now undergo one of the most trying scenes that human nature ever witnessed. You are to travel a rough and rugged road, beset with dangers on every side, where you will meet with ruffians, and you may meet with death—for some have suffered death who have traveled this road before you. In your preceding degrees you had a brother to pray for you, but in this one you must pray for yourself. You will now be hood-winked, and go and kneel at the altar, where you can pray either mentally or orally. When you get through, please to signify the same by rising.

The candidate is hood winked and conducted towards the altar, and while conducting him, the Senior Deacon says—Brother, it was the custom of our Grand Master, Hiram Abiff, every day at high twelve, when the crafts were from labor to refreshment, to enter into the sanctum sanctorum, and offer up his devotions to the ever living God. Let us, in imitation of him, kneel and pray. [Candidate kneels, and acts as if in prayer.]

In many Lodges this ceremony is turned into merriment, as candidates will frequently make believe that they are terribly frightened, and that they are praying earnestly, when in truth they are but acting a part. The rest of this degree is founded on the murder of the Grand Master, Hiram Abiff, who, as he left his devotions, was assassinated by three ruffians, who had stationed themselves at the east, west, and south gates of King Solomon's Temple, to make sure of their work of murder.

In this part of the initiation, the Master and the Junior and Senior Wardens represent three ruffians, viz. : JUBELA, JUBELO, and JUBELUM. The room being darkened, the candidate rises (still hood-winked) from the altar, is conducted several times round the Lodge, and finally stops at the south gate, which is guarded by Jubela, (the Junior Warden.)

Jubela—Who comes here ?

Senior Deacon, acting as Conductor—Our Grand Master, Hiram Abiff.

Jubela—Our Grand Master, Hiram Abiff ! he is the very man I wanted to see. [Jubela thereupon seizes the candidate by the throat and handles him roughly, exclaiming,] Give me the Master Mason's word, or I will take your life !

Senior Deacon answers for candidate—I cannot give it now, but if you will wait till the Temple is completed, and the Grand Lodge assembles at Jerusalem, if you are worthy, you shall then receive it, otherwise you cannot.

Jubela—Talk not to me of Temples or Grand Lodges—give me the word, or die ! and he thereupon strikes the candidate a blow across the throat with a twenty-four inch guage.

The candidate rapidly retreats and goes towards the west gate, which is guarded by Jubelo, (the Senior Warden.)

Jubelo—Who comes there ?

Senior Deacon—Our Grand Master, Hiram Abiff.

Jubelo (seizing candidate roughly)—Give me the grip and word of a Master Mason, or die !

The candidate is excused as before, when Jubelo gives him a blow across his breast with the square. The candidate then goes to the east gate, where he encounters Jubelum, (the Master.)

Jubelum—Give me the grip and password of a Master Mason, or die !

The Master thereupon strikes him on the forehead with the gavel, when (prompted by the Senior Deacon) the candidate falls apparently lifeless upon the floor.

Jubelum—What shall we do? We have killed our Grand Master, Hiram Abiff.

Jubelo—Let us carry him out at the east gate, and cover him with the rubbish until low twelve. We can then meet and carry him a westerly course, and bury him.

At the place where the candidate was knocked down with the gavel, in the east, a blanket had been previously spread to receive him. He is now taken up in the blanket, carried back out of sight, and covered up. The Lodge con-

tinues dark for a while, the supposed ruffians skulking about. Presently the Senior Deacon strikes twelve strokes on a bell, soon after which the three ruffians meet at the east end of the Lodge and salute each other.

Jubela—The body has not been discovered.

Jubelo—No, all is safe.

Jubelum—We must bury our Grand Master immediately, for I perceive he begins to smell a little already, and we shall be discovered. Take him up and carry him to the brow of Mount Moria, where I have dug his grave.

The candidate is again taken up in the blanket, carried several times round the Lodge, and then deposited, on his back, near the Senior Warden in the west, his feet towards the east, and covered up with chairs, benches, &c.

Jubelum—Let us mark his grave with this sprig of cassia. [He sticks down a sprig of evergreen near candidate's head.] We will now endeavor to get a passage to Ethiopia.

While the supposed ruffians are looking for their passage, (i. e. groping round the Lodge,) King Solomon arrives at the Temple, being personified by the Worshipful Master, who calls the Lodge to order by a rap with the gavel.

Master (acting as King Solomon) to Senior Warden—What is the cause of all this confusion?

Senior Warden—Our Grand Master, Hiram Abiff, is missing; and there are no plans or designs laid down on the trestle-board for the crafts to pursue their labors.

Master—Our Grand Master missing! He has always been very punctual in his attendance, and I fear he may be indisposed. Assemble the crafts, and search in and about the Temple to see if he can be found.

The brethren now shuffle about the Lodge a few minutes, as though in search of the missing Master, when the Worshipful Master calls them to order by a rap with the gavel.

Master to Senior Warden—What success?

Senior Warden—We cannot find our Grand Master, my lord.

Master—The Secretary will call the roll of workmen and see if any of them are missing.

Secretary calls the roll, and then addresses the Master, who is still acting as King Solomon.

Secretary—I have called the roll, my lord, and I find there are three of the workmen missing, viz. : Jubela, Jubelo, and Jubelum.

Master—This brings to my mind a circumstance that took place this morning. Twelve Fellow Crafts, clothed in white gloves, and aprons, in token of their innocence, came to me and confessed that they twelve, with three others, had conspired to extort the Master Mason's word from their Grand Master, Hiram Abiff, and in case of refusal, to take his life; they twelve had recanted, but they feared the other three had been base enough to carry their atrocious designs into execution.

Master (still acting as King Solomon) to Senior Warden—You will draw twelve Fellow Crafts from the banks of workmen, clothe them in white gloves and aprons in token of their innocence, and send three of them east, three west, three north and three south, in search of these missing men. When they are found, cause them to be brought forward.

The Senior Warden repeats this order to his Junior, who imparts it to the brethren, and then there is more shuffling around the Lodge, while the twelve are supposed to be in search of the missing men. Finally some one near the Senior Warden's seat addresses an old man who is dressed for the occasion, and just come from the preparation room.

Mason—Old man, have you seen any travelers passing this way?

Old man—Yes; as I was down near the coast of Joppa this morning, I saw three, and from their dress and appearance I supposed them to be men of Tyre, and workmen from the Temple. They sought a passage to Ethiopia, but could not obtain one, in consequence of an embargo recently laid on all the shipping. I believe they returned into the country.

Master (still acting as King Solomon) gives a rap with the gavel, and inquires —What tidings, brethren?

Some one replies—None from the east, Worshipful.

Another says—None from the South.

A third exclaims, in a loud voice—T? dings from the west, my lord!

Master—What tidings from the We: ?

The third answers—As we three Fe'- low Crafts were steering a westerly course, we fell in with a wayfaring man, who informed us he saw three men that morning down near the coast of Joppa, and from their dress and appearance he supposed them to be men of Tyre, workmen from the Temple; they sought a passage to Ethiopia, but could not pro-

3

cure one in consequence of an embargo which had been recently laid on all the shipping, and they returned back into the country.

Master—I had this embargo laid, to prevent the fugitives from making their escape. You will go and search again, and search till you find them, if possible. If they are not found, the twelve who confessed to have been originally in the lot must be considered as the murderers, and suffer accordingly.

The shuffling around the Lodge is continued under pretence of a further search, until one of the brothers (the same who had announced the tidings in the Lodge) seats himself on the floor in the west, near the candidate's head, and as he rises he catches hold of the sprig of evergreen that had been stuck there. He immediately stamps his foot three times and exclaims, "Companions assemble!" Two brothers rush towards him, when he says:

Brothers, a very singular circumstance has just taken place. I was fatigued and sat down here to rest, and on rising from my seat I caught hold of this sprig of cassia, and drew it out of the ground. On a close examination I find that it has lately been broken off and stuck there.

The three then begin to look down at the spot where the candidate lays, when one says—This looks like a grave! on which they prepare to remove the chairs, benches, &c., when three other brothers, who sit near by, personate the three fugitive ruffians.

Jubela, the first murderer, murmurs—O that my throat had been cut across, my tongue torn out, and my body buried in the rough sands of the sea at low water-mark, where the tide ebbs and flows twice in twenty-four hours, ere I had been accessary to the death of so good a man as our Grand Master, Hiram Abiff!

Jubelo, the second one—O that my left breast had been torn open, and my heart and vitals taken from thence, and thrown over my left shoulder, carried into the valley of Jehosaphat, there to become a prey to the wild beasts of the field, and vultures of the air, ere I had conspired the death of so good a man as our Grand Master, Hiram Abiff!

Jubelum, the third one—O that my body had been severed in two in the midst, and divided to the north and south, my bowels burnt to ashes in the center, and the ashes scattered by the four winds of heaven, that there might not the least track or trace of remembrance remain among men, or Masons, of so vile and perjured a wretch as I am—Ah, Jubela and Jubelo, it was I that struck him harder than you both—it was I that gave him the fatal blow—it was I that killed him!

The three brethren who are removing the benches and chairs, stop and overhear these murmurs of the three murderers.

One says—These are undoubtedly the assassins—what shall we do? there are three of them.

Another says—Our cause is good—let us seize them.

The three brothers personating the ruffians are thereupon seized by the three searching for the body, and the prisoners are carried before King Solomon, who is represented by the Worshipful Master in the east. The three prisoners are here made to kneel.

Master, giving a rap with the gavel—What tidings from the west?

One of the brethren replies—Worshipful, as we three Fellow Crafts were steering a due west course, I, becoming more weary than my companions, sat down on the brow of Mount Moria, to rest and refresh myself, and as I was rising, I accidentally caught hold of a sprig of cassia, which easily giving way, excited my curiosity. Upon this, I hailed my companions, and while we were consulting upon the mystery of the incident, we heard the voices of three ruffians crying from a cleft of the rock near by; we discovered them to be Jubela, Jubelo and Jubelum. We rushed upon, seized and bound them, and have brought them before you, and wait your further orders.

Master, rising—Jubela, you are suspected and accused of being accessary to the death of our Grand Master, Hiram Abiff. Are you guilty, or not guilty?

Jubela—Guilty, my lord.

Master—Vile and impious wretch, hold up your head and hear your sentence. It is my order that you be taken without the walls of the Temple, and there have your throat cut across from ear to ear, your tongue torn out by the roots, your body buried in the rough sands of the sea, where the tide ebbs and flows twice in twenty-four hours.

Master—Jubelo, you are accused of the same offence; are you guilty, or not guilty?

Jubelo—Guilty, my lord.

Master—Vile and impious wretch, hold up your head and hear your sentence. It is my order that you be taken without the gates of the Temple, and there have your left breast torn open, your heart and vitals taken from thence and thrown over your left shoulder, and carried to the valley of Jehosaphat, there to become a prey to the wild beasts of the field, and vultures of the air.

Master—Jubelum, you are suspected of the murder of our Grand Master, Hiram Abiff; are you guilty, or not guilty?

Jubelum—Guilty, my lord.

Master—Vile and impious wretch, hold up your head and hear your sentence. It is my order that you be taken without the walls of the Temple, and there have your body severed in two, and divided to the north and south, your bowels burnt to ashes in the center, and scattered to the four winds of heaven. Brother Senior, (to Senior Warden,) you will see that these penalties are executed.

The Senior Warden gives the Master's order to his Junior, who in turn orders the Deacons to execute it.

The three ruffians are thereupon dragged out into the preparation room with some violence, where they stamp and groan a few minutes, when the Senior Deacon returns and says—Worshipful, the penalties of their several obligations have been duly executed upon the three murderers of our Grand Master, Hiram Abiff.

Master—It is well. You will now go in search of the body; and it is my opinion he is buried near where his three murderers were arrested, viz.: on the brow of Mount Moria.

The brethren again shuffle about the Lodge in search of the body. One of them approaches where the candidate is laying, in the west, and says—Here is something that looks like a grave. Let us dig down and see.

A number of brethren now come forward and remove the things which have covered up the candidate. As soon as he is uncovered, they all start back, turning their faces a little one side, and each holding his open right hand with the palm downward, up in front, as if to guard his nostrils from an offensive smell.

One says—We will go back to the Temple and inform King Solomon of our discovery.

Master (seeing them approach)—What tidings from Mount Moria?

A Brother—Worshipful, we have found the grave of our Grand Master, Hiram Abiff. It is situated due east and west, near the brow of Mount Moria. We dug down six feet perpendicularly till we came to the body, and involuntarily raised our hands in this position, [he gives the due-guard of this degree, as on page 30,] to guard our nostrils from the effluvia rising from the body. We searched on and about the body for the Master Mason's word, or a key to it, but could not find it, though we discovered a faint resemblance to the letter G marked on the left breast.

Master (rising, and giving the grand hailing sign of distress, as on page 29)—Nothing but a faint resemblance of the letter G! that is not the Master's word, nor a key to it. I fear the Master's word is forever lost! [Master repeats the sign and the words three times, and after the third time, adds:] O Lord, my God, is there no help for the widow's son?

Master, to Senior Warden—You will summon twelve Fellow Crafts and go with me to the grave, in order to raise our Grand Master.

The Senior Warden delivers this order to his Junior, who communicates it to the Lodge, when the members shuffle round as before. The Master now leaves his seat and goes to the west, where the candidate is lying, when twelve brothers (the Fellow Crafts aforesaid) form a circle round him and kneel.

Master (standing)—Let us pray. [He then recites, or reads from a text-book, this prayer:] Thou, O God, knowest our down-sitting and up-rising, and understandest our thoughts afar off; shield and defend us from the evil intentions of our enemies, and support us under the trials and afflictions we are destined to endure, while traveling through this vale of tears. Man that is born of woman, is of few days, and full of trouble. He cometh forth as a flower, and is cut down; he fleeth also as a shadow, and continueth not. Seeing his days are determined, the number of his months are with thee; thou hast appointed his bounds, that he cannot pass. Turn from him, that he may rest till he shall accomplish his day. For there is hope of a tree, if it be cut down, that it will sprout again, and that the tender branch thereof will not cease. But man dieth and wasteth away; yea, man giveth up the ghost, and where is he? As the waters fail from the sea, and the flood decayeth and dryeth up, so man lieth down, and riseth not again, till the heavens shall be no more. Yet, O Lord, have compassion on the children of thy creation; give them comfort in time of trouble, and save them with an everlasting salvation. Amen. So mote it be.

The twelve now rise, when the Master directs one of them to search the body and see if the Master's word cannot be found. He searches, and soon reports— No trace of it, my lord !

The Master and brethren all give the grand hailing sign of distress (page 29) and exclaim—O Lord, my God, I fear the Master's word is forever lost !

The Master directs that the body be raised by the Entered Apprentice's grip.

A brother takes the candidate by that grip (page 11) and pulls so as to raise him a little, then lets him back and says—My lord, the body cannot be raised by the Entered Apprentice's grip ; the skin cleaves from the flesh.

The Master and brethren again give the grand hailing sign of distress and repeat aloud—O Lord, my God, I fear the Master Mason's word is forever lost !

The Master orders another of the twelve to raise the body by the Fellow Craft's grip. He takes hold of the candidate by that grip, pulls him partly up, lets him fall back, and says—My lord, the body cannot be raised by the Fellow Craft's grip ; the flesh cleaves from the bone. All again raise their hands, as in the hailing sign of distress, and exclaim, O Lord, my God, I fear the Master's word is forever lost ! was there no help for the widow's son ?

Master—I shall now raise the body of our Grand Master by the lion's grip, the strong grip of a Master Mason ; and as the Master's word is now lost, the first word spoken after the body is raised, shall be a substitute for the Master's word, until future generations shall find out the right one.

The Master now takes the candidate by the Master Mason's grip, (see above,) and bracing his right foot against him, raises him upon the five points of fellowship. This is done by putting the inside of your right foot to the inside of the right foot of the one to whom you are going to give the word, the inside of your own knee to his, laying your breast close against his, your left hands on each other's back, and each one putting his mouth to the other's right ear; in which position alone you are permitted to give the Master's word, which is MAH-HAH-BONE.

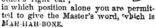

The Master's grip is given by taking hold of each other's right hand, as though you were going to shake hands, and sticking the nails of each of your fingers into the joint of the other's wrist where it unites with the hand. In this condition

the candidate is raised, he keeping his whole body stiff, as though dead. The Master in raising him is assisted by some of the brethren, who take hold of the candidate by the arms and shoulders. As soon as he is raised to his feet they step back, and the Master whispers the word MAH-HAH-BONE in his ear, and causes the candidate to repeat it, telling him at the same time that he must never give it in any manner other than that in which he receives it. He is also told that Mah-hah-bone signifies marrow in the bone. They then separate, and the Master makes the following explanation, respecting the five points of fellowship.

Master to candidate—Brother, foot to foot teaches you that you should, whenever asked, go on a brother's errand, if within the length of your cable-tow, even if you should have to go barefoot and bareheaded. Knee to knee, that you should always remember a Master Mason in your devotions to Almighty God. Breast to breast, that you should keep the Master Mason's secrets, when given to you in charge as such, as secure and inviolable in your breast as they were in his own, before communicated to you. Hand to back, that you will not speak evil of a Master Mason either behind his back or before his face. Mouth to ear, that you will give a brother Master Mason due and timely notice of all approaching danger, when you know that such danger threatens.

The candidate is now further instructed in the signs, &c., (already given,) and the charge in this degree is read to him from a text-book. He is then informed that he has taken the third degree in Masonry, and is entitled to a seat in any Master Mason's Lodge.

Master to the candidate—Brother, you have on this occasion represented one of the greatest men that ever lived, and the tragical catastrophe of his death, burial and resurrection; I mean Hiram Abiff, the widow's son, who was murdered by three ruffians, at the building of King Solomon's Temple, and who, in his inflexibility, integrity and fortitude, never was surpassed by man. The history of that momentous event is developed in the latter part of this degree, and will be thus handed down to posterity through all time. [In some Lodges the Master recites to the candidate a recapitulation of the history of the murder of the Grand Master, Hiram Abiff, but this repetition is now usually dispensed with.]

CLOSING LECTURE—FIRST SECTION.

Master to Senior Warden—Are you a Master Mason?

Senior Warden—I am; try me. Disprove me if you can.

Master—Where were you prepared to be made a Master Mason?

Senior Warden—In a room adjacent to the body of a just and lawfully constituted Lodge of such, duly assembled in a room, representing the sanctum sanctorum, or holy of holies, of King Solomon's Temple.

Master—How were you prepared?

Senior Warden—By being divested of all metals; neither naked nor clothed, barefooted nor shod; with a cable tow three times about my naked body; in which posture I was conducted to the door of the Lodge, where I gave three distinct knocks.

Master—What did those three distinct knocks allude to?

Senior Warden—To the third degree in Masonry; it being that on which I was about to enter.

Master—What was said to you from within?

Senoir Warden—Who comes there? &c. [The remainder of this lecture is a repetition of the questions and answers given and received in advancing a candidate to the Master's degree, (see pages 28 to 31,) the Warden answering in detail, and explaining in a past tense exactly how he was advanced up to the time that he resumed his usual clothing.]

SECOND SECTION.

Master—Did you ever return to the sanctum sanctorum, or holy of holies, of King Solomon's Temple?

Senior Warden—I did.

Master—Was there any particular event that marked your return?

Senior Warden—There was, viz.: I was accosted by three ruffians, who demanded of me the Master Mason's word.

Master—Did you ever give it to them?

Senior Warden—I did not, but bid them wait, with time and patience, till the Grand Lodge assembled at Jerusalem; and then, if they were found worthy, they should receive it; otherwise they could not.

Master—In what manner was you accosted?

Senior Warden—In attempting to retire at the south gate, I was accosted by one of them, who demanded of me the Master Mason's word, and, on my refusing to comply with his request, he gave me a blow with the twenty-four inch guage, across my throat; on which I fled to the west gate, where I was accosted by the second with more violence, and, on my refusing to comply with his request, he gave me a severe blow with the square, across my breast; on which I attempted to make my escape at the east gate, where I was accosted by the third with still more violence, and, on my refusing to comply with his request, he gave me a violent blow, with the common gavel, on the forehead, and brought me to the floor.

Master—Whom did you represent at that time?

Senior Warden—Our Grand Master, Hiram Abiff, who was slain at the building of King Solomon's Temple.

Master—Was his death premeditated?

Senior Warden—It was;—by fifteen Fellow Crafts, who conspired to extort from him the Master Mason's word; twelve of whom recanted; but the other three were base enough to carry their atrocious designs into execution.

Master—What did they do with the body?

Senior Warden—They carried it out at the west gate of the Temple, and buried it till low twelve at night, when they three met, agreeably to appointment, and carried it a westerly course from the Temple, and buried it under the brow of a hill, in a grave six feet due east and west, six feet perpendicular, and they then made their escape.

Master—What time was he slain?

Senior Warden—At high twelve at noon, when the crafts were from labor to refreshment.

Master—How came he to be alone at that time?

Senior Warden—Because it was the usual custom of our Grand Master, Hiram Abiff, every day, at high twelve, when the crafts were from labor to refreshment, to enter into the sanctum sanctorum, or holy of holies, and offer up his adorations to the ever living God, and draw out his plans and designs on his tressle-board for the crafts to pursue their labor.

Master—At what time was he missing?

Senior Warden—At low six in the morning, when King Solomon came up to the Temple, as usual, to view the work, and found the crafts all in confusion; and, on inquiring the cause, he was informed that their Grand Master, Hiram Abiff, was missing, and no plans or designs were laid down on the tressle-board for the crafts to pursue their labor.

[The questions and answers in this lecture, relative to the disposition of the body and its discovery, are precisely like those on pages 32, 33 and 34.

Master—How long had the body of the Grand Master, Hiram Abiff, remained in the grave on Mount Moria?

Senior Warden—Fourteen days.

Master—What did they do with the body?

Senior Warden—Raised it in a Masonic form, and carried it up to the Temple for more decent interment.

Master—Where was it buried?

Senior Warden—Under the sanctum sanctorum, or holy of holies, of King Solomon's Temple, over which they erected a marble monument, with this inscription delineated thereon :—A virgin weeping over a broken column, with a book open before her; in her right hand a sprig of cassia; in her left, an urn—Time standing behind her, with his hands infolded in the ringlets of her hair.

Master—What do they denote?

Senior Warden—The weeping virgin denotes the unfinished state of the Temple; the broken column, that one of the principal supporters in Masonry had fallen; the book open before her, that his memory was on perpetual record; the sprig of cassia, the timely discovery of his grave; the urn in her left hand, that his ashes were safely deposited under the sanctum sanctorum, or holy of holies, of King Solomon's Temple; and Time, standing behind her with his hands infolded in the ringlets of her hair, that time, patience, and perseverance will accomplish all things.

THIRD SECTION.

Master—What does the Master's Lodge represent?

Senior Warden—The sanctum sanctorum, or holy of holies, of King Solomon's Temple.

Master—How long was the Temple building?

Senior Warden—Seven years; during which it rained not in the day time, that the workmen might not be obstructed in their labor.

Master—What supported the Temple?

Senior Warden—Fourteen hundred and fifty-three columns, and two thousand, nine hundred and six pilasters; all hewn from the finest Parian marble.

Master—What further supported it?

Senior Warden—Three grand columns, or pillars.

Master—What were they called?

Senior Warden—Wisdom, Strength, and Beauty.

Master—What did they represent?

Senior Warden—The pillar of Wisdom represented Solomon, King of Israel, whose wisdom contrived the mighty fabric; the pillar of Strength, Hiram, King of Tyre, who strengthened Solomon in his grand undertaking; the pillar of Beauty, Hiram Abiff, the widow's son, whose cunning craft and curious workmanship beautified and adorned the Temple.

Master—How many were there employed in the building of King Solomon's Temple?

Senior Warden—Three Grand Masters; three thousand three hundred Masters, or overseers of the work; eighty thousand Fellow Crafts; and seventy thousand Entered Apprentices: all those were classed and arranged in such a manner, by the wisdom of Solomon, that neither envy, discord, nor confusion were suffered to interrupt that universal peace and tranquility that pervaded the work at that important period.

Master—How many constitutes an Entered Apprentice's Lodge?

Senior Warden—Seven; one Master and six Entered Apprentices.

Master—Where did they usually meet?

Senior Warden—On the ground floor of King Solomon's Temple.

Master—How many constitutes a Fellow Craft's Lodge?

Senior Warden—Five; two Masters and three Fellow Crafts.

Master—Where did they usually meet?

Senior Warden—In the middle chamber of King Solomon's Temple.

Master—How many constitutes a Master's Lodge?

Senior Warden—Three Master Masons.

Master—Where did they usually meet?

Senior Warden—In the sanctum sanctorum, or holy of holies, of King Solomon's Temple.

Master—Have you any emblems in this degree?

Senior Warden—We have several, and they are divided into two classes.

Master—What are the first class?

Senior Warden—The Pot of Incense, the Bee-hive, the Book of Constitutions, guarded by the Tyler's Sword, the Sword pointing to a Naked Heart, the All-seeing Eye, the Anchor and Ark, the Forty-seventh Problem of Euclid, the Hour-glass, the Scythe, and the Three Steps on the Master's Carpet.

Master—How are they explained?

Senior Warden—The POT OF INCENSE is an emblem of a pure heart, which is always an acceptable sacrifice to the Deity; and as this glows with fervent heat, so should our hearts continually glow with gratitude to the great and beneficent Author of our existence, for the manifold blessings and comforts we enjoy.

The BEE-HIVE is an emblem of industry, and recommends the practice of that virtue to all created beings, from the highest seraph in heaven to the lowest reptile of the dust. It teaches us, that, as we came into the world rational and intelligent beings, so we should ever be industrious ones; never sitting down contented while our fellow creatures around us are in want, when it is in our power to relieve them without inconvenience to ourselves.

The BOOK OF CONSTITUTIONS, guarded by the Tyler's Sword, reminds us that we should be ever watchful and guarded, in our thoughts, words, and actions, and particularly when before the enemies of Masonry; ever bearing in remembrance those truly Masonic virtues, Silence and Circumspection.

The SWORD POINTING TO A NAKED HEART demonstrates that justice will sooner or later overtake us; and, although our thoughts, words and actions may be hidden from the eyes of men, yet, that ALL-SEEING EYE whom the sun, moon, and stars obey, and under whose watchful care even comets perform their stupendous revolutions, pervades the inmost recesses of the human heart, and will reward us according to our merits.

The ANCHOR and ARK are emblems of a well-grounded hope and well spent life. They are emblematical of that Divine Ark which safely wafts us over this tempestuous sea of troubles, and that Anchor which shall safely moor us in a peaceful harbor, where the wicked cease from troubling, and the weary shall find rest.

The FORTY-SEVENTH PROBLEM OF EUCLID was an invention of our ancient friend and brother, the great Pythagoras, who, in his travels through Asia, Africa and Europe, was initiated into several orders of priesthood, and raised to the sublime degree of a Master Mason. He drew out many problems in Geometry, or Masonry, and on erecting this one he exclaimed, EUREKA! signifying *I have found it.* It teaches Masons to be general lovers of arts and sciences.

The HOUR-GLASS is an emblem of human life. As the sands run, thus wastes man. To-day, he puts forth the tender leaves of hope; to-morrow, blossoms, and bears his blushing honors thick upon him; the next day comes a frost, which nips the shoot, and when he thinks his greatness is still ripening, he falls, like autumn leaves, to enrich our mother earth.

The SCYTHE is an emblem of Time, which cuts the brittle thread of life and launches us into Eternity—showing that every one of us must be cut down by this all-devouring scythe, and be gathered into the unknown land of shadows.

The THREE STEPS usually delineated on the Master's Carpet, are emblematical of the three principal stages of human life, viz.: Youth, Manhood, and Age. In youth, as Entered Apprentices, we ought industriously to occupy our minds in the attainment of useful knowledge; in manhood, as Fellow Crafts, we should apply our knowledge to the discharge of our respective duties to God, our neighbors, and ourselves; so that, in age, as Master Masons, we may enjoy the happy reflections consequent on a well spent life, and die in the hope of a glorious immortality.

Master—What are the second class of emblems?

Senior Warden.—The Spade, the Coffin, the Death-head and Marrow-bones, and the Sprig of Cassia. They are thus explained:

The SPADE opens the vault to receive our bodies, where our active limbs will soon moulder to dust.

The COFFIN, DEATH-HEAD and MARROW-BONES are emblematical of the death and burial of our Grand Master, Hiram Abiff, and as such are worthy our serious attention.

The SPRIG OF CASSIA is emblematical of that immortal part of man that never dies, and should remind us that a correct and upright life here will enable us to enter into the Celestial Lodge above, where the Grand Master of the Universe presides.

This ends the Master Mason's degree, and the whole of the first three degrees of Masonry. Very few Masons take enough interest to be advanced further than to become a Master, and consequently never get the pass-word that was lost by the tragical death of Hiram Abiff.

The reader will wonder why this pass-word is represented as being utterly lost, when it must have been known to King Solomon, and to Hiram, King of Tyre, who were both Grand Masters, ranking as such, in building the Temple, equally with Hiram Abiff. The answer is, that by their oaths the pass-word of a Master Mason could not be given unless the three Masters were present; and as King Solomon, Hiram, King of Tyre, and Hiram Abiff were the only Master Masons in the world, the word could not be given at all after Hiram Abiff's death, and was therefore practically lost for all future Master Masons. King Solomon is said to have substituted in place of the lost one, the word now used in the Master Mason's degree, viz.: MAH-HAH-BONE. Yet the missing word was found after four hundred and seventy years, and was then, and still is used in the Royal Arch degree, as will be seen in the ceremonies of that degree.

Many years ago, after William Morgan published his book revealing the mysteries of the three first degrees, the Grand Lodge of the State of New York ordained and established a new Test-oath and Word for the Master Mason's degree, to prevent book-masons from gaining admittance into the Lodges. It was as follows:

A stranger who desired to visit a Lodge, presented himself at the door and rapped in the usual manner.

Tyler, looking out—Do you wish to visit this Lodge?

Stranger—Yes, if thought worthy.

Tyler—By what are you recommended?

Stranger—By my fidelity.

Tyler (opening the door, and extending his right arm obliquely forward and upward to an angle of about forty-five degrees, his hand open and thumb pointing upward)—Prove that.

Stranger comes forward and places the back of his left hand against the palm of the Tyler's extended right hand, leans forward and whispers in his ear L-O-S, and pronounces LOS.

This word is the reverse of SOL, the Sun. The Grand Lodge also made each Master Mason, on his initiation, solemnly swear, in addition to his other obligations, not to reveal this word and sign, under penalty of being forever disgraced and dishonored as a man, and despised, degraded and expelled as a Mason.

MARK MASTER'S DEGREE.

OPENING A LODGE OF MARK MASTERS.

Eight officers are necessary to open a Lodge in this degree, viz.: Right Worshipful Master, Master Overseer, Senior and Junior Overseers, Senior and Junior Wardens, Senior and Junior Deacons, Secretary and Treasurer.

The interior arrangements of the Lodge, and the positions of the Master, Wardens, Deacons, Secretary and Treasurer, are the same as those in the Entered Apprentice's degree, (page 5.) The Master Overseer takes his seat on the right of the Right Worshipful Master in the east. The Senior Overseer sits on the right of the Senior Warden in the west, and his Junior on the right of the Junior Warden in the south.

Right Worshipful Master [giving a rap with his gavel]—Brethren, I am about to open a Lodge of Mark Master Masons in this place, for the dispatch of business. I will thank you for your attention and assistance. If there is any person present who has not taken this degree, he is requested to retire. [To Senior Warden]—Brother Senior, are you satisfied that all present are Mark Masters?

Senior Warden—Right Worshipful, I wish the pass-word might be given by the brethren.

The two Deacons thereupon go round and receive the word, which is JOPPA, in same manner as in the Fellow Craft's degree, (page 19.)

Master (giving one rap)—Brother Junior Deacon, the first care of congregated Masons?

Junior Deacon (rising and giving the due-guard in this degree, as on page 42) —To see the Lodge tyled, Right Worshipful.

Master—Perform that part of your duty, and inform the Tyler that we are about to open a Lodge of Mark Master Masons in this place for the dispatch of business; and direct him to tyle accordingly.

The Junior Deacon then walks very quick to the door, and gives four raps, which are answered by four without, from the Tyler; the Junior Deacon then gives one, which is answered by the Tyler with one; the door is then partly opened, when the Junior Deacon delivers his message. He then returns, gives the due-guard again, and says—The door is tyled, Right Worshipful.

Master—How tyled?

Junior Deacon—With secresy and brotherly love; also by a brother of this degree, with a drawn sword in his hand.

Master—His duty there?

Junior Deacon—To keep off cowans and eaves-droppers, see that none pass or re-pass without due qualification, or permission from the Right Worshipful Master.

Master—Let us be clothed, brethren. [Here the officers and members put on their aprons and jewels.] The Master gives two raps with his gavel, which brings all the subordinate officers on their feet; and each standing in his place, recites his duty on being questioned.

Master—The Junior Overseer's station in the Lodge?

Junior Overseer—At the south gate.

Master—Your duty there, Brother Junior Overseer?

Junior Overseer—To inspect all materials brought up for the building of the Temple; and, if approved, pass them on to the Senior Overseer, at the west gate, for further inspection.

Master—The Senior Overseer's place in the Lodge?

Senior Overseer—At the west gate.

Master—Your business there, Brother Senior Overseer?

Senior Overseer—To inspect all materials brought up for the building of the Temple; and, if approved, pass them on to the Master Overseer, at the east gate, for further inspection.

Master—The Master Overseer's place in the Lodge?

Master Overseer—At the east gate.

Master—Your business there, Brother Master Overseer?

Master Overseer—To preside at the inspection of all materials brought up for the building of the Temple; and, if disapproved, to call a council of my brother Overseers.

Master—The Junior Deacon's place in the Lodge?

Junior Deacon—At the right, in front of the Senior Warden.

Master—Your duty there, Brother Junior?

Junior Deacon—To carry messages from the Senior Warden in the west, to the Junior Warden in the south; and elsewhere about the Lodge, as he may direct.

Master—The Senior Deacon's place in the Lodge?

Senior Deacon—At the right, in front of the Right Worshipful Master in the east.

Master—Your duty there, Bro. Senior?

Senior Deacon—To carry messages from the Right Worshipful Master in the east, to the Senior Warden in the west, and elsewhere about the Lodge, as he may direct. To assist in the preparation and initiation of candidates, and to welcome and clothe all visiting brethren.

Master—The Secretary's station in the Lodge?

Secretary—At the left hand of the Right Worshipful Master in the east.

Master—Your duty there, Brother Secretary?

Secretary—To record the doings of the Lodge, collect all money, pay it over to the Treasurer, and keep a true and correct account of the same.

Master—The Treasurer's station in the Lodge?

Treasurer—At the right hand of the Worshipful Master in the east.

Master—Your duty there, Brother Treasurer?

Treasurer—To receive all money from the hands of the Secretary, to keep a true and correct account of the same, and pay it out by order of the Right Worshipful Master, with the consent of the brethren.

Master—The Junior Warden's place in the Lodge?

Junior Warden—In the south, Right Worshipful.

Master—Your duty there, Bro. Junior?

Junior Warden—As the sun is in the south at high twelve, which is the glory and beauty of the day, so stands the Junior Warden in the south, to call the crafts from labor to refreshment, and from refreshment to labor, that the Right Worshipful Master may have profit and pleasure thereby.

Master—The Senior Warden's place in the Lodge?

Senior Warden—In the west, Right Worshipful.

Master—Your duty there, Bro. Senior?

Senior Warden—As the sun sets in the west, to close the day, so stands the Senior Warden in the west, to assist the Right Worshipful Master in opening and closing his Lodge, pay the crafts their wages, if any be due, and see that none go away dissatisfied ; harmony being the strength and support of all institutions, but more especially of ours.

Master—The Right Worshipful Master's station in the Lodge ?

Senior Warden—In the east, Right Worshipful.

Master—His duty there, Brother Senior ?

Senior Warden—As the sun rises in the east, to open and adorn the day, so rises the Right Worshipful Master in the east, to open and adorn his Lodge, and set the craft to work with proper instructions for their labor.

Master (rising)—After that manner so do I. It is my will and pleasure that a Lodge of Mark Master Masons be opened in this place, for the dispatch of business. Brother Senior, you will please communicate the same to the Junior Warden in the south, that the brethren may have due and timely notice thereof.

Senior Warden to his Junior—Brother Junior, it is the Right Worshipful Master's order that a Lodge of Mark Master Masons be opened in this place for the dispatch of business. You will please inform the brethren thereof.

Junior Warden (giving three raps with the gavel)—Brethren, it is our Right Worshipful Master's order that a Lodge of Mark Master Masons be opened in this place for the dispatch of business. You are ordered to take due notice thereof, and govern yourselves accordingly.

Master—Attend to the signs, brethren.

The members present first give the Entered Apprentice signs, (page 7,) the Fellow Craft signs, (page 22,) and the Master Mason's signs, (pages 29 and 30.) The Mark Master's signs are then given as follows : First, interlace the fingers of both hands, and hold them down in front opposite to the right hip, then draw them upward as if you held a weight in them, and bring them to the left side of the neck in a manner to indicate that you have thrown the weight over your left shoulder, the palms of your hands facing the shoulder. This is called HEAVE-OVER, and alludes to the rejection of the key-stone in this de-

Heave Over.

gree. You then drop your arms down, the last two fingers of the right hand clenched, the first two and thumb open, parallel with each other and about one inch apart.— It alludes to the manner the candidate is directed to carry the key-stone. You then raise the right hand to your right ear, still holding the thumb and the two first fingers open, and with a circular motion of the hand the fingers should be passed round the ear, as though you were combing back your ear-lock, the ear passing between the two fingers and thumb. The hand is then dropped partly down, the palm open and in a horizontal position, then lift up the left hand and bring it down edgewise upon the wrist of the right. This alludes to the penalties of the obligation in this degree, viz : to have both the ear and the right hand cut off. The third sign is made by extending in front the right arm at full length, the thumb and two first fingers open, about one inch apart, the third and little fingers clenched, palm of the hand up. It

Due-guard.

alludes to the peculiar manner in which the Mark Master is taught to receive wages.

The Master now reads from a text-book the following : Wherefore my brethren, lay aside all malice and guile, and hypocrisies, and envies, and all evil speaking. If so be, ye have tasted that the Lord is gracious ; to whom coming, as unto a living stone, disallowed indeed of men, but chosen of

God, and precious; ye also, as living stones, be ye built up a spiri al house, an holy priesthood, to offer up sacrifices acceptable to God. Brethren, this is the will of God, that with well-doing ye put to silence the ignorance of foolish men. As free, and not as using your liberty for a cloak of maliciousness, but as the servants of God.

The Right Worshipful Master then gives two raps with his gavel; Senior Warden two, and Junior Warden two, which raps are then repeated.

Master—I now declare this Lodge of Mark Master Masons opened in due and , ancient form, and hereby forbid all improper conduct whereby this Lodge may be disturbed, under no less penalty than the by-laws, or a majority of the Lodge may see fit to inflict. Master (to Junior Deacon)—Brother Junior, please to inform the Tyler the Lodge is open.

Junior Deacon informs the Tyler, and returns to his seat.

The Lodge being opened and ready for business, the Right Worshipful Master directs the Secretary to read the minutes of the last meeting, which generally brings to view the business of the present. If there are any candidates to be brought forward, that is generally the first business. A Master Mason wishing for further light in Masonry, sends a petition to the Chapter, and requests to be advanced to the honorary degree of Mark Master Mason ; he is balloted for in the same manner as in the Entered Apprentice's degree, (page 8.)

The Senior Deacon, who prepares and conducts the candidate in the first part of the ceremonies, passes out of the Lodge into the adjoining room, where the candidate is in waiting, pulls off his coat, and rolls up his shirt sleeves to the shoulder, and directs the candidate to do the same ; he then takes in his right hand a small block of white marble about four inches square, and six inches long, weighing about eleven pounds, holding it between the thumb and two first fingers, the other fingers clenched, the arm extended down ; the candidate is furnished with a key stone, of the same material and weight, which he is directed to carry in like manner ; the door is then opened without ceremony, and the Junior Deacon, as Conductor, enters, about three paces in advance of the candidate, and walks four times round the Lodge, and halts at the Junior Overseer's station at the south gate, where the Conductor gives four raps with his heel on the floor.

Junior Overseer—Who comes here ?

Senior Deacon—A craftsman from the quarries, bringing up work for inspection.

Junior Overseer—Have you a specimen of your work ?

Senior Deacon—I have.

Junior Overseer—Present it.

The Senior Deacon presents his stone to the Junior Overseer, who applies his small trying square to its different angles, and they agreeing with the angles of the square, he says—This is good work—square work—just such work as is wanted for the building , [returning the block to the Senior Deacon.] You will pass on to the Senior Overseer at the west gate, for further inspection.

Senior Deacon goes only a few steps, until the candidate has been examined. Candidate comes up to Junior Overseer in imitation of his Conductor, and gives four raps with his heel.

Junior Overseer—Who comes here ?

Candidate—A craftsman from the quarries, bringing up work for inspection.

Junior Overseer—Have you a specimen of your work ?

Candidate—I have.

Junior Overseer—Present it.

Candidate presents the key stone.

Junior Overseer (applying his square to it, and finding it does not fit)—This is a curious wrought stone indeed : it is neither oblong or square ; square work is only such as we have orders to receive ; neither has it the mark of any of the craft upon it. Is that your mark ?" [pointing to the letters on the key stone.]

Candidate—It is not.

Junior Overseer—Owing to its singular form and beauty, I feel unwilling to reject it; you will pass on to the Senior Overseer at the west gate for further inspection.

The same scene then occurs with the Senior Overseer at the west gate, who directs both the Senior Deacon and candidate to the Master Overseer at the east gate. Senior Deacon presents his stone to him.

Master Overseer (applying his square)—This is good work—square work—just such work as is wanted for the building, you are entitled to your wages; pass on. Conductor passes and takes his seat.

Candidate then presents his key stone, as before.

Master Overseer (applying his square) —This is a curiously wrought stone. It appears to be neither oblong nor square, nor is there any mark upon it. [Looking sternly at candidate]—Is this your work ?

Candidate—It is not.

Master Overseer—Where did you get it?

Candidate—I picked up this stone in the quarry.

Master Overseer—Why do you bring another man's work to impose upon the Overseers? You will stand aside.

The Master Overseer now stamps on the floor four times with his foot, which brings up the other two Overseers.

Master Overseer—Brother Junior Overseer, did you suffer this work to pass your inspection?

Junior Overseer—I did; I observed to the young craftsman, at the time, the stone was not such as we had orders to receive; but owing to its singular form and beauty, I felt unwilling to reject it, and suffered it to pass to the Senior Overseer at the west gate.

Senior Overseer—I made the same observations to the young craftsman, and for the same reason permitted it to pass to the Master Overseer at the east gate.

Master—Why, you see the stone is neither oblong or square, neither has it the *mark* of any of the craft upon it. Do you know this mark that is upon it?

Junior Overseer—I do not.

Senior Overseer—Neither do I.

Master Overseer—What shall I do with it?

Junior Overseer—I propose we heave it over among the rubbish.

Master Overseer—Agreed: it shall be done.

The Master and Senior Overseers take up the key stone, and swinging it four times back and forth between them, the fourth time the Junior Overseer catches it over the left shoulder of the Master Overseer (in imitation of the sign of heave over), and throws it aside. At this moment all the brethren begin to shuffle around the room, leaving their seats.

Master (giving one rap with his gavel) —What is the cause of this disturbance among the workmen?

Senior Warden—It is the sixth hour of the sixth day of the week, and the craft are impatient to receive their wages.

Master—Brother Senior Warden, it is my order that you assemble the craft, and march in procession to the office of the Senior Grand Warden, to receive wages.

The members now form two and two, (candidate behind,) and march round the Lodge, singing the song, "Mark Masters, all appear," &c., from the Text-book.

As they finish the second verse, each brother walks up in his turn to the Senior Warden, who stands behind a lattice window, and thrusts his hand through the hole in the window, receives his penny, withdraws his hand, and passes on, and so on, until the candidate, who comes last, puts his hand through, for his penny. The Senior Warden seizes his hand, and bracing his foot against the window, draws the candidate's arm through to the shoulder, and exclaims vehemently, "An impostor! an impostor!" another person exclaims, "Strike off his hand!" and at the same time runs up with a drawn sword to give the blow. The Senior Deacon now intercedes for the candidate, and says, "Spare him; he is not

an impostor; I know him to be a crafts-man; I have wrought with him in the quarries."

Senior Warden—He is an impostor, for he has attempted to receive wages without being able to give the *token*, and the penalty must be inflicted.

Senior Deacon—If you will release him, I will take him to our Right Wor-shipful Master, and state his case to him. and if the penalty must be inflicted, I will see it duly executed.

Senior Warden—On those conditions I will release him, provided he can satisfy me he is a Fellow Craft Mason.

* The candidate now withdraws his arm, and gives the sign of a Fellow Craft Ma-son, as on page 22.

The members of the Lodge then take their seats.

Senior Deacon (taking candidate to Master)—Right Worshipful, this young craftsman has been detected as an im-postor, at the office of the Senior Grand Warden, in attempting to receive wages without being able to give the *token*.

Master (looking sternly at the candi-date)—Are you a Fellow Craft Mason?

Candidate—I am.

Master—Give me the sign of a Fellow Craft Mason?

Candidate gives the sign, as before.

Master to Senior Deacon—It is well. He is undoubtedly a Fellow Craft. [Turn-ing to candidate.] You have attempted to receive wages without being able to give the token—I am astonished that so intelligent a looking young craftsman should thus attempt to impose upon us. Such conduct requires severe punish-ment. The penalty you have incurred is to have your right hand struck off. Have you ever been taught how to re-ceive wages?

Candidate—I have not.

Master—Ah, this in a measure serves to mitigate your crime. If you are in-structed how to receive wages, will you do better for the future?

Candidate—I will.

Master—On account of your youth and inexperience, the penalty is remitted. Brother Senior Deacon, you will take this young craftsman, and give him a severe reprimand, and take him with you to the quarries, and there teach him how to bring up a regular wrought stone.

Senior Deacon (taking candidate by the collar)—Young man, it appears you have come up here this evening to im-pose upon us; first, by presenting work which was not fit for the building, and then by claiming wages when there was

not one farthing your due. Your work was not approved; you are not entitled to any wages, and had it not been for my timely interference, you would have lost your right hand, if not your life. Let this be a striking lesson to you, never to attempt to impose upon the craft here-after. But go with me to the quarries, and there exhibit some specimens of your skill and industry; and if your work is approved, you shall be taught how to re-ceive wages in a proper manner. Come, I say, go with me. [Shakes the candi-date severely, and hurries him off into the preparation room.]

The Senior Deacon returns to his seat in the Lodge, and the Junior Deacon prepares the candidate for the degree, by divesting him of his outward apparel, and all money and valuables, his breast bare, and a cable-tow four times round his bo-dy; in which condition he is conducted to the door, and gives four distinct knocks.

Senior Deacon—Right Worshipful, while we are peaceably at work on the fourth degree in Masonry, the door of our Lodge appears to be alarmed.

Master—Brother Senior, attend to the cause of that alarm.

The Senior Deacon then steps to the door, and answers the alarm by four knocks. This is responded to from the outside by one knock, which is returned by the Senior Deacon. The door is then partly opened.

Senior Deacon—Who comes there?

Junior Deacon—A worthy brother, who has been regularly initiated as an Entered Apprentice Mason, served a proper time as such, passed to the degree of a Fellow Craft, raised to the sublime degree of a Master Mason, and now wishes for further light in Masonry, by being advanced to the more honorable degree of Mark Master Mason.

Senior Deacon—Is it of his own free will and accord he makes this request?

Junior Deacon—It is.

Senior Deacon—Is he duly and truly prepared?

Junior Deacon—He is.

Senior Deacon—Has he wrought in the quarries, and exhibited specimens of his skill in the preceding degrees?

Junior Deacon—He has.

Senior Deacon—By what further right or benefit does he expect this favor?

Junior Deacon—By the benefit of a pass-word.

Senior Deacon—Has he a pass-word?

Junior Deacon—He has not, but I have it for him.

Senior Deacon—Give it me.

Junior Deacon whispers in his ear the word JOPPA.

Senior Deacon—The pass-word is right. You will let him wait until the Right Worshipful Master is made acquainted with his request, and his answer returned.

Senior Deacon ..... to the Right Worshipful Master, where the same questions are asked, and answers returned, as at the door.

Master—Since he comes endowed with the necessary qualifications, let him enter, in the name of the Lord, and take heed on what he enters.

The door is then opened, the candidate enters, the Junior Deacon steps behind him, takes hold of his arms, draws them back, and holds them firmly behind.

Senior Deacon (approaching candidate with a mallet and engraving chisel in his hands)—Brother, it becomes my duty to place a mark upon you which you will probably carry to your grave. As an Entered Apprentice Mason, you were received upon one point of the compasses, pressing your naked left breast; as a Fellow Craft Mason, you were received upon the angle of a square, pressing your naked right breast: as a Master Mason, you were received upon both points of the compasses, extending from your naked left to right breast. They were then explained to you. The chisel and mallet [placing the edge of the chisel against his breast] are instruments used by operative Masons to hew, cut, carve, and indent their work : but we, as Free and Accepted Masons, make use of them for a more noble and glorious purpose. We use them to hew, cut, carve, and indent the mind. And as a Mark Master Mason, we receive you upon the edge of the indenting chisel, and under the pressure of the mallet.

As he pronounces the last words, he braces his feet, raises his mallet, and makes two or three false motions, and gives a violent blow upon the head of the chisel ; throws down mallet and chisel, takes hold of the cable-tow, and says to candidate—Follow me.

They walk four times round the Lodge, and each time as he passes the stations of the Master, Senior and Junior Wardens, they each give one loud rap with their mallet. The Master, in the mean time, reads from a text-book the following passages of Scripture :

The stone which the builders refused, is become the head stone of the corner. —Psalm cxviii. 22.

Did ye never read in the Scriptures, The stone which the builders rejected, is become the head of the corner ?—Gospel of St. Matthew, ch. xxi. v. 42.

And have you not read this Scripture, The stone which the builders rejected, is become the head of the corner ?—Mark, chap. xii. v. 10.

What is this, then, that is written, The stone which the builders rejected, is become the head of the corner.—Luke xx. verse 17.

The reading is so timed as to be completed just as the candidate arrives at the Junior Warden's post ; who gives an alarm of four knocks, and the same questions are asked, and answers returned, as at the door.

The Junior Warden directs him to his Senior, who, on his arrival, gives four raps, and the like questions are asked and answered. From thence he is directed to the Right Worshipful Master in the east, where the same questions are asked and the same answers given. The Master then orders that the candidate be conducted back to the Senior Warden in the west, and be taught by him to approach the east by four upright regular steps, his feet forming a square, and body erect at the altar. The candidate then kneels, and receives the obligation, as follows :

I, John Smith, of my own free will and accord, in presence of Almighty God, and this Right Worshipful Lodge of Mark Master Masons, do hereby and hereon, in addition to my former obligations, most solemnly and sincerely promise and swear, that I will not give the secrets of a Mark Master Mason to any one of an inferior degree, nor to any other person in the known world, except it be a true and lawful brother, or brethren, of this degree ; and not unto him nor unto them whom I shall hear so to be, but unto him and them only whom I shall find so to be, after strict trial and due examination, or lawful information given. Furthermore do I promise and swear, that I will support the constitution of the General Grand Royal Arch Chapter of the United States of America, also the Grand Royal Arch Chapter of this State, under which this Lodge is held, and conform to all the by-laws, rules and regulations of this or any other Lodge of Mark Master Masons, of which I may at any time hereafter become a member. Furthermore do I promise and swear, that I will obey all regular signs and summons given, handed, sent, or thrown to me from the hand of a brother Mark Master Mason, or from the body of a just and legally constituted Lodge of such, provided it be within the length of my cable-tow. Furthermore do I promise and swear, that I will not wrong this Lodge, or a brother of this degree, to the value of his wages, (or one penny) myself, knowingly, nor suffer it to be done by others if in my power to prevent it. Furthermore do I promise and swear, that I will not sell, swap, barter, or exchange my mark, which I shall hereafter choose, after it has been recorded in the book of marks, for any other one unless it be a dead mark, or one of an older date, nor will I pledge it a second time until it is lawfully redeemed from the first pledge. Furthermore do I promise and swear, that I will receive a brother's mark when offered to me requesting a favor, and grant him his request if in my power ; and if it is not in my power to grant his request, I will return him his mark with the value thereof, which is half a shekel of silver, or quarter of a dollar. To all of which I do most solemnly and sincerely promise and swear, with a fixed and steady purpose of mind in me to keep and perform the same, binding myself under no less penalty than to have my right ear smote off, that I may forever be unable to hear the word, and my right hand chopped off, as the penalty as an impostor, if I should ever prove wilfully guilty of violating any part of this my solemn oath, or obligation, of a Mark Master Mason. So help me God, and make me steadfast to keep and perform the same.

Master—Detach your hand and kiss the book four times.

As soon as the candidate has taken the obligation, some brother makes an alarm on the outside of the door.

Junior Deacon (rising)—There is an alarm at the door, Right Worshipful.

Master—Attend to the alarm, brother, and see who comes there.

Junior Deacon inquires the cause of the alarm, and returns with a letter for the Right Worshipful Master, who opens it and reads as follows, or something to this effect :

To the Right Worshipful Master,
St. Johns Mark Lodge :

Dear Brother—I am in the immediate want of the loan of twenty-five dollars, which I wish to borrow of Brother Smith. The only security which I can offer for the same, is my *mark*, which I *pledge* until the money is refunded. You will please present it to him, and send the money by the bearer.

Yours fraternally,   T. JONES.

Master, to candidate, at the same time handing him the mark—Well, can you accommodate Brother Jones with this money he asks the loan of ?

Candidate receives the mark, says he has no money about him ; he cannot grant the request.

Senior Warden—Right Worshipful, I can accommodate Brother Jones with twenty-five dollars, if he will leave his mark with me, as a pledge.

Master, to candidate—Will you return the mark, then ?

Candidate hands it back.

Master—How is this ? do you return it without the price, and thus break your oath before you rise from the altar ? Have you not sworn that where you could not grant a brother's request, you would return his mark with the price thereof, viz. : half a Jewish shekel of silver, or the fourth of a dollar ?

Candidate is generally embarrassed, and replies that all his money was taken from him in the preparation room.

Master—Are you sure that you have not even a quarter dollar about you ?

Candidate—I am.

Master—Look further. Perhaps some good friend has, in pity to your destitute situation, supplied you with that amount unknown to yourself : feel in all your pockets, and if you find, after a thorough search, that you have really none, we shall have less reason to think that you meant wilfully to violate your obligation.

The candidate feels in his pocket and finds a quarter of a dollar, which some brother had slily placed there. He protests he had no intention of concealing it ; really supposed he had none about him, and hands it to the Master, with the mark.

Master—Brother, let this scene be a striking lesson to you ; should you ever hereafter have a mark presented you by a worthy brother, asking a favor, before you deny him, make diligent search, and be quite sure of your inability to serve him ; perhaps you will then find, as in the present instance, that some unknown person has befriended you, and you are really in a better situation than you think yourself.

The Right Worshipful Master now takes the candidate by the hand, and says—Arise, brother, and I will invest you with the pass-grip and word, and also the real grip and word of a Mark Master Mason.

The pass-grip of this degree is made by extending the right arms and clasping the fingers of the right hands, as one would naturally do to assist another up a steep ascent. It is said to have originated from the fact that the banks of the river at Joppa were so steep that the workmen on the Temple had to assist each other up them while conveying the timber from the forests of Lebanon. The pass-word is JOPPA.

Master, to candidate—Will you be *off*, *or from*?

Candidate—From.

Master—From what?

Candidate—From the pass-grip to the true grip of a Mark Master Mason.

Master—Pass on.

The grip is made by locking the little fingers of the right hands, turning the backs of them together, and placing the ends of the thumbs against each other; its name is SIROC, or MARK WELL, and when properly made forms the initials of those two words, mark well.

The Right Worshipful Master, after admonishing the candidate never to give the words in any way but that in which he received them, resumes his seat, when the brethren shuffle about their feet.

Master—What means this disturbance among the workmen, Brother Senior?

Senior Warden (rising)—Right Worshipful, the workmen are at a stand for the want of a certain key stone to one of the principal arches, which no one has had orders to make.

Master—A key stone to one of the principal arches? I gave our Grand Master, Hiram Abiff, strict orders to make that key stone, previous to his assassination. [Gives two raps with his gavel, which brings the three Overseers before him.] Brothers Overseers, has there been a stone of this description brought up for inspection? [exhibiting the figure of a key stone.]

Master Overseer—There was a stone of that description brought up for inspec-

tion, but it being neither oblong nor square, nor having the mark of any of the craft upon it, and we not knowing the mark that was upon it, supposed it unfit for the building, and it was thrown over among the rubbish.

Master—Let immediate search be made for it; the Temple cannot be finished without it; it is one of the most valuable stones in the whole building. [The brethren then shuffle about the Lodge again, and find the key stone, and bring it up to the east.]

The Master receives the stone and then reads to the Overseers from text-book—This is the stone which was set at naught by you builders, which is become the head of the corner—Acts iv. 11.

The Overseers retire confounded.

Master reads to candidate from text-book—To him that overcometh will I give to eat of the hidden manna, and I will give him a white stone, and in the stone a new name written, which no man knoweth, saving him that receiveth it.—[Rev. xi. 17.] Come forward, and receive the new name.

Candidate steps forward.

Master—Brother, I will now invest you with the new name that none but a Mark Master can receive. It is a circle of letters which are the general mark of this degree, and are the initials of the following words: HIRAM TYRIAN, WIDOW'S SON, SENT TO KING SOLOMON.

$$\begin{array}{cc} & H \\ T & W \\ S & S \\ T & K \end{array}$$

Within this circle of letters every Mark Master Mason must place his own private mark, which may be any device he chooses to select.

Master reads to candidate—He that hath an ear to ear, let him hear.—Rev. chap. iii. v. 13.

The Master further instructs the candidate in the signs of the penalties of this degree. (page 42,) and then presents, or points out to him on the chart, the working tools of a Mark Master Mason, viz.: a mallet and chisel, the use of which he explains as follows:—The chisel morally demonstrates the advantages of discipline and education. The mind, like the diamond in its original state, is rude and unpolished, but as the effect of the chisel on the external coat soon presents to view the latent beauties of the diamond, so education discovers the latent beauties of the mind, and draws them forth to range the large field of matter and space, to display the summit of human knowledge, our duty to God and man. The mallet morally teaches to correct irregularities, and to reduce man to a proper level; so that by quiet deportment, he may, in the school of discipline, learn to be content. What the mallet is to the workman, enlightened reason is to the passions; it curbs ambition, it depresses envy, it moderates anger, and it encourages good dispositions, whence arises among good Masons that comely order "which nothing earthly gives, or can destroy."

Master, to candidate—Brother, in taking this degree, you have represented one of the Fellow Craft Masons who wrought at the building of King Solomon's Temple. It was their custom on the eve of the sixth day of the week to carry up their work for inspection. This young craftsman discovered in the quarries the key stone to one of the principal arches that had been wrought by the Grand Master, Hiram Abiff, and, throwing away his own work, he took it up to the Temple, where it was inspected by the Overseers, rejected as of no account, and thrown over among the rubbish. He then repaired to the office of the Senior Grand Warden to receive his wages; but not being able to give the token, he was detected as an impostor, which like to have cost him his right hand; but King Solomon pardoned him, and after a severe reprimand he was taken back to the quarries. Previous to the completion of the Temple, the progress of the work was interrupted for want of the key stone, which circumstance being communicated to King Solomon, he gave orders that search should be made for it among the rubbish, where it was found, and afterwards applied to its intended use. How it was disposed of, we cannot now inform you. You must advance further in the mysteries of Masonry, before you can know.

On the sixth hour of the sixth day of every week, the craft, being eighty thousand in number, formed in procession, and repaired to the office of the Senior Grand Wardens, to receive their wages; and in order to prevent the craft being imposed upon by unskilful workmen, each craftsman claiming wages was made to thrust his hand through a lattice window, and at the same time give this token, holding under the two last fingers of his hand, a copy of his mark.

The Senior Grand Warden cast his eye upon the corresponding mark in the book, (where all the marks of the craft, eighty thousand in number, were recorded,) and seeing how much money was due to that particular mark, placed it between the thumb and two fore-fingers of the craftsman, who withdrew his hand

and passed on; and so on, each in his turn, until all were paid off. If any person attempted to receive wages without being able to give the token, the Senior Grand Warden seized him by the hand, drew his arm through the window, held him fast, and exclaimed immediately, "An impostor!" Upon this signal, an officer who was stationed there for that purpose, would immediately strike his arm off.

The following charge is then given to the candidate, by the Right Worshipful Master:

Brother, I congratulate you on having been thought worthy of being advanced to this honorable degree of Masonry. Permit me to impress it on your mind, that your assiduity should ever be commensurate with your duties, which become more and more extensive as you advance in Masonry. In the honorable character of Mark Master Mason, it is more particularly your duty to endeavor to let your conduct in the Lodge and among your brethren, be such as may stand the test of the Grand Overseer's square: that you may not, like the unfinished and imperfect work of the negligent and unfaithful of former times, be rejected, and thrown aside, as unfit for that spiritual building, that house not made with hands, eternal in the heavens. While such is your conduct, should misfortunes assail you, should friends forsake you, should envy traduce your good name, and malice persecute you: yet may you have confidence, that among Mark Master Masons you will find friends who will administer to your distresses, and comfort your afflictions; ever bearing in mind, as a consolation under the frowns of fortune, and as an encouragement to hope for better prospects, that *the stone which the builders rejected*, possessing merits to them unknown, became the chief stone of the corner.

The brethren shuffle round the Lodge again, as before.

Master, giving one rap—Brother Senior, what is the cause of this disturbance?

Senior Warden—Right Worshipful, is the sixth hour of the sixth day of the week, and the crafts are inpatient to receive their wages.

Master—You will form them in procession, and let them repair to the office of the Senior Grand Wardens and receive their wages.

Members form two and two and march around the Lodge against the sun, and sing from the text-book the last three

4

verses of the Mark Master's Song. The ceremony of paying the wages is gone through at the Master's seat in the east, the Master acting as Senior Grand Warden, and paying "every man a penny."

The members then inquire, each of the other, "How much have you?" The answer is given, "A penny." Some one asks the candidate the. question, and he replies, "A penny." At this information, all the brethren pretend to be in a great rage, and hurl their pennies on the floor with violence, each protesting against the manner of paying the craft.

Master, giving one rap—Brethren, what is the cause of this confusion ?

Senior Deacon—The craft are dissatisfied with the manner in which you pay them. Here is a young craftsman, who has just past the square, and has received as much as we, who have borne the burden and fatigue of the day ; and we don't think it is right and just ; and we will not put up with it.

Master—This is the law, and it is perfectly right.

Junior Deacon—I don't know of any law that will justify any such proceeding. If there is any such law, I should be glad if you would show it.

Master—If you will be patient, you shall hear the law. [Reads.] For the kingdom of heaven is like unto a man that is an householder, which went out early in the morning, to hire laborers into his vineyard. And when he had agreed with the laborers for a penny a day, he sent them into his vineyard. And he went out about the third hour, and saw others standing idle in the market-place, and said unto them, Go ye also into the vineyard ; and whatsoever is right, I will give you. And they went their way. And he again went out, about the sixth and ninth hour, and did likewise ; and about the eleventh hour, he went out and found others standing idle, and saith unto them, Why stand ye here all the day idle ? They say unto him, Because no man hath hired us. He saith unto them, Go ye also into the vineyard, and whatsoever is right, that shall ye receive. So when even was come, the lord of the vineyard saith unto his steward, Call the laborers, and give them their hire, beginning from the last unto the first. And when they came that were hired about the eleventh hour, they received every man a penny. But when the first came, they supposed that they should have received more ; and they likewise received, every man a penny. And when they had received it, they murmured against the good man of the house, saying, These last have wrought but one hour, and thou hast made them equal unto us, which have borne the burden and heat of the day. But he answered one of them, and said, Friend, I do thee no wrong : didst thou not agree with me for a penny ? Take that thine is, and go thy way ; I will give unto this last, even as unto thee. Is it not lawful for me to do what I will with mine own ? Is thine eye evil, because I am good ? So the last shall be first, and the first last : for many are called, but few chosen. MATTHEW xx. 1 to 16.

Master—Are you content ?

Brethren (picking up their pennies)—We are satisfied.

CLOSING LECTURE—FIRST SECTION.

Master, to Senior Warden—Are you a Mark Master Mason ?

Senior Warden—I am ; try me.

Master—By what will you be tried ?

Senior Warden—By the engraving chisel and mallet.

Master—Why by the engraving chisel and mallet ?

Senior Warden—Because they are the true and proper Masonic implements of this degree.

Master—On what was the degree founded ?

Senior Warden—On a certain key stone which belonged to the principal arch of King Solomon's Temple.

Master—Who formed this key stone ?

Senior Warden—Our worthy Grand Master, Hiram Abiff.

Master—What were the preparatory steps relative to your advancement to this degree ?

Senior Warden—I was caused to represent one of the Fellow Crafts at the building of King Solomon's Temple, whose custom it was, on the eve of every sixth day, to carry up their work for inspection.

Master—Why was you caused to represent these Fellow Crafts ?

Senior Warden—Because our worthy Grand Master, Hiram Abiff, had completed this key stone, agreeable to the original plan ; and before he gave orders to have it carried up to the Temple, was slain by three ruffians ; and it so happened that on the eve of a certain sixth day, as the craft were carrying up work for inspection, a young Fellow Craft discovered this stone in the quarry, and from its singular form and beauty, supposing it to belong to some part of the Temple, carried it up for inspection.

Master—Who inspected it ?

Senior Warden—The Overseers, placed at the east, west, and south gates.

Master—How did they inspect it ?

Senior Warden—On its being presented to the Junior Overseer at the south gate, he observed that it was neither an oblong or a square, neither had it the regular mark of the craft upon it ; but from its singular form and beauty was unwilling to reject it therefore ordered it to be passed to the Senior Overseer at the west gate, for further inspection ; who, for similar reasons, suffered it to pass to the Master Overseer at the east gate, who held a consultation with his brother Overseers, and they observed, as before, that it was neither an oblong or square, neither had it the regular mark of the craft upon it ; and neither of them being Mark Master Masons, supposed it of no use in the building, and hove it over among the rubbish.

Master—How many Fellow Crafts were there engaged at the building of the Temple ?

Senior Warden—Eighty thousand.

Master—Were not the Master Overseers liable to be imposed upon by receiving bad work from the hands of such a vast number of workmen ?

Senior Warden—They were not.

Master—How was this imposition prevented ?

Senior Warden—By the wisdom of King Solomon, who wisely ordered, that the craftsman who worked, should choose him a particular mark and place it upon all his work ; by which it was known and distinguished when carried up to the building, and if approved, to receive wages.

Master—What was the wages of a Fellow Craft ?

Senior Warden—A penny a day.

Master—Who paid the craftsmen ?

Senior Warden—The Senior Grand Warden.

Master—Was not the Senior Grand Warden liable to be imposed upon by impostors, in paying off such a vast number of workmen ?

Senior Warden—He was not.

Master—How was this imposition prevented ?

Senior Warden—By the wisdom of King Solomon, who also ordered that every craftsman applying to receive wages, should present his right hand through a lattice window of the door of the Junior Grand Warden's apartment, with a copy of his mark in the palm thereof, at the same time giving a token.

Master—What was that token ?

Senior Warden holds out his right hand with the little finger and the next middle finger to it, clenched. (Page 42.)

Master—What did it allude to ?

Senior Warden—To the manner of receiving wages ; it was also to distinguish a true craftsman from an impostor.

Master—What is the penalty on an impostor ?

Senior Warden—To have his right hand chopped off.

SECOND SECTION.

Master—Where was you prepared to be made a Mark Master Mason ?

Senior Warden—In the room adjoining the body of a just and lawfully constituted Lodge of such, duly assembled in a room, or place, representing a work shop that was erected near the ruins of King Solomon's Temple.

Master—How was you prepared ?

Senior Warden—By being divested of my outward apparel and all money ; my breast bare, with a cable-tow four times about my body ; in which situation I was conducted to the door of a Lodge, where I gave four distinct knocks.

Master—What do those four distinct knocks allude to ?

Senior Warden—To the fourth degree of Masonry ; it being that on which I was about to enter.

Master—What was said to you from within ?

Senior Warden—Who comes here, &c.

The Master continues his questions as to the manner of initiating a Mark Master. These, and the answers to them, are precisely the same as the questions and answers on page 43 at the initiation of a candidate, except that they are given and answered in the past tense, the Master asking what was done, and the Senior Warden telling him.

Master—After your initiation into the Mark Master's degree, what followed ?

Senior Warden—I was more fully instructed in its mysteries.

Master—Of what do they consist ?

Senior Warden—Of signs and tokens.

Master—Have you a sign ?

Senior Warden—I have.

Master—What is it called ?

Senior Warden—Heave over.

Master—What does it allude to ?

Senior Warden—To the manner of heaving over work that the Overseers said was unfit for the Temple ; also, the manner the key stone was hove over.

Master—Have you any other sign ?

Senior Warden—I have, (giving the due-guard, as on page 42.)

Master—What is that?

Senior Warden—The due-guard of a Mark Master Mason.

Master—What does it allude to?

Senior Warden—To the penalty of my obligation; which is, that my right ear should be smote off, that I might forever be unable to hear the word, and my right hand be chopped off, as the penalty of an impostor, if I should ever prove wilfully guilty of revealing any part of my obligation.

Master—Have you any further sign?

Senior Warden—I have.

Master—What is that?

Senior Warden—The grand sign, or sign of distress.

Master—What does it allude to?

Senior Warden—To the manner the Fellow Crafts carry their work up to the Temple for inspection; also the manner I was taught to carry my work, on my advancement to this degree.

Master—Have you any other sign?

Senior Warden—I have not; but I have a token. (Gives the pass-grip.)

Master—What is this?

Senior Warden—The pass-grip of a Mark Master Mason.

Master—What is the name of it?

Senior Warden—JOPPA.

Master—What does it allude to?

Senior Warden—The City of Joppa.

Master—Have you any other token?

Senior Warden—I have.

Master—What is this?

Senior Warden—The real grip of a Mark Master Mason.

Master—What is the name of it?

Senior Warden—MARK WELL.

Master—What does it allude to?

Senior Warden—To a passage of Scripture, where it says, "Then he brought me back the way of the gate of the outward sanctuary, which looketh towards the east, and it was shut; and the Lord said unto me, son of man, mark well, and behold with thine eyes, and hear with thine ears, all that I say unto thee concerning all the ordinances of the house of the Lord, and the laws thereof, and mark well the entering in of the house, with the going forth of the sanctuary."

Master—Who founded this degree?

Senior Warden—Our three ancient Grand Masters, viz.: Solomon, King of Israel, Hiram, King of Tyre, and Hiram Abiff.

Master—Why was it founded?

Senior Warden—Not only as an honorary reward, to be conferred on all who have proved themselves meritorious in the preceding degrees, but to render it impossible for a brother to suffer for the immediate necessities of life, when the price of his mark will procure them for him.

Master—A brother, pledging his mark, and asking for a favor, who does he represent?

Senior Warden—Our worthy Grand Master, Hiram Abiff, who was a poor man, but on account of his great skill and mysterious conduct at the building of King Solomon's Temple, was most eminently distinguished.

Master—A brother receiving a pledge, and granting a favor, whom does he represent?

Senior Warden—King Solomon, who was a rich man, but renowned for his benevolence.

———

NOTE.—The following is the Song before alluded to, and either the whole or a few verses of it are always sung before closing a Lodge of Mark Masters.

MARK MASTER'S SONG.

Mark Masters, all appear,
Before the Chief O'erseer:
   In concert move;
Let him your work inspect,
For the Chief Architect,
If there be no defect,
   He will approve.

You who have passed the square,
For your rewards prepare,
   Join heart and hand;
Each with his mark in view,
March with the just and true,
Wages to you are due,
   At your command.

Hiram, the widow's son,
Sent unto Solomon
   Our great key-stone;
On it appears the name
Which raises high the fame
Of all to whom the same
   Is truly known.

Now to the westward move,
Where, full of strength and love,
   Hiram doth stand;
But if imposters are
Mix'd with the worthy there,
Caution them to beware
   Of the right hand.

Now to the praise of those
Who triumph'd o'er the foes
   Of Mason's arts:
To the praiseworthy three
Who founded this degree,
May all their virtues be
   Deep in our hearts.

PAST MASTER'S DEGREE.

After having received the degree of Master Mason, you cannot yet preside over a Lodge of such until the Past Master's Degree is conferred upon you. Masons usually take this degree before offering themselves as a candidate for presiding in a Master's Lodge, but should it so happen that a Master is elected Master of a Lodge who is not a Past Master, the Past Master's degree may be conferred upon him without any other ceremony than that of administering the obligation. In such a case it is usually done by a Chapter of Royal Arch Masons.

The Past Master's Lodge consists of seven officers, as follows:

1. Right Worshipful Master; 2. Senior Warden; 3. Junior Warden; 4. Secretary; 5. Treasurer; 6. Senior Deacon; 7. Junior Deacon.

The interior arrangement is the same as in the first degrees, and the officers are similarly seated. [See page 6.] All the officers and members keep their hats on while at work in this degree. They open and close their Lodge in the same manner as in the Entered Apprentice's Degree.

A Master Mason wishing to enter on the degree of Past Master, petitions the Lodge and is balloted for in the same way that a candidate would be in one of the first degrees; but he is received very differently. Having had the requisite ballot, the Junior Deacon conducts him into the Lodge, places him on a seat, and then repairs to his own station near the Senior Warden in the west. Soon after a heavy alarm is given at the outer door.

Junior Deacon, to the (Master rising)—There is an alarm at the outer door, Right Worshipful.

Master—Attend to the alarm, and see who comes there.

Junior Deacon goes to the door, and soon returns, bringing a letter to the Master. who opens it, and reads aloud to the Lodge as follows:

Dear Husband—I am in great distress. Our little boy has upset a tea-kettle of boiling water, and scalded himself so shockingly, that I fear for his life. You must come home immediately.

From your loving wife,   JULIE.

Master (addressing the Lodge)—Brethren, you see by the tenor of this letter to me that it is necessary I should leave immediately. You must appoint some one to fill the chair, for I cannot stay to confer this degree.

Junior Warden—Right Worshipful, I certainly sympathise with you for the afflicting calamity which has befallen your family, and am sorry that it seems so urgently necessary for you to leave; but could you not stop a few moments? Brother Smith has come on purpose to receive this degree, and expects to receive it. I believe he is in the room, and can speak for himself; and unless he is willing to put off the ceremony, I do not see how you can avoid staying.

The candidate, sympathising with the Master, says he consents to wait, and by no means desires the Right Worshipful to stay one moment on his account.

Junior Warden—I thank our brother for his courtesy, but I have other reasons, Right Worshipful, why I desire you should stay to confer this degree to-night. In the first place, it is uncertain when I myself shall be able to attend again—then we might not get so many brethren together at another meeting; and as this is a very difficult degree to confer, I feel that you ought to stay.

Master—Brethren, it is impossible for me to stay. You will therefore appoint some one to fill the chair. There are a number of brethren present who are well qualified to confer the degree; you will therefore please to nominate.

Junior Warden—I nominate our Brother Senior Warden to fill the chair.

Master—Brethren, it is moved and seconded that Brother Senior Warden fill the chair this evening, to confer this degree on Brother Smith. All those in favor, will signify it by saying aye. [Two or three of the members respond by saying aye.]. Those opposed will say no. [Nearly all the members exclaim, No!] It is not a vote. Brethren will please nominate a new Master.

Senior Warden—I nominate Brother Junior Warden to fill the chair.

The Master puts the question with a similar result, when some member nominates Brother Smith, (the candidate,) who is unanimously voted for and declared duly elected.

Master—Brother Smith, you are elected Master of this Lodge. Will you please to step this way and take the chair?

The candidate goes forward to take the chair, when the Right Worshipful Master pushes him back and says:

Master—Before you occupy the Master's chair you must first assent to the ancient regulations, and take an obligation to discharge with fidelity the duty of Master of the Lodge.

The candidate, having no objection, the Master addresses him as follows:

1. You agree to be a good man, and true, and strictly to obey the moral law?

2. You agree to be a peaceable subject, and cheerfully to conform to the laws of the country in which you reside?

3. You promise not to be concerned in any plots or conspiracies against government; but patiently to submit to the decisions of the supreme legislature?

4. You agree to pay a proper respect to the civil magistrates, to work diligently, live creditably, and act honorably by all men?

5. You agree to hold in veneration the original rules and patrons of Masonry, and their regular successors, supreme and subordinate, according to their stations, and to submit to the awards and resolutions of your brethren, when convened, in every case consistent with the constitution of the Order?

6. You agree to avoid private piques and quarrels, and to guard against intemperance and excess?

7. You agree to be cautious in carriage and behaviour, cautious to your brethren, and faithful to your Lodge?

8. You promise to respect genuine brethren, and discountenance impostors, and all dissenters from the original plan of Masonry?

9. You agree to promote the general good of society, to cultivate the social virtues, and to propagate the knowledge of the arts?

10. You promise to pay homage to the Grand Master for the time being, and to his office when duly installed, strictly to conform to every edict of the Grand Lodge, or general assembly of Masons, that is not subversive of the principles and groundwork of Masonry?

11. You admit that it is not in the power of any man, or body of men, to make innovations in the body of Masonry?

12. You promise a regular attendance on the committees and communications of the Grand Lodge, on receiving proper notice, and to pay attention to the duties of Masonry on all convenient occasions?

13. You admit that no new Lodge can be formed without permission of the Grand Lodge, and that no countenance be given to any irregular Lodge, or to any person clandestinely initiated therein, being contrary to the ancient charges of the Order?

14. You admit that no person can be regularly made a Mason in, or admitted a member of, any regular Lodge, without previous notice, and due inquiry into his character?

15. You agree that no visitors shall be received into your Lodge without due examination, and producing proper vouchers of their having been initiated into a regular Lodge?

Do you submit to these charges, and promise to support these regulations, as Masters have done in all ages before you?

Candidate—I do.

Master—You will now take upon yourself the obligation of this degree. Please to kneel at the altar.

The candidate is conducted to the altar, kneels on both knees, lays both hands on the Holy Bible, square and compasses, and takes the following oath:

I, John Smith, of my own free will and accord, in presence of Almighty God, and this Worshipful Lodge of Past Master Masons, do hereby and hereon, most solemnly and sincerely promise and swear, in addition to my former obligations, that I will not give the secrets of Past Master Mason, or any of the secrets pertaining thereto, to any one of an inferior degree, nor to any person in the known world, except it be to a true and lawful brother, or brethren, Past Master Masons, or within the body of a just and lawfully constituted Lodge of such; and not unto him or unto them whom I shall hear so to be, but unto him and them only whom I shall find so to be, after strict trial and examination, or lawful information.

Furthermore do I promise and swear, that I will obey all regular signs and summonses sent, thrown, handed or given from the hand of a brother of this degree, or from the body of a just and lawfully constituted Lodge of Past Masters.

Furthermore do I promise and swear, that I will support the constitution of the General Grand Royal Arch Chapter of the United States; also, that of the Grand Chapter of the State in which this Lodge is located, and under which it is held, and conform to all the by-laws, rules and regulations of this, or any other Lodge of which I may at any time become a member, so far as in my power.

Furthermore do I promise and swear, that I will not assist, or be present at the conferring of this degree upon any person who has not, to the best of my knowledge and belief, regularly received (in addition to the degrees of Entered Apprentice, Fellow Craft, and Master Mason), the degree of Mark Master, or been elected Master of a regular Lodge of Master Masons.

Furthermore do I promise and swear, that I will aid and assist all poor and indigent Past Master Masons, their widows and orphans, wherever dispersed round the globe, they applying to me as such, and I finding them worthy, so far as is in my power without material injury to myself or family.

Furthermore do I promise and swear, that the secrets of a brother of this degree, delivered to me in charge as such, shall remain as secure and inviolable in my breast, as they were in his own before communicated to me, murder and treason excepted, and those left to my own election.

Furthermore do I promise and swear, that I will not wrong this Lodge, nor a brother of this degree, to the value of one cent, knowingly, myself, nor suffer it to be done by others, if in my power to prevent it.

Furthermore do I promise and swear, that I will not govern this Lodge, or any other over which I may be called to preside, in a haughty and arbitrary manner; but will, at all times, use my utmost endeavors to preserve peace and harmony among the brethren.

Furthermore do I promise and swear, that I will never open a Lodge of Master Masons unless there be present three regular Master Masons, besides the Tyler; nor close the same without giving a lecture, or some section, or part of a lecture, for the instruction of the Lodge.

Furthermore do I promise and swear, that I will not sit in a Lodge where the presiding officer has not taken the degree of Past Master Mason. To all of which I do most solemnly and sincerely promise and swear, with a fixed and steady purpose of mind to keep and perform the same; binding myself under no less penalty than (in addition to all my former penalties) to have my tongue split from tip to root, that I might for ever thereafter be unable to pronounce the word, should I ever prove wilfully guilty of violating any part of this, my solemn oath, or obligation, of a Past Master Mason. So help me God, and make me steadfast to keep and perform the same.

Master to candidate—Kiss the book five times.

The obligation having been administered, the candidate rises, when the Master proceeds to give him the sign, word and grip of this degree, as follows:

Master to candidate—You now behold me approaching you from the east, under the step, sign, and due-guard of a Past Master Mason.

The Master now steps off with his left foot, and then places the heel of his right foot at the toe of the left so as to bring the two feet at right angles, and make them the right angle of a square. He then gives this sign, placing the thumb of his right hand (fingers clenched) upon his lips. It alludes to the penalty to have his tongue split from tip to root. He gives a second sign by placing his right hand upon the left side of his neck, and drawing it edgewise downward in a diagonal direction towards the right side, so as to cross the three former penalties.

Master—Brother, let me now have the pleasure of conducting you into the oriental chair of King Solomon. [Places a large cocked hat on his head, and seats him in a chair in front of the Master's chair.] That wise king, when old and decrepit, was attended by his two friends, Hiram, King of Tyre, and Hiram Abiff, who raised and seated him in his chair by means of the Past Master's grip.

The Master and Senior Warden now take the candidate by this grip and raise him on his feet several times, each time letting him sit back in the chair again. The Senior Warden then goes back to his seat, the candidate rises, and the Right Worshipful Master instructs him in the grip and word of a Past Master Mason. They first take each other by the Master Mason's grip, [page 36,] the Master saying, and the candidate repeating, "from a grip to a span." At that moment they slip their right hands so as to catch each other by the wrist, and raise their left hands, catching each other's right elbow. This is the regular Past Master's grip.

Master—A three-fold cord is strong

Candidate—A four-fold cord is not easily broken.

The Rt. Worshipful Master seats the candidate in the Master's chair, places a hat on his head, and then comes down in front, and says: Worshipful brother, I now present you with the furniture and various Masonic implements of our profession; they are emblematical of our conduct in life, and will now be enumerated and explained as presented.

The Holy Writings, that great light in Masonry, will guide you to all truth; it will direct your path to the temple of happiness, and point out to you the whole duty of man.

The Square teaches to regulate our actions by rule and line, and to harmonize our conduct by the principles of morality and virtue.

The Compass teaches to limit our desires in every station; thus rising to eminence by merit, we may live respected, and die regretted.

The Rule directs, that we should punctually observe our duty; press forward in the path of virtue, and, neither inclining to the right nor to the left, in all our actions have eternity in view.

The Line teaches the criterion of moral rectitude; to avoid dissimulation in conversation and action, and to direct our steps to the path that leads to immortality.

The Book of Constitutions you are to search at all times; cause it to be read in your Lodge, that none may pretend ignorance of the excellent precepts it enjoins.

Lastly, you receive in charge the By-Laws of your Lodge, which you are to see carefully and punctually executed. I will also present you with the Mallet; it is an emblem of power. One stroke of the mallet calls to order, and calls up the Junior and Senior Deacons; two strokes call up all the subordinate officers; and three, the whole Lodge.

Master—Brethren, please to salute your new Master.

All the brethren present, headed by the Master, now walk in front of the chair, give the sign of an Entered Apprentice, and pass on. This is repeated with the sign of each degree in Masonry up to that of Past Master.

Master to candidate—I now leave you to the government of your Lodge. [Master takes his seat with the brethren.]

The Senior Warden now steps forward and delivers up his jewel and his gavel to the new Master, and each of the other officers of the Lodge does the same, taking his turn according to rank. Presently the retired Master rises.

Retired Master (addressing the Chair)—Right Worshipful, in consequence of my resignation, and the election of a new Master, the seats of the Wardens have become vacant. It is necessary you should have Wardens to assist you in the government of your Lodge. I presume the brethren who have held these stations will continue to serve if you so request. [The new Master requests the Senior Warden to resume his jewel and gavel, when the other officers (who had left their places) also resume their seats.]

Retired Master—Right Worshipful, I would respectfully suggest to you that as the office of Treasurer is one of considerable responsibility—he holding all the funds and property of the Lodge—you should direct that he be nominated and elected by the members present. This has been customary, and if you order a nomination to be made in this manner, I have no doubt that we shall select some one who will be satisfactory to you.

Candidate (acting as Master)—The brethren will please nominate a Treasurer for this Lodge.

Here a scene of confusion takes place, which is not easily described. The newly installed Worshipful is made the butt for every worthy brother to exercise his wit upon. Half-a-dozen are up at a time, soliciting the Master to nominate them, urging their several claims, and decrying the merits of others with much zeal, crying out—"Order, Worshipful! keep order!" Others propose to dance, and request the Master to sing for them; others whistle, or sing, or jump about the room; or scuffle, and knock down chairs or benches. One proposes to call from labor to refreshment; another compliments the Worshipful Master on his dignified appearance, and knocks off his hat, or pulls it down over his face, and sometimes he is even dragged from his chair on the pretence that a lady wishes

to see him. The Senior Warden, or some other brother, makes a long speech about reducing the price of the Chapter degrees, from twenty dollars to twelve, and recommends that it be paid in country produce, &c. His motion is seconded, and the new Master is pressed on all sides to put the question. If the question is put, the brethren all vote against it, and accuse the new Master of breaking his oath, when he swore he would support the Constitution of the General Grand Royal Arch Chapter, which establishes the price of the four Chapter degrees, at twenty dollars. If the Master attempts to exercise the power of the gavel, it often has the contrary effect; for if he gives more than one rap, and calls to order, every one obeys the signal, with the utmost promptness, and drops on the nearest seat. The next instant, before the Master can utter a word, all are on their feet again, and as noisy as ever. Some brother now proposes that the Lodge be closed; another one hopes it will be closed in a short way.

Retired Master, to candidate—Right Worshipful, it is moved and seconded that this Lodge be closed. You can close it as you please. You can merely declare the Lodge closed, or in any other way.

The candidate, being much embarrassed, will often attempt to close the Lodge by rapping with his gavel, and declaring it closed. Should he do so, the retired Master stops him as follows:

Retired Master—Right Worshipful, you swore in your obligation, that you would not close this or any other Lodge over which you should be called to preside, without giving a lecture or some part thereof. Do you intend to break your oath?

Candidate—I had forgotten that in this confusion. I hope the brethren will excuse me.

A brother goes and whispers to the candidate, telling him that he can resign the chair to the old Master, and have him close the Lodge, if he so prefers. The candidate is very glad to do this, and cheerfully abdicates his seat.

Master (resuming the chair)—Brother, the lesson we have just given, notwithstanding its apparent confusion, is designed to convey to you, in a striking manner, the necessity of at all times abstaining from soliciting, or accepting any office or station that you do not know yourself amply qualified to fill.

The Master now delivers the Lecture in this degree. It is divided into five sections. The first treats of the manner of constituting a Lodge of Master Masons. The second treats of the ceremony of installation, including the manner of receiving candidates to this degree, as given above. The third treats of the ceremonies observed at laying the foundation stones of public structures. The fourth section, of the ceremony observed at the dedications of Masonic Halls. The fifth, of the ceremony observed at funerals, according to the ancient custom, with the service used on the occasion. The Lecture is usually read from a Monitor which is kept in every Lodge.

The foregoing includes all the ceremonies ever used in conferring the degree of Past Master; but the ceremonies are frequently shortened by the omission of some part of them; the presenting of the various implements of the profession, and their explanations, are often dispensed with; and still more often, the charge.

MOST EXCELLENT MASTER.

No Mason can receive the degree of Most Excellent Master until after he has become a Past Master, and presided in a Lodge, or in other words, been inducted into the Oriental Chair of King Solomon. When the Temple of Jerusalem was finished, those who had proved themselves worthy by their virtue, skill, and fidelity, were installed as Most Excellent Masters; and even at this date none but those who have a perfect knowledge of all preceding degrees are (or should not be) admitted.

A Lodge of Most Excellent Masters is opened in nearly the same manner as Lodges in the preceding degrees. The officers are a Master, Senior and Junior Wardens and Deacons, Secretary and Treasurer, and of course a Tyler. They are stationed as in the Entered Apprentice's Degree, described on page 6. The Master presiding, calls the Lodge to order, and says:

Master to the Junior Warden—Brother Junior, are they all Most Excellent Masters in the south?

Junior Warden—They are, Most Excellent.

Master to the Senior Warden—Brother Senior, are they all Most Excellent Masters in the west?

Senior Warden—They are, Most Excellent.

Master—They are also in the east.

Master gives one rap, which calls up the two Deacons.

Master to Junior Deacon—Brother Junior, the first care of a Mason?

Junior Deacon—To see the door tyled, Most Excellent.

Master—Attend to that part of your duty and inform the Tyler that we are about to open this Lodge of Most Excellent Masters, and direct him to tyle accordingly.

Junior Deacon goes to the door and gives six knocks, which the Tyler from without answers by six more. He then gives one knock, which the Tyler answers with one, and he then partly opens the door and informs the Tyler that by order of the Most Excellent Master a Lodge of Most Excellent Masters is now about to be opened in this place, and he must tyle accordingly. He then returns to his place and addresses the Master:

Junior Deacon—The Lodge is tyled, Most Excellent.

Master—By whom?

Junior Deacon—By a Most Excellent Master Mason without the door, armed with the proper implements of his office.

Master—His duty there?

Junior Deacon—To keep off all cowans and eaves-droppers, and see that none pass or repass without permission of the Most Excellent Master.

The Master now questions each officer of the Lodge as to his duties, which are recited by them as in the other degrees.

Master to Senior Warden—Brother Senior, you will assemble the brethren round the altar for our opening.

Senior Warden—Brethren, please to assemble round the altar for the purpose of opening this Lodge of Most Excellent Master Masons.

The brethren now assemble round the altar, and form a circle, and stand in such a position as to touch each other, leaving a space for the Most Excellent Master; they then all kneel on their left knee, and join hands, each giving his right hand brother his left hand, and his left hand brother his right hand; their left arms uppermost, and their heads inclining downward: all being thus situated, the Most Excellent Master reads the following verses from Psalm xx v.:

The earth is the Lord's, and the fulness thereof; the world, and they that dwell therein. For he hath founded it upon the seas, and established it upon the floods. Who shall ascend into the hill of the Lord? and who shall stand in his holy place? He that hath clean hands, and a pure heart; who hath not lifted up his soul unto vanity, nor sworn deceitfully. He shall receive the blessing from the Lord, and righteousness from the God of his salvation. This is the generation of them that seek him, that seek thy face, O Jacob. Selah. Lift up your heads, O ye gates; [here the kneeling brethren alternately raise and bow their heads as the reading proceeds] and be ye lifted up, ye everlasting doors; and the King of glory shall come in. Who is this King of glory? The Lord, strong and mighty; the Lord, mighty in battle. Lift up your heads, O ye gates; even lift them up, ye everlasting doors; and the King of glory shall come in. Who is this King of glory? The Lord of hosts; he is the King of glory. Selah.

While reading these verses the Most Excellent Master advances towards the circle of kneeling brethren, taking his steps only when reading those passages relative to the King of glory.

The reading being ended, the Most Excellent Master then kneels, joins hands with the others, which closes the circle, and they all lift their hands, as joined together, up and down, six times, keeping time with the words, as the Most Excellent Master repeats them: "one, two, three; one, two, three." This is Masonically called balancing. They then rise, disengage their hands, and lift them up above their heads, with a moderate and somewhat graceful motion, and cast up their eyes; turning at the same time to the right, they extend their arms, and then suffer them to fall loose and somewhat nerveless by their sides. This sign is said by Masons to represent the sign of astonishment made by the Queen of Sheba, on first viewing Solomon's Temple.

The Most Excellent Master resumes his seat and says—Brethren, attend to the signs. He himself then gives all the signs from an Entered Apprentice up to this degree, and the brethren join and imitate him.

Master to the Senior Warden—Brother Senior, it is my will and pleasure that this Lodge of Most Excellent Masters be now opened for dispatch of business, strictly forbidding all private committees, or profane language, whereby the har-mony of the same may be interrupted, while engaged in their lawful pursuits, under no less penalty than the by-laws enjoin, or a majority of the brethren may see cause to inflict.

The Senior Warden repeats this to his Junior, and the Junior announces it to the Lodge as follows:

Junior Warden—Brethren, you have heard our Most Excellent Master's will and pleasure as just communicated to me—so let it be done.

The Lodge being opened, the ordinary business of the evening is gone through with, as in the former degrees. If a candidate is to be initiated, the Junior Deacon goes to the preparation room, where he is in waiting, and prepares him. He takes off the candidate's coat, puts a cable-tow six times round his body, and conducts him to the door of the Lodge, where he gives six distinct knocks (which are answered by the Senior Deacon from within,) and then one knock, which is answered in the same manner.

Senior Deacon (partly opening the door)—Who comes there?

Junior Deacon—A worthy brother, who has been regularly initiated as an Entered Apprentice Mason; passed to the degree of Fellow Craft; raised to the sublime degree of Master Mason; advanced to the honorary degree of a Mark Master Mason; presided in the chair as Past Master; and now wishes for further light in Masonry, by being received and acknowledged as a Most Excellent Master.

Senior Deacon—Is it of his own free will and accord he makes this request?

Junior Deacon—It is.

Senior Deacon—Is he duly and truly prepared?

Junior Deacon—He is.

Senior Deacon—Is he worthy and well qualified?

Junior Deacon—He is.

Senior Deacon—Has he made suitable proficiency in the preceding degrees?

Junior Deacon—He has.

Senior Deacon—By what further right, or benefit, does he expect to obtain this favor?

Junior Deacon—By the benefit of pass-word.

Senior Deacon—Has he a pass-word?

Junior Deacon—He has it not: but I have it for him.

Senior Deacon—Give it to me.

Junior Deacon whispers in the ear of the Senior Deacon the word RABONI. [In many Lodges, the Past Master's word, Giblem, is used as pass-word for this degree, and the word Raboni, as the réal word.]

Senior Deacon—The word is right. You will wait until the Most Excellent Master is made acquainted with your request, and his answer returned.

Senior Deacon repairs to the Most Excellent Master in the east, and gives six raps at the door.

Master—Who comes there?

Senior Deacon—A worthy brother who has been regularly initiated as an Entered Apprentice; passed to the degree of a Fellow Craft; raised to the sublime degree of a Master Mason; advanced to the honorary degree of Mark Master; presided as Master in the chair, and now wishes for further light in Masonry, by being received and acknowledged as a Most Excellent Master.

Master—Is it of his own free will and accord he makes this request?

Senior Deacon—It is.

Master—Is he duly and truly prepared?

Senior Deacon—He is.

Master—Is he worthy and qualified?

Senior Deacon—He is.

Master—Has he made suitable proficiency in the preceding degrees?

Senior Deacon—He has.

Master—By what further right or benefit does he expect to obtain this favor?

Senior Deacon—By the benefit of a pass-word.

Master—Has he a pass-word?

Senior Deacon—He has not; but I have it for him.

Master—Give it.

Senior Deacon whispers in the ear, the word RABONI.

Master—The pass is right. Since he comes endowed with all these necessary qualifications, let him enter this Lodge of Most Excellent Masters, in the name of the Lord.

The door is then flung open, and the Senior Deacon receives the candidate upon the Key-Stone. The candidate is then walked six times round the Lodge, by the Senior Deacon, moving with the sun. The first time they pass round the Lodge, when opposite the Junior Warden, he gives one rap with the gavel; when opposite the Senior Warden, he does the same; and likewise when opposite the Most Excellent Master. The second time round, each gives two blows; the third, three; and so on, until they arrive to six. During this time, the Most Excellent Master reads the following verses from Psalm cxxii.:

I was glad when they said unto me, Let us go into the house of the Lord.

Our feet shall stand within thy gates, O Jerusalem. Jerusalem is builded as a city that is compact together: Whither the tribes go up, the tribes of the Lord, unto the testimony of Israel, to give thanks unto the name of the Lord. For there are set thrones of judgment, the thrones of the house of David. Pray for the peace of Jerusalem: they shall prosper that love thee. Peace be within thy walls, and prosperity within thy palaces. For my brethren and companions' sakes, I will now say, Peace be within thee. Because of the house of the Lord, our God, I will seek thy good.

The reading of the foregoing is so timed, as not to be fully ended until the Senior Deacon and candidate have performed the sixth revolution. Immediately after this the Senior Deacon and candidate arrive at the Junior Warden's station in the south, when the same questions are asked and the same answers returned, as at the door: (Who comes there? &c.) The Junior Warden then directs the candidate to pass on to the Senior Warden in the west, for further examination; where the same questions are asked and answers returned as before. The Senior Warden directs him to be conducted to the Right Worshipful Master in the east, for further examination. The Right Worshipful Master asks the same questions and receives the same answers, as before.

Master to Senior Deacon—Please to conduct the candidate back to the west, from whence he came, and put him in the care of the Senior Warden, and request him to teach the candidate how to approach the east, by advancing upon six upright regular steps to the sixth step, and place him in a position to take upon him the solemn oath, or obligation of a Most Excellent Master Mason.

The candidate is conducted back to the west, and the Senior Warden teaches him how to approach the east in this degree. First, by taking the first step in Masonry, as in the Entered Apprentice's degree, that is, stepping off with the left foot, and bringing up the right foot so as to form a square; then taking the steps as directed in the Fellow Craft degree, and so on up to this one—beginning always with the Entered Apprentice's step.

On arriving at the altar the candidate kneels on both knees, and places both hands on the Bible, square and compasses. The Master then comes forward and addresses him:

Master—Brother, you are now placed in a proper position to take upon you the solemn oath or obligation of a Most Excellent Master Mason, which I assure you, as before, is neither to affect your religion or politics. If you are willing to take it, repeat your name and say after me :

I, John Smith, of my own free will and accord, in presence of Almighty God, and this Lodge of Most Excellent Master Masons, do hereby and hereon, most solemnly and sincerely promise and swear, in addition to my former obligations, that I will not give the secrets of Most Excellent Master to any one of an inferior degree, nor to any person in the known world, except it be to a true and lawful brother of this degree, and within the body of a just and lawfully constituted Lodge of such; and not unto him nor them whom I shall hear so to be, but unto him and them only whom I shall find so to be, after strict trial and due examination, or lawful information.

Furthermore do I promise and swear, that I will obey all regular signs and summonses handed, sent, or thrown to me from a brother of this degree, or from the body of a just and lawfully constituted Lodge of such; provided it be within the length of my cable-tow.

Furthermore do I promise and swear, that I will support the constitution of the General Grand Royal Arch Chapter of the United States; also, that of the Grand Chapter of this State, under which this Lodge is held, and conform to all the by-laws, rules and regulations of this, or any other Lodge of which I may hereafter become a member.

Furthermore do I promise and swear, that I will aid and assist all poor and indigent brethren of this degree, their widows and orphans, wheresoever dispersed around the globe, as far as in my power, without injuring myself or family.

Furthermore do I promise and swear, that the secrets of a brother of this degree, given to me in charge as such, and I knowing them to be such, shall remain as secret and inviolable in my breast, as in his own, murder and treason excepted, and the same left to my own free will and choice.

Furthermore do I promise and swear, that I will not wrong this Lodge of Most Excellent Master Masons, nor a brother of this degree, to the value of anything, knowingly, myself, nor suffer it to be done by others, if in my power to prevent it.

Furthermore do I promise and swear, that I will dispense light and knowledge to all ignorant and uninformed brethren

at all times, as far as is in my power, without material injury to myself or family. To all which I do most solemnly swear, with a fixed and steady purpose of mind in me to keep and perform the same; binding myself under no less penalty than to have my breast torn open, and my heart and vitals taken from thence, and exposed to rot on the dunghill, if ever I violate any part of this, my solemn oath, or obligation, of a Most Excellent Master Mason. So help me God, and keep me steadfast in the due performance of the same.

Master to the candidate—Detach your hands and kiss the book six times [Candidate obeys.] You will now rise and receive from me the sign, grip and word of a Most Excellent Master Mason.

The sign is given by placing your two hands, one on each breast, the fingers meeting in the centre of the body, and jerking them apart as though you were trying to tear open your breast: it alludes to the penalty of the obligation.

The grip is given by taking each other by the right hand, and clasping them so that each compress the third finger of the other with his thumb. [If one hand is large and the other small, they cannot both give the grip at the same time.] It is called the grip of all grips, because it is said to cover all the preceding grips.

Master (holding candidate by his hand and placing the inside of his right foot to the inside of candidate's right foot) whispers in his ear—RABONI.

Should there be more than one candidate for initiation, the ceremony stops here until the others are advanced thus far, and then they all receive the remainder together.

A noise of shuffling feet is now heard in the Lodge, which is purposely made by some of the members.

Master to Senior Warden—What is the cause of all this confusion?

Senior Warden—Is not this the day set apart for the celebration of the cope-stone. Most Excellent?

Master—Ah, I had forgotten. [To Secretary.] Is it so, Brother Secretary?

Secretary (looking at his book)—It is, Most Excellent.

Master to Senior Warden—Brother Senior, assemble the brethren and form a procession for the purpose of celebrating the cope-stone.

The candidate now stands aside, while the brethren assemble and form a procession, double file, and march six times round the Lodge, against the course of sun, singing from the text-book the first three verses of the Most Excellent Master's Song, "All hail to the morning," &c. The Key-Stone is now brought forward, and placed in its proper place; that is, two pillars or columns, called Jachin and Boaz, each about five feet high, are set up, and an arch placed on them, made of plank, or boards, in imitation of block work, in the centre of which is a mortice left for the reception of a key-stone; the Most Excellent Master takes the key-stone and steps up into a chair, and places it into the arch, and drives it down to its place by giving it six raps with his gavel.

As soon as this ceremony is through, all the brethren move around as before, continuing the song:

> There is no more occasion
> For level or plum line,
> For trowel or gavel,
> For compass or square;

As they come to these words, all the brethren divest themselves of their jewels, aprons, sashes, &c., and hang them on the arch as they pass round.

> Our works are completed,
> The ark safely seated,
> And we shall be greeted
> As workmen most rare.

The Ark, which all this time has been carried round by four of the brethren, is brought forward and placed on the altar, and a pot of incense is placed on the ark.

> Now those that are worthy,
> Our toils who have shared,
> And proved themselves faithful,
> Shall meet their reward;
> Their virtue and knowledge,
> Industry and skill,
> Have our approbation—
> Have gained our good will.

The brethren now all halt, and face inward to the altar, and beckon the candidate to come forward and join in the ceremonies, which he does.

> We accept and receive them,
> Most Excellent Masters,
> Invested with honor
> And power to preside,
> Among worthy craftsmen,
> Where'er assembled,
> The knowledge of Masons,
> To spread far and wide.

As they begin the next verses, each one throws up his hands and rolls his eyes upwards,——giving a sign of admiration or astonishment like that described (p. 59) as having been expressed by the Queen of Sheba on first viewing Solomon's Temple——and keeps them in that position while singing these two verses of the song:

> Almighty Jehovah,
> Descend now, and fill
> This Lodge with thy glory,
> Our hearts with good-will;
> Preside at our meetings,
> Assist us to find
> True pleasure in teaching
> Good-will to mankind.
>
> Thy wisdom inspired
> The great Institution,
> Thy strength shall support it
> Till Nature expire,
> And when the creation
> Shall fall into ruin,
> Its beauty shall rise
> Through the midst of the fire.

The brothers now all join hands as in opening, and while in this attitude the Master reads the first four verses of the seventh chapter of Chronicles, as follows:

Now when Solomon had made an end of praying, the fire came down from Heaven, and consumed the burnt-offering and the sacrifices; and the glory of the Lord filled the house. And the priests could not enter into the house of the Lord, because the glory of the Lord had filled the Lord's house. And when all the children of Israel saw how the fire came down, and the glory of the Lord upon the house, they bowed themselves with their faces to the ground upon the pavement, and worshipped, and praised the Lord, saying, For He is good, [here the Master, who is High Priest of the Chapter, kneels and joins hands with the rest,] for his mercy endureth for ever.

They all then repeat in concert the words, "For He is good, for his mercy endureth for ever," six times, each time bowing their heads low towards the floor. The members now balance six times, as in opening, rise and balance six times more, then disengaging themselves from each other, take their seats.

Master to candidate—Brother, your admittance to this degree of Masonry is a proof of the good opinion the brethren of this Lodge entertain of your Masonic abilities. Let this consideration induce you to be careful of forfeiting, by misconduct and inattention to our rules, that esteem which has raised you to the rank you now possess. It is one of your great duties, as a Most Excellent Master, to dispense light and truth to the uninformed Mason ; and I need not remind you of the impossibility of complying with this obligation without possessing an accurate acquaintance with the lectures of each degree. If you are not already completely conversant in all the degrees heretofore conferred on you, remember that an indulgence, prompted by a belief that you will apply yourself with double diligence to make yourself so, has induced the brethren to accept you. Let it, therefore, be your unremitting study to acquire such a degree of knowledge and information as shall enable you to discharge with propriety the various duties incumbent on you, and to preserve unsullied the title now conferred upon you of a Most Excellent Master.

This charge closes the initiation, and a motion is generally made to adjourn, and close the Lodge.

Master to the Junior Warden. Brother Junior, you will please assemble the brethren round the altar, for the purpose of closing this Lodge of Most Excellent Masters.

The brethren immediately assemble round the altar in a circle, and kneel on the right knee, put their left arms over and join hands, as before. While kneeling in this position, the Master reads the following verses from the one hundred and thirty-fourth Psalm :

Behold, bless ye the Lord, all ye servants of the Lord, which by night stand in the house of the Lord. Lift up your hands in the sanctuary and bless the Lord. The Lord that made heaven and earth bless thee out of Zion.

The Master then closes the circle as in opening, when they balance six times, rise and balance six times more, disengaging their hands, and giving the signs from this degree downwards, and he then declares the Lodge closed.

The engraving below shows the position of the brethren as they prostrate themselves round the altar previous to the delivery of the charge.

ROYAL ARCH DEGREE.

A society of Royal Arch Masons is called a Chapter, and not a Lodge, as in the previous degrees. The several degrees of Mark Master, Present or Past Master, and Most Excellent Master are given only under the sanction of the Royal Arch Chapter, and a Master Mason who applies for these degrees, usually enters the Chapter also, and sometimes the four degrees are given at once. If he takes the four he is only balloted for once, viz., in the Mark Master's degree. It is a point of the Royal Arch degree not to assist, or be present, at the conferring of this degree upon more or less than three candidates at one time. If there are not three candidates present, one or two companions, as the case may be, volunteer to represent candidates, so as to make the requisite number, or a "team," as it is technically styled, and accompany the candidate or candidates through all the stages of exaltation.

At the destruction of Jerusalem by Nebuchadnezzar, three Most Excellent Masters were carried captives to Babylon, where they remained seventy years, and were liberated by Cyrus, King of Persia. They returned to Jerusalem to assist in rebuilding the Temple, after traveling over rugged roads on foot. They arrived at the outer veil of the Tabernacle, which was erected near the ruins of the Temple. This tabernacle was an oblong square, inclosed by four veils, or curtains, and divided into separate apartments, by four cross veils, including the west end veil, or entrance.

The veils were parted in the centre, and guarded by four guards, with drawn swords.

At the east end of the Tabernacle, Haggai, Joshua, and Zerubbabel usually sat in grand council, to examine all who wished to be employed in the noble and glorious work of rebuilding the Temple. Since that time, every Chapter of Royal Arch Masons, if properly formed, is a correct representation of the Tabernacle, and our engraving shows the interior arrangement of a Chapter of the Royal Arch Degree.

These three Most Excellent Masters, on their arrival, were introduced to the Grand Council, (consisting of the High Priest, King and Scribe,) and employed, furnished with tools, and directed to commence their labors at the north-east corner of the ruins of the old Temple, and to clear away and remove the rubbish, in order to lay the foundation of the new. The Grand Council also gave them strict orders to preserve whatever should fall in their way, (such as specimens of ancient architecture, &c.) and bring it up for their inspection.

Among the discoveries made by the three Masters was a secret vault in which they found treasures of great benefit to the craft, &c. The ceremony of exalting companions to this degree is a recapitulation of the adventures of these three Most Excellent Masters, and hence it is that three candidates are necessary for an initiation.

A Chapter of Royal Arch Masons consists of nine officers, as follows:

1. High Priest, or Master.
2. King, or Senior Warden.
3. Scribe, or Junior Warden.
4. Captain of the Host, (as Marshal, or Master of Ceremonies,) or Senior Deacon.
5. Principal Sojourner, who represents the Junior Deacon.
6. Royal Arch Captain, who represents the Master Overseer.
7. Grand Master of the Third Veil, or Senior Overseer.
8. Grand Master of the Second Veil, or Junior Overseer.
9. Grand Master of the First Veil.

In addition to these, three other officers are usually present, viz., a Secretary, a Treasurer and a Tyler.

The officers and companions of the Chapter being stationed as in the engraving, the High Priest proceeds to business as follows:

High Priest—Companions, I am about to open a Chapter of Royal Arch Masons in this place, for the dispatch of business, and will thank you for your attention and assistance. If there is any person present who is not a companion Royal Arch Mason, he is requested to retire from the room.

After waiting for any stranger, or bro-ther not of this degree, to retire, he gives one rap with the gavel, which brings up the Captain of the Host.

High Priest—Companion Captain, the first care of congregated Masons?

Captain (placing the palm of his right

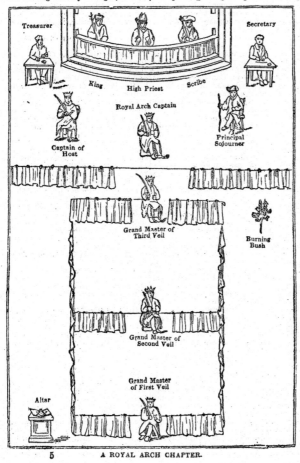

Treasurer

Secretary

King　High Priest　Scribe

Royal Arch Captain

Captain of Host

Principal Sojourner

Grand Master of Third Veil

Burning Bush

Grand Master of Second Veil

Grand Master of First Veil

Altar

5　A ROYAL ARCH CHAPTER.

hand to his forehead as if to shade his eyes—To see the Tabernacle duly guarded, Most Excellent. [This due-guard is explained hereafter.]

High Priest—Attend to that part of your duty, and inform the Guard that we are about to open a Chapter of Royal Arch Masons in this place for the dispatch of business; direct him to guard accordingly.

The Captain of the Host stations the Guard at the outside of the door, gives him his orders, closes the door, and makes an alarm of three times three, on the inside, to ascertain that the Guard is on his post; the Guard answers by nine corresponding raps; the Captain of the Host then gives one, and Guard does the same. The Captain then returns to his post.

Captain to High Priest—The Chapter is duly guarded, Most Excellent.

High Priest—How guarded?

Captain—By a companion of this degree at the outer avenue, with a drawn sword in his hand.

High Priest—His duty there?

Captain—To observe the approach of all cowans and eaves-droppers, and see that none pass or repass, but such as are duly qualified.

High Priest—Companions, we will be clothed.

The companions place the furniture of the Chapter in proper order, clothe with their various jewels, robes, and badges of this degree, and draw aside the veils, which brings the hall into one apartment, and resume their seats. The High Priest then gives two raps with the gavel, which brings all the officers on their feet, while the following lecture is given, or questions asked by the High Priest, and answered by the Captain of the Host.

High Priest—Companion Captain of the Host, are you a Royal Arch Mason?

Captain—I am, that I am.

High Priest—How shall I know you to be a Royal Arch Mason?

Captain—By three times three.

High Priest—Where was you made a Royal Arch Mason?

Captain—In a just and legally constituted Chapter of Royal Arch Masons, consisting of Most Excellent High Priest, King and Scribe, Captain of the Host, Principal Sojourner, Royal Arch Captain, and the three Grand Masters of the veils, assembled in a room or place, representing the Tabernacle erected by our ancient brethren, near the ruins of King Solomon's Temple.

High Priest—Where is the High Priest stationed, and what are his duties?

Captain—He is stationed in the sanc-tum sanctorum. His duty, with the King and Scribe, is to sit in the Grand Council, to form plans, and give directions to the workmen.

High Priest—The King's station and duty?

Captain—Station, at the right hand of the High Priest; duty, to aid him by his advice and counsel, and in his absence, to preside.

High Priest—The Scribe's station and duty?

Captain—Station, at the left hand of the high priest; duty, to assist him and the King in the discharge of their duties, and to preside, in their absence.

High Priest—The Captain of the Host's station and duty?

Captain—Station, at the right hand in front of Grand Council; duty, to receive orders, and see them duly executed.

High Priest—The Principal Sojourner's station and duty?

Captain—Station, at the left hand in front of Grand Council; duty, to bring the blind by a way that they know not; to lead them in paths they have not known; to make darkness light before them, and crooked things straight.

High Priest—The Royal Arch Captain's station and duty?

Captain—Station, at the inner veil, or entrance to the sanctum sanctorum: duty, to guard the same, and see that none pass but such as are duly qualified, and have the proper pass-words, and the signet of truth.

High Priest—What is the color of his banner?

Captain—White, and is emblematical of that purity of heart, and rectitude of conduct, which is essential to obtain admission into the divine sanctum sanctorum above.

High Priest—The stations and duties of the three Grand Masters of the veils?

Captain—Station, at the entrance of their respective veils; duty, to guard the same, and see that none pass but such as are duly qualified, and in possession of the proper pass-words and tokens.

High Priest—What are the colors of their banners?

Captain—That of the third, scarlet; which is emblematical of fervency and zeal, and the appropriate color of the Royal Arch degree. It admonishes us to be fervent in the exercise of our devotions to God, and zealous in our endeavors to promote the happiness of men. Of the second, purple; which being produced by a due mixture of blue and scarlet, the former of which is the characteristic color of the symbolic, or three first degrees. It teaches us to cultivate and improve that spirit of harmony between the brethren of the symbolic degrees, and the companions of the sublime degrees, which should ever distinguish the members of a society founded upon the principles of everlasting truth and universal philanthropy. Of the first, blue; the peculiar color of the three ancient, or symbolical degrees. It is an emblem of universal friendship and benevolence, and instructs us, that in the mind of a Mason, those virtues should be as expansive as the blue arch of heaven itself.

High Priest—The Treasurer's station and duty?

Captain—Station, at the right hand in rear of the Captain of the Host; his duty, to keep a just and regular account of all the property and funds of the Chapter, placed in his hands, and exhibit them to the Chapter, when called upon for that purpose.

High Priest—The Secretary's place in the Chapter?

Captain—Station, at the left in rear of the Principal Sojourner; his duty, to issue the orders and notifications of his superior officers, record the proceedings of the Chapter proper to be written, to receive all moneys due the Chapter, and pay them over to the Treasurer.

High Priest—Guard's place and duty?

Captain—His station is at the outer avenue of the Chapter; his duty to guard against the approach of cowans and caves-droppers, and suffer none to pass, or repass, but such as are duly qualified.

High Priest (addressing the Chapter)—Companions, you will assemble round the altar for the purpose of assisting me in opening a Chapter of Royal Arch Masons.

All the members present (except the three principal officers) approach the altar, and, forming a circle, kneel, each upon his right knee. An opening in the circle is left for the High Priest, the King, and the Scribe. The High Priest rises and reads from the Second Epistle of Paul to the Thessalonians, chapter iii., v. 6 to 18.

Now we command you, brethren, in the name of our Lord Jesus Christ, that ye withdraw yourselves from every brother that walketh disorderly, and not after the tradition which ye received of us. For yourselves know how ye ought to follow us; for we behaved not ourselves disorderly among you; neither did we eat any man's bread for naught; but wrought with labor and travail night and day, that we might not be chargeable to any

of you; not because we have not power, but to make ourselves an ensample unto you to follow us, &c.

After the reading, the High Priest, the King and the Scribe approach the altar and take their places in the circle, kneeling with the rest, the King on the right, and the Scribe on the left of the High Priest. Each one now crosses his arms and gives his right hand to his left hand companion, and his left hand to his right hand companion. This constitutes the living arch under which the Grand Omnific Royal Arch Word must be given, but it must also be given by three times three, as hereafter explained.

The High Priest now whispers in the King's ear the pass-word, RABONI.

The King whispers it to the companion on his right, and he to the next one, and so on until it comes round to the Scribe, who whispers it to the High Priest.

High Priest—The word is right.

The companions now all balance three times three with their arms; that is, they raise their arms and let them fall upon their knees three times in concert, after a short pause three times more, and after another pause, three times more. They then rise and give all the signs from the Entered Apprentice up to this degree, after which they join in squads of three for giving the Grand Omnific Royal Arch Word, as follows: Each one takes hold with his right hand of the right wrist of his companion on the left, and with his left hand takes hold of the left wrist of his companion on the right.

Each one then places his right foot forward with the hollow in front so that the toe touches the heel of his companion on the right. This is called "three times three," that is, three right feet forming a triangle, three left hands forming a triangle, and three right hands forming a triangle. In this position each repeats the following:

As we three did agree,
In peace, love, and unity,
The Sacred Word to keep,
So we three do agree
In peace, love, and unity,
The Sacred Word to search ;
Until we three,
Or three such as we, shall agree
To close this Royal Arch.

They then balance three times three, bringing the right hand with some violence down upon the left. The right hands are then raised above their heads, and the word, Jah-buh-lun Je-ho-vah, G-o-d, are given at low breath, each companion pronouncing the syllables or letters alternately, as follows :

Jah..........buh.... ......lun.
.............Jah........ ....buh
lun.............................
...........................Jah
buh..........lun.
Je........ ......ho...........vah.
....Je...........ho .
vah...............................
...........................Je .
ho...... .....vah.
G ....o....... ......d.
..............G...............o
d. ....
....G
o.... ....d.

After the word is thus given, the High Priest inquires if the word is right ?

Each squad replies that it is right.

The officers and companions resume their seats. The High Priest raps three times with his gavel, the King repeats it, as also the Scribe ; this is done three times.

High Priest (rising)—I now declare this Chapter of Royal Arch Masons opened in due and ancient form ; and I hereby forbid all improper conduct whereby the peace and harmony of this Chapter may be disturbed, under no less penalties than the by-laws, or a majority of the Chapter may see fit to inflict.

High Priest to Captain of the Host—Companion Captain, please to inform the Gu. d that the Chapter is open.

T e Captain proceeds on this duty, while the Secretary reads the minutes of the last meeting. Should there be any candidates to ballot for, this is the first business in order. If one or more candidates are waiting without, the Principal Sojourner goes to the preparation room to get them ready. If there are not

three of them, a companion or companions volunteer to make the trio, as not less than three can perform the ceremonies. The three take off their coats, when the Principal Sojourner ties bandages over their eyes, and taking a long rope, coils it seven times round the body of each, leaving about three feet slack between. He then proceeds with them, to the door of the Chapter and gives seven distinct knocks.

Captain (rising)—There is an alarm at the door, Most Excellent.

High Priest—Attend to the cause of it, and see who comes there.

The Captain of the Host goes to the door and raps on it nine times. The Principal Sojourner, outside, answers this by three times three, and then gives one rap, which the Captain answers by one, and then partly opens the door.

Captain—Who comes there ?

Principal Sojourner—Three worthy brothers, who have been initiated, passed, and raised to the sublime degree of Master Masons, advanced to the honorary degree of Mark Master, presided as Master in the chair, and, at the completion and dedication of the Temple, were received and acknowledged Most Excellent Masters ; and now wish for further light in Masonry, by being exalted to the august sublime degree of the Holy Royal Arch.

Captain to candidates—Is it of your own free will and accord you make this request ?

First Candidate—It is.

Captain to Principal Sojourner—Are they duly and truly prepared ?

Principal Sojourner—They are.

Captain—Have they made suitable proficiency in the preceding degrees ?

Principal Sojourner—They have.

Captain—By what further right, or benefit, do they expect to gain admission to this Chapter of Royal Arch Masons ?

Principal Sojourner—By the benefit of a pass.

Captain—Have they that pass ?

Principal Sojourner—They have it not, but I have it for them.

Captain—Advance, and give it.

Principal Sojourner whispers in his ear the word RABONI.

Captain—The word is right; you will wait a time, until the Most Excellent High Priest be informed of their request, and his answer returned.

The Captain of the Host closes the door, and returns to his place in the Chapter, gives the alarm, which is answered by the High Priest, who asks the same questions, and receives the same answers from the Captain of the Host, as were asked and given at the door.

High Priest—Since this is the case, you will let them enter this Chapter of Royal Arch Masons, and be received under a Living Arch.

The Captain of the Host goes to the door, opens it and says—It is our Most Excellent High Priest's order, that the candidates enter this Chapter of Royal Arch Masons, and be received under a Living Arch.

Principal Sojourner (leading the candidates by the rope)—Companions, you will follow me. [Leads them in.] I will bring the blind by a way they know not; I will lead them in paths they have not known; I will make darkness light before them, and crooked things straight. These things will I do unto them, and will not forsake them. Stoop low, brethren: he that humbleth himself, shall be exalted.

Meantime the brethren, or companions of the Chapter, form two lines facing each other, from the door to the centre of the room, and each one takes hold and locks his fingers with those of his opposite companion. As the candidates pass under this Living Arch, each couple place their knuckles upon the necks and backs of the candidates, kneading them pretty hard sometimes, and prostrating them on the floor. Thus they have a good deal of difficulty in forcing their way through. When they do get through they are first conducted round the Chapter, and then to the altar, where they must kneel to receive the obligation.

Principal Sojourner to the candidates—Brethren, as you advance in Masonry, your obligation becomes more binding. You are now kneeling at the altar for the seventh time; and about to take a solemn oath, or obligation, which, like your former obligations, is not to interfere with the duty you owe to your country, or Maker. If you are willing to proceed, you will repeat your christian and surnames, and say after me:

I, John Smith, of my own free will and accord, in presence of Almighty God, and this Chapter of Royal Arch Masons, erected to God, and dedicated to Zerub' babel, do hereby and hereon, most solemnly and sincerely promise and swear, in addition to my former obligations, that I will not reveal the secrets of this degree to any of an inferior degree, nor to any being in the known world, except it be to a true and lawful companion Royal Arch Mason, or within the body of a just and legally constituted Chapter of such;

and never unto him, or them, whom I shall hear so to be, but him and them only whom I shall find so to be, after strict trial and due examination, or lawful information given.

I furthermore promise and swear, that I will not wrong this Chapter of Royal Arch Masons, or a companion of this degree, out of the value of anything, myself, nor suffer it to be done by others, if in my power to prevent it.

I furthermore promise and swear, that I will not reveal the key to the ineffable characters of this degree, nor retain it in my possession, but will destroy it whenever it comes to my sight.

I furthermore promise and swear, that I will not speak the Grand Omnific Royal Arch word, which I shall hereafter receive, in any manner, except in that in which I shall receive it, which will be in the presence of three companions Royal Arch Masons, myself making one of the number; and then by three times three, under a living arch, and at low breath.

I furthermore promise and swear, that I will not be at the exaltation of candidates in a clandestine Chapter, nor converse upon the secrets of this degree with a clandestine made Mason, or with one who has been expelled or suspended, while under that sentence.

I furthermore promise and swear, that I will not assist, or be present at the exaltation of a candidate to this degree, who has not received the degrees of Entered Apprentice, Fellow Craft, Master Mason, Mark Master, Past Master, and Most Excellent Master.

I furthermore promise and swear, that I will not be at the exaltation of more nor less than three candidates, at one and the same time.

I furthermore promise and swear, that I will not be at the forming or opening of a Chapter of Royal Arch Masons, unless there be present nine Royal Arch Masons, myself making one of that number.

I furthermore promise and swear, that I will not speak evil of a companion Royal Arch Mason, behind his back, nor before his face, but will apprise him of all approaching danger, if in my power.

I furthermore promise and swear, that I will support the Constitution of the General Grand Royal Arch Chapter of the United States of America; together with that of the Grand Chapter of this State, under which this Chapter is holden; that I will stand to, and abide by all the by-laws, rules, and regulations of this Chapter, or of any other Chapter of which I may hereafter become a member.

I furthermore promise and swear, that I will answer and obey all due signs and summonses, handed, sent, or thrown to me from a Chapter of Royal Arch Masons, or from a companion Royal Arch Mason, if within the length of my cabletow.

I furthermore promise and swear, that I will not strike a companion Royal Arch Mason, so as to draw his blood, in anger.

I furthermore promise and swear, that I will employ a companion Royal Arch Mason, in preference to any other person of equal qualifications.

I furthermore promise and swear, that I will assist a companion Royal Arch Mason when I see him engaged in any difficulty, and will espouse his cause so far as to extricate him from the same, whether he be right or wrong.

I furthermore promise and swear, that I will keep all the secrets of a companion Royal Arch Mason (when communicated to me as such, or I knowing them to be such,) without exceptions.

I furthermore promise and swear, that I will be aiding and assisting all poor and indigent companions Royal Arch Masons, their widows and orphans, wheresoever dispersed around the globe ; they making application to me as such, and I finding them worthy, and can do it without any material injury to myself or family.

To all which I do most solemnly and sincerely promise and swear, with a firm and steadfast resolution to keep and perform the same, without any equivocation, mental reservation, or self-evasion of mind in me whatever ; binding myself under no less penalty, than to have my skull smote off, and my brains exposed to the scorching rays of the meridian sun, should I knowingly or wilfully violate or transgress any part of this my solemn oath or obligation of a Royal Arch Mason. So help me God, and keep me steadfast in the due performance of the same.

Principal Sojourner—Kiss the book seven times.

The candidate kisses the book as directed.

Principal Sojourner—Companions, you will arise and follow me. For although you are obligated Royal Arch Masons, yet as the secrets of this degree are of infinitely more importance than any that precede it, it is necessary that you should travel through rough and rugged ways, and pass through many trials, in testimony of your fidelity to the Order, before you can be instructed in the more important secrets of this degree.

The candidates are conducted once around the Chapter, and then again directed to kneel, while the Principal Sojourner reads the following prayer :

Supreme and inscrutible Architect of universal Nature, who, by thine Almighty word, didst speak into being the stupendous arch of heaven, and for the instruction and pleasure of thy rational creatures, didst adorn us with greater and lesser lights, thereby magnifying thy power, and endearing thy goodness unto the sons of men, we humbly adore and worship thine unspeakable perfection. We bless thee, that, when man had fallen from his innocence and his happiness, thou didst leave him the powers of reasoning, and capacity of improvement and pleasure. We thank thee, that, amidst the pains and calamities of our present state, so many means of refreshment and satisfaction are reserved to us, while traveling the rugged path of life ; especially would we, at this time, render thee our thanksgiving and praise for the institution, as members of which we are, at this time, assembled, and for all the pleasures we have derived from it. We thank thee, that the few here assembled before thee, have been favored with new inducements, and been laid under new and stronger obligations of virtue and holiness. May these obligations, O blessed Father ! have their full effect upon us. Teach us, we pray thee, the true reverence of thy great, mighty, and terrible name. Inspire us with a firm and unshaken resolution in our virtuous pursuits. Give us grace diligently to search thy word in the book of nature, wherein the duties of our high vocation are inculcated with divine authority. May the solemnity of the ceremonies of our institution be duly impressed on our minds, and have a happy and lasting effect on our lives ! O, thou, who didst aforetime appear unto thy servant Moses in a flame of fire out of the midst of a bush, enkindle, we beseech thee, in each of our hearts, a flame of devotion to thee, of love to each other, and of charity to all mankind ! May all thy miracles and mighty works fill us with thy dread, and thy goodness impress us with a love of thy holy name ! May Holiness to the Lord be engraven upon all our thoughts, words, and actions ! May the incense of piety ascend continually unto thee, from the altar of our hearts, and burn day and night, as a sacrifice of a sweet smelling savor, well pleasing unto thee ! And since sin has destroyed within us the first temple of purity and innocence, may thy heavenly grace guide and assist us in rebuilding a second temple of reformation, and may the glory of this latter house be greater than the glory of the former! Amen, so mote it be.

Principal Sojourner—Companions, arise and follow me.

He now conducts them once around the Chapter, during which time he reads from the text-book the first six verses of the third chapter of Exodus:

Now Moses kept the flock of Jethro his father-in law, the priest of Midian; and he led the flock to the back side of the desert, and came to the mountain of God, even to Horeb. And the angel of the Lord appeared unto him in a flame of fire out of the midst of a bush; and he looked, and behold, the bush burned with fire, and the bush was not consumed, &c.

The reading of these verses is so timed that just when they are finished the candidates have arrived in front of a representation of the burning bush, placed in a corner of the Chapter: when the Principal Sojourner directs them to halt, and slips up the bandages from their eyes.

One of the members now personates the Deity, behind the bush, and calls out Moses! Moses!

Principal Sojourner (answering for candidates)—Here I am.

Companion behind the bush—Draw not nigh hither: put off thy shoes from off thy feet, for the place whereon thou standest is holy ground. I am the God of thy fathers, the God of Abraham, the God of Isaac, and the God of Jacob.

Principal Sojourner directs the candidates to kneel, and he covers their faces again, and then says—And Moses hid his face, for he was afraid to look upon God.

Principal Sojourner to candidates—Arise, and follow me.

He then leads them three times around the Chapter, during which time he reads from the text-book Chronicles, chapter xxvi., verses 11 to 20:

Zedekiah was one-and-twenty years old when he began to reign, and he reigned eleven years in Jerusalem. And he did that which was evil in the sight of the Lord his God, and humbled not himself before Jeremiah the prophet, speaking from the mouth of the Lord. And he also rebelled against King Nebuchadnezzar, and stiffened his neck, and hardened his heart from turning unto the Lord God of Israel. Moreover, all the chief of the priests and the people transgressed very much, after all the abominations of the heathen, and polluted the house of the Lord, which he had hallowed in Jerusalem. And the Lord God of their fathers

sent to them by his messengers, because he had compassion on his people, and on his dwelling place. But they mocked the messengers of God, and despised his word, and misused his prophets, until the wrath of the Lord arose against his people, till there was no remedy. Therefore he brought upon them the King of the Chaldees, who slew their young men with the sword, in the house of their sanctuary, and had no compassion upon young men or maidens, old men, or him that stooped for age; he gave them all into his hand. And all the vessels of the house of God, great and small, and the treasures of the house of the Lord, and the treasures of the king, and his princes; all these he brought to Babylon. And they burnt the house of God, and brake down the wall of Jerusalem, and burnt all the palaces thereof with fire, and destroyed all the goodly vessels thereof. And them that had escaped from the sword carried he away to Babylon; where they were servants to him and his sons, until the reign of the kingdom of Persia.

When the Principal Sojourner arrives at that part of the above reading which alludes to the Chaldees killing the young men with the sword, the companions of the Chapter begin to make all sorts of queer and unearthly noises, such as rolling cannon balls on the floor, clashing old swords, discharging pistols, shouting, groaning, whistling, stamping, throwing down benches, &c. This noise continues during the remainder of the reading, the object being to represent the siege and destruction of Jerusalem. During this confusion the three candidates are siezed, thrown upon the floor, bound hand and foot and carried bodily into the preparation room, when the door is closed.

In a few minutes the companions begin to shout, "Hurrah for the captives!" repeating it several times.

Captain of the Host goes and opens the door and says—Come forth! you are at liberty to return! for Cyrus has issued his proclamation to build a second Temple at Jerusalem.

Principal Sojourner (who is with the candidates)—Will you read the proclamation?

Captain of the Host reads the first three verses of the first chapter of Ezra, as follows:

Now in the first year of Cyrus, King of Persia, the Lord stirred up the spirit of Cyrus, King of Persia, that he made a proclamation throughout all his kingdom, and put it also in writing, saying: Thus saith Cyrus, King of Persia, the Lord

God of Heaven hath given me all the kingdoms of the earth, and he hath charged me to build him an house at Jerusalem, which is in Judah. Who is there among you of all his people? His God be with him, and let him go up to Jerusalem, which is in Judah, and build the house of the Lord God of Israel, which is in Jerusalem.

Captain of the Host—What say you to the proclamation? are you willing to go up to Jerusalem?

Principal Sojourner (consulting candidates)—Yes, we are willing to go, but we have no pass-word whereby to make ourselves known to the brethren when we get there. What shall we say to them?

Captain of the Host reads verses 13 and 14 of the third chapter of Exodus:

And Moses said unto God, Behold! when I come unto the children of Israel, and shall say unto them, The God of your fathers hath sent me unto you, and they shall say to me, What is his name? what shall I say to them? And God said unto Moses, I AM THAT I AM: And thus thou shalt say unto the children of Israel, I AM hath sent me unto you.

We were directed to use the words, "I AM THAT I AM," as a pass-word.

Principal Sojourner—We will go up. Companions, you will follow me: our pass-word is, I AM THAT I AM.

As they enter the Chapter, they again pass under the Living Arch.

Principal Sojourner—Stoop low, brethren. He that humbleth himself shall be exalted.

On one side of the hall or Chapter, the Living Arch is formed, as before described; on the other side is what is called the rugged road. This is generally made of blocks and logs of wood, old chairs, benches, &c.

The companions who form the Living Arch press harder on the candidates each time they go through, and they now go through three times. While passing through, the Principal Sojourner says:

Principal Sojourner—This is the way many great and good men have traveled before you; never deeming it derogatory to their dignity to level themselves with the fraternity. I have often traveled this road from Babylon to Jerusalem, and generally find it rough and rugged. However, I think I never saw it much smoother than it is at the present time.

The candidates after passing the Living Arch, stumble over the rugged road, and arrive again at the entrance of the arch.

Principal Sojourner—Companions, here is a very difficult and dangerous place

ahead, which lays directly in our way. Before we attempt to pass it, we must kneel down and pray. [Reads Psalm cxli.]

Lord, I cry unto thee, make haste unto me; give ear unto my voice. Let my prayer be set forth before thee as incense:

and the lifting up of my hands as the evening sacrifice. Set a watch, O Lord, before my mouth; keep the door of my lips. Incline not my heart to any evil thing, to practice wicked works with men that work iniquity. Let the righteous smite me; it shall be a kindness: and let him reprove me; it shall be an excellent oil. Mine eyes are unto thee, O God, the Lord: in thee is my trust; leave not my soul destitute. Keep me from the snare which they have laid before me, and the gins of the workers of iniquity. Let the wicked fall into their own nets, whilst that I withal escape.

The candidates rise and again pass under the Living Arch and over the rugged road. They then kneel again.

Principal Sojourner—Let us pray. [Reads from text-book Psalm cxlii.]

I cried unto the Lord with my voice; with my voice unto the Lord did I make my supplication, &c.

They then pass round the third time as before, when the candidates again kneel.

Principal Sojourner reads Psalm cxliii. from the text-book:

Hear my prayer, O Lord, give ear to my supplications; in thy faithfulness answer me, and in thy righteousness, &c.

Principal Sojourner—We have now arrived in sight of the ruins of the old Temple, near the outer veil of the Tabernacle.

The companions now put up the veils throughout the hall, as seen in the engraving, and the officers (except the Principal Sojourner) take their seats.

Principal Sojourner makes an alarm by stamping nine times on the floor, which brings out the Master from the First Veil.

Master of First Veil—Who comes there? Who dares approach this outer Veil of our sacred Tabernacle? Who are you?

Principal Sojourner—Three weary travelers from Babylon.

Master of First Veil—What are your intentions?

Principal Sojourner—We have come to assist in the noble and glorious work of rebuilding the house of the Lord, without the hope of fee or reward.

Master of First Veil—How do you expect to enter here?

Principal Sojourner—By a pass-word that we received in Babylon.

Master of First Veil—Give it to me.

Principal Sojourner—I AM THAT I AM.

Master of First Veil—The pass is right. You have my permission to enter.

The candidates now enter the First Veil, when the bandages are removed from their eyes.

Master of First Veil—You surely could not have come thus far unless you were three Most Excellent Masters; but further you cannot go, without my words, sign, and word of exhortation. My words are, Shem, Ham, and Japhet; my sign is this, [holding out a cane,] in imitation of one given by God to Moses, when he commanded him to cast his rod upon the ground thus, [casting down the cane,] and it became a serpent; but putting forth his hand, and taking it up by the tail, it became a rod in his hand as be

fore. My word of exhortation is explanatory of this sign, and is to be found in the writings of Moses, viz.: the first verses of the fourth chapter of Exodus:

And the Lord said unto Moses, What is that in thy hand? And he said, A rod. And the Lord said, Cast it on the ground, and he cast it, and it became a serpent, and Moses fled from before it, &c.

Principal Sojourner—Companions, we have passed the first guard, and will make an alarm at the Second Veil. [Stamps on the floor, as before.]

Master of Second Veil—Who comes there? Who dares approach this Second Veil of our sacred Tabernacle?

Principal Sojourner—Three weary sojourners from Babylon, who have come to assist in rebuilding the house of the Lord, without the hope of fee or reward.

Master of Second Veil—How do you expect to enter the Second Veil?

Principal Sojourner—By the words, sign, and word of exhortation of the Master of the First Veil.

Master of Second Veil—Give them.

Principal Sojourner—Shem, Ham and Japhet. [Gives the sign by casting down a cane and taking it up by the end, as before explained.]

Master of Second Veil—They are right. You have my permission to enter the Second Veil.

The candidates, led by the Principal Sojourner, pass in.

Master of Second Veil—Three Most Excellent Masters you must have been, or thus far you could not have come;

but further you cannot go without my words, sign, and word of exhortation. My words are Shem, Japhet, and Adoniram ; my sign is this, [thrusting his hand in his bosom;] it is in imitation of one given by God to Moses, when he commanded him to thrust his hand into his bosom, and taking it out it became as leprous as snow. My word of exhortation is explanatory of this sign, and is found in the writings of Moses, viz.: fourth chapter of Exodus :

And the Lord said unto Moses, Put now thine hand into thy bosom ;— and he put his hand in his bosom ; and when he took it out, behold his hand was leprous as snow, &c.

Principal Sojourner—Companions, we will pass on, and make an alarm at the Third Veil. [Stamps nine times.]

Master of the Third Veil—Who comes there? Who dare approach this Third Veil of our sacred Tabernacle ?

Principal Sojourner—Three weary sojourners from Babylon, who have come to assist in the rebuilding of the house of the Lord, without the hope of fee or reward.

Master of Third Veil—How do you expect to enter ?

Principal Sojourner—By the words, sign, and word of exhortation of the Master of the Second Veil.

Master of Third Veil—Give them.

Principal Sojourner—Shem, Japhet and Adoniram. [Thrusts his hand into his bosom as Master of Second Veil had done.]

Master of Third Veil—They are right. You can enter the Third Veil.

The candidates enter.

Master of Third Veil to candidates—Three Most Excellent Masters you must have been, or thus far you could not have come. But you cannot go further without my words, sign, and word of exhortation. My words are Haggai, Joshua and Zerubbabel. My sign is this : [Holds out a tumbler of water and pours out a little on the floor.] It is in imitation of one given by God to Moses, when he commanded him to pour water upon the dry land, and it became blood. My word of exhortation is explanatory of this sign, and is found in the writings of Moses, viz.: the fourth chapter of Exodus :

And it shall come to pass, if they will

not believe in the two former signs, thou shalt take the water of the river and pour it upon dry land ; and the water shall become blood upon the dry land.

Master of Third Veil—I also present you with the Signet of Truth, which is that of Zerubbabel. [Presents a triangular piece of metal with ZER-UBBA-BEL, engraved on it.]

Principal Sojourner to candidates—Companions, we have now passed the Third Veil ; let us make an alarm at the Fourth. [Stamps as before.]

Royal Arch Captain—Who comes there? Who dares approach the Fourth Veil of our sacred Tabernacle, where incense burns, day and night, upon the holy altar? Who are you, and what are your intentions?

Principal Sojourner—Three weary sojourners from Babylon, who have come up thus far to aid and assist in the noble and glorious work of rebuilding the house of the Lord, without the hope of fee or reward.

Royal Arch Captain—How do you expect to enter this Fourth Veil of our sacred Tabernacle ?

Principal Sojourner—By the words, sign, and word of exhortation of the Master of the Third Veil.

Royal Arch Captain—Give them.

Principal Sojourner—Haggai, Joshua and Zerubbabel. [Pours a little water from a tumbler, or cup, upon the floor, for the sign.]

Royal Arch Captain—They are right. You have my permission to enter the Fourth Veil.

The Veils are now drawn aside, and the candidates enter amidst a dazzling light, and behold the High Priest, King and Scribe sitting in Grand Council. The light is usually made by igniting gum camphor in an urn upon the altar.

Royal Arch Captain—Three Most Excellent Masters you must have been, or thus far you could not have come. I wil present you to the Grand Council. [Stamps his foot nine times.]

High Priest—Who comes here?

Principal Sojourner—Three weary sojourners from Babylon, who have come up thus far to aid and assist in rebuilding the house of the Lord, without the hope of fee or reward.

High Priest—Have you the signet of Zerubbabel?

Principal Sojourner—We have. [Presents the signet given him by Master of Third Veil.]

High Priest takes it, and reads from the second chapter of Haggai:

In that day will I take thee, O Zerubbabel, my servant, the son of Shealtiel, saith the Lord, and will make thee a signet: for I have chosen thee.

High Priest to King (showing him the signet)—Companion, are you satisfied that this is the signet of Zerubbabel?

King (taking the signet, and scrutinizing it)—I am satisfied, Most Excellent, that it is.

High Priest (showing signet to Scribe) —Companion Scribe, think you this is the true signet of Zerubbabel?

Scribe (looking shrewdly at it)—I am satisfied that it is, Most Excellent.

High Priest (drawing signet across his forehead in imitation of the penalty, or due-guard)—Signet of Truth, and Holiness to the Lord!

The King and the Scribe each in turn puts his hand to his forehead, repeating—Holiness to the Lord.

High Priest to candidates—It is the opinion of the Grand Council, that you have presented the true signet of Zerubbabel. But owing to difficulties having arisen from the introduction of strangers among the workmen, none are allowed to undertake in the noble and glorious work, but the true descendants of the twelve tribes. It is necessary you should be very particular in tracing your genealogy. Who are you, and what are your intentions?

Principal Sojourner—We are your own kindred, the descendants of those noble families of Giblemites, who wrought so hard at the building of the first Temple. We have been regularly initiated as Entered Apprentice Masons, passed to the degree of Fellow Craft, raised to the sublime degree of Master Mason, advanced to the honorary degree of Mark Master, presided as Master in the chair, and at the completion and dedication of the Temple, were acknowledged as Most Excellent Masters. We were present at its destruction by Nebuchadnezzar, and by him were carried away captives to Babylon; where we remained servants to him and his successors, until the reign of Cyrus, King of Persia, by whose proclamation we were liberated, and have come up thus far to aid and assist in the noble and glorious work of rebuilding the house of the Lord, without the hope of fee or reward.

High Priest—Let the captives be unbound, and brought to light Companion King, I think we had better employ these sojourners. They look like good hardy men: just such men as we want about the building. What say you?

King—It is my opinion, Most Excellent, they are very expert workmen. I wish they might be examined.

High Priest—What is your opinion, companion Scribe?

Scribe—If they can satisfy us they are Free Masons, I shall be in favor of employing them immediately.

High Priest—You say you are Entered Apprentice Masons? Satisfy the Grand Council.

The three candidates give the signs of Entered Apprentice, as on page 7.

High Priest to King and Scribe—Companions, are you satisfied?

The King bows gracefully, and the Scribe answers—We are satisfied, Most Excellent.

High Priest to candidates—The Grand Council are satisfied that you are Entered Apprentice Masons. Have you been advanced to the Fellow Craft's degree?

Candidates give the Fellow Craft signs as on page 22, when the High Priest asks his companions of the Grand Council if they are satisfied, as before, and then informs the candidates that the Grand Council approves them as true Fellow Crafts, &c.

The same questions and answers are given in like manner as to each degree up to, and including that of Most Excellent Master, and the candidates give all the signs of those degrees to the Grand Council in detail.

High Priest (after consultation with th King and Scribe)—Companions, we are satisfied that you are three worthy Most Excellent Masters. As such, we will employ you on the Temple. What part of the work will you undertake?

Principal Sojourner—We will take any service, however servile or dangerous, for the sake of forwarding so great and noble an undertaking.

High Priest to Royal Arch Captain—You will furnish them with the working tools, and direct them to repair to the north-east corner of the ruins of the old Temple, with orders to remove the rubbish, preparatory to laying the foundation of the new Temple. Advise them 1) carefully preserve everything of service to the craft that falls in their way, and bring it to the Grand Council.

The candidates are presented, one with a pick-ax, one with a crow, and the other with a shovel, which are generally made of wood, and kept for the purpose in the Lodge or Chapter.

Principal Sojourner to the candidates—Follow me.

Each candidate shoulders his working tool and follows the Principal Sojourner, going single file to a corner of the room where a quantity of blocks, or bricks are scattered around. These they stir up a little, when they come to a ring in a trap door, which they pull up and find it shaped like a key-stone of an arch. Each one examines it, and then looks down the trap, when the Principal Sojourner suggests that it be at once taken up to the Grand Council. He then leads the candidates back.

High Priest—Companion King, have you further business to lay before this Grand Council?

King—I have nothing, Most Excellent.

High Priest to Scribe—Have you anything, worthy companion?

Scribe—I know of nothing, Most Excellent.

High Priest—I know of nothing, unless the workmen from the ruins have articles for inspection. The workmen will please come forward and give an account of their labors.

Principal Sojourner—Most Excellent, in pursuance of orders of this Grand Council, we repaired to the ruins and commenced our labors. After laboring several days, we discovered what seemed a rock, but on striking it with a crow, it gave a hollow sound, and upon closer examination, we discovered in it an iron ring, by help of which we succeeded in removing it from its place, when we found it to be the key-stone of an arch, and through the aperture there appeared to be an immense vault curiously arched. We have brought this key-stone up, that it may be examined by the Grand Council.

High Priest—You will present it.

Principal Sojourner presents the key-stone, or trap.

High Priest (looking closely at it)—Companion King, this is a very valuable discovery indeed. It must be a key stone of a Mark Master Mason.

King—I think that is the stone wrought by our Grand Master, Hiram Abiff.

High Priest—What think you of it, Companion Scribe?

Scribe—It is undoubtedly the stone wrought by our Grand Master, Hiram Abiff.

High Priest (drawing key-stone across his forehead, and giving the sign)—The Key-stone of a Mark Master! Holiness to the Lord.

King and Scribe do and say the same.

High Priest to candidates—This is a very valuable discovery indeed. No doubt it will lead to some important treasure, of inestimable value to the craft. Are you willing to pursue your labors, and endeavor to penetrate this secret vault?

Principal Sojourner, (after consulting candidates)—We are, even to the risk of our lives.

High Priest—Go: and may the God of your fathers be with you. Preserve everything that falls in your way.

The Principal Sojourner returns with the candidates to the place where they lifted the trap, and they there consult together as to who shall descend into the vault. One of the candidates agreeing to go, they put a rope seven times around his body, leaving two long ends.

Principal Sojourner to candidate who is about to descend—Companion, it is necessary you should take a little precaution. Should you wish to descend still lower, pull the rope in your left hand: if you wish to ascend, pull that in your right hand.

Two companions take hold of each end of the rope, letting the candidate down eight or ten feet, to another trap-door, where he finds three small trying squares; and giving the signal of ascending, is drawn up.

Each candidate taking a square, they repair to the Grand Council. As they present themselves, the High Priest reads the following passage from the fourth chapter of Zechariah:

The hands of Zerubbabel have laid the foundation of this house; his hands shall also finish it; and thou shalt know that the Lord of hosts hath sent me unto you. For who hath despised the day of small things? for they shall rejoice, and shall see the plummet of Zerubbabel, with those seven.

High Priest to the King—Companions, have you any further business for the Grand Council?

King—I have nothing, Most Excellent.

High Priest to Scribe—Have you anything, worthy companion?

Scribe—Nothing, Most Excellent.

High Priest—I know of nothing, unless the workmen from the ruins have something for our inspection.

Principal Sojourner—We have examined the secret vault, Most Excellent, and here is what we have found in it, [presenting the three trying squares.]

High Priest (drawing one of the squares across his forehead)—The jewels of our ancient Grand Masters, King Solomon, Hiram, King of Tyre, and Hiram Abiff! Holiness to the Lord.

The King and the Scribe each take one and imitate the High Priest.

High Priest to candidates—Are you willing to continue your labors and still further penetrate this secret vault?

Principal Sojourner—We are, even to the risk of our lives.

High Priest—Go, and may the God of your fathers be with you; and remember that your labors shall not go unrewarded.

The Principal Sojourner leads the candidates back as before, and winds the rope round one of them, who is let down the trap, still further down than before, where he finds the Ark, when he gives the signal and is drawn up.

The party immediately returns to the Grand Council, two of them carrying the Ark, where they present themselves in the same manner as before, and the High Priest directs them to come forward and give an account of their labors.

Principal Sojourner—Most Excellent, in pursuance of your orders, we repaired to the secret vault, and let down one of our companions. The sun at this time was at its meridian height, the rays of which enabled him to discover a small box, or chest, standing on a pedestal, curiously wrought, and overlaid with gold. On discovering it, he involuntarily found his hands raised in this position, [giving due-guard, as on page 79,] to guard his eyes from the intense light and heat reflected from it. The air becoming offensive, he gave the signal for ascending, and was immediately drawn out. We have brought this chest up for the examination of the Grand Council.

High Priest (looking with surprise at the Ark)—Companion King, this is the Ark of the Covenant of God.

King (looking at it)—It is undoubtedly the true Ark of the Covenant, Most Excellent.

Scribe (looking at the Ark)—That is also my opinion.

High Priest (taking the Ark)—Let us open it, and see what valuable treasure it may contain. [Opens the Ark, and takes out a Look.]

High Priest to King—Companion, here is a very ancient looking book; what can it be? Let us read in it. [Reads first three verses of first chapter of Genesis:]

In the beginning God created the heaven and the earth, &c.

After reading these verses, the High Priest turns over to Deuteronomy xxxi., and reads from the 24th to the 26th verses, as follows:

And it came to pass, when Moses had made an end of writing the words of this law in a book, until they were finished, that Moses commanded the Levites which

bare the Ark of the Lord, saying, Take this book of the law, and put it in the side of the Ark of the Covenant of the Lord your God, that it may be there for a witness against thee.

The High Priest then turns back to Exodus xx. and reads the 21st verse, as follows:

And thou shalt put the mercy seat above, upon the Ark; and in the Ark thou shalt put the testimony that I shall give thee.

High Priest—This is a book of the law—long lost, but now found. Holiness to the Lord. [He repeats this again twice.]

King—A book of the law—long lost, but now found. Holiness to the Lord!

Scribe repeats the same.

High Priest to candidates—You now see that the world is indebted to Masonry for the preservation of this sacred volume. Had it not been for the wisdom and precaution of our ancient brethren, this, the only remaining copy of the law, would have been destroyed, at the destruction of Jerusalem.

High Priest (taking a little pot out of the Ark)—Companion King, what can this be? a pot of manna? We will read in the book of the law and see what that says. [Reads Hebrews ix., v. 2 to 5:]

For there was a tabernacle made: the first wherein was the candlesticks, and the table, and the shew-bread, which is called the sanctuary: and after the second veil, the tabernacle, which is called the holiest of all: which had the golden censer, and the ark of the covenant, overlaid round about with gold; wherein was the golden pot that had manna; and Aaron's rod, that budded, and the tables of the covenant; and over it the cherubims of glory, overshadowing the mercy seat; of which we cannot now speak particularly.

High Priest—A Pot of Manna! Holiness to the Lord!

King—A Pot of Manna! Holiness to the Lord!

Scribe repeats the same.

High Priest—Companions, we read in the book of the law, that He that overcometh, will I give to eat of the hidden manna. Come forward, companions, you are entitled to it. [Each one receives a small lump of sugar.] But how it came deposited here, we cannot now particularly speak. You must go higher in Masonry before you can know.

The High Priest looks again into the Ark, and finds a stick with some buds upon it, which he shows to the King and

Scribe, and after a consultation, they decide that it is Aaron's Rod, and the fact is thus proclaimed in the same manner as the discovery of the manna.

Looking again into the Ark, the High Priest takes out four pieces of paper, which he examines closely, consults with the King and Scribe, and then puts together so as to show a key to the ineffable characters of this degree.

a b c d e f g h i j k l m

n o p q r s t u v w x y z

After examining the Key, he proceeds to read, by the aid of it, the characters on the four sides of the Ark.

High Priest (reading first side)—Deposited in the year three thousand. Second side—By Solomon, King of Israel. Third side—Hiram, King of Tyre, and Hiram Abiff. Fourth side—For the Good of Masonry, generally, but the Jewish nation in particular.

High Priest to candidates—Companions, here are three mysterious words, in a triangular form, upon the Ark, which, when first found, was covered with three squares, the jewels of our three ancient Grand Masters; and from this circumstance, we supposed it to be the long lost Master Mason's word; and on applying the Key to it, it proved our suspicions to be correct. It is the name of Deity in three languages, viz.: Chaldeac, Hebrew, and Syriac, which is the long lost Master Mason's word, and has now become the Grand Omnific Royal Arch word. This word was anciently written only in those sacred characters, and thus preserved from one generation to another. It was lost by the death of Hiram Abiff, was found again at the building of the Temple, and will now be given to you; and you will remember the manner you receive it, and that you have sworn never to give it to others except in that particular manner.

The candidates, instructed by the Principal Sojourner, now learn the Grand Omnific Royal Arch Word, as follows: Each one takes hold with his right hand of the right wrist of his companion on the left, and with his left hand takes hold of the left wrist of his companion on the right. Each one then places his right foot forward with the hollow in front so that the toe touches the heel of his companion on the right. This is called "three times three," that is, three right feet forming a triangle, three left hands forming a triangle, and three right hands forming a triangle. They balance in the same manner, and then, with hands raised, repeat the words Jah-buh-lun, Jeho-vah, G-o-d, at low breath, as described at length on page 68.

The signs of this degree are now given to the candidates, as follows:

First, raise the right hand to the forehead, the hand and arm horizontal, the thumb towards the forehead; draw it briskly across the forehead, and drop it perpendicularly by the side. This constitutes the due-guard of this degree, and refers not only to the penalty of the obligation, but alludes also to the manner in which the brother who descended into the vault, and found the Ark, found his hands involuntarily placed to protect his head from the rays of the meridian sun.

Due-guard.   Grand Sign.

The grand sign is made by locking the fingers of both hands together, and carrying them to the top of the head, the palms upward. This alludes to the penalty of having the scull clove off, &c.

High Priest (placing crowns upon the heads of candidates)—Companions, you are now invested with all the important secrets of this degree, and crowned and received as worthy companions Royal Arch Masons.

The High Priest then reads to them from a book the charge in this degree, informing them that the degree owes its origin to Zerubbabel and his associates, who rebuilt the Temple by order of Cyrus, King of Persia. He likewise informs them that the discovery of the secret vault and the inestimable treasures, with the long lost word, actually took place in the manner represented in conferring this degree, and that it is the circumstance upon which the degree is principally founded.

The initiation being over, the High Priest begins the closing lecture, which is a repetition, by questions and answers, of the opening of a Chapter, and the advancement of a companion of this degree. It begins as follows:

High Priest to Captain of the Host—Are you a Royal Arch Mason?

Captain—I am, that I am.

High Priest—How shall I know you to be a Royal Arch Mason?

Captain of Host—By three times three.

High Priest—Where was you made a Royal Arch Mason?

Captain of the Host—In a just and legally constituted Chapter of Royal Arch Masons, consisting of Most Excellent High Priest, King, and Scribe, Captain of the Host, Principal Sojourner, Royal Arch Captain, and the three Grand Masters of the Veils, assembled in a room or place representing the Tabernacle erected by our ancient brethren, near the ruins of King Solomon's Temple.

The High Priest continues his questions as to the station and duties of each officer of the Chapter, and every particular relative to the organization thereof, the initiation or advancement of candidates, &c. The Captain of the Host rehearses, or describes the whole precisely as we have given it. These closing lectures are intended to perfect members in the full understanding of each degree.

After the lecture the Chapter is closed in the same manner as the opening, up to the raising of the Living Arch. The companions join hands by threes, in the same manner, and say in concert—

As we three did agree,
The Sacred Word to keep—
As we three did agree
The Sacred Word to search;
So we three do agree
To close this Royal Arch.

They then break, and the High Priest reads the following prayer:

By the wisdom of the Supreme High Priest may we be directed, by his strength may we be enabled, and by the beauty of virtue may we be incited, to perform the obligations here enjoined upon us, to keep inviolable the mysteries here unfolded to us, and invariably to practice all those duties out of the Chapter, which are inculcated in it.

Companions—So mote it be. Amen.

High Priest—I now declare this Chapter of Royal Arch Masons closed.

ROYAL MASTER'S DEGREE.

This degree can only be conferred on a perfect Royal Arch Mason—one who has not only taken all the preceding degrees, but is well posted in them. It originated in the following manner:

At the building of the Temple, King Solomon, Hiram, King of Tyre, and Hiram Abiff, the three ancient Grand Masters, resolved to reward all those Master Masons whose fidelity, industry and skill placed them above their companions, by communicating to them the Omnific Word. After several consultations as to when this word should be conferred, it was proposed by Hiram Abiff that it should not be given until the Temple was completed, and then only in the presence of all three, and by their free consent then to be expressed. This plan was adopted, and the three Grand Masters bound themselves by solemn oaths to a strict observance of it.

One day, soon after this agreement, Hiram Abiff went into the sanctum sanctorum, as was his usual custom at high 12, to offer prayers, and to draw designs on the tressle-board. As he was returning, he was accosted near the entrance by Adoniram, a worthy Master, as follows:

Adoniram—Most Excellent, at what time shall I receive the Omnific Word?

Hiram Abiff—My worthy friend, it is uncertain when, or whether you will ever receive it at all; for the Omnific Word cannot be given until the Temple is completed, and then only by the free consent of the three Grand Masters.

Adoniram—Supposing one of you three were removed hence by death, how then shall I expect to receive it?

Hiram Abiff (tapping the floor three times with his foot)—When I die, they'll bury it there. [He alluded to his own violent death, the details of which are recorded in the Master Mason's degree.]

The Lodge, or Chapter, in this degree, is organized similar to that in the Royal Arch, only arranged differently. The Ark is set in the middle of the inner veil, and the members assemble round it at the opening, each one taking his companion by the wrist, as hereafter explained, when the presiding officer reads the 27th verse of 1 Kings vi. as follows :

And he set the cherubims within the inner house, and they stretched forth the wings of the cherubims, so that the wing of the one touched the one wall, and the wing of the other touched the other wall, and their wings touched one another in the midst of the house.

When a companion is to be advanced to this degree, the members assemble round the altar, taking each other's wrists in the same manner as at the opening. While in this position, the Grand Master, or presiding officer, enters and goes to the altar, kneels, [meantime the candidate has been led in,] and reads the following prayer :

Thou, O God, knowest our downsitting and uprising, and understandest our thoughts afar off : shield and defend us from the evil intentions of our enemies, and support us under the trials and afflictions we are destined to endure while traveling this vale of tears. Man that is born of woman is of few days, and full of trouble. He cometh forth as the flower, and is cut down : he fleeth also as a shadow, and continueth not ; seeing his days are determined, the number of his months are with Thee ; Thou hast appointed his bounds that he cannot pass : turn from him, that he may rest, till he shall accomplish his day ; for there is hope of a tree, if it be not cut down, that it will sprout again, and that the tender branches thereof will not cease. But man dieth and wasteth away ; yea, man giveth up the ghost, and where is he ? As the waters fail from the sea, and the flood decayeth and drieth up, so man lieth down, and riseth not up till the heavens shall be no more. Yet, O Lord, have compassion on the children of thy creation ; administer them comfort in time of trouble, and save them with an everlasting salvation. Amen, so mote it be.

The Grand Master then rises, and passes out of the circle under the extended arms of the companions. [He personates Hiram Abiff, who came in at high noon to pray] As he goes out, the candidate accosts him thus :

Candidate (prompted by conductor)—Most Excellent, at what time shall I receive the Omnific Word ?

Master—My worthy friend, it is uncertain when, or whether you will ever receive it at all ; for the Omnific Word cannot be given except by the free consent of three Grand Masters, and at a time only when they together shall agree to give it.

The Master passes to his seat, and the candidate approaches the altar and kneels, when the following promise is administered :

Master—Companion, do you solemnly promise, on the oath of a Royal Arch Mason, to keep sacred the secrets of this degree ?

Candidate—I do.

The candidate is then instructed in the grip, which is as follows : Each takes hold of his left wrist with his right hand, and with his left hand takes hold of his companion's right wrist. This forms a square. It is the same as when we see two children making a seat for a third with their hands.

Royal Master's Grip.   Due-guard.

The words are given in this manner : let go your own wrist, and let your left hand fall at your side, keeping hold of your companion's right wrist, and placing your right feet together, toe to heel, so as to form two sides of a triangle. Looking down at the feet, one says in a low voice, "Alas, poor Hiram! The candidate repeats the same words. The sign, or due-guard, is made by placing the fore finger of the right hand upon the lips. It is a caution to a companion when you wish him to keep silent.

Master to candidate (tapping the floor three times with his toe)—Do you know about this ?

Candidate (instructed)—I know something about it.

6

Master—What do you know about it ?

Candidate—I know something about the beginning of it. [Taps three times with his toe.]

The same questions are repeated, when the candidate answers that he also knows something about the ending of it.

Master—What is the beginning ?

Candidate (instructed)—Alpha.

Master—What is the ending ?

Candidate—Omega.

Master—I am Alpha and Omega, the beginning and the end.

The Master then reads verses 12 to 14 of the twenty-second chapter of Revelations, as follows:

And behold I come quickly; and my reward is with me, to give every man according as his work shall be. I am Alpha and Omega, the beginning and the end, the first and the last. Blessed are they that do his commandments, that they may have a right to the tree of life, and may enter in at the gates of the city.

There is little formality in this degree, and different Lodges or Chapters give it in different ways. The above is the usual manner of giving it in New York.

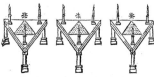

SELECT MASTER'S DEGREE.

At the building of the Temple, the Grand Masters entered into a solemn agreement that they would not confer the Master's Degree until the Temple should be completed, and then only on such as should have rendered themselves worthy, by their skill, their virtue and their inflexible fidelity to the craft. Their agreement was such, that all three must be present when it should be conferred, lest partiality for a friend might occasion the admission of an unworthy member; they also caused their obligation to be such, that if either should be taken away by death prior to the finishing of the Temple, the Master's degree would of course be lost. They also possessed a firm belief, that if the children of Israel continued not in the belief of the Supreme Judge, to obey his commands, their enemies would be let loose against them, their city and Temple would be sacked, and destroyed, and themselves carried

into captivity, and thus the knowledge of the arts and sciences, together with the patterns and valuable models, which were contained in the Temple, and the writings of Moses, would be for ever lost.

To prevent such a catastrophe, they agreed to build a secret vault under ground, leading from King Solomon's most retired apartment, a due west course, and ending under the sanctum sanctorum, to be divided into nine separate apartments, or arches, the ninth to be under the sanctum sanctorum, all of which were to be erected or built by themselves, and such companions as they should select, for the special purpose. The Ninth Arch was to be the place for holding their Grand Council, and also a deposit for a true copy of all those things which were contained in the sanctum sanctorum above. There were selected to work in the other eight arches, twenty-three from Gebul, a city in Phenicia, who were stone squarers, who, together with Adoniram, were well skilled in the arts and sciences, particularly sculpture; their hours of labor were from nine at night to twelve, when they retired to rest. During the erection of this secret vault, a circumstance occurred which characterizes this degree.

A particular friend of King Solomon, whose name was Izabud, discovered that a secret work was going on about the Temple, of which he was not informed by his friend; and he for some time grieved in silence : at length he communicated his suspicions to King Solomon, and begged to know how he had forfeited his confidence. The king told him that his confidence in him remained the same, and desired him to be contented for the present, for the time would soon arrive when a door would be left open for his reception, (meaning when the Temple should be finished and he received the Master's degree.) This for a time satisfied him, but one evening, having some particular business with King Solomon, he went as usual to seek him in his most retired room, and finding the door of the secret vault open and not guarded as usual, by the Grand Steward Ahishar, he took it for granted that it was left open for his reception, agreeably to the king's promise. He therefore boldly entered, but was soon accosted by Adoniram, the captain of the guards, who sternly challenged him, and took him into custody.

With this historical explanation, the conferring of this degree will be understood as described in the following pages

The Council are seated as in the engraving, which represents the interior arrangement of a Lodge or Chapter in this degree, with the Ark curtained round in the centre. The place of meeting is supposed to be a secret vault under the Temple, where Solomon deposited his choicest treasures. The first, or presiding officer, represents King Solomon, and is styled Thrice Illustrious Grand Master. He is dressed in purple robes, a golden cro   on his head, a sceptre in his hand, an

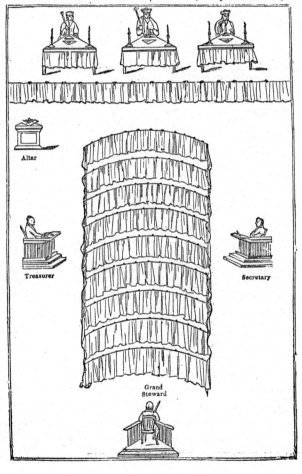

gold trimmed collar on his neck, to which is suspended a gold trowel.

The second officer sits on his right, with the same dress and decorations. He represents Hiram, King of Tyre, and is styled Deputy Illustrious Grand Master.

The third officer is seated on the left of the first. He is dressed in yellow robes, trimmed with blue; a collar on his neck, and a gold hammer in his hand. He represents Hiram Abiff, and is called Principal Conductor of the work.

Before each of the three first officers is a triangular table, upon each angle of which is a burning taper; and in the centre, a triangular plate of gold. A veil or curtain separates them from the rest of the officers and companions, as is represented in the engraving.

The next three officers in rank, are seated in other parts of the hall, so as to form a triangle, viz. :

The Secretary, who is the fourth officer, in the south.

The fifth, Treasurer, in the north.

The sixth is seated in the west, with a drawn sword, representing Adoniram, the Grand Steward. He acts as Tyler, and is to guard the inside of the door.

The officers being seated, the veil is drawn aside, making the room one apartment, with the Ark (veiled) in the centre.

Grand Master—Companions, I am about to open a Council of Select Masters. If there are any present not of this degree, they will please to retire.

After waiting to ascertain if all present are Select Masters, he addresses the Deputy Grand Master on his right :

Grand Master—Worthy Companion of Tyre, shall we resume our labors, and complete the secret work which has been so happily begun ?

Deputy—Thrice Illustrious, it is my most ardent wish to see it completed, and the sacred treasure therein safely deposited ; that I may return to my own country with the satisfaction of having faithfully discharged my duty to the craft.

Grand Master to Conductor, on his left —Companion Conductor, are our numbers complete ?

Conductor—Thrice Illustrious, I find the number of three times nine.

Grand Master—You will see that the secret vault is made secure.

Conductor goes out, returns, and says—Thrice Illustrious, all is in security.

Grand Master to Deputy—What is it o'clock ?

Deputy—Nine at night, Thrice Illustrious, when all prying eyes are closed in sleep, and stillness pervades all nature.

Grand Master—Such being the hour, it is my pleasure that a Council of Select Masters be now opened for the dispatch of business. Companion Conductor, you will order the companions to their several stations, and after the regular alarm shall be given, let them proceed in their labors, according to the directions they have received.

Conductor—Companions, it is our Illustrious Grand Master's orders that a Council of Select Masters be now opened for the dispatch of business; and after the regular alarm of the mysterious number nine is given, each will resume his labor.

Grand Master knocks eight quick and one slow, and all the officers imitate him in their turn, according to rank.

Then all the companions knock eight quick and one slow, with their hands.

Grand Master—Attend to giving the signs, companions.

All the companions rise on their feet, and give the signs from Entered Apprentice to Royal Master, as before described.

The signs of a Select Master are then given as follows : The first is similar to the sign of distress of a Master Mason. The fists are both clenched, in allusion to one of the penalties of the obligation, which is to have both hands chopped off to the stumps.

First Sign, or Due guard.   Second Sign.

The second sign is made by crossing the hands and arms, as in the engraving ; with a quick motion draw the hands edgewise across the body downwards, as though you were in the act of quartering the body, and let them drop by your sides. This is in imitation of a part of the penalty of this degree, which is to have the body quartered.

The third sign is given by placing the hands over each eye, as in the engraving, and with a quick motion, throw the arms downwards at an angle of forty-five degrees, as though you was tearing the eyeballs from the sockets, and dashing them on the ground, then drop the arms by the sides. This is also a part of the penalty.

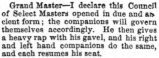

The fourth sign alludes to that part of the penalty of being thrown among the rubbish of the Temple. It is made by placing the left hand upon the upper part

of the forehead, the palm downwards, and cover it with the right, the body erect, heels together, step off with the right foot, and plant it about eighteen inches in front with a stamp, at the same time dart the hands forward.

The most popular signs of this degree among Masons are made in this manner: Place the palm of the the right hand upon the heart, and pronounce the word SECRESY, and immediately raise the left hand, and place the palm over the mouth, the first finger against the upper lip, the others a little off from it, the thumb against the side of the nose, and speak the word SILENCE; raise the right hand from the breast and place it over the eyes, and pronounce, SILENCE and DARKNESS.

Grand Master—I declare this Council of Select Masters opened in due and ancient form; the companions will govern themselves accordingly. He then gives a heavy rap with his gavel, and his right and left hand companions do the same, and each resumes his seat.

In an initiation in this degree, the candidate is conducted to an antechamber, and is told to remain there until he sees the door open, when he must walk into the Council.

The Tyler (or Grand Steward) takes his post on the inside of the door to guard the same, and after walking back and forth, sits down by the door, and feigns himself sleeping. [This is a very difficult part to act: the loudest snorers are always selected.] The door is now thrown open, and the candidate (who represents Izabud) enters.

Captain of Guards—Who comes there?

Candidate—A zealous brother, who wishes to partake of your labors.

Captain—Give me the word, sign, and token of your entrance.

Candidate—I have none.

Captain—An intruder! an intruder!

Companions all exclaim—Put him to death instantly!

Grand Master—What is the cause of this confusion?

Captain of Guards—An intruder has invaded our secret vault.

Grand Master—Put him to death immediately.

Captain of the Guards seizes candidate by the collar, and placing the point of his sword at his breast, looks him in the face, and then drops the point of it.

Captain to Grand Master—Thrice Illustrious, consider for a moment on whom you are about to inflict this awful penalty. This is your particular friend Izabud.

Grand Master—Bind him fast, then, and see that he is forthcoming when called for. Your life shall answer for his escape.

Captain of the Guards binds candidate and takes him out of the room.

The three presiding officers leave their seats, and are supposed to go to the Ninth Arch.

Grand Master to his Deputy—Worthy Companion, I do not see how we can prevent this sacrifice.

Deputy—It is impossible, Thrice Illustrious. Only three can be employed in each arch—twenty-seven in all. None can pass beyond, and none can enter unless they know our secret, and thus forfeit their lives.

Grand Master—It is, then, out of my power to pardon my friend.

Conductor—It is truly out of your power, Thrice Illustrious.

The Grand Master and his aids now return to their seats.

Grand Master to Captain of Guards—Bring in your prisoner.

Candidate is brought forward.

Grand Master to candidate—Alas, my unfortunate friend Izabud, your disobedience and curiosity have forfeited your life. I have consulted with my colleagues, and find them inflexible. My obligation, also, is of such a nature, that I have not the power to pardon you.

Candidate—Thrice Illustrious, I pray you to remember how great and sincere my attachment has ever been to your sacred person, to your services and secrets. Of late, finding a private work going on, with which I was not made acquainted, I feared I had lost all the confidence of my sovereign, and grieved in silence. At length I took the liberty of mentioning the matter to your majesty, and you directed me to rest contented; for the time would soon arrive when a door would be left open for my reception. This assurance satisfied me; and this evening, having some particular business with your majesty, I sought you in the retired room; and finding the door open and unguarded, I took it for granted it was for my reception, and entered accordingly. But I beg your majesty to believe that it was not a spirit of disobedience or curiosity which prompted me to do it.

Deputy to Grand Master—Thrice Illustrious, I find your friend is not guilty of the charge alleged against him. His offence is rather owing to some imprudent observation of your own; he must therefore be pardoned, and admitted.

Grand Master—Worthy Companion of Tyre, how can that be done? is not our number already full?

Conductor—Thrice Illustrious, it is true our numbers are full; but Ahishar, the Guard, is no longer worthy of our confidence. He was found sleeping at his post, and he alone is guilty. Let him be discharged and immediately executed; and let Izabud be placed in his stead.

Grand Master—I thank you, my worthy companion, for your advice: it shall be done. Izabud, are you willing to take a solemn obligation to keep inviolable the secrets of our Order?

Candidate—I am willing.

Grand Master—Free him of his shackles, and conduct him to the altar.

Captain of the Guards conducts candidate to the altar, and makes him kneel, when the Grand Master directs him to take the oath, which he does as follows:

I, John Smith, in the presence of the Grand Architect of the Universe, and before this illustrious assembly, dedicated to the most puissant, most terrible, most merciful Creator, do solemnly swear, that I will never discover the signs, tokens, and words belonging to a Select Master, nor to any one living, the secret of this royal vault, neither by speaking, writing, engraving, carving, or painting; or by any dumb sign, or motion, in any unlawful way, whereby the least hint might be taken, that in this place existed a secret work, or that any secrets are deposited here.

I furthermore swear that I never will penetrate into the secrets of the ninth arch, unless legally authorized by our Thrice Illustrious Grand Masters. All this I swear, with a firm and steady resolution, without any mental reservation or self-evasion of mind in me whatever; binding myself under no less penalty, besides all my former penalties, to have my hands chopped off to the stumps, my eyes plucked out from the sockets, my body quartered, and then thrown among the rubbish of the Temple; that there may remain no more remembrance of such a vile wretch, if ever I should wilfully violate this my obligation. So help me God, and keep me steadfast in the same. Amen.

Grand Master to candidate—Kiss the book nine times.

Candidate obeys.

Grand Master (taking him by the hand and raising him up)—I now greet you a Companion Select; therefore, in future, be ever blind and dumb to everything you have seen or heard in this Council, and keep in mind the words SECRESY and SILENCE, as they will now be given to you, [placing his hands as in the engraving.]

Candidate is instructed in the signs, &c., as given on pages 84–85.

The Grand Master then reads to him the following history:

After the Ninth Arch was completed, the three Grand Masters deposited therein a true copy of those things which were of importance to the Craft, and to the

Jewish nation—such as the Ark of the Covenant, the Pot of Manna, the Rod of Aaron, the Book of the Law, &c. ; and that they might be known and duly appreciated, if ever found, by future generations, they agreed to place their names on three of the sides of the Ark, and on the fourth side they placed the date of, by whom, and for what purpose they were thus deposited ; which was for the good of the craft in general, and the Jewish nation in particular ; and that, should the Temple be destroyed, and the people carried away into captivity, yet on their release, and rebuilding the house of their God, they might possibly discover these valuable treasures.

After this deposit was made, and prior to the completion of the Temple, our Grand Master Hiram Abiff was assassinated, in a manner related in a preceding degree ; and by his death, the Master's word was lost. The two kings were willing to do all in their power to preserve the sacred word, and as they could not communicate it to any, by reason of the death of their friend Hiram Abiff, they agreed to place it in the secret vault, that if the other treasures were ever brought to light, the word might be found also ; they therefore placed it on the top of the Ark of the Covenant, in the Hebrew, Syriac, and Chaldaic languages ; and that it might be known as the true word, when discovered, they placed the three Grand Master's jewels, one on each language, well knowing that a description of those jewels would be handed down to the latest posterity ; and by these means the Royal Arch, or rather the ancient Master's word, was finally discovered ; being the same which was communicated by God himself to Enoch, and in use three thousand years, when it was lost by the death of Hiram Abiff, and afterwards brought to light at rebuilding the second Temple, and has been in use ever since, and will continue to be the same till time shall be no more.

The ceremony of receiving the candidate being through, the officers and companions all resume their seats, as before described, and the Grand Master reads 24th to 26th verses xxxi. Deuteronomy :

And it came to pass, when Moses had made an end of writing the words of this law in a book, until they were finished, that Moses commanded the Levites which bore the Ark of the Covenant of the Lord saying, Take this Book of the Law, and put it in the side of the Ark of the Covenant of the Lord your God, that it may be there for a witness against thee.

When the reading is finished, four companions bearing the Ark advance to the centre of the Council, and place it upon the altar, open it, and put the Book of the Law into it, and return to their seats.

The Grand Master reads verses 33 and 34 of xvi. Exodus :

And Moses said unto Aaron, Take a pot, and put an omer full of manna therein, and lay it up before the Lord, to keep for your generations. As the Lord commanded Moses, so Aaron laid it up before the testimony to be kept.

A companion brings the Pot of Manna and puts it into the Ark.

The Grand Master reads verse 10 of xvii. chapter of Numbers :

And the Lord said unto Moses, Bring Aaron's Rod again before the testimony, to be kept for a token.

In like manner Aaron's Rod is deposited.

The Grand Master reads 89th verse of vii. chapter of Numbers :

And when Moses was gone into the tabernacle of the congregation to speak with him, then he heard the voice of one speaking unto him from off the mercy seat, that was upon the ark of the testimony, from between the two cherubims ; and he spake unto him.

The Thrice Illustrious Grand Master, Deputy Grand Master and Grand Conductor, (personating Solomon, Hiram, King of Tyre, and Hiram Abiff,) now approach the altar, and place the name of God upon three sides of the Ark in three languages, viz., Hebrew, Chaldaic and Syriac. They also place upon it the date it was deposited, who by, and for what purpose, &c., written in the ineffable characters before described, upon its sides and top. They put into the Ark a key to the ineffable characters, (as on page 79.) They then place their three jewels (or squares) in a triangular form upon it. The Ark is then put through a trap in the floor and placed in the position described as having been found, in the Royal Arch Degree.

This finishes the business, and the companions take their proper stations, when the charge is read to the candidate, as follows :

Grand Master—Companion, having attained to this degree, you have passed the circle of perfection in ancient Masonry. In the capacity of Select Master, you must be sensible that your obligations are increased in proportion to your privileges. Let it be your constant care to prove yourself worthy of the confidence reposed in you, and the high honor conferred on you, in admitting you to this select degree. Let uprightness and integrity attend your steps; let justice and mercy mark your conduct. Let fervency and zeal stimulate you in the discharge of the various duties incumbent on you: but suffer not an idle, or impertinent curiosity to lead you astray, or betray you into danger. Be deaf to every insinuation which would have a tendency to weaken your resolution, or tempt you to an act of disobedience. Be voluntarily dumb and blind, when the exercise of those faculties would endanger the peace of your mind, or the probity of your conduct; and let silence and secresy, those cardinal virtues of a Select Master, on all necessary occasions, be scrupulously observed. By a steady adherence to the important instructions contained in this degree, you will merit the approbation of the select number with whom you are associated, and will enjoy the high satisfaction of having acted well your part in the important enterprise in which you are engaged; and after having wrought your regular hours, you may be admitted to participate in all the privileges of a Select Master.

The Grand Master then proceeds to close the Council, as follows:

Grand Master to Captain of Guards—Companion Captain, are you a Select Master?

Captain—I am acknowledged as such, and have wrought my regular hours in the secret vault.

Grand Master—What are the regular hours?

Captain—From nine at night until midnight.

Grand Master—How gained you admission there?

Captain—Through fervency and zeal, which was mistaken for curiosity and disobedience, and had well nigh cost me my life; but justice and mercy prevailed, and I was admitted.

Grand Master—How was that?

Captain—My fervency and zeal led me into a place, through a misconstruction of King Solomon's promise; by which I forfeited my life; but mercy triumphed over justice, and I was admitted a member among them.

Grand Master—What is meant by a Select Master?

Captain—Those who are selected to build the royal vault. Men whose skill, integrity and secresy were well known to our Grand Master.

Grand Master—How many were there?

Captain—Twenty-two, from Gebal, to-

gether with Ahishar, Adoniram, and our three Grand Masters; making in all, twenty-seven, and no more.

Grand Master—Why but twenty-seven?

Captain—Because there were but nine arches, and three only could be employed in each.

Grand Master—Where did this royal vault begin?

Captain—At King Solomon's most retired room.

Grand Master—Where did it end?

Captain—Under the sanctum sanctorum, or holy of holies, of King Solomon's Temple.

Grand Master—When were you to be admitted into the Ninth Arch?

Captain—When the Temple should be completed; but owing to the death of Hiram Abiff, it was then closed from our eyes.

Grand Master—What countryman are you?

Captain—A Phœnician.

Grand Master—In what city was you born?

Captain—In Gebal.

Grand Master—What is your name?

Captain—Giblem, or stone squarer.

Grand Master—What is it o'clock?

Captain—Low twelve; the usual time to call from labor to refreshment.

Grand Master—What remains now to be done?

Captain—To retire in peace, practice virtue, and meditate in silence.

Grand Master—Companion Captain of the Guards, you will give notice to the companions by the mysterious Number Nine that this Council is now about to be closed.

Captain of the Guards knocks eight quick and one slow, which is repeated by the Deputy Grand Master and the Grand Conductor.

Grand Master knocks one, and calls to order, and gives the sign of Silence, with his left hand on his mouth, and his right hand on his breast, which is repeated by all the companions, and Ish Soudy is repeated by all.

Grand Master—Companions, this Council is closed.

In some Lodges this degree is made more of than here described; for instead of disposing of the unfaithful Guard, Ahishar, so summarily, he is brought forward and has his trial and sentence before the Grand Master. Other incidents, too, are more fully illustrated. But we have made our description from the condensed mode now practiced.

SUPER-EXCELLENT MASTER.

A Lodge of Super-Excellent Masters consists of the following officers, viz. :

Most Excellent King (representing Zedekiah, the last King of Israel) presides, and sits in the east.

Companion Gedaliah (so called) is the second officer, and is seated in the west.

First Keeper of the Temple is seated on the right of Gedaliah.

Second Keeper of the Temple takes his seat on the left of Gedaliah.

Third Keeper of the Temple is seated at the door inside the hall, to guard it.

Three Heralds, stationed outside the door, with bugles in their hands.

Three Royal Guards, (including Captain,) stationed near the King.

A Recorder, or Secretary, sitting at the right in front of the King.

The Altar is placed in the centre of the hall, and the general business is conducted similar to that in other degrees. The Council is opened as follows :

Captain.   King.   Royal Guards.

Recorder.

Altar.

3d Keeper.   2d Keeper.   Gedaliah.   1st Keeper.

The King does not take his seat at first, and the business of opening devolves on Gedaliah, who calls the Council to order with one rap of the gavel.

Gedaliah to First Keeper of the Temple—Companion First Keeper, are all present Super Excellent Masters?

First Keeper—They are.

Gedaliah—As a Super-Excellent Master, Keeper of the Temple, let it be your first duty and last care, to see the Sanctuary duly guarded.

First to Third Keeper of the Temple—Companion, are we duly guarded?

Third Keeper—We are : the Sanctuary is secure.

First Keeper—Companion Gedaliah, the Sanctuary is duly guarded.

Gedaliah—Where is the King?

First Keeper—In one of the apartments of the Temple.

Gedaliah—What is the hour?

First Keeper—It is the time of the second watch.

Gedaliah gives three raps with the gavel, when the companions all rise.

Gedaliah—Companions, since it is the time of the second watch, let us repair to the holy altar, and there offer up our fervent aspirations to Deity, that he would be pleased to vouchsafe to us, as heretofore, his protecting care and favor.

The companions assemble round the altar, kneel on the left knee, the right elbow resting on the right knee, and the forehead leaning on the right hand, in imitation of silent devotion. They remain a short time in this position.

Gedaliah (rising)—Let us arise and attend to giving the signs.

The companions give all the signs from an Entered Apprentice up to and including those of this degree, hereafter described.

Gedaliah—Let each take his station.

First Herald sounds.

Third Keeper of Temple—A Herald!

First Keeper—A Herald approaches.

Herald (coming in at the door and advancing towards Gedaliah)—Nebuchadnezzar, King of Babylon, approaches with innumerable forces, and fills the city : they are formidable and victorious, approaching the king's palace, and within a few furlongs of the Temple ; and everywhere may be seen unhallowed ravage and devastation.

The Second Herald sounds, and comes in and gives the same intelligence.

Third Herald sounds.

Third Keeper of Temple—A Herald!

The King now enters, protected by his Guards, the Captain of the Guards in front of him, and one Guard on each side.

First Keeper of the Temple—The King approaches.

Gedaliah gives three raps, when all the companions rise and face the King, who then takes his seat in the east.

Gedaliah (addressing the King)—Most Excellent, the Council is assembled, the officers stationed, and we all await your orders.

King (rising)—I proclaim this Council of Super-Excellent Masters duly organized. [Pauses, and then says]—Companion Recorder, is there any business before the Council?

Recorder—Most Excellent, a worthy companion of the Royal Arch is desirous of being advanced to the degree of Super-Excellent Master.

King—Let him come forward.

The candidate (hoodwinked) is brought in, when just as he gets in front of the King, the First Herald sounds.

Third Keeper of Temple—A Herald!

First Keeper—A Herald?

Third Keeper—A Herald approaches.

First Herald (coming in and advancing towards the King) — Nebuchadnezzar, King of Babylon, with battering rams assaults the Temple, and the Courts are filled with carnage.

King—Companion Gedaliah, is there no way of escape?

Gedaliah—There is none, Most Excellent, except by way of the King's garden, by the private entrance between the walls, leading out to the plains of Jericho.

King—Let us make our escape.

The companions now make a great noise by stamping, throwing over benches, and running about ; the King goes out, and then the noise ceases.

First Herald sounds.

Third Keeper of Temple—A Herald!

First Keeper—A Herald?

Third Keeper—A Herald approaches.

Herald enters and comes forward.

Gedaliah—What tidings from the King?

Herald—The King, and all the men of war fled by night, by the way of the gate between two walls, which is by the King's garden, and the King went the way towards the plain, and the army of the Chaldees pursued after the King and overtook him on the plains of Jericho, and all his army was scattered from him ; so they took the King, and brought him up to the King of Babylon, to Riblah, and they gave judgment upon him, and they slew his sons before his eyes, and they put out the eyes of our Most Excellent King, and bound him in fetters of brass, and carried him to Babylon.

Gedaliah—Companions, the sword of

the enemy prevails; our young men are captives, and our old men slaves. In this extremity what remains to be done?— Let us repair to the holy altar, and there pledge our faith and renew our vows.

The companions now form a circle around the altar; the candidate is caused to kneel at the altar within the circle— both hands on the Holy Bible, square and compasses—and take the following obligation:

I, John Smith, of my own free will and accord, in the presence of the most puissant, most holy, and most merciful Creator, and this Council of Super-Excellent Masters, dedicated to him, do hereby and hereon, most solemnly and sincerely promise and swear, that I will not bow down to other gods, nor pay religious adoration to idols. And I promise and swear, that I will not worship the sun, moon, or stars of heaven; but in good faith and conscience, to the best of my abilities, will serve and worship the only true and living God: And I promise and swear, that I will always hail and conceal the secrets of this degree, and never reveal them except it be to a true and lawful companion Super-Excellent Master, or in a legally constituted Council of such; and neither unto him nor them till first by strict trial and due examination or lawful information I shall have found him, or them, as lawfully entitled to the same as I am, or shall be myself: And I promise and swear, that I will give meat, drink, and lodging to a poor but worthy brother in necessity; will defend him in danger, and vindicate his character, so far as honor, justice and good faith may warrant. And I promise and swear, that I will not derogate from the character of a Super-Excellent Master, now about to be conferred on me. To all this I do most solemnly promise and swear, with fixed and steadfast resolution to keep and perform the same, without any hesitation, equivocation, or self-evasion of mind in me whatever; binding myself under no less penalty than to have my thumbs cut off, my eyes put out, my body bound in fetters of brass, and conveyed captive to a strange land. So help me God, and keep me steadfast in this my solemn oath and obligation of a Super-Excellent Master.

As soon as the obligation is pronounced, the First Herald sounds.

Third Keeper of the Temple—A Herald approaches!

Herald (coming forward)—The enemy is upon us!

A great noise is now made by the companions, who had assembled for the purpose outside, such as huzzaing, shouting and stamping. They rush in, led by the Captain of the Guards, seize the candidate with violence, and carry him out of the hall into the preparation room.

First Keeper of the Temple (taking bandage from candidate's eyes, and leading him into the hall)—I will now introduce you to our Companion Gedaliah, who will instruct you in your duties.

Gedaliah comes forward, takes the candidate by the hand, and explains to him the signs, pass word and grand word of this degree.

The pass-word is SAUL, THE FIRST KING OF ISRAEL.

First sign—Cross the arms at right angles in front, on your body, the right one uppermost, the fingers clenched, and the thumbs pointing upward. It alludes to the penalty of the obligation.

Second sign—Raise the right hand and elbow as high as the eyes, extending the two first fingers like a fork, the thumb and other fingers being clenched—then draw it back over the right shoulder, and with a quick motion dart the extended fingers forward in a horizontal direction. It alludes to the penalty of gouging out the eyes of a traitor.

Grand Word is NAHOD ZABOD BONE.

This finishes the initiation. The Council is then closed, as follows:

Gedaliah to First Keeper of the Temple—Companion Keeper, where do Super-Excellent Masters convene in council?

First Keeper—In a place representing the Sanctuary.

Gedaliah—Their first and last care?

First Keeper—To see the Sanctuary duly guarded.

Gedaliah—Please to attend to that part of your duty.

First to Third Keeper—Companion Third Keeper, are we duly guarded?

Third Keeper—We are duly guarded, and the Sanctuary is secure.

Gedaliah—Companion First Keeper, where is the King?

First Keeper—In the prison of Babylon: his thumbs have been cut off, his eyes put out, and his body bound in fetters of brass. He has been conveyed captive to a strange land as the *penalty of perjury.*

Gedaliah—What is the hour?

First Keeper—It is the third watch.

Gedaliah—Companions, since it is the time of the third watch, let us repair to the holy altar, and offer our fervent aspirations to Deity, for his protecting care and favor.

The companions assemble round the altar as at the opening; each kneels on his left knee, places his elbow on his right knee, and bows his head on the right hand in imitation of secret prayer. They remain in this position a moment.

Gedaliah (rising)—Let us arise.

They all rise and give the signs, beginning with that of this degree, and going back in detail to the sign of Entered Apprentice.

Gedaliah resumes his seat and gives ten raps with the gavel.

First Keeper of the Temple raps ten.

Second Keeper gives ten raps.

Gedaliah—I declare this Council closed.

SECRET MONITOR,

OR MASONIC TRADING DEGREE.

This is a side degree that may be conferred by a single brother upon any worthy brother Master Mason. There is no form of initiation, the candidate merely taking an oath on the Bible, or on the Bible, square and compasses on the altar. The following is the obligation:

I, John Smith, in presence of Almighty God and this witness, do hereby and hereon, solemnly and sincerely swear, in addition to my former obligations, that I will not confer this degree of Secret Monitor on any person in the known world, except it be a worthy Master Mason.

I furthermore promise and swear, that I will caution a brother Secret Monitor, by sign, word, or token, wherever I see him doing, or about to do, anything contrary to the true principles of Masonry.

I furthermore promise and swear, that I will caution a brother Secret Monitor by sign, word, or token, wherever I see him doing, or about to do, anything contrary to his interest in buying or selling.

I furthermore promise and swear, that when I am so cautioned myself by a brother Secret Monitor, I will pause and reflect on the course I am pursuing.

I furthermore promise and swear, that I will assist a brother Secret Monitor, in preference to any other person, by introducing him to business, by sending him custom, or in any other manner in which I can throw a penny in his way.

I furthermore promise and swear, that I will immediately commit this obligation to memory.

To all of which I do most solemnly and sincerely promise and swear, without any mental reservation or self-evasion of mind in me whatever; binding myself under no less penalty than that of having my heart thrust through with the arrow of an enemy, and to be without friends in the hour of trouble. So help me God, and keep me steadfast in this my solemn oath and obligation of a Secret Monitor. [Kisses the book.]

The history of this degree is then usually given to the new member by reading to him the following passages from the text-book, taken from the twentieth chapter of 1st Samuel:

So Jonathan made a covenant with the house of David, saying, Let the Lord even require it at the hands of David's enemies. And Jonathan caused David to swear again, because he loved him: for he loved him as he loved his own soul. Then Jonathan said to David, To-morrow is the new moon: and thou shalt be missed, because thy seat will be empty. And when thou hast stayed three days, then thou shalt go down quickly, and come to the place where thou didst hide thyself when the business was in hand, and shalt remain by the stone Ezel. And I will shoot three arrows on the side thereof, as though I shot at a mark. And behold, I will send a lad, saying, Go, find out the arrows. If I expressly say unto the lad, Behold, the arrows on this side of thee, take them; then come thou: for there is peace to thee, and no hurt; as the Lord liveth. But if I say thus unto the young man, Behold, the arrows are beyond thee; go thy way, for the Lord hath sent thee away. And as touching the matter which thou and I have spoken of, behold, the Lord be between thee and me for ever. * * * * * *

And it came to pass in the morning, that Jonathan went out into the field at the time appointed with David, and a little lad with him. And he said unto the lad, Run, find out now the arrows which I shoot. And as the lad ran, he shot an arrow beyond him. And when the lad was come to the place of the arrow which Jonathan had shot, Jonathan cried after the lad, and said, Is not the arrow beyond thee? And Jonathan cried after the lad, Make speed, haste, stay not. And Jonathan's lad gathered up the arrows, and came to his master. But the lad knew not any thing: only Jonathan and David knew the matter. And Jonathan gave his artillery unto his lad, and said unto him, Go, carry them to the city. And as soon as the lad was gone, David arose out of a place toward the south, and fell on his face to the ground, and bowed himself three times: and they kissed one another, and wept one with another, until David exceeded. And Jonathan said to David, Go in peace, forasmuch as we have sworn both of us in the name of the Lord, saying, The Lord be between me and thee, and between my seed and thy seed for ever. And he arose and departed; and Jonathan went into the city.

Brother to candidate—I am David.

Candidate—I am Jonathan.

Brother—David and Jonathan knew the matter.

Candidate—The lad knew nothing.

The signs, words and tokens are now explained to the candidate. They are negatives and affirmatives, as follows:

The negative sign is made by extending the right arm, forming a square at the elbow, holding the hand pointing upwards, the two first fingers extended, and the other fingers and thumb clenched. It is given whenever you see a brother doing, or about to do, anything contrary to his interest in buying or selling, &c. It means desist; and the brother who receives the sign, is bound by his oath to pause and reflect.

The sign of approbation is given by holding up one finger in same manner. It is given whenever you wish secretly to advise a brother in any traffic or dealing to his profit or interest. It means proceed.

Grips are given and received in the same admonishing way. When you take the hand of a brother, if you grip him in the centre of the hand, with two fingers, it means desist; if you grip with one finger, it means proceed.

To caution a brother by word. If you see a brother doing anything contrary to his interest, in buying or selling, say to him, You had better buy two; two is better than one. It means desist. If you say to him, One is as good as two, it means proceed, and he will directly understand you, and act accordingly.

Thus you can caution a brother, by sign, token, or word, whenever you see him doing anything contrary to the principles of Masonry, or his interest; and he, so cautioned, is bound to pause and reflect, before he further goes, under the penalties of having the arrow of an enemy thrust through his heart, &c. There is also another way to caution a brother. If you say to him, The arrows are beyond thee, it means desist. If you say to him, The arrows are this side of thee, it means proceed.

The due-guard of this degree is given by placing yourself in the attitude of springing a bow. It is in imitation of Jonathan shooting his arrows, and alludes to the penalty of the obligation.

HEROINE OF JERICHO.

This is a side degree, which may be given to Royal Arch Masons, their wives, or their widows ; and it can only be administered by a Royal Arch Mason. It is seldom conferred in a Lodge, but usually at the residence of some Royal Arch Mason. It cannot be given by any Mason to his own wife. The parties assemble in different rooms—the Heroines in one room, and those who have not taken the degree in another. Only one can receive the degree at the same time.

The candidate (if a female) is conducted into the Lodge of Heroines, and seated in a chair near the centre of the room.

A brother of the degree (not her husband) comes forward and addresses her, extolling the beauties of Masonry, and then seats him before her, laying a Bible in his lap.

Brother to candidate—Sister Smith, you will find this a beautiful degree, though not at all like Masonry in any of its bearings. There is an obligation to take before you can be made acquainted with its mysteries. Are you willing to take it ?

Candidate—I am.

Brother—You will please to repeat your name, and say after me :

I, Sarah Smith, of my own free will and accord, in the presence of Almighty God, and these Heroines of Jericho, do hereby and hereon, solemnly and sincerely promise and swear, that I will not communicate the secrets of Heroine of Jericho to any person in the known world, except it be to a true and lawful brother or sister Heroine of Jericho.

I furthermore promise and swear, that I will not confer this degree upon any person in the known world.

I furthermore promise and swear, that I will keep the secrets of a brother or sister Heroine of Jericho, when they are communicated to me as such, or whenever their interest or safety shall require it.

I furthermore promise and swear, that I will answer and obey all due signs and summonses, handed, sent, or thrown to me from a brother or sister Heroine of Jericho.

I furthermore promise and swear, that I will not give the hailing sign of distress of a Heroine of Jericho, unless I am in real distress ; and should I see this sign given, I will fly to the relief of the person giving it, and extricate them from difficulty, if in my power.

I furthermore promise and swear, that I will not speak the word of Heroine of Jericho, which I shall hereafter receive, in any manner, except in that in which I shall receive it.

I furthermore promise and swear, that I will not speak evil of a brother or sister Heroine behind their backs, or before their faces ; but will give them due and timely notice of all approaching danger.

To all of which do I solemnly and sincerely promise and swear, with a firm and steady purpose to keep and perform the same ; binding myself under no less penalty than to have my head struck off and carried to the highest mountain. So help me God, and keep me steadfast in the due performance of the same. [Kisses the book.]

After the oath is administered, the brother opens the Bible at the second chapter of the book of Joshua, and reads as follows :

And Joshua, the son of Nun, sent out to Shittim two men to spy secretly, saying, Go, view the land, even Jericho. And they went, and came into a harlot's house, named Rahab, and lodged there. And it was told the king of Jericho, saying, Behold, there came men in hither to-night of the children of Israel, to search out the country. And the King of Jericho sent unto Rahab, saying, Bring forth the men that are come to thee, which are entered into thy house : for they be come to search out all the country. And the woman took the two men, and hid them, and said thus, There came men unto me, but I wist not whence they were : And it came to pass about the time of shutting the gate, when it was dark, that the men went out : whither the men went, I wot not : pursue after them quickly ; for ye shall overtake them. But she had brought them up to the roof of the house, and hid them with the stalks of flax, which she had laid in order upon the roof. And the men pursued after them the way to Jordan unto the fords: and as soon as they which pursued after them were gone out, they shut the gate. And before they were laid down, she came up unto them upon the roof: And she said unto the men, I know that the Lord hath given you the land, and that your terror is fallen upon us, and that all the inhabitants of the land faint because of you. For we have heard how the Lord dried up the water of the Red Sea for you, when ye came out of Egypt; and what ye did unto the two kings of the Amorites that were on the other side of Jordan, Sihon and Og, whom ye utterly destroyed. And as soon as we heard these things, our hearts did melt, neither did there remain any more courage in any man, because of you: for the Lord your God, he is God in heaven above and in earth beneath. Now therefore, I pray you swear unto me by the Lord, since I have showed you kindness, that ye will also show kindness unto my father's house, and give me a true token: And that ye shall save alive my father, and my mother, and my brethren, and my sisters, and all that they have, and deliver our lives from death. And the men answered her, Our life for yours, if ye utter not this our business. And it shall be, when the Lord hath given us the land, that we will deal kindly and truly with thee. Then she let them down by a cord through the window: for her house was upon the town wall, and she dwelt upon the wall, &c.

The initiating brother now rises and instructs the candidate in giving the signs, and in the word, as follows:

First sign is in imitation of the scarlet line that Rahab let down from the window of her father's house to assist in the escape of the spies. She takes a red handkerchief, places one corner of it in her mouth, lets it hang down in front, and crosses her hands on her breast over it.

Second sign—She takes the handkerchief by the corner between her right thumb and fore finger, and holds it up even with the corner of her right eye, a little distance off from the eye, the other corner hanging down.

The grand hailing sign of distress is given by holding your arm out sidewise and upward from the body at an angle of forty-five degrees, and holding the handkerchief by a corner between the thumb and finger, letting a corner hang down.

The word is thus given: The initiating brother places the inside of his right foot against the inside of the lady candidate's foot—toe to heel—then putting his right hand on her left shoulder, bends forward and speaks in her ear, My life! She replies by putting her right hand on his shoulder, bending forward and saying, For yours. The brother then puts his left hand on the lady's other shoulder, and says, If ye utter not. She does the same, and says, This is our business. He then whispers in her ear, RAHAB, which is the word in this degree.

Brother—It is very dark to-night.

Candidate—Yes, but not so dark but that I can see.

Brother—What can you see?

Candidate—A scarlet line.

Brother—Why a scarlet line?

Candidate—Because it saved my life in the hour of danger.

This usually closes this degree, when the initiating brother makes some remarks alluding to the history of the degree, and assures the candidate that it was actually founded by Rahab, &c.

KNIGHTS OF THREE KINGS.

All Master Masons are entitled to this degree if they are in good standing. It is usually conferred in a Lodge or Chapter after the other business is finished. The initiation is as follows:

A brother, duly qualified, leaves the Lodge and goes into the preparation room. The candidate then kneels at the altar, when the following obligation is administered to him:

I, John Smith, of my own free will and accord, in the presence of Almighty God, and these witnesses, do hereby and hereon solemnly and sincerely promise and swear, that I will not confer the degree of Knights of Three Kings upon any person except it be a worthy Master Mason.

I furthermore promise and swear, that I will not be offended at any of the ceremonies of this degree.

I furthermore promise and swear, that I will not confer this degree, unless by the unanimous consent of all present.

Here an interruption occurs.

Brother (returning from preparation room)—How is this? I have not consented that this degree should be conferred on Brother Smith to-night.

Brother (who was administering the oath)—I did not expect that you had any objection to the candidate, and therefore I commenced giving the oath. You should have made your objection before you left the room.

Objecting Brother (vehemently)—I did make my objection known before I left the room! I stated to you and the rest of the brethren that there was difficulty existing of a very serious nature between Brother Smith and myself, and unless he promptly gave me satisfaction, I should oppose him.

All the brethren now interpose to settle the difficulty. They say they are very sorry that two brother Masons should quarrel, especially at this time; it is very wrong to carry their prejudices into the Lodge.

The candidate rises from the altar apparently much surprised, says he was not aware until the present moment that Brother —— was offended at him; he wishes he would tell wherein he had done him any injury, and if it is in his power he will give him satisfaction.

The offended brother then very gravely relates his aggrievances; he accuses the candidate of slandering him in various ways. You have reported, says he, that I am a common drunkard, [or that I quarrel with my wife, that I am dis-

honest in dealing, that I speak disrespectfully of Masonry, &c., &c.]

The candidate generally promptly denies ever making any such statements, and demands the name of the author.

He is told it came from Brother ——, (naming some Mason who is not present.)

The candidate says it is an absolute falsehood, circulated to injure him.

The objecting brother says he believes the candidate has reported the story; it is just like him, he is always meddling with other men's affairs.

A general war of words now ensues, and not unfrequently hard names are called—the candidate by this time being nearly worked up into a passion, and the other brother feigning himself so.

Some brother now makes a proposition that all shall leave the room, and leave them alone to settle their difficulty.

The candidate and his antagonist being left alone, they dispute the matter a little while, when a brother comes in and inquires, Have you agreed?

The offending or objecting brother replies—The difficulty is not settled, neither is it likely to be.

They are again left alone for a short time, when the brother comes a second time and inquires, Have you agreed?

The objecting brother replies, No.

He now offers to submit their case to a third person to decide, and abide his decision, which being acceded to on the part of the candidate, the rest of the brethren return to the hall.

A brother inquires—Have you agreed?

Objecting brother—We choose Brother —— as an umpire to settle our differences.

Brother named as umpire—If you can agree in the dark, you can in the light.

He then takes his seat, and directs the candidate to kneel at the altar and receive the remaining part of the obligation. The candidate kneels again at the altar, and repeats as follows:

I furthermore promise and swear, that I will not confer this degree upon any one without the hope of fee or reward.

To all of which I do solemnly and sincerely promise and swear, with a firm and steady resolution to keep and perform the same, binding myself under no less penalty than crucifixion, and to die a lingering death upon the cross. So help me God and keep me steadfast. [Kisses the book once.]

After the candidate has taken the obligation, the person who was chosen judge gives his opinion as follows: The candidate, and the brother who opposed his taking the degree, shall approach each other upon the five points of fellowship, and give the Master Mason's word, which balances all difficulties.

HISTORY OF THIS DEGREE.—Masonic tradition informs us, that the circumstances upon which the degree of Three Kings was founded, are briefly these: At the dedication of the Temple, King Solomon invited all the eastern Kings and Princes to attend and assist in the ceremonies. It so happened that two of the kings were at war. Solomon repeatedly attempted to effect a reconciliation between them, but to no purpose; whereupon he wisely determined to effect by force what he could not by argument. He therefore invited them into a small apartment in the Temple, locked the door, and left them to meditate in silence, telling them that whenever they settled their difficulties and agreed to live in peace, they would be liberated, and until that time they would be shut up in total darkness, and kept on bread and water. The next day King Solomon went in to see them, and inquired if they had agreed. They informed him they had not, neither was there a probability they would. King Solomon again left them, and on the next day went in as before, and received a like answer. On the third day he went in, when they informed him they had agreed.

King Solomon advancing towards them, holding in each hand a lighted taper, said —If you can agree in the dark, you can in the light, bowing at the same time.

This, then, is the sign in this degree, viz.: Holding your arms out straight from your body, with a candle in each hand. Alludes to the penalty, crucifixion.

The watch-word, and the word of caution is AGREED.

7

KNIGHTS OF THE RED CROSS.

The history of this degree is briefly as follows: After the death of Cyrus, King of Persia, who had ordered the rebuilding of the Temple at Jerusalem, the enemies of the Jews found means to prevent the progress of that glorious undertaking, and the work upon it ceased. Zerubbabel, a prince of Judah, and a personal friend of Darius, the new king, thereupon resolved to make his way through the Persian dominions to the capital, to obtain an interview with Darius, and persuade him to direct that the work on the Temple should be continued to completion. Notwithstanding the dangers of the journey, he made it successfully, obtained the desired interview, and Darius not only accorded permission to rebuild the city and Temple of Jerusalem, but he restored to the Jews all the holy vessels remaining at Babylon since the destruction of the first Temple. Being desirous also of perpetuating a remembrance of this renewal of his friendship with Zerubbabel, Darius then instituted a new Order called Order of the Knights of the East, the name of which was subsequently altered to Knights of the Red Cross, in Palestine—the banner of the Knights having a red cross conspicuously upon it.

The Council chamber of this degree is arranged as follows:

The Sovereign Master sits on a throne in the east; and above it is suspended a green banner, with a red cross in the centre, and also a triple triangle; underneath are arranged other emblems of the Order. On his right sits the Chancellor, and the Prelate, and on his left is the Master of the Palace. On the right and left in front of the throne are the Treasurer and Secretary, who in this degree are called Master of Finances and Master of Dispatches. Past Sovereign Masters who may be present usually sit at the right of the Prelate.

The Standard Bearer sits in the west, at the end of the room opposite to the throne. At his right sits the Sword Bearer, and the Warder sits on his left. The duties of the several officers are fully detailed in opening the Council.

At the sound of the trumpet the line is formed on the left from east to west, with the Master of Cavalry on the right towards the throne, and Master of Infantry on the left.

Master of Cavalry to Warder—Sir Knight Warder, when a Council of Red Cross Knights is about to be opened, what is the first duty?

Warder—To see that the Sentinels are at their respective posts, and the Council chamber duly guarded.

Master of Cavalry—Attend to that part of your duty, and inform the Captain of the Guards that we are about to open a Council of Red Cross Knights for the dispatch of business.

The Warder goes and stations the Guard (Tyler) and returns to his post.

Warder to Master of Cavalry—Sir Knight, the Sentinels are at their respective posts, and the Council chamber is duly guarded.

Master of Cavalry—Are all present Knights of the Red Cross?

Warder—All present are true Red Cross Knights.

Master of Cavalry—Attention, Sir Knights; handle sword; draw sword; carry sword. You will count yourselves into first and second divisions, beginning on the right.

The Knights count themselves into two divisions, as follows: The first one says First, the second one Second, third one First, fourth one Second, fifth one First, sixth one Second, and so on all through the line. The persons who counted First, are the first division, and those who counted Second are the second division.

Master of Cavalry—Attention, first division; you will form a line three paces in front—forward, march.

Those of the first division step three paces in front of the line.

Master of Cavalry—Halt !—to the right about—face.

The first division faces the second, and Master of Cavalry takes his station on the right of it.

Master of Cavalry to Master of Infantry—Sir Knight, you will inform our Sovereign Master that the lines are formed for inspection and review.

The Master of Infantry, accompanied by the Sword Bearer and Warder, goes up in front and informs the Sovereign Master that the lines are formed, waiting his pleasure.

As the Sovereign Master rises, the trumpet sounds. He passes down between the two divisions uncovered, instructing the first as he goes, and the second on his return.

Master of Cavalry—Recover arms; poise arms.

Sovereign Master, with Chancellor and Prelate on his right, and Master of Palace on his left, form a line across from the right of the second to the front of the first division.

Sovereign Master says—Attention, Sir Knights: give your attention to the several signs of Masonry. As I do, so do you.

The signs are now given from Entered Apprentice up to, and including those of Select Master.

Sovereign Master says—Attention, Sir Knights: handle sword: draw sword: Sir Knights, you will attend to giving the signs of the Red Cross degree.

Sovereign Master says to Chancellor—Attention, Sir Knight, [Chancellor faces him and recovers sword:] advance and communicate the Jewish Pass. This is given with three cuts, *over* an arch of steel, as follows: Master and Chancellor bring their swords to a recover, advance with the right foot, and at the same time clash their swords together with some violence. This is the first cut. They then cut one and four as in infantry exercise, holding their swords together at cut four, and then stepping forward with the left foot, each raises his left hand and seizes the other by the shoulder, their position being as in the engraving.

Chancellor says—JUDAH.

Sovereign Master—BENJAMIN.

Chancellor—BENJAMIN.

Sovereign Master—JUDAH.

They then resume their former positions, and the Sovereign Master pauses a moment, and then turns to Chancellor.

Sovereign Master to Chancellor—The word is right: you will receive it from Sir Knight on your right.

Chancellor to Knight on his right—Attention, Sir Knight, [Knight faces him:] advance and communicate the Jewish Pass.

The pass is communicated in the same way as by the Chancellor to the Master, before described.

Sir Knight, who has thus communicated the pass, makes the same demand from the Knight on his right, and he from the next, and so on until it reaches the Master of Cavalry on the right of the first division.

Meantime the Sovereign Master demands and receives the Jewish pass in the same manner from the Master of the Palace on his left; the Master of the Palace demands and receives it from Sir Knight at his left, the Knight from his neighbor on the left, and so on, until it reaches the Master of Infantry at the left of the second division.

Master of Infantry says—Attention, Sir Knight Master of Cavalry: advance and communicate the Jewish Pass.

Both Masters advance to the centre of the space between the two divisions, when the Master of Cavalry communicates the pass in the same manner as before described, and returns to his post.

Master of Infantry (standing in centre) —Sovereign Master, I have the Jewish Pass.

Sovereign Master—Sir Knight, you will advance and communicate it.

Master of Infantry advances towards Sovereign Master, and when within three paces, brings his sword to a recover, and communicates the pass in the manner before described.

Sovereign Master—The word has come up right. Attention, Sir Knight—to the right about face—to your post—march !

Master of Infantry goes to his post on the left of second division.

Sovereign Master (turning to his left) —Attention, Sir Knight, Master of the Palace. Advance and communicate the Persian Pass.

Master of Palace and Sovereign Master meet with drawn swords, and cut, as in infantry exercise, two, one, four, two, and the word is given *under* an arch of steel,

seizing each other by the shoulder, as in the engraving.

Master of Palace—TETNAI.

Sovereign Master—SHETHARBOZNAI.

Master of Palace—SHETHARBOZNAI.

Sovereign Master—TETNAI.

They then resume their places.

Sovereign Master to Master of Palace —The word is right: you will receive it from Sir Knight on your left.

The Master of the Palace demands and receives the pass in the same manner from the Knight on his left, this Knight from the next one, and so on down to the Master of Infantry.

Meantime the Sovereign Master receives it from the Chancellor on his right, and the Chancellor from the Knight on his right, and so it passes down the division line to the Master of Cavalry.

Master of Cavalry says—Attention, Sir Knight Master of Infantry: advance and communicate the Persian Pass.

The two step out in the centre of the space, as before, when the pass is given, and the Master of Infantry returns to his post.

Master of Cavalry to Sovereign Master—Most Illustrious, I have the Persian Pass.

Sovereign Master—Sir Knight, you will advance and communicate it.

Master of Cavalry advances within three paces of Sovereign Master, and then gives the Persian Pass as described.

Sovereign Master—The pass is right. Attention, Sir Knight—to the right about face—to your post—march !

Master of Cavalry goes to his post on the right of the first division.

Sovereign Master—Attention, first division: you will advance and communicate to the second division the Red Cross Word.

The Knights of the first division advance as directed, and each gives the word to his opposite companion, as follows:

Give the cuts one, two and four, as in infantry exercise, and step forward with the left foot, placing it side by side, parallel with the left foot of your companion; at the same time seize each other by the right shoulder, and draw back your sword with a quick, threatening motion, as though you intended to stab your companion to the heart: then he of the first division whispers VERITAS, and he of the second division answers, RIGHT.

They then step back with the left foot, and bring up the right.

Sovereign Master—Attention, second division: you will advance and communicate to the first division the sign, grip and word of a Red Cross Knight.

The Knights all advance towards each other, as did the Sovereign Master and Chancellor when giving the Jewish Pass, (page 98,) and meet on the guard, or first cut, clashing their swords together. Each then raises his left hand, places the thumb and fore finger against his lips, the other fingers spread open towards the left eye in a similar position to the hand of a person who is giving a blast with a horn. Carry off the hand in a horizontal direction to the left, till it sweeps a semi-circle, then drop it by your side: then give three other cuts, viz., one, four, two, as in infantry exercise, advance, and place your left foot by the side of your companion's, interlace the fingers of the left

hand, and he of the second division pronounces the word LIBERTAS. The Knight of the first division replies, "the word is right"

Sovereign Master—Sir Knights, you will form around the altar for the purpose of opening this Council of Red Cross Knights.

The Sovereign Master takes his seat on the throne, with his officers each side, while the Masters of Cavalry and Infantry form their divisions round the altar, facing inward.

Sovereign Master says—Attention, Sir Knights: to the right about, face—deposit swords.

Knights take off their swords.

Sovereign Master—Deposit helmets.

Knights obey.

Sovereign Master—To the right about, face—to your devotions.

The Knights all kneel round the altar, each on his left knee: they then cross their arms and each interlaces his fingers with his right and left hand companion. They then all repeat the Lord's prayer, after which each Knight whispers the word VERITAS in the ear of his left hand companion.

Sovereign Master says—Attention, Sir Knights; [all the Knights rise upon their feet:] to the right about, face—recover helmets.

The Knights take their helmets.

Sovereign Master—Recover swords: [Knights take their swords:] return, swords: to your posts, march!

Each one now takes his proper place, when the Sovereign Master addresses some one Knight, chosen for the purpose, as to the station and duties of the officers of the Council, as follows :

Sovereign Master—Sir Knight, are you a Knight of the Red Cross?

Knight—That is my profession.

Sovereign Master—By what will you be tried?

Knight—By the test of truth.

Sovereign Master—Why by the test of truth?

Knight—Because none but good men and true, are entitled to the honors of the Order.

Sovereign Master—Where did you receive the honors?

Knight—In a just and regular Council of Knights of the Red Cross.

Sovereign Master—What number compose a Council?

Knight—There is an indispensable number, and a constitutional number.

Sovereign Master—What is the indispensable number?

Knight—Three.

Sovereign Master—Under what circumstances are they authorized to form a Council of Knights of the Red Cross?

Knight—Three Knights of the Red Cross, being also Knights Templars, and hailing from three different commanderies, may, under the sanction of a warrant or charter from a Grand Encampment, form and open a Council of Red Cross Knights, for dispatch of business.

Sovereign Master—What is the constitutional number?

Knight—Five, seven, nine, eleven, or more.

Sovereign Master—When composed of eleven, of whom does it consist?

Knight—Sovereign Master, Chancellor, Master of Palace, Prelate, Master of Cavalry, Master of Infantry, Master of Finance, Master of Dispatches, Standard Bearer, Sword Bearer, and Warder.

Sovereign Master—Warder's station in the Council?

Knight—On the left of the Standard Bearer in the west.

Sovereign Master—His duty there?

Knight—To announce the approach of the Sovereign Master, to see that the Sentinels are at their respective posts, and the Council chamber duly guarded.

Sovereign Master—Sword Bearer's station?

Knight—On the right of the Standard Bearer in the west.

Sovereign Master—His duty there?

Knight—To assist in the protection of the banners of our Order, to watch all signals from the Sovereign Master, and see his orders duly executed.

Sovereign Master—Standard Bearer's station?

Knight—In the west.

Sovereign Master—His duty there?

Knight—To display, support, and protect the banners of our Order.

Sovereign Master—Why is the Standard Bearer's station in the west?

Knight—That the brilliant rays of the rising sun, shedding their lustre upon the banners of our Order, may encourage and animate all true and courteous Knights, and dismay and confound their enemies.

Sovereign Master—Station of Master of Dispatches?

Knight—In front of the Master of the Palace.

Sovereign Master—His duty?

Knight—To observe with attention the transactions of the Council; to keep a just and regular record thereof, collect the revenue, and pay the same over to the Master of Finance.

Sovereign Master—Station of Master of Finance?

Knight—In front of the Chancellor.

Sovereign Master—His duty?

Knight—To receive in charge the funds and property of the Council, pay all orders drawn upon the Treasurer, and render a just and regular account when called for.

Sovereign Master—Station of the Master of Infantry?

Knight—On the left of the second division, when separately formed; on the left of the whole, when formed in line.

Sovereign Master—His duty?

Knight—To command the second division or line of infantry, teach them their duty and exercise; also to prepare all candidates, attend them on their journey, answer all questions for them, and finally introduce them into the Council chamber.

Sovereign Master—Station of Master of Cavalry?

Knight—On the right of the first division, when separately formed, and on the right of the whole, when formed in line.

Sovereign Master—His duty?

Knight—To command the first division or line of cavalry, teach them their duty and exercise; to form the avenue for the reception and departure of the Sovereign Master, and prepare the lines for inspection and review.

Sovereign Master—Prelate's station?

Knight—On the right of the Chancellor.

Sovereign Master—His duty?

Knight—To preside in the Royal Arch Council; administer at the altar; to offer up prayers and adorations to the Deity.

Sovereign Master—Station of Master of the Palace?

Knight—On the left of the Sovereign Master in the east.

Sovereign Master—His duty?

Knight—To see that the proper officers make all due preparations for the several meetings of the Council; to take special care that the Council chamber is in suitable array for the reception of candidates, and dispatch of business; to receive and communicate all orders issued by the Sovereign Master through the officers of the line.

Sovereign Master—Chancellor's station?

Knight—On the right of the Sovereign Master.

Sovereign Master—His duty?

Knight—To receive and communicate all orders and petitions, to assist the Sovereign Master in the discharge of his various duties, and in his absence to preside in the Council.

Prelate   Chancellor   Sovereign Master   Master of Palace

Master of Finances.   Master of Dispatches.

Altar.

Warder   Sw'd Bearer   Stan'd Bearer

Sovereign Master—Sovereign Master's station?

Knight—In the east.

Sovereign Master—His duty?

Knight—To preside in the Grand Council; confer this Order of Knighthood upon those whom his Council may approve; to preserve inviolate the laws and constitution of our Order; to dispense justice, reward merit, encourage truth, and diffuse the sublime principles of universal benevolence.

Sovereign Master—Sir Knight Chancellor, it is my will and pleasure that a Council of Knights of the Red Cross be now opened, and stand open for the dispatch of such business as may regularly come before it at this time, requiring all Sir Knights now assembled, or who may come at this time, to govern themselves according to the sublime principles of our Order.

Chancellor to Master of Palace—Sir Knight, it is the will and pleasure of our Sovereign Master that a Council of Knights of the Red Cross be now opened for the dispatch of business. You will communicate it to the Sir Knights, that they may govern themselves accordingly.

The Master of the Palace addresses the Knights in same manner.

Sovereign Master—Sir Knights, this Council is now opened for the dispatch of business.

The chamber is now divided into two apartments by a veil. In some halls three rooms are made. The King, Chancellor, and Master of Palace remain in their seats, but the Prelate goes and sits in a seat prepared for him behind the altar, which is in the outer apartment, where he presides over the Royal Arch Council. The division commanded by the Master of Infantry is stationed in this apartment, the Knights seating themselves in a semi-circle with their hats on. The division of the Master of Cavalry guards the Council chamber, and represents the Persian Guards, while that in the outer chamber represents the Jewish Guards.

If a candidate is to be advanced to the degree of Red Cross Knight, the Master of Infantry goes out into a side room to prepare him, and then comes and raps three times three upon the door.

Warder to Prelate—Most Excellent, there is an alarm at the door.

Prelate—Attend to the alarm, and see who comes there.

Warder goes to the door, raps three times three, opens the door and says—Who comes there?

Master of Infantry—A worthy companion, who has been regularly initiated, passed, and raised to the sublime degree of Master Mason—advanced to the honorary degree of Mark Master, presided as Master in the chair—has been received and acknowledged as Most Excellent Master, and exalted to the more august sublime degree of Royal Arch Mason—now solicits the honor of being created a Knight of the Illustrious Order of the Red Cross.

Warder—Is it of his own free will and accord he makes this request?

Master of Infantry—It is.

Warder—Is he worthy and well qualified?

Master of Infantry—He is.

Warder—Has he made suitable proficiency in the preceding degrees?

Master of Infantry—He has.

Warder—By what further right and benefit does he expect to gain admittance here?

Master of Infantry—By the benefit of a pass; and with your assistance we will give it.

Warder—Advance and give it.

The pass is JAH-BU-LUN, and is now given in same manner as the Royal Arch Word, (page 68.)

Warder—The pass is right: let the candidate wait a time with patience, until the Most Excellent Prelate be informed of his request, and his answer returned.

The Warder closes the door and goes to the Prelate, who he informs that a worthy companion of the Royal Arch is craving admittance.

The Prelate asks the same questions of the Warder that the Warder had asked the Master of Infantry, and receives the same answers relative to the candidate.

Prelate—Let him be admitted.

Master of Infantry conducts candidate to the centre of the hall, seats him in a chair, and takes a seat by his side.

Prelate (addressing candidate)—Companion, the Council you here see assembled, represents the Grand Council assembled at Jerusalem in the first year of Darius, King of Persia, to deliberate upon their unhappy situation, and to devise means whereby they could obtain the favor and assistance of their new sovereign, in rebuilding the house of the Lord. If you are desirous of joining us in our deliberations, you must assume the name and character of Zerubbabel, one of the princes of the house of Judah, whose hands laid the foundation of the first Temple, and whose hands the Lord promised should finish it.

Candidate signifies his assent, bowing.

Prelate—Companions, we will attend to a lesson from the records of our fathers.

The companions, sitting in a semi-circle, as in the engraving, take off their hats, drop their elbows on their knees, and support their heads, each with his right hand.

Prelate now reads from text-book verses 8 to 11 of Ezra iii. :

Now in the second year of their coming unto the house of God at Jerusalem, in the second month, began Zerubbabel the son of Shealtiel, and Jeshua the son of Jozadak, and the remnant of their brethren, the priests and the Levites, and all they that were come out of the captivity unto Jerusalem ; and appointed the Levites, from twenty years old and upward, to set forward the work of the house of the Lord, &c.

Prelate then reads from Ezra iv. :

Now when the adversaries of Judah and Benjamin heard that the children of the captivity builded the Temple unto the Lord God of Israel ; then they came to Zerubbabel, and to the chief of the fathers, and said unto them, Let us build with you : for we seek your God, as ye do ; and we do sacrifice unto him since the days of Esarhaddon, King of Assur, who brought us up hither. But Zerubbabel, and Jeshua, and the rest of the chief of the fathers of Israel, said unto them, Ye have nothing to do with us to build an house unto our God ; but we ourselves together will build unto the Lord God of Israel, as King Cyrus the King of Persia hath commanded us, &c. [See text-book.]

Master of Infantry (rising and introducing candidate to Prelate)—Most Excellent, in consequence of our sovereign lord Darius the King, having ascended the throne of Persia, new hopes are inspired of protection and support in the noble and glorious undertaking of rebuilding the House of the Lord, in which we have been so long and so often interrupted by our adversaries on the other side of the river ; for Darius, when a private man in life, made a vow to God, that should he ever ascend the throne of Persia, he would send all the holy vessels remaining in Babylon back to Jerusalem. Our most excellent and faithful companion Zerubbabel, who was formerly honored with the favorable notice and friendship of the sovereign, now offers his services to encounter the hazardous enterprise of traversing the Persian dominions, and seeking admission to the presence of the sovereign, where the first favorable moment will be seized to remind the king of his vow, and impress on his mind the almighty force and importance of truth ; and from his known piety, no doubt can be entertained of obtaining his consent, that our enemies be removed far hence, and that we be no longer hindered or impeded in the noble and glorious undertaking of rebuilding the House of the Lord, in which we have so laudably engaged.

Prelate—Companion Zerubbabel, the Council with great joy accept your noble and generous offer, and will invest you with the necessary passports, by the means of which you will be enabled to make yourself known to the friends of our cause, wherever you may find them ; but on entering upon an undertaking of such vast importance to the craft, it is necessary that you take a solemn obligation to be faithful to the trust reposed in you. I will invest you with this sword, [presents him with a sword,] by the use of which you will be enabled to defend yourself against your enemies : you will now kneel at the altar, and receive your obligation.

The candidate kneels at the altar on his left knee, his body erect, his right hand grasping the hilt of his sword, his left resting on the Holy Bible, square and compass, on which are placed two swords at right angles.

Prelate—Companion, you are now about to take an obligation appertaining to this degree, which, like your former obligations, will not interfere with your duty to your country or Maker; if you are willing to proceed, you will repeat your christian and surname, and say after me:

I, John Smith, of my own free will and accord, in the presence of the Supreme Architect of the Universe, and these witnesses, do hereby and hereon, most solemnly and sincerely promise and swear, that I will always hail, forever conceal, and never reveal, any of the secret arts, parts or points of the mysteries appertaining to this Order of Knight of the Red Cross, unless it be to a true and lawful companion Sir Knight of the Order, or within the body of a just and lawful Council of such; and not unto him or them, until by true trial, strict examination or lawful information, I find him or them lawfully entitled to receive the same.

I furthermore promise and swear, that I will answer and obey all due signs and regular summonses, which shall be sent to me from a regular Council of Knights of the Red Cross, or given to me from the hands of a companion Sir Knight of the Red Cross, if within the distance of forty miles, natural infirmities and unavoidable accidents only excusing me.

I furthermore promise and swear, that I will not be present at the conferring of this Order of Knighthood upon any person, unless he shall have previously regularly received the several degrees of Entered Apprentice, Fellow Craft, Master Mason, Mark Master, Past Master, Most Excellent Master, and Royal Arch degree, to the best of my knowledge and belief.

I furthermore promise and swear, that I will not assist or be present at the forming and opening of a Council of Knights of the Red Cross, unless there be present at least five regular Knights of the Order, or the representatives of three different Encampments, acting under the sanction of a legal warrant.

I furthermore promise and swear, that I will vindicate the character of a courteous Sir Knight of the Red Cross, when wrongfully traduced: that I will help him on a lawful occasion in preference to any brother of an inferior degree, and so far as truth, honor and justice may warrant.

I furthermore promise and swear, that I will support and maintain the by-laws of the Council of which I may hereafter become a member, the laws and regulations of the Grand Encampment under which the same may be holden, together with the constitution and ordinances of the General Grand Encampment of the United States of America, so far as the same shall come to my knowledge.

To all which I do most solemnly promise and swear, binding myself under no less penalty than of having my house torn down, the timbers thereof set up, and I hanged thereon; and when the last trump shall blow, that I be forever excluded from the society of all true and courteous Knights, should I ever wilfully or knowingly violate any part of this solemn obligation of Knight of the Red Cross. So help me God, and keep me steadfast to keep and perform the same.

The candidate is directed to kiss the book, which he does, and then rises.

Prelate—Companion Zerubbabel, the Master of Infantry will now invest you with the Jewish Pass, by means of which you will be able to make yourself known to friends of our cause wherever you may find them, and which will insure to you their friendship and protection.

Master of Infantry gives him the Jewish Pass, as on page 98.

Prelate (presenting candidate with a green sash)—Companion, I now invest you with this sash, as a mark of our peculiar friendship and esteem: you will wear it as a constant memorial to stimulate you to the performance of every duty. Its color is green, and will remind you that the memory of him who falls in a just and virtuous cause is blessed, and will flourish like the green bay tree. Fare you well, companion; may success attend your enterprise.

Master of Infantry to candidate—Follow me.

The candidate is (or should be) conducted through several doors into different apartments. On arriving at the first door, and giving the alarm—

First Guard says—Who comes there?
Master of Infantry—A friend.
Guard—Advance and give the pass.
Master of Infantry gives the Jewish Pass, as on page 98.

Candidate is also examined and gives the pass, when they pass on to the second door, where they are challenged, and each gives the pass in the same manner.

They now approach the third door, which is open, and before it is placed a little frame in imitation of an arched bridge.

Master of Infantry—Companion, we have now arrived in sight of the Persian dominions: I can accompany you no further. This bridge you see here, over which you have to pass alone, separates the Jewish from the Persian de minions. Fare you well; may success attend your enterprise.

Candidate walks over the bridge, gives an alarm, and is accosted by a guard.

Guard—Who comes there?

Candidate gives three cuts with his sword, and advances to give the Jewish Pass: guard throws up candidate's sword: candidate whispers Judah.

Guard (as if not understanding him)— What?

Candidate (louder)—JUDAH!

Guard (looking sternly)—What?

Candidate (very loud)—JUDAH!

Guard—An enemy! an enemy! seize him!

The guards lay hold of the candidate, disarm him and divest him of his green sash: hand-cuffs and fetters are put on his hands and feet: these are made of chains of four parts, each about eighteen inches long, fastened in the middle: at the ends are rings like hand-cuffs, which are fastened around the ankles and wrists with bolts.

Master of Infantry (coming forward as prompter to candidate)—Why do you use this violence? Why treat me thus? I am no enemy: I am a prince of the house of Judah, and demand an audience with your sovereign.

Master of Cavalry (acting as Captain of Persian Guards)—You a prince of the house of Judah! You are my slave, and you can only appear in the presence of our sovereign as such. Do you yield yourself?

Candidate (instructed) after a pause— I consent to be your slave: take me before your king.

Master of Cavalry puts a sackcloth over candidate's head, and leads him to the door of the Council chamber, where he raps four times two.

The Warder, who at this time is in the Council chamber, draws the curtains apart in the centre, and demands—Who comes there?

Master of Cavalry—A detachment of his majesty's guards, having made prisoner of one, who says he is a prince of the house of Judah.

Warder—Where is he from?

Master of Infantry—From Jerusalem.

Warder—What is his name?

Master of Infantry—Zerubbabel, the first among his equals, a Mason, free by rank, but a captive and slave by misfortune.

Warder—What does he desire?

Master of Infantry—An audience with his majesty, if possible.

Warder—Wait with patience, and the Sovereign Master will soon return his orders.

Warder returns and reports to the Sovereign Master the same that has passed at the veil.

Sovereign Master—Having ascertained that he is armed with no hostile weapon, you may let him enter.

Warder returns and inquires—Is he armed with any hostile weapon?

Master of Cavalry—He is not.

Warder—He has the sovereign's permission to enter the Council chamber.

The veil or curtain is now parted in the middle, and the candidate is conducted before the Sovereign Master, guarded on his right by the Master of Cavalry, with drawn sword, and on his left by Master of Infantry.

Sovereign Master to Council, on seeing him enter—This is no enemy, but a friend and companion of my youth.

Sovereign Master to candidate—Zerubbabel, having now gained admittance into our presence, we demand that you immediately declare the particular motives which induced you, without our permission, and with force and arms, to pass the lines of our dominions?

Master of Infantry (answering for candidate)—Sovereign Master, the tears and complaints of my companions at Jerusalem, who have been so long and so often impeded in the noble and glorious undertaking in which they were permitted to engage by our late Sovereign Lord Cyrus the King; but our enemies having made that great work to cease by force and power, I have now come up to implore your majesty's clemency, that you would be pleased to restore me to favor, and grant me employment among the servants of your household.

Sovereign Master—Zerubbabel, I have often reflected with much pleasure upon our early intimacy and friendship, and I have frequently heard, with great satisfaction, of your fame as a wise and accomplished Mason, and having myself a profound veneration for that ancient and honorable institution, and having a sincere desire to become a member of the same, I will this moment grant your request, on condition that you will reveal to me the secrets of Free Masonry, which distinguish the architects of the Jews from those of all other nations.

Master of Infantry (for candidate)— Sovereign Master, when our Grand Master Solomon, King of Israel, first instituted the Fraternity of Free and Accepted Masons, he taught us that truth was a divine attribute, and the foundation of every virtue : to be good and true is the first lesson we are taught in Masonry. My engagements are sacred and inviolable ; I cannot reveal our secrets. If I can obtain your Majesty's favor only at the expense of my integrity, I humbly beg leave to decline your royal protection, and will cheerfully submit to an honorable exile, or a glorious death.

Sovereign Master—Zerubbabel, your virtue and integrity are truly commendable, and your fidelity to your engagements is worthy of imitation ; from this moment you are free—my guards will divest you of those chains and that garb of slavery, and clothe you in suitable habiliments to attend me at the banquet hall. Zerubbabel, you are free : guards, strike off those chains ; and may those emblems of slavery never again disgrace the hands of a Mason, more particularly a prince of the house of Judah ; Zerubbabel, we assign you a seat of rank and honor among the princes and rulers of our assembly.

While this conversation with the Sovereign Master has been passing in the Council, the Sir Knights prepare a banquet (refreshments) in the other room.

Warder to Sovereign Master—We are ready, Most Illustrious, to escort you to the banquet hall.

The Sovereign Master and his officers now pass out between two lines of Sir Knights, accompanied by candidate.—Sovereign Master sits at the head of the table, Chancellor on his right, Master of Palace on his left ; on the right of the Chancellor sits Zerubbabel and Master of Infantry. The Knights being all seated at the table, commence eating and drinking. After having participated in the refreshments for ten or fifteen minutes, the Sir Knights begin to withdraw, one by one, until they have all left but the officers and candidate.

Sovereign Master—It has been the custom, from time immemorial, among the kings and sovereigns of this realm, on occasions like this, to propose certain questions ; and he who should be found to give the most satisfactory answer, should be clothed in purple, drink in a golden cup, wear a silken tiara, and a golden chain about his neck. There has a question occurred to my mind, which I will propose for discussion, viz. : Which is the greatest, the strength of wine, of the king, or of women ?

Chancellor (rising)—Sovereign Master, I think wine is the strongest.

Master of Palace—Sovereign Master, I think the king is the strongest.

Master of Infantry (speaking for candidate)—Sovereign Master, I think women are stronger ; but above all things, truth beareth the victory.

Sovereign Master to candidate—Companion Zerubbabel, you have made a very important addition to the question, which needs further consideration : it being late at night, we will retire. To-morrow you will assemble in the Council chamber to hear the question debated.

Master of Cavalry—Attention, Sir Knights : you will form an avenue to escort the Sovereign Master and his companion Zerubbabel to the Council chamber.

The lines are formed as before, and the Sovereign Master and his officers, accompanied by candidate, return to their seats in Council.

After a pause (until next day) the Sovereign Master says—Sir Knight, I will now hear from each his defence of the position taken last evening in certain questions proposed by me in accordance with the ancient custom. Sir Knight Chancellor, yours first.

Chancellor (rising)—O ye princes and rulers, how exceeding strong is wine ! It causeth all men to err that drink it : it maketh the mind of the king and the beggar to be all one ; of the bondman and the freeman, of the poor man and of the rich ; it turneth, also, every thought into jollity and mirth, so that a man remembereth neither sorrow nor debt ; it changeth and elevateth the spirits, and enliveneth the heavy hearts of the miserable. It maketh a man forget his brethren, and draw his sword against his best friends. O ye princes and rulers, is not wine the strongest, that forceth us to do these things ?

Sovereign Master—Sir Knight Master of the Palace, we will now hear your defence.

Master of Palace—It is beyond dispute, O princes and rulers, that God has made man master of all things under the sun ; to command them, to make use of them, and apply them to his service as he pleases : but whereas men have only dominion over other sublunary creatures kings have an authority even over men themselves, and a right of ruling them by will and pleasure. Now, he that is master of those who are masters of all things else, hath no earthly thing above him.

Sovereign Master—We will now hear you, my friend, Zerubbabel.

Master of Infantry (for candidate)—O princes and rulers, the force of wine is not to be denied; neither is that of kings, that unites so many men in one common allegiance; but the super-eminency of *women* is yet above all this; for kings are but the gifts of women, and they are also the mothers of those that cultivate our vineyards. Women have the power to make us abandon our very country and relations, and many times to forget the best friends we have in the world, and forsake all other comforts, to live and die with them. But when all is said, neither they, nor wine, nor kings, are comparable to the almighty force of *truth*. As for all other things, they are mortal and transient; but truth alone is unchangeable and everlasting; the benefits we receive from it are subject to no variations or vicissitudes of time and fortune. In her, judgment is no unrighteousness, and she is the Wisdom, Strength, Beauty, Power, and Majesty of all ages. Blessed be the God of Truth.

Sovereign Master and companions then exclaim—Great is truth, and mighty above all things.

Sovereign Master then says—Zerubbabel, ask what thou wilt, and I will give thee; because thou are found the wisest among thy companions.

Master of Infantry (for candidate)—O king, remember thy vow which thou hast vowed, to build Jerusalem in the day when thou shouldst come to thy kingdom, and to restore the holy vessels which were taken away out of Jerusalem. Thou hast also vowed to build up the Temple which was burned, when Judah was made desolate by the Chaldees. And now, O king, this is that I desire of thee, that thou make good the vow, the performance whereof with thine own mouth thou hast vowed to the KING OF HEAVEN.

Sovereign Master—Zerubbabel, it shall be done. I will punctually fulfil my vow: letters and passports shall be immediately issued to my officers throughout the realm, and they shall give you and those who accompany you, safe conveyance to Jerusalem, and you shall be no longer hindered or impeded in rebuilding your city and Temple, until they shall be completed.

The Sovereign Master then invests the candidate with a green sash, and says— This green sash, of which you were deprived by my guards, I now with pleasure restore to you, and will make it one of the insignia of a new Order, calculated to perpetuate the remembrance of the event which caused the renewal of our friendship. Its color will remind you that truth is a divine attribute, and shall prevail, and shall for ever flourish in immortal green. I will now confer on you the highest honor in our power at this time to bestow, and will create you the first Knight of an Order, instituted for the express purpose of inculcating the almighty force and importance of truth.

Sovereign Master then directs the candidate to kneel, which he does.

Sovereign Master—By virtue of the high power in me vested, as the successor and representative of Darius, King of Persia, I now constitute and create you a Knight of the illustrious Order of the Red Cross. [Lays the blade of his sword first upon the right shoulder, then upon the left, and then upon the head of the candidate.]

Sovereign Master (taking candidate by the hand)—This sword, of which you was deprived by my guards, I now with pleasure restore to you, in the hand of a true and courteous Knight. It is endowed with three most excellent qualities: its hilt with Faith, its blade with Hope, and its point with Charity; which teaches this important lesson, that when we draw our swords in a just and virtuous cause, having faith in God, we may reasonably hope for victory, ever remembering to extend the hand of charity to a fallen foe. Take it, and return it to its scabbard, and there let it remain until it is consumed by rust, rather than to draw it in the cause of injustice and oppression.

The Sovereign Master now instructs candidate in the Persian Pass and countersign, under the arch of steel, (page 99,) then invests him with the Red Cross Word, VERITAS, (page 100,) then with the grand sign, grip and word of Knight of the Red Cross, as follows: The grand sign is given by bringing the thumb and finger of the left hand to the mouth, and carrying it off in an oblique direction, as though you were blowing a trumpet—the grip is given by interlacing the fingers of the left hands—the word is LIBERTAS. The sign, grip and word is given under the arch of steel. [See page 100.]

The Sovereign Master explains to candidate that the grand sign alludes to the blowing of the trumpet upon the walls and watch-towers of the Council, but more particularly to that part of the obligation which says that "when the last trump shall sound, I shall be for ever excluded from the society of all true and faithful Sir Knights," &c.

This ends the initiation, and the Council is now closed with a lecture.

The trumpet sounds, and the Knights resume their stations as at the opening.

The Sovereign Master begins the lecture by questioning one of the Sir Knights selected for the purpose as to his being a true Knight of the Red Cross, the manner of his reception into the Illustrious Order, &c. The questions and answers are a repetition of the initiation into this degree, and the lecture is given to perfect each Knight in his part. The Council is then closed as follows:

Sovereign Master—Sir Knight Chancellor, it is my will and pleasure that this Council of Knights of the Red Cross be now closed.

The Chancellor communicates this to the Master of the Palace, who in turn proclaims to the Sir Knights that the Council is closed.

ORDER OF KNIGHTS TEMPLARS.

Three Knights Templars, from three different Commanderies, may form an Encampment ; but the constitutional number is not less than seven, and eleven is the required number to form a regular Encampment. The officers are named and stationed as follows:

Most Eminent Grand Commander, seated on a throne in the east.

Generalissimo, seated at the right of the throne.

Captain General, seated on the left.

Prelate, on the right of Generalissimo.

Treasurer, on the right, in front of Generalissimo.

Recorder, on the left, in front of the Captain General.

Senior Warden, at the north-west angle of the triangle, and on the left of the Second Division.

Junior Warden, at the south-west angle of the triangle, and on the right of the First Division.

Standard Bearer is stationed in the west, holding his standard aloft.

Sword Bearer, on his right, and on the right of the Third Division.

Warder, on the left of the Standard Bearer, and left of the Third Division.

In front of the throne is a triangle, as in the engraving, and above it is suspended a banner with a cross surmounted by rays of light. On each side are sky-blue banners—that on the right having on it the paschal lamb and a Maltese cross, with the motto " The Will of God," and the other having emblems of the Order upon it.

The Knights are usually dressed in black, and wear black velvet sashes trimmed with silver lace. The sash hangs from a black rose on the right shoulder across to the left side, and suspended to it is a poinard, or small dirk, and a Maltese cross. On the left breast is worn a nine-pointed star, having in its centre a cross and serpent of gold surmounted by a circle on which is engraved " In hoc signo vinces." The apron is of black velvet, trimmed with silver lace. It is of triangular form, and has on it a cross with a serpent entwined thereon, and a skull and cross-bones, and stars arranged in the triangular form, with the red cross in the centre of each.

The organization is somewhat similar to the opening of a Council in the Red Cross Degree, except that the Knights Templars are counted off into three divisions, the third one stationed across the end of the hall in front of the Standard Bearer in the west, and the other two formed down from the base of the triangle. After the Knights have formed the lines, the Senior Warden addresses the Warder as follows:

Senior Warden—Sir Knight Warder, you will inform the Captain of the Guards that we are about to open a Council of Knights Templars, for the dispatch of business, and direct that he will station the Sentinels at their respective posts, and see that the Council is duly guarded.

Warder goes out, and returns and says:

Warder to Senior Warden—Sir Knight, the Sentinels are at their posts, and we are duly guarded.

Senior Warden—Are all present Knights Templars?

Warder—All present are true Knights Templars.

Senior Warden then instructs Junior Warden, who informs the Most Eminent Grand Commander that the Council is duly guarded, the lines formed, and that the Sir Knights await his pleasure.

Grand Commander inspects the Lines, and then returns to his seat,

Grand Commander — Attention, Sir Knights : you will now give the signs.

All the signs in Masonry are given by each Knight, from Entered Apprentice up to those of Red Cross Knights.

The signs in this degree are then given in detail, as explained hereafter.

Grand Commander — Attention, Sir Knights : you will form around the altar, for the purpose of opening this Council of Knights Templars.

The Knights kneel around the altar, and the proceedings of opening are similar to those in a Council of Red Cross Knights. After all is ready, the Grand Commander says :

Grand Commander — Sir Knights, this Council of Knights Templars is now open for the dispatch of business, and you will govern yourselves according to the sublime principles of our Order.

The veil is now drawn, and the hall divided. That part occupied by the Grand Commander is called the Assilum, and

Altar.

Warder   Sw'd Bearer   Stan'd Bearer

the other part the Council chamber. When initiations take place, it is doubly divided, two veils being drawn, unless there are different rooms used. The Warder sits at the right in front of the Grand Commander during the ceremonies of initiation.

When a candidate is to be admitted to this degree, he is first put in charge of the Junior Warden, who conducts him (hoodwinked) to the chamber of reflection, a small adjoining apartment, the walls and furniture painted black, and lighted with a small taper. Here he is requested to sit down, and he sits in a chair beside a table, when the Junior Warden says to him:

Junior Warden—Companion, you are now seated in the chamber of reflection; before you, on the table, you will find the Holy Bible, that great light in Masonry, and also a paper upon which is written three questions: you are required to write answers to these questions—yes, or no, as you see fit, and to sign your name to each answer. You will likewise find on the table a bowl of pure water, and a napkin: wash your hands in the water and wipe them on the napkin, in token of the purity of your intentions in the business in which you are engaged. When I go out, I will give three distinct knocks on the door, and you will then remove the bandage from your eyes, and proceed in the duties I have pointed out. When you are through with them, please to give me the same signal, and I will return to you.

Junior Warden leaves the room, and candidate removes the bandage and discovers in addition to the Bible, bowl of water, &c., a human skull and cross-

bones facing him on the table! This will often disconcert him not a little, if he is a timid man. He proceeds to read the three questions, as follows:

First—Should you ever be called upon to draw your sword, will you wield it in defence of the Christian religion?

The answer should be—Yes! and signed with the candidate's name—John Smith.

Second—Does your conscience upbraid you for any known or overt act unrepented of?

As the candidate is presumed to have nothing heavy on his conscience, he would answer—No! John Smith.

Third—Do you solemnly promise to conform to all the ceremonies, rules, and regulations of this Encampment, as all valiant and magnanimous Sir Knights have done who have traveled this way before you?

Candidate writes—Yes! John Smith.

Candidate washes his hands as directed, wipes them on the napkin, and then raps three times on the door.

Junior Warden (coming in)—Have you written down the answers to the questions proposed?

Candidate—Yes.

Junior Warden—Please to give them to me. Presuming them to be satisfactory, I will present them at once to the Most Eminent Grand Commander in the east, and will return you his answer.

Junior Warden takes the paper, goes out and shuts the door. He then repairs to the Veil, which separates the hall, and stamps four times on the floor, repeating this twice, (called three times four.)

Grand Commander—Sir Knight Warder, attend to the cause of that alarm, and see who comes there.

Warder (going up close to the Veil)—Who comes there?

Junior Warden—A worthy companion, who, having taken all the necessary preceding degrees, now solicits the honor of being dubbed and created in this Encampment a Knight of the valiant and magnanimous Order of the Knights Templars, or Knights of Malta, or the Order of St. Johns of Jerusalem.

Warder—Has he given answers to the usual questions proposed?

Junior Warden—He has made them in writing, and, in token of his sincerity, has performed the necessary ablution.

Warder—You will present them, and wait a time until the Most Eminent Grand Commander be informed of your request, and his answer returned.

Warder returns to his post.

Grand Commander—Sir Knight Warder, what is the cause of that alarm? who comes there?

Warder—A worthy companion, who, having taken all the necessary preceding degrees, now solicits the honor of being dubbed and created in this Encampment a Knight of the valiant and magnanimous Order of Knights Templars, and Knights of Malta, or Order of St. Johns of Jerusalem.

Grand Commander—Has he given answers to the questions proposed?

Warder—He has made them in writing, and, in token of his sincerity, has performed the necessary ablution.

Grand Commander—Present the questions.

Warder reads the questions and answers.

Grand Commander—The questions are answered satisfactorily; but as a trial of his patience and perseverance, I enjoin upon him seven years' pilgrimage, which he will perform under the direction of the Junior Warden dressed in pilgrim's weeds.

Warder returns to the Veil, and addresses the Junior Warden—Our Most Excellent Grand Commander is pleased to decide that the questions are answered satisfactorily; but as a trial of the patience and perseverance of the worthy companion, he enjoins upon him a seven years' pilgrimage, which he will perform under your direction, dressed in pilgrim's weeds.

The Junior Warden returns to the chamber of reflection, and gives the answer to candidate, at the same time informing him that in addition to his sandals, staff and scrip, he must take some bread and a bottle of water to sustain him on his journey.

Junior Warden (after dressing the candidate in pilgrim's weeds as in the engraving)—Follow me.

He goes out followed by the candidate.

In some Lodges there are several different rooms erected suitable to the conferring of this degree. Where there are not, a second curtain is suspended in the hall. The Junior Warden and candidate come to the door of the first room.

Guard—Who comes there?

Junior Warden—A weary pilgrim, traveling from afar, to join with those who oft have gone before him, to offer his devotions at the holy shrine.

Guard—Pilgrim, I greet thee: walk into my tent; sit down: silver and gold have I none; but such as I have I give thee: here is some good bread and pure water, just such as pilgrims need; help yourself. [Pilgrim eats.] I will examine your scrip, and see how your bread holds out; [feeling in his scrip,] your bread is almost gone, I will put in some; your water is also almost spent, I will replenish your bottle. Help yourself, brother pilgrim, to what you like best.

The candidate having sufficiently refreshed himself, the Guard says—Pilgrim, hearken now to a lesson to cheer thee on thy way, and assure thee of success.

Reads from Text Book.

And Abraham rose up early in the morning, and took bread, and a bottle of water, and gave it unto Hagar (putting it on her shoulder), and the child, and sent her away, and she departed, and wandered in the wilderness; and the water was spent in the bottle, and she cast the child under one of the shrubs; and the angel of God called to Hagar out of heaven, saying, Arise, lift up the lad, and hold him in thine hand; for I will make him a great nation: and God opened her eyes and she saw a well of water. By faith, Abraham sojourned in the land of promise as in a strange country, dwelling in tabernacles; for he looked for a city which hath foundations, whose builder and maker is God. Be ye therefore followers of God as dear children, rejoicing in the Lord always; and again I say, rejoice.

Guard—Farewell, Pilgrim. God speed thee.

Junior Warden and pilgrim pass into another room, where they are again accosted:

Second Guard—Who comes there?

Junior Warden—A weary pilgrim, traveling from afar, to offer his devotions at the holy shrine.

Second Guard—Pilgrim, I greet thee: come thou into my tent and refresh your-

sent. [Examines his scrip, and offers him bread and water as the other Guard had done.] Hearken now to a lesson to cheer thee on thy journey.

Reads from Text Book.

If a brother or sister be naked and destitute of daily food, and one of you say, Depart in peace, be ye warmed and filled, and ye give them not of those things which are needful for the body, what doth it profit? To do good and to communicate, forget not, for with such sacrifices God is well pleased. Beware lest any man spoil you through philosophy and vain deceit, after the traditions of men; after the rudiments of the world, and not after Christ: For in him dwelleth all the fullness of the Godhead bodily.

Second Guard—Farewell, Pilgrim. God speed thee.

They pass into a third room, where the third Guard treats them with bread and water as before, and reads the following lesson from the Text Book:

He that receiveth you, receiveth me, and he that receiveth me receiveth him that sent me: Come unto me all ye that labor and are heavy laden, and I will give you rest. Take my yoke upon you and learn of me, for I am meek and lowly in heart, and ye shall find rest unto your souls; for my yoke is easy and my burden is light. Whosoever shall give to drink unto one of these little ones a cup of cold water only, in the name of a disciple, verily I say unto you, he shall in no wise lose his reward.

Third Guard—Farewell, Pilgrim. God speed thee.

They then pass on and the Junior Warden makes an alarm at the entrance of the assilum.

Grand Commander—Sir Knight Warder, attend to that alarm, and see who comes there.

Warder (going to the Veil)—Who comes there?

Junior Warden—A weary pilgrim, traveling from afar, who having passed full three long years of pilgrimage, is most desirous, if it please the Grand Commander, forthwith to dedicate the four remaining years to deeds of more exalted usefulness; and if found worthy, his strong desire is to be now admitted among those valiant Knights, whose well-earned fame has spread both far and wide for acts of charity and pure beneficence.

Warder—What surety does he offer that he is no impostor?

Junior Warden—The commendation of a valiant and magnanimous Knight, our

Junior Warden, who recommends to the Grand Commander a remission of the four remaining years of pilgrimage.

Warder—Let him wait a time with patience and perseverance, and soon an answer will be returned to his request.

Warder returns to his post.

Grand Commander—Who comes there?

The Warder replies in same manner that Junior Warden had replied—A weary pilgrim, traveling from afar, &c.

Grand Commander—This being true, Sir Knight, you will take this weary pilgrim to the holy altar, where, having sworn him for ever to be faithful, forthwith invest him with the sword and buckler, that as a pilgrim warrior he may perform seven years of warfare.

Senior Warden—Attention, Sir Knights; you will form an avenue, to escort our Most Excellent Prelate to the holy altar.

The Veil is drawn aside, and the avenue is formed by the Sir Knights, standing in two lines, and forming an arch with their swords; the Prelate takes the candidate by the arm, leading him down the avenue to the lower end of the Council chamber. The candidate kneels at the altar, upon two cross swords, places his hands upon the Holy Bible, on which is placed two cross swords; the Senior Warden stands on the right and the Junior Warden on the left of the candidate, with drawn swords. The Prelate takes his place in front of the candidate, in an elevated seat, and addresses him as follows:

Prelate—Companion, you are kneeling at the altar for the purpose of taking a solemn oath and obligation appertaining to the degree of Knight Templar, which is not to interfere with the duty you owe to your country or Maker. If you are willing to proceed, you may repeat your christian and surname, and say after me:

I, John Smith, of my own free will and accord, in the presence of Almighty God, and this Encampment of Knights Templars, do hereby and hereon most solemnly promise and swear that I will always hail, for ever conceal, and never reveal, any of the secret arts, part or points appertaining to the mysteries of this Order of Knights Templars, unless it be to a true and lawful companion Sir Knight, or within the body of a just and lawful Encampment of such; and not unto him, or them, until by due trial, strict examination, or lawful information, I find they are lawfully entitled to receive the same.

Furthermore do I promise and swear, that I will answer and obey all due signs

8

and regular summonses which shall be given or sent to me from a regular Encampment of Knights Templars, if within the distance of forty miles, natural infirmities and unavoidable accidents only excusing me.

Furthermore do I promise and swear, that I will help, aid and assist with my counsel, my purse, and my sword, all poor and indigent Knights Templars, their widows and orphans, they making application to me as such, and I finding them worthy, so far as I can do it without material injury to myself, and so far as truth, honor, and justice may warrant.

Furthermore do I promise and swear, that I will not assist, or be present at the forming and opening of an Encampment of Knights Templars, unless there be present seven Knights of the Order, or the representatives of three different Encampments, acting under the sanction of a legal warrant.

Furthermore do I promise and swear, that I will go to the distance of forty miles, even barefoot and on frosty ground, to save the life, and relieve the necessities of a worthy Knight, should I know that his necessities required it, and my abilities permit.

Furthermore do I promise and swear, that I will wield my sword in the defence of innocent maidens, destitute widows, helpless orphans, and the Christian religion.

Furthermore do I promise and swear, that I will support and maintain the by-laws of the Encampment of which I may hereafter become a member, the edicts and regulations of the Grand Encampment of the United States of America, so far as the same shall come to my knowledge.

To all this I most solemnly and sincerely promise and swear, with a firm and steady resolution to perform and keep the same, without any hesitation, equivocation, mental reservation or self-evasion of mind in me whatever; binding myself under no less penalty than to have my head struck off and placed on the highest spire in christendom, should I knowingly or willingly violate any part of this my solemn obligation of a Knight Templar. So help me God, and keep me steadfast to perform and keep the same.

Candidate kisses the book and rises.

Prelate—Pilgrim, thou hast craved permission to pass through our solemn ceremonies and enter the assilum of our Encampment; by thy sandals, staff, and scrip, I judge thee to be a child of humility: charity, and hospitality, are the grand characteristics of this magnanimous Order. In the character of Knights Templars, we are bound to give alms to poor and weary pilgrims traveling from afar, to succor the needy, feed the hungry, clothe the naked, and bind up the wounds of the afflicted. We here wage war against the enemies of innocent maidens, destitute widows, helpless orphans, and the Christian religion. If you are desirous of enlisting in this noble and glorious warfare, lay aside thy staff, and take up the sword, fighting manfully thy way, and with valor running thy course: and may the Almighty, who is a strong tower and defence to all those who put their trust in him, be thy support and thy salvation.

Prelate here invests candidate with sword and buckler, as in the engraving.

Prelate—Pilgrim, having laid aside the staff, and taken up the sword, we expect you will make a public declaration of the cause in which you wield it. You will now repeat after me, and do as I do.

Prelate makes this declaration—I will wield my sword in defence of innocent maidens, of destitute widows, helpless orphans, and the christian religion.

The candidate repeats the same, word by word, after the Prelate, and at each pause gives his sword a flourish above his head.

Prelate—With confidence in this your profession, our Senior Warden will invest you with the Pilgrim Warrior's Pass; and under his direction, we assign you seven years' warfare, which you will perform as a token of your constancy and courage. May success and victory attend you.

The Senior Warden then invests the candidate with the Pilgrim Warrior's Pass, which is MAHER-SHALAL-HASHBAZ. It is given by four cuts of the sword and under an arch of steel, as in the Red Cross degree, on page 99.

Senior Warden—Pilgrim, you will follow me, and repeat what I say. They then start on their tour of warfare, both wielding their swords, and saying:

I will wield my sword in defence of innocent maidens, destitute widows, helpless orphans, and the Christian religion.

Presently they come to the first Guard.

Guard—Who comes there?

Senior Warden—A Pilgrim Warrior.

Guard—Advance and communicate the Pilgrim Warrior's Pass.

They both give the Pass with four cuts as before described, and pass on to the second, and then the third Guard, both of whom challenge them and receive the Pass as the first Guard had done.

The Senior Warden and candidate now arrive at the assilum, when the Senior Warden stamps three times four on the floor.

Grand Commander—Sir Knight Warder, attend to the cause of that alarm, and see who comes there.

Warder (going to the Veil)—Who comes there?

Senior Warden—A pilgrim warrior, traveling from afar, who, having passed full three long years of warfare, is most desirous, if it please the Grand Commander, to be now admitted to the honors and rewards that await the valiant Templar.

Warder—What surety does he offer tha..c is no impostor?

Senior Warden—The commendations of a valiant and magnanimous Knight, our Senior Warden, who recommends to the Grand Commander a remission of the four remaining years of warfare.

Warder—By what further right or benefit, does he expect to gain admission to the assilum?

Senior Warden—By the benefit of the Pilgrim Warrior's Pass.

Warder—Let him communicate it to the Sir Knight on his right.

The Pass is given as before described.

Warder—Let him wait a time with constancy and courage; and soon an answer will be returned to his request.

The Warder returns, and reports to the Grand Commander, who asks the same questions and receives the same answers as the Warder had done at the Veil. Grand Commander then orders the candidate to enter. The veil is then drawn aside, and the candidate advances near to the base of the triangle.

Grand Commander—Pilgrim, having gained admission to the assilum, what profession have you to make in testimony of your fitness to become a Knight among our number?

Candidate (prompted by Senior Warden)—Most Eminent, I now declare in truth and soberness, that I entertain no enmity or ill will to a soul on earth that I would not freely reconcile, in case I found in him a corresponding disposition.

Grand Commander—Pilgrim, the sentiments you utter are truly commendable, and are worthy of imitation; but yet we require some stronger proof of your fidelity to us. The proofs that we demand are, that you participate with us in five libations, which being performed, we will receive you a Knight among our number. The elements of these libations are for the four first, wine and water; the fifth is pure wine. Have you any repugnance to participate?

Candidate (prompted by Senior Warden)—Most Eminent, I am willing to conform to the rules of the Order.

Grand Commander takes a wine-glass of wine and water from the triangle, and directs the candidate to do the same, and repeat after him, as follows:

First Libation—To the memory of Solomon, King of Israel, our ancient Grand Master. [Both drink, and then give the drinking sign by drawing the glass across their throats.]

Second Libation—To the memory of Hiram, King of Tyre, our ancient Grand Master. [Both drink, and give the sign.]

Third Libation—To the memory of Hiram Abiff, the widow's son, who lost his life in defence of his integrity. [Both drink and give the sign.]

Grand Commander—Pilgrim, the Order to which you wish to unite yourself, is founded upon the Christian religion. We will therefore attend to a lesson from the holy evangelist. Sir Knight, our Prelate, you will read.

The Prelate reads the 14th to 26th verses of Matthew xxvi.:

Then one of the twelve, called Judas Iscariot, went unto the chief priests, and said unto them, What will ye give me, and I will deliver him unto you? And they covenanted with him for thirty pieces of silver. And from that time he sought opportunity to betray him. Now the first day of the feast of unleavened bread, the disciples came to Jesus, saying unto him, Where wilt thou that we prepare for thee to eat the passover? And he said, Go into the city to such a man, and say unto him, The Master saith, My time is at hand; I will keep the passover at thy house with my disciples. And the disciples did as Jesus had appointed them; and they made ready the passover. Now, when the even was come, he sat down with the twelve. And as they did eat, he said, Verily I say unto you, That one of you shall betray me. And they were exceeding sorrowful, and began every one of them to say unto him, Lord, is it I? And he answered and said, He that dippeth his hand with me in the dish, the same shall betray me. The Son of man goeth, as it is written of him: but woe unto that man by whom the Son of man is betrayed! It had been good for that man if he had not been born. Then Judas, which betrayed him, answered and said, Master, is it I? He said unto him, Thou hast said.

Grand Commander—Pilgrim, the twelve burning tapers you here see upon the triangle, correspond in number with the twelve disciples of our Saviour while on earth; one of whom fell by transgression, and betrayed his Lord and Master. And as a constant admonition to you, always to persevere in the paths of honor, integrity, and truth, and as a perpetual memorial of the apostasy of Judas Iscariot, you are required by the rules of our Order to extinguish one of those burning tapers.

Candidate extinguishes one.

Grand Commander—Thus may perish the enemies of our Order; and may you ever bear it in mind, that he who basely violates his vow, is worthy of no better fate.

The relics are now uncovered, which exhibits to the candidate, in the centre of the triangle, a black coffin, supporting the Holy Bible, on which rests a human skull, and cross bones. The skull is called Old Simon.

Grand Commander—Pilgrim, you here see mortality resting on divinity, a human skull resting on the Holy Bible, which is to teach you that a faithful reliance in the truth herein revealed will afford you consolation in the gloomy hour of death, and will assure you inevitable happiness in the world that is to come. Sir Knight, our Prelate, you will read another lesson from the holy evangelist.

Prelate reads verses 36 to 50 of Matthew xxvi.:

Then cometh Jesus with them unto a place called Gethsemane, and saith unto his disciples, Sit ye here, while I go and pray yonder. And he took with him Peter and the two sons of Zebedee, and began to be sorrowful and very heavy. Then saith he unto them, My soul is exceeding sorrowful, even unto death: tarry ye here, and watch with me. And he went a little farther, and fell on his face, and prayed, saying, O my father, if it be possible, let this cup pass from me: nevertheless, not as I will, but as thou wilt. And he cometh unto the disciples, and findeth them asleep, and saith unto Peter, What! could ye not watch with me one hour? Watch and pray, that ye enter not into temptation: the spirit indeed is willing, but the flesh is weak. He went away again the second time, and prayed, saying, O my father, if this cup may not pass from me except I drink it, thy will be done. And he came and found them asleep again; for their eyes were heavy. And he left them, and went away again, and prayed a third time, saying the same words. Then cometh he to his disciples, and saith unto them, Sleep on now, and take your rest: behold, the hour is at hand, and the Son of man is betrayed into the hands of sinners. Rise, let us be going: behold, he is at hand that doth betray me. And while he yet spake, lo, Judas, one of the twelve, came; with him a great multitude with swords and staves, from the chief priests and elders of the people. Now he that betrayed him gave them a sign, saying, Whomsoever I shall kiss, that same is he; hold him fast. And forthwith he came to Jesus, and said, Hail, Master; and kissed him.

Grand Commander (rising and taking the skull in his hand)—Pilgrim, how striking is this emblem of mortality! once it was animated like ourselves, but now it ceases to act or think; its vital energies are extinct, and all the powers of life have ceased their operations. To such a state, Sir Knights, we all are hastening; therefore let us gratefully improve this present opportunity, that when our weak and frail bodies, like this memento, shall become cold and inanimate, our disembodied spirits may soar aloft to the blessed regions of light and life eternal. Sir Knight, our Prelate, we will attend to another lesson from the holy evangelist.

Prelate reads verses 24 to 38 of Matthew xxvii.:

When Pilate saw that he could prevail nothing, but that rather a tumult was made, he took water, and washed his hands before the multitude, saying, I am innocent of the blood of this just person; see ye to it. Then answered all the people, and said, His blood be on us and on our children. Then released he Barabbas unto them: and when he had scourged Jesus, he delivered him to be crucified. Then the soldiers of the governor took Jesus into the common hall, and gathered unto him the whole band of soldiers.

And they stripped him, and put on him a scarlet robe. And when they had platted a crown of thorns, they put it upon his head, and a reed in his right hand: and they bowed the knee before him, and mocked him, saying, Hail, king of the Jews! And they spit upon him, and took the reed and smote him on the head. And after that they had mocked him, they took the robe off from him, and put his own raiment on him, and led him away to crucify him. And as they came out, they found a man of Cyrene, Simon by name ; him they compelled to bear his cross. And when they were come unto a place called Golgotha, that is to say, 'A place of the skull, they gave him vinegar to drink mingled with gall : and when he had tasted thereof, he would not drink. And they crucified him, and parted his garments, casting lots : that it might be fulfilled which was spoken by the prophet ; They parted my garments among them, and upon my vesture did they cast lots. And sitting down, they watched him there : And set up over his head his accusation written, THIS IS JESUS, THE KING OF THE JEWS.

Grand Commander—Pilgrim, we will now participate in the fourth libation.

Fourth Libation—To the memory of Simon, of Cyrene, the friend of our Saviour, who bore his cross, and fell a martyr to his faith. [Both drink and give the sign.]

Grand Commander—Pilgrim, before you will be permitted to participate in the fifth libation, I shall enjoin upon you one year's penance, which you will perform as a token of your faith and humility, under the direction of the Senior and Junior Wardens, with this emblem of humility [a skull] in one hand, and this emblem of faith [a lighted taper] in the other : you will take them, and travel to the Sepulchre of our Saviour.

The candidate commences his journey, accompanied by the two Wardens, and after traveling around the hall a while, they are accosted by a Guard, stationed at the entrance of a dark room, representing the Sepulchre of our Saviour.

Guard—Who comes there ?

Senior Warden—A pilgrim penitent, traveling from afar, craves your permission here awhile to wait, and at the shrine of our departed Lord to offer up his prayers and meditations.

Guard—How does he expect to obtain this favor ?

Senior Warden—By the benefit of the Pilgrim Penitent's Pass.

Guard—Has he that pass ?

Senior Warden—He has it not ; I have it for him.

Guard—Advance and give it.

This word, or pass, is GOLGOTHA, and is given by five cuts under an arch of steel, as on page 99.

The pass being given, the Guard says —Right ; you have my permission to enter the Sepulchre of our Saviour.

The candidate steps along, and is directed to kneel at the entrance of the Sepulchre, and the Senior Warden reads to him as follows :

Although it is appointed unto all men once to die, yet as the Scriptures inform us, the Saviour of the world arose from the dead, and ascended up into heaven, there for ever seated on the throne of the majesty on high, so they also assure us, that all who have received him for their righteousness, and put their trust in him, shall rise to life everlasting. * * * * In the end of the Sabbath, as it began to dawn towards the first day of the week, came Mary Magdalene, and the other Mary, to see the sepulchre. And behold there was a great earthquake : for the angel of the Lord descended from heaven, and came and rolled back the stone from the door, and sat upon it. His countenance was like lightning, and his raiment white as snow : and for fear of him the keepers did shake, and became as dead men. And the angel answered and said unto the women, Fear not ye ; for I know that ye seek Jesus, which was crucified. He is not here ; for he is risen, as he said. Come, see the place where the Lord lay : and go quickly, and tell his disciples that he is risen from the dead ; and, behold, he goeth before you into Galilee ; there shall ye see him : lo, I have told you. And they departed quickly from the sepulchre with fear and great joy ; and did run to bring his disciples word. And as they went to tell his disciples, behold Jesus met them, saying, All hail. And they came and held him by the feet, and worshipped him. And he led them out as far as to Bethany ; and he lifted up his hands, and blessed them. And it came to pass, while he blessed them, he was parted from them, and carried up into heaven. And they worshipped him, and returned to Jerusalem with great joy.

As soon as the reading is ended, the room or hall is darkened, and the candidate rises, and beholds in another part of the Encampment, a transparency, brilliantly lighted, representing the resurrection and ascension of the Saviour. In Lodges where no properties of this kind exist, this part is omitted. The following words are now sung :

The rising God forsakes the tomb—
   Up to his Father's court he flies ;
Cherubic legions guard him home,
   And shout him welcome to the skies.

Break off your tears, ye saints, and tell
   How high our great deliv'rer reigns ;
Sing how he spoil'd the hosts of hell,
   And led the monster, death, in chains.

Say "live for ever, wond'rous king,
   Born to redeem, and strong to save !"
Then ask the tyrant, "where's thy sting?
   And where's thy vict'ry, boasting grave ?"

The singing being ended, the Prelate takes the candidate by the arm, and walks near the transparency, and thus addresses him :

Prelate—Pilgrim, the scene before you represents the splendid conclusion of the hallowed sacrifice offered by the Redeemer of the world, to propitiate the anger of an offended Deity. This sacred volume informs us, [showing him the Bible,] that our Saviour, after having suffered the pains of death, descended into the place of departed spirits, and that on the third day, he burst the bands of death, triumphed over the grave, and in due time, ascended with transcendent majesty to heaven, where he now sits on the right hand of our heavenly Father, a mediator and intercessor, for all those who have faith in him. I now invest you with an emblem of that faith. [Suspends from his neck a black cross.] It is also an emblem of our Order, which you will wear as a constant memorial, for you to imitate the virtues of the immaculate Jesus, who died that you might live. Pilgrim, the ceremonies in which you are now engaged, are calculated deeply to impress your mind; and I trust will have a happy and lasting effect upon your future character. You were first, as a trial of your faith and humility, enjoined to perform seven years' pilgrimage ; it represents the great pilgrimage of life through which we are all passing. We are all weary pilgrims, anxiously looking forward to that asylum, where we shall rest from our labors, and be at rest for ever. You were then directed, as a trial of your courage and constancy, to perform seven years' warfare ; it represents to you the constant warfare with the lying vanities and deceits of this world, in which it is necessary for us always to be engaged. You are now performing penance as a trial of your humility. Of this, our Lord and Saviour has left us a bright example. For though he was the eternal Son of God, he humbled himself to be born of a woman, to endure the pains and afflictions incident to human nature, and finally to suffer a cruel and ignominious death upon the cross : it is also a trial of that faith which will conduct you safely over the dark gulf of everlasting death, and land your enfranchised spirit in the peaceful abodes of the blessed. Pilgrim, keep ever in your memory this awful truth. You know not how soon you may be called upon to render up an account to that Supreme Judge, from whom not even the most minute act of your life is hidden : for although you now stand erect in all the strength of manhood and pride of beauty, in a few short moments, you may become a pale and lifeless corpse. This moment, even while I am yet speaking, the angel of death may receive the fatal mandate to strike you from the roll of human existence ; and the friends who now surround you, may be called upon to perform the last sad office of laying you in the earth, a banquet for worms, and this fair body become as the miserable relic you now hold in your hand. Man, that is born of a woman, is of few days and full of sorrow : he cometh up and is cut down as a flower ; he fleeth as a shadow, and continueth not. In the midst of life, we are in death : of whom may we seek succor, but of thee, O Lord, who for our sins art justly displeased ? Yet, O God, most holy, thou God most mighty, O holy and most merciful Saviour, deliver us from the pains of eternal death. I heard a voice from heaven, saying unto me, Write from henceforth, blessed are the dead that die in the Lord ; even so, saith the spirit, for they rest from their labors. Be ye also ready, and rest assured, that a firm faith in the truths here revealed, will afford you consolation in the gloomy hour of dissolution, and insure you ineffable and eternal happiness in the world to come. Amen, and amen.

The hall is again lighted up, and the candidate, accompanied by the Senior and Junior Wardens, makes another alarm at the assilum.

Grand Commander—Sir Knight Warder, attend to that alarm, and see who comes there.

Warder—Who comes there ? who dares approach this sacred assilum of our Encampment, to disturb our holy meditations ? Who are you ?

Senior Warden—A pilgrim penitent,

traveling from afar, who, having performed his term of penance, seeks now to participate in the fifth libation, thereby to seal his faith.

Warder—What surety does he offer, that he is no impostor?

Senior Warden—The commendation of two valiant and magnanimous Knights, our Senior and Junior Wardens.

Warder—By what further right or benefit does he expect to obtain this favor?

Senior Warden—By the benefit of the Pilgrim Penitent's Pass.

Warder—Has he that pass?

Senior Warden—He has it not; I have it for him.

Warder—Advance and communicate it to the Sir Knight on your left.

The pass, GOLGOTHA, is then given by the two Wardens, and the Warder returns and reports the same to the Most Eminent Grand Commander, who directs the candidate to enter. The veil is then drawn aside, and the candidate enters the assilum.

Grand Commander (rising)—Who have you there in charge, Sir Knights?

Senior Warden—A pilgrim penitent, who, having performed his term of penance, seeks now to participate in the fifth libation, thereby to seal his faith.

Grand Commander—Pilgrim, in granting your request, and admitting you a Knight among our number, we can only offer you a rough habit, coarse diet, and severe duty. If, upon these conditions, you are still desirous of enlisting under our banners, you will advance, and kneel at the base of the triangle.

Candidate kneels at base of triangle.

Grand Commander—Pilgrim, the fifth libation is taken in a very solemn way. It is emblematical of the bitter cup of death, of which we must all, sooner or later, taste; and even the Saviour of the world was not exempted, notwithstanding his repeated prayers and solicitations. It is taken of pure wine, and from this cup. [Exhibiting a human skull, he pours the wine into it, and says]—To show you that we here practice no imposition, I give you this pledge. [Drinks from the skull.] He then pours more wine into the skull, and presents it to the candidate, telling him that the fifth libation is called the sealed obligation, as it is to seal all his former engagements in Masonry.

The Grand Commander here also gives a short history of the degree. The substance of it is, that the object of the degree of Knight Templar was originally instituted to preserve Masonry, which had become much corrupted, &c.

Sometimes the candidate hesitates to drink out of the skull, in which case he is intimidated as follows:

Grand Commander—Attention, Sir Knights: [Knights form around the candidate:] Handle sword—draw sword—charge!

The Knights charge, as in the engraving.

Grand Commander—Pilgrim, you here see the swords of your companions, all drawn, ready to defend you in the discharge of every duty we require of you. They are also drawn to avenge any violation of the rules of our Order. You promised, when you entered the cham-

ber of reflection, that you would conform to all the ceremonies, rules, and regulations of this Encampment. We here have your promise in writing. We expect you will proceed. All Sir Knights who have taken this degree, have participated in the fifth libation; and if there is anything in it that you do not perfectly understand, it will be qualified and explained to your satisfaction.

Candidate takes the skull in his hand, and repeats after the Grand Commander as follows : This pure wine, I take from this cup, in testimony of my belief of the mortality of the body and the immortality of the soul ; and as the sins of the whole world were laid upon the head of our Saviour, so may the sins of the person whose skull this once was, be heaped upon my head, in addition to my own ; and may they appear in judgment against me, both here and hereafter, should I violate or transgress any obligation in Masonry, or the Orders of Knighthood which I have heretofore taken, take at this time, or may hereafter be instructed in. So help me God. [Drinks of the wine.]

Grand Commander (taking skull from candidate)—This is called the sealed obligation, because any promise of secresy, made in reference to this obligation, is considered by Knights Templars to be more binding than any other obligation can be.

The Grand Commander then resumes his seat, and directs the Prelate to read a lesson from the holy evangelist.

Prelate reads verses 15 to 27 of Acts i. :

And in those days, Peter stood up in the midst of the disciples, and said, (the number of the names together were about an hundred and twenty,) Men and brethren, this scripture must needs have been fulfilled, which the Holy Ghost, by the mouth of David, spake before concerning Judas, which was guide to them that took Jesus. For he was numbered with us, and had obtained part of this ministry. Now this man purchased a field with the reward of iniquity ; and falling headlong, he burst asunder in the midst, and all his bowels gushed out. And it was known to all the dwellers at Jerusalem ; insomuch as that field is called in their proper tongue, Aceldama, that is to say, The field of blood. For it is written in the book of Psalms, Let his habitation be desolate, and let no man dwell therein : and his bishopric, let another take. Wherefore, of these men which have companied with us, all the time that the Lord Jesus went in and out among us, beginning from the baptism of John,

unto that same day that he was taken up from us, must one be ordained to be a witness with us of his resurrection. And they appointed two, Joseph, called Barsabas, who was surnamed Justus, and Matthias. And they prayed, and said, Thou, Lord, which knowest the hearts of all men, show whether of these two thou hast chosen, that he may take part of this ministry and apostleship, from which Judas by transgression fell, that he might go to his own place. And they gave forth their lots, and the lot fell upon Matthias ; and he was numbered with the eleven apostles.

Generalissimo to Grand Commander— Most Eminent, by the extinguished taper upon the triangle, I perceive there is a vacancy in our Encampment, which I propose should be filled by some valiant Knight, who has passed through the ceremonies of our Order.

Grand Commander—Sir Knights, you will cast lots to fill this vacancy.

Knights cast lots, and candidate is chosen to fill the vacancy.

Grand Commander—Pilgrim, you are elected to fill the vacancy in our Encampment made vacant by the death of Judas Iscariot ; and in testimony of your acceptance of that appointment, you will relight that extinguished taper upon the triangle. [Candidate lights it.] Thus may the Lord lift upon you the light of his reconciled countenance, and preserve you from falling.

The candidate then arises from the triangle, and kneels before the Most Eminent Grand Commander, who draws his sword, and laying it first on the candidate's left shoulder, then on his right, and on his head, says—By the high power in me vested, as the successor and representative of Hugho de Paganis, and Godfrey Adelman, I now dub and create you a Knight of the Valiant and Magnanimous Order of Knights Templars, and Knights of Malta, or Order of St. Johns of Jerusalem.

Grand Commander (taking candidate by the hand)—Arise, Sir Knight, and with this hand receive a hearty welcome into the bosom of a society which will be ever ready to defend and protect you. I will now present you with this sword, in the hand of a valiant and magnanimous Knight. It is endowed with three most excellent qualities, viz. : its hilt with justice, its blade with fortitude, and its point with mercy ; and it teaches us this important lesson. Having faith in the justice of our cause, we must press forward with undaunted fortitude, ever remembering to extend the point of mercy to a fallen foe.

Grand Commander then instructs candidate in the Pilgrim Penitent's Pass, as described on page 117; and also in the signs, grip and word in this degree, as follows:

The due-guard is given by placing the end of the thumb of the right hand under the chin, the fingers clenched. It alludes to the penalty of the obligation, impaling the head on the highest spire in christendom.

The cross is given by drawing the hand horizontally across the throat, and darting it up perpendicularly before the face, the edge of the hand towards the mouth.

The grand hailing sign of distress is given by placing the right foot over the left, extend both arms and incline head to the right. It is the manner that the Saviour was nailed to the cross. The motto of the Order, IN HOC SIGNO VINCES, is given in this position.

The grip is given by interlacing the fingers of the right and left hands, and each, as he crosses his arms, pronounces the word EMMANUEL.

Grand Commander then tells candidate that in America the degrees of Knights Templars and Knights of Malta are given together; and that he has received the two degrees, except a few signs, which belong to the Knights of Malta, which will be then explained.

The Prelate now reads verses 1 to 6 of Acts xxviii. :

And when they were escaped, then they knew that the island was called Melita. And the barbarous people showed us no little kindness: for they kindled a fire, and received us every one, because of the present rain, and because of the cold. And when Paul had gathered a bundle of sticks, and laid them on the fire, there came a viper out of the heat, and fastened on his hand. And when the barbarians saw the venomous beast hang on his hand, they said among themselves, No doubt this man is a murderer, whom, though he hath escaped the sea, yet vengeance suffereth not to live. And he shook off the beast into the fire, and felt no harm.

This sign is then made by holding out both hands, as though you were warming them, to the fire, and immediately seize hold of the lower edge of the left hand, near the main joint of the little finger, with the thumb and fore finger of the right; raise them in this position, as high as the chin, disengage them with a quick motion, and extend them downwards on each side, at an angle of forty-five degrees from the the body, the fingers extended, and palms downward.

The Prelate reads verse 19 of St. John, chapter xix. :

And Pilate wrote a title and put it on the cross. And the writing was JESUS OF NAZARETH, KING OF THE JEWS.

This is the grand word of a Knight of Malta. INRI. It is formed by the initials of the four words that Pilate put on the cross, viz. :

Iasus Nazaresi
Rex Iudaorum.

Night Templar's Grip.

The Prelate reads verses 24 to 28 of St. John, chapter xx. :

But Thomas, one of the twelve, called Didymus, was not with them when Jesus came. The other disciples therefore said unto him, We have seen the Lord. But he said unto them, Except I shall see in his hands the print of the nails, and put my finger into the print of the nails, and thrust my hand into his side, I will not believe. And after eight days, again his disciples were within, and Thomas with them. Then came Jesus, the doors being shut, and stood in the midst, and said, Peace be unto you. Then saith he to Thomas, Reach hither thy finger, and behold my hands; and reach hither thy hand, and thrust it into my side ; and be not faithless, but believing. And Thomas answered and said unto him, My Lord, and my God.

Grand Commander now explains the grip and word of a Knight of Malta. He says to candidate —Thomas, reach hither thy finger, and feel the print of the nails ; [they join right hands, and force the first finger into the centre of the palm ;] reach hither thy hand, and thrust it into my side.— Each extends out his left hand, and presses his fingers into the left side of his companion, still holding on by the grip. With arms thus crossed, one pronounces the words My Lord ! the other says, And my God !

The candidate is informed that he has taken the degree of Knights Templars, and Knights of Malta, and is directed to take a seat.

If there is no more business before the Encampment, the ceremonies of closing commence, the Senior Warden first giving a lecture. He interrogates one of the Sir Knights as to what constitutes a Knight Templar, the number of Knights requisite to form an Encampment, names of the officers, &c. He then asks the stations and duties of the officers, viz. :

Senior Warden—Where is the Warder's station in the Encampment ?

Knight—On the left of the Standard Bearer in the west, and on the left of the third division.

Senior Warden—His duty ?

Knight—To observe the orders and directions of the Grand Commander ; to see that the Sentinels are at their respective posts, and that the Encampment is duly guarded.

Senior Warden—You will proceed, and describe to me the Sword Bearer's station in the Encampment ?

Knight—On the right of the Standard Bearer in the west, and on the right of the third division.

Senior Warden—His duty ?

Knight—To assist in the protection of the banners of our Order , to watch all signals from the Grand Commander, and see his orders duly executed.

Senior Warden—Standard Bearer's station in the Encampment ?

Knight—In the west, and in the centre of the third division.

Senior Warden—His duty ?

Knight—To display, support, and protect the banners of our Order.

Senior Warden—Why is the Standard Bearer's station in the west ?

Knight—That the brilliant rays of the rising sun, shedding their lustre apon the banners of our Order, may encourage and animate all true and courteous Knights, and dismay and confound their enemies.

Senior Warden—Recorder's station in the Encampment ?

Knight—On the left, in front of the Captain General.

Senior Warden—His duty ?

Knight—To observe with attention the order of the Encampment , keep a just and regular record of the same ; collect the revenue, and pay the same over to the Treasurer.

Senior Warden—Treasurer's station in the Encampment ?

Knight—In front of the Generalissimo.

Senior Warden—His duty ?

Knight—To receive in charge all funds and property of the Encampment ; pay all orders drawn upon him, and render a just and faithful account when required.

Senior Warden—Station of the Junior Warden in the Encampment ?

Knight—At the south-west angle of the triangle, and on the left of the first division.

Senior Warden—His duty ?

Knight—To attend to all poor and weary pilgrims traveling from afar ; to accompany them on their journey ; answer all questions for them, and finally introduce them into the assilum.

Senior Warden—Senior Warden's station in the Encampment ?

Knight—At the north-west angle of the triangle, and on the right of the second division.

Senior Warden—His duty there?

Knight—To attend on pilgrim warriors traveling from afar; to comfort and support pilgrims penitent, and, after due trial, to recommend them to the hospitality of the Generalissimo.

Senior Warden—Prelate's station in the Encampment?

Knight—Right of the Generalissimo.

Senior Warden—His duty there?

Knight—To administer at the altar, and offer up prayers and adorations to the Deity.

Senior Warden—The Captain General's station?

Knight—On the left of the Grand Commander.

Senior Warden—His duty?

Knight—To see that the proper officers make all suitable preparations for the several meetings of the Encampment, and take special care that the assilum is in a suitable array for the introduction of candidates and dispatch of business, also, to receive and communicate all orders from the Grand Commander to the officers of the line.

Senior Warden—The Generalissimo's station?

Knight—On the right of the Grand Commander.

Senior Warden—His duty?

Knight—To receive and communicate all orders, signals and petitions, and assist the Grand Commander in the discharge of his various duties, and in his absence to govern the Encampment.

Senior Warden—Grand Commander's station?

Knight—In the east.

Senior Warden—His duty?

Knight—To distribute alms, and protect weary pilgrims, traveling from afar; to encourage pilgrim warriors, to sustain pilgrims penitent; feed the hungry, clothe the naked, bind up the wounds of the afflicted; to inculcate hospitality, and govern his Encampment with justice and moderation.

This ends the first section. The second section recapitulates the manner of initiating a candidate into the illustrious Order, the Junior Warden inquiring how it was done, and the Knight describing, in detail, in reply to questions, the whole ceremony.

After the lecture, the Encampment is closed by giving the signs, kneeling at the altar, &c., similar to the ceremonies in the Red Cross Degree.

KNIGHTS OF CHRISTIAN MARK,

AND GUARDS OF THE CONCLAVE.

This is a Conclave, governed by an Invincible Knight of the Order of St. Johns of Jerusalem.

The officers are as follows:

Invincible Knight, presiding, sits in the east.

Senior and Junior Knights on his right and left in front.

Six Grand Ministers, who are stationed in the north.

Conductor and Guard in the west.

Invincible to the Junior Knight—Sir Knight, are we all secret and secure from the prying eyes of the profane?

Junior Knight—We are, Invincible.

Invincible to Senior Knight—Sir Senior, you will instruct the Knights to assemble in due form for the purpose of opening this Invincible Order.

Senior Knight—Attention, Sir Knights —form the circle for devotion.

Knights kneel on both knees in a circle, each with his right hand on his heart, and his left hand on his forehead.

Invincible Knight now offers the following prayer:

Eternal source of life, of light, and perfection, Supreme God and Governor of all things, liberal dispenser of every blessing! We adore and magnify thy holy name for the many blessings we have received from thy hands, and acknowledge our unworthiness to appear before thee; but for the sake and in the name of thy atoning Son, we approach thee as lost and undone children of wrath; but through the blood of sprinkling, and the sanctification of the Holy Ghost, we come imploring a continuation of thy favors, for thou hast said, that he who cometh to thee through faith in the Son of thy love, thou wilt in no wise cast out; therefore, at the foot of the cross we come, supplicating pardon for our past offences, that they may be blotted out from the book of thy remembrance, and be seen no more, and that the remainder of our days may be spent as becometh the followers of the Holy One of Israel; and graciously grant that love, harmony, peace, and unity may reign in this Council; that one spirit may animate us—one God reign over us—and one heaven receive us, there to dwell in thine adorable presence, for ever and ever. Amen.

Invincible Knight takes the Bible, and waves it four times over his head, saying, Rex Regnantium et Dominus Dominantium, [King of Kings and Lord of Lords.] Kisses the book and passes it to the Knight on his right.

Each Knight takes the Bible, waves and kisses it in the same manner, repeating the same words, until it comes round the circle to the Invincible Knight, who takes it again and reads from Matthew v.:

Blessed are the poor in spirit, for theirs is the kingdom of heaven. Blessed are they that mourn, for they shall be comforted, &c.

Invincible Knight orders the sign to be given, viz.: each Knight interlaces the fingers of his left hand with the left hand of a companion, when each draws his sword, and presenting it towards his heart, pronounces the words TAMMUZ TOULIMETH.

Invincible Knight—I pronounce this Convention opened in ample form. Let us repair to our several stations, and strictly observe silence.

If a candidate is to be admitted, he is shown into a side room by the Conductor, who clothes him in a gown of brown stuff, and leads him to the door of the Council chamber, where he knocks two, six and two—2, 6 and 2.

Junior Knight—Invincible, some one knocks for admission.

Invincible Knight—See who it is, and make report.

Junior Knight (after going to the door and back)—One that is faithful in good works, wishes admission here.

Invincible Knight—What good works hath he performed?

Junior Knight—He hath given food to the hungry, drink to the thirsty, and clothed the naked with a garment.

Invincible Knight—Thus far he hath done well; but there is still much for him to do. To be faithful in my house, saith the Lord, he should be filled with love for my people. If so, let him enter under the penalties of his symbolic obligation.

Candidate enters with Conductor, and Junior Knight conducts him to the altar, making the signs meanwhile.

Candidate kneels, the Knights assemble round him, and the Invincible Knight administers to him the following vow:

I, John Smith, do promise and vow, with this same volume clasped in my hands, [taking up Bible,] that I will keep secret the words, signs, tokens, and grips of this Order of Knighthood, from all but those Knights of St. Johns of Jerusalem, who have shown a Christian disposition to their fellow-men, are professors of the Christian faith, and have passed through the degrees of symbolic Masonry, and that I will protect and support, as far as in me lies, the followers of the Lord Jesus Christ, feed them, if hungry, give them drink, if thirsty; if naked, clothe them with garments; teach them, if ignorant, and advise them for their good and their advantage: All this I promise in the name of the Father, of the Son, and of the Holy Ghost; and, if I perform it not, LET ME BE ANATHEMA MARANATHA! ANATHEMA MARANATHA! [accursed at the coming of the Lord.]

The Invincible Knight then interlaces the fingers of his left hand with those of the candidate, who lays his right hand on his heart. The Invincible Knight draws his sword; the Senior Knight does the same; they cross them on the back of the candidate's neck.

Invincible Knight—By virtue of the high power in me vested, by a bull of His Holiness, Pope Sylvester, I dub you a Knight of the Christian Mark, member of the Grand Council, and Guard of the Grand Conclave. [Whispers in his ear TAMMUZ TOULIMETH.]

The Knights resume their places, and the Senior Knight takes his seat. The candidate continues standing, while the Conductor goes and brings a white robe.

Senior Knight reads from text-book as follows:

Thus saith the Lord, he that believeth and endureth to the end shall overcome, and I will cause his iniquities to pass from him, and he shall dwell in my presence for ever and ever. Take away his filthy garments from him, and clothe him with a change of raiment. For he that overcometh, the same shall be clothed in white raiment, and his name shall be written in the book of life, and I will confess his name before my father and his holy angels. He that hath an ear to hear, let him hear what the Spirit saith to the true believer. Set ye a fair mitre upon his head, place a palm in his hand, for he shall go in and out and minister before me, saith the Lord of hosts; and he shall be a disciple of that rod taken from the branch of the stem of Jesse. For a branch has grown out of his root, and the Spirit of the Lord hath rested upon it; the spirit of his wisdom, and might, and righteousness, is the girdle of his loins, and faithfulness the girdle of his vine; and he stands as an Insignia to the people, and him shall the Gentiles seek, and his rest shall be glorious. Cause them that have charge over the city to draw near, every one with the destroying weapon in his hand.

The six Grand Ministers come forward from the north with swords and shields. The first is clothed in white, and has an inkhorn in his hand, and stands before the Invincible.

Invincible Knight—Go through the city; run in the midst thereof and smite; let not thine eye spare, neither have pity; for they have not executed my judgments with clean hands, saith the Lord of Hosts.

Candidate (instructed)—Wo is me, for I am a man of unclean lips, and my dwelling has been in the tents of Kedar, and among the children of Meshec.

First Minister (taking a live coal in the tongs from the altar, and touching candidate's lips with it)—If ye believe, thine iniquities shall be taken away, thy sins shall be purged: I will that these be clean with the branch that shall be given up before me. All thy sins are removed, and thine iniquities blotted out. For I have trodden the wine press alone, and with me was none of my people: For behold, I come with dyed garments from Bozrah, mighty to save. Refuse not, therefore, to hearken; draw not away thy shoulders; shut not thine ear that thou shouldest not hear.

The six Ministers now flourish their swords as if they were about to commence a great slaughter.

Senior Knight to First Minister—Stay thine hand: proceed no further until thou hast set a mark on those that are faithful in the house of the Lord, and trust in the power of his might. Take ye the signet, and set a mark on the forehead of my people that have passed through great tribulation, and have washed their robes, and have made them white in the blood of the Lamb which was slain, from the foundation of the world.

First Minister takes the signet and presses it on candidate's forehead, leaving an impression in red letters, "King of Kings, and Lord of Lords." The Minister then opens a scroll.

First Minister to Invincible Knight—Sir Knight, the number of sealed are one hundred and forty-four thousand.

Invincible Knight raps four, and all the Knights stand up before him, when he says—Salvation belongeth to our God,

who sitteth upon the throne of heaven, and unto the Lamb.

Knights (falling on their faces)—Amen, Blessing, honor, glory, wisdom, thanksgiving, and power, might, majesty, and dominion, be unto our God, for ever and ever, Amen.

Knights now cast down crowns and palm branches, and rise up and say—Great and numberless are thy works, thou King of Saints. Behold, the star which I laid before Joshua, on which is engraved seven eyes, as the engraving of a signet, shall be set as a seal on thine arm—as a seal on thine heart; for love is stronger than death; many waters cannot quench it: If a man would give all the treasures of his house for love, he cannot obtain it: It is the gift of God, through Jesus Christ, our Lord.

Invincible Knight now delivers the following charge to candidate—Sir Knight, I congratulate you on your having been found worthy to be promoted to this honorable Order of Knighthood. It is highly honorable to all those worthy Knights, who, with good faith and diligence, perform its many important duties. The honorable situation to which you are now advanced, and the illustrious office which you now fill, is one that was much desired by the first noblemen of Italy; but ambition and jealousy caused his Highness, Pope Alexander, to call on his ancient friend, the Grand Master of the Knights of St. Johns, of Jerusalem, to guard his person and the Holy See, as those knights were known to be well grounded in the faith, and zealous followers of the Lord. The members of this guard were chosen by their countenances, for it is believed that a plain countenance is an indication of the heart; and that no stranger should gain admission and discover the secrets of this august assembly, this Order of the Christian Mark was conferred on those who went about doing good, and following the example of their Illustrious Master, Jesus Christ. Go thou and do likewise.

This ends the initiation, and if there is no business before the Knights, they form round the altar, give signs, &c., the closing ceremonies being similar to those of opening.

The Motto of the Order is—Christus regnat, vincit, triumphat: Rex regnantium, et Dominus dominantium. [Christ rules, conquers, triumphs, &c.]

Insignia—On the left breast a triangular plate of gold, seven eyes engraved on one side, on the other the letter G in the five points.

ORDER OF KNIGHTS OF THE
HOLY SEPULCHRE.

The history of this degree is briefly as follows: St. Helen, mother of Constantine the Great, made a journey to the Holy Land in the year 296, to search out the true cross. After considerable search three crosses were found, but it was difficult to determine which was the true one. Pope Marcellimus, in order to test the matter, had the three conveyed to the bed of a dying woman. Touching the first, nor the second, did not affect her, but the moment she laid her hand upon the third, she was almost instantly restored to perfect health. This, then, was the true cross. In gratitude for her own success, St. Helen erected a church on the spot where the crosses were found, and instituted the Order of Knights of the Holy Sepulchre. The Knights were bound by a sacred vow to guard the Holy Sepulchre, protect pilgrims, and fight infidels, and enemies of the Cross of Christ.

A Council of Knights of the Holy Sepulchre represents a cathedral church, the altar covered with black, and upon which is placed three large candles, a cross, and in the centre a skull and cross bones.

The Principal, or Prelate, stands on the right side of the altar, with a Bible in one hand, and a staff in the other; soft music plays, and the veil is drawn up, and discovers the altar. The choir recite:

Hush, hush, the heavenly choir,
They cleave the air in bright attire:
See, see, the lute each angel brings,
And hark divinely thus they sing:

To the power divine,
All glory be given,
By man upon earth,
And angels in heaven.

Prelate (stepping before the altar)—Kyrie Elieson; Christe Elieson; Kyrie Elieson; Amen: Gloria Sibi Domino! I declare this Grand Council opened, and ready to proceed to business.

The Priests and Ministers now take their several stations.

When one or more candidates are to be admitted, they are prepared in the outer room by the Verger, who leaves them and returns to his place.

If there are less than seven, a number of the brethren make up the number to seven; and they all go to the door, and they rap seven times.

Prelate to Verger—See the cause of that alarm, and report.

Verger goes to the door, opens it a little, looks out, and then returns to his place.

Verger—Right Reverend Prelate, there are seven brethren who solicit admission to this Grand Council.

Prelate—On what is their desire founded?

Verger—On a true Christian principle, to serve the church and its members, by performing the seven corporeal works of mercy, and to protect and guard the Holy Sepulchre from the destroying hands of our enemies.

Prelate—Admit them, if you please, that we may know them.

Candidates come forward.

Prelate—Are you followers of the Captain of our salvation?

Verger—We are, Right Reverend Prelate.

Prelate—Attend, then, to the sayings of our Master, Jesus Christ. Thou shalt love the Lord thy God with all thy heart, with all thy mind, with all thy soul, and with all thy might. This is the first great commandment, and the second is like unto it; thou shalt love thy neighbor as thyself: on these two commandments hang all the law and the prophets. Will you take the vows of our Order?

Candidates assent by bowing.

The Verger and Beadle now hold the Bible, on which each of the seven places his right hand, and repeats after the Prelate as follows:

I, John Smith, in the name of the high and undivided Trinity, do promise and vow to keep and conceal the high mysteries of this noble and invincible Order of Knights of the Holy Sepulchre, from all but such as are ready and willing to serve the church of Christ, by acts of valor and charity, and its members, by performing all the corporeal works of mercy; and that, as far as in me lies, I will defend the church of the Holy Sepulchre from pillage and violence, and guard and protect pilgrims on their way to and from the Holy Land; and if I perform not this, my vow, to the best of my abilities, let me become inanimatus, [dead.]

By direction of the Prelate the seven interlace their fingers, cross their arms and say, De mortuis, nil nisi bonum; [concerning the dead, say nothing but good.]

Prelate to candidates—Take the sword, and travel onward—guard the Holy Sepulchre—defeat our enemies—unfurl the banner of our cross—protect the Roman Eagle—return with victory and safety.

The candidates depart, going towards

the south, where they meet a band of Turks—a desperate conflict ensues—the Knights are victorious—they seize the crescent, and return to the Cathedral in triumph, and place the banner, eagle, and crescent before the altar, and take their seats.

The Prelate reads a chapter from the New Testament, and the choir sings:

Creator of the radiant light,
Dividing day from sable night,
Who, with the light, bright origin,
The world's creation didst begin.

Prelate then says—Let our prayer come before thee, and let our exercise be acceptable in thy sight. [Candidates kneel at the foot of the altar.]

Prelate (offering them bread)—Brethren, eat ye all of this bread in love, that ye may learn to support each other. [Taking a cup]—Drink ye all of this cup to ratify the vow that ye have made, and learn to sustain one another.

The Prelate now raises candidates up by the grip (interlace the fingers).

Prelate to first candidate—Sir, I greet thee a Knight of the Holy Sepulchre; go feed the hungry.

To second candidate—Give drink to the thirsty.

To third candidate—Clothe the naked with a garment.

To fourth candidate—Visit and ransom the captives.

To fifth candidate—Harbor the harborless, give the orphan and widow where to lay their heads.

To sixth candidate—Visit and relieve the sick.

To seventh candidate—Go and bury the dead.

Candidates all make crosses, and say—In nomini patria filio et spiritus sancto. Amen.

Prelate—Brethren, let us recommend to each other the practice of the four cardinal virtues—prudence, justice, temperance, fortitude.

This ends the initiation.

In closing the Council, the Knights all rise, stand in a circle, interlace their fingers, and say—Sepulchrum.

Prelate—Gloria patri, et filio, et spiritus sancto. [Glory to father, son, and holy spirit.]

Knights—Sicut erat in principio, et nunc, et semper et in secula seculorum. Amen. [As it was in the beginning, is now, and shall be, world without end.]

Prelate then pronounces the benediction as follows—Blessed be thou, O Lord, our God! Great first cause and governor of all things! &c.—which closes

ORDER OF THE CROSS.

None but Knights Templars can take this degree. The officers are Most Illustrious Sovereign Prefect, seated in the east; Worshipful Provost, Senior and Junior Inductor, Herald, Guards, &c.

The Council having assembled, the Sovereign Prefect says:

Prefect—Most Worshipful Provost, what is the hour?

Provost (rising, facing the east, and raising his mark in his right hand)—Most Illustrious, it is now the first hour of the day, the time when our Lord suffered, and the veil of the temple was rent asunder; when darkness and consternation was spread over the earth, when the confusion of the old covenant was made light in the new, in the temple of the cross. It is the third watch, when the implements of Masonry were broken—when the flame, which led the wise men of the east, reappeared—when the cubic stone was broken, and the word was given.

Sovereign Prefect to Herald—Worthy Herald, it is my will that this House of God be closed, and the remembrance of those solemn and sacred events, be here commemorated: make this known to the Most Worshipful Provost, in due and ancient form.

Herald bows to Sovereign Prefect, retires, and approaches the Provost, to whom he bows thrice, and then faces about and gives a blast with his horn. This calls up the Sir Knights, who file in threes around him.

Herald—Most Worshipful Provost, it is the sovereign will of Count Albertus, of Pergamus, that this House of God be closed, and that those solemn and sacred events in the new covenant be here commemorated: you will observe this. [Herald bows.]

Provost to Senior Inductor (rising)—Worthy Senior Inductor, it is the will of the Most Illustrious Prefect that here now be opened a Council of Knights of the Cross: what therein becomes your duty?

Senior Inductor—To receive the commands of my superiors in the Order, and pay obedience thereto—to conduct and instruct my ignorant pass-brethren; and to revere, and inculcate reverence in others, for the Most Holy and Almighty God.

Provost (speaking fiercely)—By what right do you claim this duty?

Senior Inductor—By the right of a sign, and the mark of a sign.

Provost—Will you give me a sign?

Senior Inductor—I could if I should.

Most Worshipful Provost partly extends both arms, pointing downwards to an angle of about forty degrees, with the palms open, and upwards, to show they are not sullied with iniquity and oppression, and says—Worthy Senior Inductor, you may give it.

Senior Inductor looks him full in the face, and with his fore finger touches his right temple, and lets fall his hand, and says—This is a sign.

Provost— A sign of what?

Senior Inductor—Aye, a sign of what?

Provost—A penal sign.

Senior Inductor—Your sign is ——

Provost—The last sign of my induction. But you have the mark of a sign.

Senior Inductor—The sign whereof my mark is a mark, I hope is in the Council above.

Provost—But the mark ——

Senior Inductor—Is in my bosom.

Senior Inductor produces his mark in his left hand, and with the fore finger of his right on the letter S, on the cross, asks—What's that?

Provost—Lisha.

Worshipful Provost puts his finger on the letter H, and asks—What is this?

Senior Inductor—Sha.

Worthy Senior Inductor then puts his finger on the letter I, and asks—What is this?

Provost—Baal. What is your mark?

Senior Inductor—Baal, Sha-Lisha ; [Lord of the three ;] I am the Lord.

Provost—You are my brother. and the duty is yours of ancient right; please announce the Council open.

When a new member is to receive this Order, the following are the ceremonies :

The Senior Inductor steps to the door and gives three raps, and is answered by some Knight from without, who is then admitted, and the Senior Inductor gives the conditional sign, (which is by partly extending both arms, as before described ;) the Knight answering by putting his finger to his right temple, as before shown.

Senior Inductor to Sovereign Prefect— Most Illustrious, a professing brother is within the Council by virtue of a sign.

Prefect—Worthy Herald, go to this professing brother, and see him marked before the chair of the most Worshipful Provost ; conduct him thither.

Herald to candidate—Worthy Sir, know you the sacred cross of our Council?

Candidate—I am a Christian.

Herald—Follow me.

Herald conducts the candidate in front of the Provost, and says—Most Worthy Provost, by order of our Sovereign Prefect, I here bring you to be marked a professing brother of the Cross.

Provost—Know you the Cross of our Council?

Candidate—I am a Christian.

Provost—No more. Administer the obligation.

The first obligation is then administered, as follows :

You, John Smith, do now, by your honor, and in view of the power and union of the Thrice Illustrious Order of the Cross, now first made known to you, and in the dread presence of the Most Holy and Almighty God, solemnly and sincerely swear and declare, that, to the end of your life, you will not, either in consideration of gain, interest, or honor, nor with good or bad design, ever take any, the least, step or measure, or be instrumental in any such object, to betray or communicate to any person, or being, or number of the same, in the known world, not thereto of cross and craft entitled, any secret or secrets, or ceremony or ceremonies, or any part thereof appertaining to the Order and Degree known among Masons as the Thrice Illustrious Order of the Cross. That you will not, at any time or times whatever, either now or hereafter, directly or indirectly, by letter, figure, or character, however or by whoever made, ever communicate any of the information and secret mysteries heretofore alluded to. That you will never speak on or upon, or breathe high or low, any ceremony or secret appertaining thereto, out of Council, where there shall not be two or more Knights companions of the Order present, besides yourself, and that in a safe and sure place, whereby my opinion, even of the nature and general principles of the institution, can be formed by any other person, be he Mason or otherwise. than a true Knight companion of the Cross; nothing herein going to interfere with the prudent practice of the duties enjoined by the Order, or arrangement for their enforcement.

You further swear, that, should you know another to violate any essential part of this obligation, you will use your most decided endeavors, by the blessing of God, to bring such person to the strictest and most condign punishment, agreeably to the rules and usages of our ancient fraternity, and this by pointing him out to the world as an unworthy vagabond; by opposing his interest, by deranging his business, by transferring his character after him wherever he may go, and by exposing him to the contempt of the whole fraternity and the world, but of our illustrious Order more especially, during his whole natural life: nothing herein going to prevent yourself, or any other, when elected to the dignity of Thrice Illustrious, from retaining the ritual of the Order, if prudence and caution appear to be the governing principle in so retaining it, such dignity authorizing the elected to be governed by no rule but the dictates of his own judgment, in regard to what will best conduce to the interest of the Order; but that he be responsible for the character of those whom he may induct, and for the concealment of the said ritual.

Should any Thrice Illustrious Knight, or acting officer of any Council which may have them in hand, ever require your aid in any emergency in defence of the recovery of his said charge, you swear cheerfully to exercise all assistance in his favor, which the nature of the time and place will admit, even to the sacrifice of life, liberty, and property.

To all, and every part thereof, we then bind you, and by ancient usage you bind yourself, under the no less infamous penalty than dying the death of a traitor, by having a spear, or other sharp instrument, like as our divine Master, thrust in your left side, bearing testimony, even in death, of the power and justice of the mark of the holy cross.

Provost—Mr. Smith, before you can be admitted to the benefits of this Thrice Illustrious Order, it becomes my duty to ask you certain questions relative to your past life, and resolutions for the future. We shall expect true and candid answers from you. Have you given me your true baptismal and family name, your correct age, birth-place, and present residence?

Candidate—I have.

Provost—It is well. Were your parents free, and not slaves; and had they right or title in the soil of the earth, and were they devoted to the religion of the Cross?

Candidate—They were free, and devoted to the true religion, and thus was I educated.

Provost—Have you searched the spiritual claims of that religion on your gratitude and your affections; and have you continued steadfast in that faith from choice and a conviction of your duty to heaven, or from education?

Candidate—From duty and choice.

Provost—It is well. Have you ever,

up to this time, lived according to the principles of that religion, by acting upon the square of virtue with all men, not defrauding any, nor defamed the good name of any, nor indulged sensual appetites unreasonably, but more especially to the dishonor of the matrimonial tie, nor extorted on, or oppressed the poor.

Candidate—I have not been guilty of these things.

Provost—You have then entitled yourself to our highest confidence, by obeying the injunctions of our Thrice Illustrious Prefect in Heaven, of "doing to all men even as you would that they should do unto you." Can you so continue to act, that yearly on the anniversary of St. Albert, you can solemnly swear for the past season you have not been guilty of the crimes enumerated in these questions?

Candidate—By the help of God, I can.

Provost—Be it so, then, that annually, on the anniversary of St. Albert, you swear to these great questions; and the confidence of the Knights Companions of the Order in you, rests on your being able so to do. [Provost pauses, and then continues]—For the future, then, you promise to be a good man, and to be governed by the moral laws of God and the rules of the Order, in always dealing openly, honorably, and above deceit, especially with the Knights Companions of the Order?

Candidate—I do.

Provost—You promise so to act with all mankind, but especially with the fraternity, as that you shall never be justly called a bad paymaster, ungrateful, a liar, a rake, or a libertine, a man careless in the business of your vocation, a drunkard, or a tyrant?

Candidate—I do.

Provost—You promise to lead a life as upright and just in relation to all mankind as you are capable of, but in matters of difference to preserve the interest of a companion of the Order, or of a companion's friend for whom he pleads, to any mere man of the world?

Candidate—I do.

Provost—You promise never to engage in mean party strife, nor conspiracies against the government or religion of your country, whereby your reputation may suffer, nor ever to associate with dishonorable men even for a moment, except it be to secure the interest of such person, his family or friends, to a companion, whose necessities require this degradation at your hands?

Candidate—I do.

9

Provost—You promise to act honorably in all matters of office or vocation, even to the value of the one-third part of a Roman penny, and never to take any advantage therein, unworthy the best countenance of your companions, and this, that they shall not, by your unworthiness, be brought into disrepute?

Candidate—I do.

Provost—It is well. Administer the oath.

The candidate now takes the following final oath, or obligation:

I, John Smith, do now, by the honor and power of the mark of the Holy and Illustrious Order of the Cross, which I do now hold to Heaven in my right hand as an earnest of my faith, and in the dread presence of the most holy and Almighty God, solemnly swear and declare, that I do hereby accept of, and for ever will consider the cross and mark of this Order as my only hope : that I will make it the test of faith and fellowship ; and that I will effect its objects and defend its mysteries to the end of my days, with my life and with my property—and first, that in the state of collision and misunderstanding impiously existing among the princes and pilgrims, defenders and champions of the Holy Cross of Jesus our Lord, now assembled in the land and city of their peace, and considering that the glory of the Most High requires the greatest and strictest unanimity of measures and arms, the most sacred union of sentiment and brotherly love in the soldiers who there thus devote themselves to his cause and banner, I swear strictly to dedicate myself, my life and my property for ever hereafter to his holy name and the purposes of our mark, and to the best interest of all those who thus with me become Knights of the Cross : I swear for ever to give myself to this holy and illustrious Order, confiding fully and unreservedly in the purity of their morals and the ardor of their pious enthusiasm, for the recovery of the land of their fathers, and the blessed clime of our Lord's sufferings, and never to renounce the mark of the Order nor the claims and welfare of my brethren.

2d. And that the holy and pious enthusiasm of my brethren may not have slander or disgrace at my hands, or the Order be injured by my unworthiness, I swear for ever to renounce tyranny and oppression in my own person and place, whatever it may be, and to stand forth against it in others, whether public or private ; to become the champion of the cross ; to observe the common good ; be the protector of the poor and unfortunate ; and ever to observe the common rights of human nature without encroachment, or permitting encroachment thereon, if in my power to prevent or lessen it. I will, moreover, act in subordination to the laws of my country, and never countenance any change in the government under which I live, without good and answerable reasons for so doing, that ancient usages and immemorial customs be not overturned.

3d. I swear to venerate the mark as the wisdom and decree of Heaven, to unite our hands and hearts in the work of the holy crusade, and as an encouragement to act with zeal and efficacy, and I swear to consider its testimonies as the true and only proper test of an illustrious brother of the cross.

4th. I swear to wear the mark of this Order, without any the least addition, except what I shall be legally entitled to by induction, for ever, if not without the physical means of doing so, or it being contrary to propriety ; and even then, if possible, to wear the holy cross ; and I swear to put a chief dependence for the said worthy and pious objects therein.

5th. I swear to put confidence unlimited in every illustrious brother of the cross, as a true and worthy follower of the blessed Jesus, who has sought this land, not for private good, but pity, and the glory of the religion of the Most High and Holy God.

6th. I swear never to permit political principles nor personal interest to come counter to a brother's, if forbearance and brotherly kindness can operate to prevent it ; and never to meet him if I know it, in war or in peace, under such circumstances that I may not, in justice to myself, my cross, and my country, wish him unqualified success ; and if perchance it should happen without my knowledge, on being informed thereof, that I will use my best endeavors to satisfy him, even to the relinquishing of my arms and purpose. I will never shed a brother's blood nor thwart his good fortune, knowing him to be such, nor see it done by others if in my power to prevent it.

7th. I swear to advance my brother's interest, by always supporting his military fame and political preferment in opposition to another ; and by employing his arms or his aid in his vocation under all circumstances where I shall not suffer more by doing so, than he, by my neglecting to do so, but this never to the sacrifice of any vital interest in our holy religion, or in the welfare of my country.

8th. I swear to look on his enemies as my enemies, his friends as my friends, and stand forth to mete out tender kindness or vengeance accordingly; but never to intrude on his social or domestic relations to his hurt or dishonor, by claiming his privileges, or by debauching or defaming his female relations or friends.

9th. I swear never to see calmly, nor without earnest desires and decided measures to prevent, the ill treatment, slander, or defamation, of any brother Knight, nor ever to view danger or the least shadow of injury about to fall on his head, without well and truly apprising him thereof; and, if in my power to prevent it, never to fail, by my sword or counsel, to defend his welfare and good name.

10th. I do swear never to prosecute a brother before those who know not our Order, till the remonstrances of a Council shall be inadequate to do me justice.

11th. I swear to keep sacred my brother's secrets, both when delivered to me as such, and when the nature of the information is such as to require secresy for his welfare.

12th. I swear to hold myself bound to him, especially in affliction and adversity, to contribute to his necessities my prayers, my influence, and my purse.

13th. I swear to be under the control of my Council, or, if belonging to none, to that which is nearest to me, and never to demur to, or complain at, any decree concerning me, which my brethren, as a Council, shall conceive me to deserve, and enforce on my head, to my hurt and dishonor.

14th. I swear to obey all summonses sent from any Council to me, or from any Most Illustrious Knight, whether Illustrious Counsellor for the time being, or by induction, and to be governed by the constitution, usages, and customs of the Order without variation or change.

15th. I swear never to see nor permit more than two candidates, who, with the Senior Inductor, will make three, to be advanced at the same time, in any Council where I shall be, nor shall any candidate, by suffrage, be inducted without a unanimous vote of the illustrious brethren in Council; nor shall any Council advance any member, there not being three Illustrious Knights, or one Most Illustrious and four Illustrious Knights of the Cross present, which latter may be substituted by Most Illustrious Induction; nor yet where there shall not be a full and proper mark of the Order, such as usage had adopted to our altar, of metal, or other durable and worthy material,

contained within the apartment of Council, as also the Holy Bible; nor will I ever see a Council opened for business, without the ceremony of testing the mark, exercised on the character of every brother, prayers, and the reading of the 35th Psalm of David; nor will I ever see, consent to, or countenance, more than two persons of the same business or calling in life, to belong to, or be inducted and advanced in any one Council of which I am a member, at the same time; nothing therein going to exclude members from other parts of the country, or from foreign parts, from joining us, if they consent formally and truly to stand in deference and defence, first, of their special bar-brethren in the council, nor to prevent advancements to fill vacancies, occasioned by death or removal. To all this, and every part thereof, I do now, as before, by the honor and power of the mark, as by an honorable and awful oath, which confirmeth all things in the dread presence of the Most Holy and Almighty God, solemnly and in truth, bind and obligate my soul; and in the earthly penalties, to wit, that, for the violation of the least matter or particle of any of the here taken obligations, I become the silent and mute subject of the displeasure of the Illustrious Order, and have their power and wrath turned on my head, to my destruction and dishonor, which, like the nail of Jael, may be the sure end of an unworthy wretch, by piercing my temples with a true sense of my ingratitude—and for a breach of silence in case of such an unhappy event, that I shall die the infamous death of a traitor, by having a spear, or other sharp weapon, like as my Lord, thrust in my left side—bearing testimony, even in death, of the power of the mark of the Holy and Illustrious Cross, before I. H. S. our Thrice Illustrious Counsellor in Heaven, the Grand Council of the good. To this I swear.

The closing of the Council is somewhat similar to the opening ceremonies—the Most Illustrious Prefect first inquiring the duties of the several officers, as in other degrees.

Herald then faces the Worthy Provost, bows, turns and gives a blast with his horn, and says—Most Worthy Provost, it is the will of the Most Illustrious Prefect that this Council be now closed. Give notice accordingly.

The Provost notifies Senior Inductor, when the signs are given, with the usual ceremony, and the Council is then declared closed.

INEFFABLE DEGREES,

OR, THE LODGE OF PERFECTION.

Brothers or Companions of these degrees receive the name of God as it was revealed to Enoch, and are sworn not to pronounce it but once in their lives.

SECRET MASTER.

Soon after the completion of the Temple, King Solomon selected seven worthy and expert brethren from the Craft, and appointed them Secret Masters, or guards of the sanctum sanctorum, and the sacred furniture of the holy place.

A Lodge of Secret Masters represents the Sanctuary of King Solomon's Temple, adjoining the Sanctum Sanctorum. It is hung with black, sprinkled with white tears. The furniture is covered with black crape. There should be nine candlebras of nine lights each, but this number is generally reduced to three times three.

The Master is seated in the east, before a triangular table, and represents King Solomon. He is dressed in royal robes, with a sceptre in his hand. He also wears a large blue ribbon, extending from the right shoulder to the left hip. at the end of which is suspended a golden triangle. He is styled Thrice Potent.

The second officer is seated in the west, and represents Adoniram, son of Abda, who had the inspection of the work on Mount Lebanon. He is styled Grand Inspector, and is clothed in a black robe and cap, and is decorated with a white ribbon, bordered with black, with a black rosette on it, and an ivory key suspended therefrom, with a figure of Z upon it.

All the other brethren wear black robes and caps, with white arpons and gloves, the strings of the aprons black; the flap of the apron is blue, with a golden eye upon it. The Lodge should be enlightened by eighty-one candles, distributed by nine times nine.

At the opening of the Lodge the Thrice Potent Master raps five, when the Grand Marshal rises.

Master—Your place in the Lodge?

Grand Marshal—In the north, Thrice Potent.

Master—Your business there?

Grand Marshal—To see that the Sanctum Sanctorum is duly guarded.

Master—Please to attend to your duty, and inform the guards that we are about to open a Lodge of Secret Masters by the mysterious number.

Grand Marshal goes to the door, returns and says—It is done, Most Powerful.

Master—How are we guarded?

Grand Master—By seven Secret Masters stationed before the veil of the Sanctum Sanctorum.

Master raps six.

Adoniram, the Inspector, rises.

Master—Brother Adoniram, are you a Secret Master?

Inspector—I have passed from the square to the compasses: I have seen the tomb of our respectful Master, Hiram Abiff, and shed tears at the same.

Master—What is the hour?

Inspector—The dawn of day has driven away darkness, and the great light begins to shine in this Lodge.

Master raps seven, when all the brethren rise.

Master—If the great light is a token of the dawn of day, and we are all Secret Masters, it is time to begin our labors. Brother Adoniram, you will give notice that I am about to open a Lodge of Secret Masters by the mysterious number.

Adoniram proclaims this to the brethren, when the signs are given by them from Entered Apprentice up to and including Royal Arch, and also that of Silence, which belongs to this degree, as follows:

Master places the two fore fingers of his right hand on his lips, and the brethren all answer this sign by each placing the two fore fingers of his left hand on his lips.

All clap their hands seven times.

Master—I declare this Lodge of Secret Masters open, and in order for business. Brother Grand Marshal, please to inform the Guards.

When a candidate for this degree is to be admitted, he is prepared by the Master of Ceremonies in an outer room and led to the door of the Lodge, where seven distinct knocks are given.

Adoniram (goes to the door and knocks seven times, then opens the door a little)—Who is there?

Master of Ceremonies—A brother, who is well qualified, wishes to receive the degree of Secret Master.

Adoniram—You will wait until the pleasure of our Thrice Potent Master is consulted.

Adoniram goes to Master in the east, and says, that a brother, well qualified, &c., desires to receive the degree of Secret Master.

Master—Is his integrity, zeal and good conduct, duly vouched for?

Adoniram—It is.

Master—Let him be admitted.

Candidate is led in, and advances to the altar; his right knee on the floor; head bound, and a square fastened on his forehead by the bandage; a great light in the right hand. A crown of laurel and olive leaves lays upon the altar.

The obligation is now administered. It enjoins secresy, and to obey the orders and decrees of Council of Princes of Jerusalem, under penalties of all former degrees.

After the obligation, the Master (taking the crown of laurel and olive from the altar) says—My brother, you are now received as a Secret Master.

The words and signs are now given to the candidate. The words are SHADDAI, ADONAI, and JUHA. The password is ZIZON. The sign is given by placing the two fore fingers of right hand on the lips.

The token is thus given: join hands as in the Master Mason's grip, (page 36,) at same time crossing the legs.

Master to the candidate—Brother, you have hitherto only seen the thick veil that covers the sanctum sanctorum of God's Temple; your fidelity, zeal and constancy have gained you the favor that I now grant of showing you our treasure, and introducing you into the secret place.

Candidate is now invested with the decorations of the degree, before described, blue ribbon, scarf, &c.

Master to candidate—As an approved Secret Master you now take rank among the Levites. In this quality you are to become the faithful guardian of the sanctum sanctorum, and I put you in the number of seven, to be one of the conductors of the works which are raising to the divinity. The eye upon your apron is to remind you to have a careful watch over the conduct of the Craft in general.

After the initiation, if there is no other business, the Master begins a lecture, prior to closing.

Master to Adoniram—Your duty as a Secret Master?

Adoniram—To guard the sanctum sanctorum, and sacred furniture of the holy place.

Master—What is that furniture?

Adoniram—The altar of incense, the two tables of shew-bread, and the golden candlesticks.

Master—How are they placed?

Adoniram—The altar of incense stands nearest the Sanctum Sanctorum, and the tables and candlesticks are placed, five on the north, and five on the south of the holy place.

Master—What is meant by the eye of our Lodge?

Adoniram—That Secret Masters should keep a careful watch over the conduct of the Craft in general.

Master—What is your age?

Adoniram—Three times twenty-seven, and accomplished, eighty-one.

Master raps five, and Grand Marshal rises.

Master—Brother Grand Marshal, what is the last as well as the first care of a Lodge of Secret Masters?

Grand Marshal—To see that the Sanctum Sanctorum is duly guarded.

Master—Please attend to your duty, and inform the Guards that we are about to close this Lodge of Secret Masters by the mysterious number.

Grand Marshal goes and informs the Guards, and returns and says—It is done Most Potent.

Master raps six. Adoniram rises.

Master—Brother Adoniram, what is the hour?

Adoniram—The end of the day.

Master—What remains to do?

Adoniram—To practice virtue, fly from vice, and remain in silence.

Master—Since there remains nothing to do but to practice virtue and fly vice, let us enter again into silence, that the will of God may be accomplished.

The signs are now given of Secresy and Silence, by placing the two fore fingers on their lips, as in the opening, and the brethren all clap their hands seven times.

Master—I declare this Lodge of Secret Masters duly closed.

PERFECT MASTER

The Lodge is hung with green tapestry, on eight columns, four on each side, placed at equal distances; illuminated with sixteen lights, placed at the four cardinal points. A table stands before the canopy covered with black. A pyramid in the north with open compasses on it. One at the south with a blazing star upon it.

Right Worshipful and Respectable Master, seated under a canopy in the east, represents Adoniram, he being the first of the seven who was chosen Secret Master by King Solomon. He commanded the works of the Temple before Hiram Abiff arrived at Jerusalem, and afterwards had the inspection of the works at Mount Libanus. He is decorated with the ornaments of perfection, and is a Prince of Jerusalem.

Warden sits in the west, and represents Stolkyn as Grand Inspector.

Master of Ceremonies represents Zerbal, and is seated in the south.

Grand Marshal in the north.

The assistants, being at least Perfect Masters, ought to be decorated with a large green ribbon hung to the neck, with a jewel suspended thereto, being compasses extended to sixty degrees.

The brethren wear black robes and caps, and have aprons of white leather with green flaps; on the middle of the apron must be embroidered a square stone, surrounded by three circles, with the letter J in the centre.

On opening, the Master raps two, when the Grand Marshal rises.

Master—Brother Grand Marshal, are we all Perfect Masters?

Grand Marshal—We are, Right Worshipful and Respectable.

Master—Your place in the Lodge?

Marshal—In the north, Right Worshipful and Respectable.

Master—Your business there?

Marshal—To see that the Lodge is duly tyled.

Master—Please to attend to your duty and inform the Tyler that we are about to open a Lodge of Perfect Masters.

Grand Marshal informs the Tyler, and then reports that the Lodge is duly tyled.

Master raps three, and the Warden and Master of Ceremonies rise.

Master—Brother Stolkyn, are you a Perfect Master?

Warden—I have seen the tomb of our respectable Master, Hiram Abiff, and have in company with my brethren shed tears at the same.

Master—What is the hour?

Warden—It is four.

Master then knocks four, upon which all the brethren rise.

Master—If it is four, it is time to set the workmen to labor. Give notice that I am going to open a Lodge of Perfect Masters by four times four.

Warden gives notice, when the brethren give the signs of all the degrees, with those of this one, hereafter explained.

Master raps four, Warden four, Master of Ceremonies four, and Grand Marshal four—then all the brethren clap their hands four times four.

Master—I declare this Lodge of Perfect Masters open for business. Brother Marshal, please to inform the Tyler that the Lodge is open.

Grand Marshal goes and informs the Tyler, and returns to his seat and reports that the Lodge is duly tyled.

When a candidate is to be advanced to this degree, he puts on the dress of a Secret Master, and is prepared outside by the Master of Ceremonies, who places a green cord round his neck, a green sprig in his left hand, and leads him to the door of the Lodge, where he gives four distinct knocks.

Warden answers the knocks, and reports to the Master—Right Worshipful, while the Craft are engaged in lamenting the death of our Grand Master, Hiram Abiff, an alarm is heard at the inner door of the Lodge.

Master—Attend to the cause of it.

Warden orders the Tyler to open the door. Tyler raps four, and opens it; then reports to Warden, who reports to Master, that there is in the ante-chamber a Secret Master, desirous of being raised to this degree.

Master—Is he worthy and qualified?

Warden—He is.

Master—Let him be introduced according to the ancient due form.

Candidate is then conducted into the Lodge by the Master of Ceremonies, and brought before the Master.

Master—What is your request?

Candidate—To receive the honorable degree of Perfect Master.

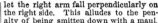

Master—Before you can be admitted to this privilege, it will be necessary for you to join the funeral procession of Hiram Abiff.

Candidate is then conducted several times round the Lodge, the brethren joining in the procession, and singing a dirge from text-book, after which he passes to the tomb of Hiram Abiff, joined by the Master, (personating King Solomon.)

Master (looking at inscription J. M. B. on the tomb, and making sign of admiration)—It is accomplished and complete.

The brethren now make the same sign of admiration, viz. : raise hands and eyes upward, and then let the arms fall crossed upon the abdomen, looking downwards.

Master and brethren now resume their proper places, while the Master of Ceremonies instructs the candidate how to approach the east, and to take upon himself the obligation in this degree, as follows : by four times four steps from a pair of compasses, extended from an angle of seven to that of sixty degrees. Candidate then takes the obligation, which enjoins secresy, and to obey the orders and decrees of Council of the Princes of Jerusalem, under penalties in all former degrees, and of being smitten to the earth with a setting maul, &c.

Master (drawing green cord from candidate's neck)—I now draw you from your vicious life, and, by the favor I have received from the most powerful of kings, I raise you to the degree of Perfect Master, on condition that you strictly adhere to what shall be presented to you by our laws.

The Master now instructs the candidate in all the signs, words, tokens and history of this degree, as follows :

First sign—Place the palm of the left hand upon the right temple, at the same time stepping back with the right foot ; then bring the foot forward again, and let the right arm fall perpendicularly on the right side. This alludes to the penalty of being smitten down with a maul.

Second sign is that of admiration—Raise the hands and eyes upwards, as in the engraving, then let the hands fall crossed in front, at the same time casting the eyes downwards.

The pass-word is ACCASSIA.

The token is that of a Mark Master, given on the five points of fellowship, [page 42.] Mysterious word, JEVA, pronounced Je-vau.

Master then invests candidate with the jewel and apron of a Perfect Master, and informs him that the jewel should remind him to measure his conduct by the exact rule of equity.

Master then instructs candidate in the history of the degree, as follows :

After the body of Hiram Abiff had been found, Solomon requested Adoniram to make suitable arrangements for his burial. The brethren were ordered to attend with white aprons and gloves, and he forbade that the marks of blood, which had been spilled in the Temple, should be effaced until the assassins had been punished. In the meantime, Adoniram furnished a plan for a superb tomb and obelisk of white and black marble, which were finished in nine days. The tomb was entered by passing between two pillars, supporting a square stone surrounded by three circles. On the stone was engraved the letter J. On the tomb was a device representing a virgin, &c., (as in third degree.) The heart of Hiram Abiff was enclosed in a golden urn, which was pierced with a sword to denote the desire of the brethren to punish the assassins. A triangular stone was affixed to the side of the urn, and on it were the letters J. M. B. surrounded by a wreath of cassia. This urn was placed on the top of the obelisk which was erected on the tomb. Three days after the interment, Solomon repaired with his court to the Temple, and all the brethren being arranged as at the funeral, he directed his prayer to heaven, examined the tomb and the inscription on the urn : struck with admiration, he raised his hands and eyes to heaven, and said in the joy of his heart, "It is accomplished and complete."

In closing the Lodge, the Master raps two, as in the opening, when the Grand Marshal rises.

Master—The last as well as the first care of a Perfect Master ? &c.

The Master continues, and asks all the questions as in opening, and then declares the Lodge duly closed.

INTIMATE SECRETARY.

The Lodge is hung in black, spangled with white tears, and represents the Hall of Audience of King Solomon. It should be lighted with three candlebras, each with nine branches, and each containing a candle—one in the east, one in the west, and one in the south.

Most Illustrious Master, representing King Solomon, and Hiram, King of Tyre, seated in the hall of audience in the east, behind a triangular table on which is a scroll and two cross swords. They wear long blue robes and caps, and their aprons are white, lined and bordered with red, and a scroll and golden triangle on each —the letters A P P in the corners of the triangle: a red ribbon, with a golden triangle suspended, same letters engraved on each corner, which is the jewel in this degree: white gloves, bordered with red.

Master raps nine, Grand Marshal rises.

Master—Are all Intimate Secretaries?

Marshal—We are, Most Illustrious.

Master—Your place, Brother Grand Marshal?

Marshal—In the ante-chamber, at the head of the Guards, Most Illustrious.

Master—Your business there?

Marshal—To see that the hall of audience is duly guarded.

Master—How are we guarded?

Marshal—By a full guard of Perfect Masters.

Master—I appoint Brother Terbel Lieutenant of the Guards to aid you in your duties: repair to your station, and see that none approach without permission.

The brethren now fall, each on his right knee, and they cross their hands and hold them up so that the thumb of the right hand touches the left temple, and left thumb the right temple, when each speaks the word JEVA in a low voice, pronouncing it Je-vau, and repeats it three times.

Master raps twice nine.

Hiram rises, and, together with the brethren, make all the signs up to this one, and then the signs of this degree as hereafter explained.

[In the Ineffable Degrees, when the signs are given, they begin with Entered Apprentice, and go usually up to Master Mason, when they skip over to Secret Master, the first of the Ineffable grade.]

Master raps three times nine, and declares the Lodge open for the dispatch of business.

Grand Marshal places a triple triangle on the Bible, which lays on the altar.

When a candidate is to be advanced to this degree, he is placed by the Lieutenant of the Guards outside the veil or door of the hall of audience, which is left partly open, or drawn, and is directed to listen to what is going on inside.

Hiram turns his head, sees candidate, and speaks to Master in an agitated manner—My brother, there is a listener!

Master—It is impossible, since the guards are without.

Hiram (rushing to the door, and dragging candidate in)—Here he is!

Master—What shall we do with him?

Hiram (drawing his sword)—We must kill him.

Master leaves his seat and goes to Hiram, places his hand on Hiram's, and says—Stop, brother.

Master raps nine, and Guards enter and salute him.

Master—Take this prisoner, keep him secure, and let him be forthcoming when called for.

Guards go out with prisoner, leaving Master and Hiram alone a few minutes.

Master raps nine, and Guards bring in candidate and take seats near the foot of the triangle in the east.

Master to candidate—I have, by my entreaties, prevailed upon my worthy ally, Hiram, King of Tyre, whom your vain curiosity had offended, to remit the sentence of death which he pronounced upon you. I have not only obtained your pardon, but have gained his consent to receive you an Intimate Secretary to the alliance we have contracted. Do you promise to keep inviolate the secrets entrusted to you in this degree, and will you take an obligation for that purpose, in the most solemn manner?

Candidate—I promise, and will take the obligation.

The obligation in this degree is now administered. Candidate kneels before the altar, and promises to obey the mandates and decrees of the Grand Council of Princes of Jerusalem, under penalty of having his body dissected, his bowels and vitals taken out, his heart cut to pieces, and the whole thrown out to be devoured by the wild beasts of the field.

Master (raising up candidate from his knees)—I now receive you an Intimate Secretary, on your promise to be faithful to the Order in which you have just now entered. We hope, brother, that your fidelity will be proof to every trial, and that this sword, with which we arm you, will defend you from the attacks of those who may try to extort from you those secrets which we are now about to confer upon you.

Master then instructs candidate in the signs, pass-word, &c., as follows:

First sign—Close the right hand, and draw it from the left shoulder to the right hip. It alludes to the penalty of dissecting the body, &c.

Second sign—Cross your arms in front, and hold up your hands so that the right thumb touches the left temple, and your left thumb the right temple, and speak in a low voice JEVA—pronouncing it Je-vau. This is the mysterious word.

Grip—Join the right hands, and turn them downward thrice, saying, the first time, Berith—second time, Nedir—and the third time, Shelemoth.

Pass-words—Joabert—response, Terbel, being the names of the listener, and the Lieutenant of the Guards.

Master now invests candidate with the jewel and apron of this degree, and says:

Master—Brother, the color of your ribbon is intended to remind you of the blood of Hiram Abiff, the last drop of which he chose to spill, rather than betray his trust; may you be equally faithful. The triple triangle is emblematical of the three theological virtues, faith, hope, and charity; it is also emblematical of the three Masons who were present at the opening of the first Lodge of Intimate Secretaries, to wit: Solomon, King of Israel; Hiram, King of Tyre, and Joabert, a favorite Master Mason in the employ of King Solomon.

This closes the initiation. The meeting is closed with a lecture, as in the other degrees. The Master asks the questions as to the organization and initiation in this degree, the Grand Marshal answering.

In closing the Lodge, the Master raps nine, and Grand Marshal rises, when he is interrogated as to the general duties of Intimate Secretary, whether the place is duly guarded, &c., as in the opening. He then notifies the Lieutenant of the Guards that he is about to close, and directs him to repair to his station, and attend to giving the signs, &c.

Master raps twice nine, Hiram rises, and the signs are given from those of this degree backward.

Master raps three times nine, and declares the Lodge to be duly closed.

PROVOST AND JUDGE.

The Lodge in this degree is hung with red tapestry, and five candlebras are placed therein, each with five lights. One light is placed in each corner, and the fifth in the centre.

Thrice Illustrious Master, representing Tito Zadoc, Prince of Harodim, is seated in the east under a blue canopy surrounded with stars. Prince Tito was the eldest of the Perfect Grand Masters, and Intimate Secretary. He was First Grand Warden, and inspector of the three hundred architects who drew plans for the workmen.

Grand Marshal sits in the north.

Senior and Junior Wardens represent Adoniram and Abda, his father, and are seated in the West.

The brethren wear black robes and caps: white apron trimmed with red, and a red and white rosette, pocket in centre, in which to carry plans; on the flap, a gold key: a red collar, from which is suspended a gold key, the jewel of this degree.

In opening, the Master raps three, when the Grand Marshal rises.

Master—Brother Grand Marshal, are we all Provosts and Judges?

Marshal—We are, Thrice Illustrious.

Master—Your place in the Lodge?

Marshal—In the north.

Master—Your business there?

Marshal—To see that the middle chamber is duly tyled.

Master—Attend to your duty, and inform the Tyler that we are about to open this Lodge of Provosts and Judges.

Marshal goes and informs the Tyler outside the door, and returns to his place.

Master raps four, and the Wardens both rise.

Master—Brother Junior Warden, where is the Master placed?

Junior Warden—Everywhere.

Master—Why so?

Junior Warden—To superintend the workmen, direct the work, and render justice to every man.

Master to Senior Warden—What is the hour?

Senior Warden—Break of day: eight, two and seven.

Master raps five, and brethren all rise.

Master—It is time to begin our labors: take notice that I am about to open a Lodge of Provosts and Judges by four and one.

The brethren give all the signs, up to Intimate Secretary, and then the signs of this degree, hereafter explained.

Master, two Wardens, and Grand Marshal each rap four and one in succession, and the brethren clap four and one with their hands, when the Master declares the Lodge duly opened.

If a candidate is to be advanced, he is prepared outside by the Master of Ceremonies, who conducts him to the door and knocks four and one.

Senior Warden to Master (rising)—Thrice Illustrious, while the Provosts and Judges are here engaged in rendering justice to all men without distinction, an alarm is heard at the door of the lodge.

Master—Attend to the cause of it.

Senior Warden goes to the door, raps four and one, partly opens the door, and inquires who is there. Master of Ceremonies informs him that a brother duly qualified craves the honor of a seat among the Provosts and Judges.

Senior Warden—By what further right does he claim this honor?

Master of Ceremonies—By the right of a pass. [Whispers Tito.]

Senior Warden—The pass is right. You will wait until our Thrice Illustrious Master is informed of your request, and his answer returned.

Senior Warden goes and informs the Master that a brother is without who desires a seat with the Provosts and Judges.

Master—You will see that he is well examined, and if found worthy, introduce him in due and ancient form.

Senior Warden goes and directs the Master of Ceremonies to examine him further, and then introduce him. He then resumes his seat.

Master of Ceremonies conducts candidate to the south-west corner of the Lodge, where [under instruction] he kneels on his right knee and pronounces the word Beroke.

Master—Kumi, [meaning rise.]

Candidate rises, and is conducted three times round the Lodge, at the same time giving the signs in the previous degrees. He is then led to the altar, and takes the obligation in this degree, which is the same as that in Perfect Master, with the addition that he will justly and impartially decide all matters of difference between brethren of this degree, if in his power to do so, under penalty of being punished as an unjust judge, by having his nose cut off.

Master now gives candidate the signs, tokens and words as follows:

First sign—Place the two first fingers of your right hand up to the side of the nose, the thumb under the chin, forming a square with the fingers and thumb.

Second sign, or response—Place first finger of right hand on tip of the nose, and the thumb under the chin.

Token—Clench the three first fingers of the right hand over the thumb, and join hands by interlacing the little fingers. In some Lodges the hands are kept open while the little fingers are locked, and each taps the other seven times with his thumb in the palm.

Pass-word is TITO: other words are Jova, Civi, Ky, Hiram, Stokin, Geometros, Xinchen, Yzire, Ivan, &c.

Master invests candidate with the jewel, apron and gloves of this degree, and addresses him as follows:

Respectable Brother, it gives me joy, that I am now about to recompense. &c. This key opens a small ebony box, in which are contained the plans for the building of the Temple, and this key opens a small ivory box containing all the keys of the Temple. I clothe you with a white apron, lined with red, having a pocket in its centre, and in which you are intended to carry the plans for the building of the Temple, that they may be laid out on the tressel-board for the use of the workmen when wanted. I also give you a balance in equilibrio, as a badge of your office. Let it remind you of that equity of judgment which should characterize your decisions.

Master gives candidate a rap on each shoulder and says—By the power with which I am invested, I constitute you Provost and Judge over all the works and workmen of the Temple. Be impartial, just, prudent, discreet, and merciful. Go salute the Junior and Senior Wardens as a Provost and Judge, and return here for further instruction.

This closes the initiation.

The Lecture is then given, in two sections. The first recapitulates the initiation. The second is historical of the degree, as follows:

Master—What did you observe in the middle chamber?

Senior Warden—A curtain, behind which was suspended a small ebony box containing the plans for the construction of the Temple.

Master—What else did you see?

Senior Warden—A triangle enclosing the letters G. A.

Master—Their meaning and use?

Senior Warden—Grand Architect, and are designed to make us remember him in all our decisions and actions.

Master—Did you see any thing more?

Senior Warden—I saw the letters I H. S. with the sprig of cassia.

Master—What is meant thereby ?

Senior Warden—Imitate Hiram's Silence, and Justice, Humanity and Secrecy, which are designed to teach Provosts and Judges that while their decisions are just, they should be tempered with humanity, or mercy, and that all differences which may arise among the Craft, should be kept secret from the world.

Master—What was the intention of Solomon in instituting this degree ?

Senior Warden—To strengthen the means of preserving order among such a vast number of workmen ; the duty of Provosts and Judges being, to decide all differences arising among the brethren.

Master—Who was the first that was made Provost and Judge ?

Senior Warden—Joabert, being honored with the intimate confidence of King Solomon, received this new mark of distinction. Solomon first created Tito, Adoniram, and Abda, his father, Provosts and Judges, and gave them orders to initiate Joabert into the mysteries of this degree, and to give him all the keys of the Temple, which were inclosed in a small ivory box suspended in the Sanctum Sanctorum, under a rich canopy. When Joabert was first admitted into this sacred place, he involuntarily fell in a kneeling posture, and said, Beroke ; Solomon seeing him, said Kumi, (rise.)

Master—Whence came you as a Provost and Judge ?

Senior Warden—I came from, and am going everywhere.

Master in closing the Lodge, raps three, and Grand Marshal rises.

Master—The last as well as the first care of a Provost and Judge ?

Marshal—To see that the middle chamber is duly tyled.

Master—Attend to your duty, and inform the Tyler that we are about to close this Lodge of Provosts and Judges by four and one.

Marshal goes and informs the Tyler

Master raps four, and Wardens rise.

Master—What is the hour ?

Senior Warden—Break of day—eight, two and seven.

Master—Brother Junior, how so ?

Junior Warden—Because Provosts and Judges should be ready at all times to render justice to all men.

Master raps four and one, and brethren all rise and give the signs from this degree back to Entered Apprentice.

Master raps four and one, then each officer four and one, and the brethren clap four and one with their hands, when the Master declares the Lodge closed.

INTENDANT OF THE BUILDING,

OR, I. B.

A Lodge in this degree is hung with red, and has three candlebras of nine lights each, and an additional one with five lights in the east. It should also have an illuminated transparent triangle in the east, with a circle in the centre of it, and the letters J A I N around the circle, and three Js on a blazing star in its centre.

Thrice Potent Master (represents King Solomon,) is seated in the east, dressed in royal robes, with crown and sceptre.

Thrice Illustrious Inspector, or Senior Warden, (representing Tito Zadoc,) in the west.

Junior Warden (representing Adoniram, son of Abda,) is the Conductor, and is seated in the south.

Grand Marshal in the north.

The junior officers and brethren are dressed in black robes and caps : white apron lined with red and bordered with green ; on the apron is a star with nine points, a sprig of cassia, and a balance ; it also has a triangular flap with the letters B A J, one at each angle. The collar is a broad red ribbon, from which is suspended a golden triangle with the same letters in each corner, and J J J in the centre : on the reverse side three Js in the corners and letter G in the centre.

In opening, Thrice Potent Master raps three, and Grand Marshal rises.

Master—Brother Grand Marshal, are we all I. Bs. ?

Marshal—We are. Thrice Potent.

Master—Your place in the Lodge ?

Marshal—In the north.

Master—Your business there ?

Marshal—To see the Lodge duly tyled.

Master—Attend to your duty, and inform the brethren that we are about to open a Lodge of I. B. by the number five.

Marshal proclaims to the Lodge what the Master has ordered.

Master raps four, and Wardens rise.

Master—Brother Senior Warden, what is the hour ?

Senior Warden—Break of day.

Master raps five. and brethren all rise.

Master—If it is break of day, it is time to begin our labors ; Brother Senior Warden, you will give notice that I am about to open a Lodge of I. B.

Senior Warden proclaims that it is break of day, and that our Thrice Potent Master is about to open a Lodge, &c.

The signs are now given by the brethren as in the other degrees, and then those of this degree, hereafter described.

All the officers now rap five, and the brethren clap five with their hands, when the Master declares the Lodge to be duly opened.

A candidate admitted to this degree represents Joabert, and is introduced as follows:

Master raps seven, and Senior Warden rises, when the Master says—My excellent brother, how shall we repair the loss of our worthy Hiram Abiff? he is now removed from us, and we are thereby deprived of his counsel and services : can you give me any advice in this important matter?

Senior Warden—The method I would propose, would be to select a chief from the five Orders of Architecture, upon whom we may confer the degree of I. B. and by his assistance fill the secret chamber of the third story.

Master—I approve of your advice, and to convince you of my readiness to follow it, I appoint you and Brother Adoniram to carry the same into execution. Excellent brothers, let Adoniram go into the middle chamber and see if he can find a chief of the five Orders of Architecture.

Junior Warden goes out of the Lodge into the ante-chamber, and finding the candidate, thus addresses him:

Junior Warden—Is there here a chief of the five Orders of Architecture?

Candidate—I am one.

Junior Warden—My dear brother, have you the zeal to apply yourself with attention to that which our Thrice Potent Master shall request of you?

Candidate—I have, and will comply with his request, and raise this edifice to his honor and glory.

Junior Warden—Give me the signs, words and tokens of preceding degrees.

Candidate gives them.

Junior Warden then conducts candidate to the door of the Lodge, and gives five distinct knocks.

Senior Warden (inside) rises and says —Thrice Potent, we are disturbed in our deliberations by an alarm at the inner door of the secret chamber.

Master—See to the cause of the alarm.

Senior Warden goes to the door, raps five, partly opens it, and says—Who comes there?

Junior Warden—A chief of the five Orders of Architecture, who is to be employed in works of the secret chamber.

Senior Warden—By what further right does he claim admittance?

Junior Warden—By the right and benefit of a pass-word.

Senior Warden—Give it to me.

Junior Warden—Bonahim, [pronounced Bo-nau-heem.]

Senior Warden—You will wait until our Thrice Potent Master is informed of the request, and his answer returned.

Senior Warden now repairs to the east, and informs Master of what has occurred at the door.

Master—Let Joabert be introduced in due form.

Senior Warden goes and opens the door and admits the candidate, who is conducted to the altar, when (under instruction) he recedes five steps, and then advances to the altar again by five regular steps.

Junior Warden then lays down the candidate, and Senior Warden puts a sprig of cassia in his right hand, in which position (lying prostrate) he takes the obligation in this degree.

The obligation enjoins secrecy, and obedience to orders of the Grand Council of Princes of Jerusalem, under penalty of having his eyes put out, body cut in two, and bowels taken out.

Master to candidate—Your present posture is that of a dead man, and is designed to remind you of the fate of our worthy Hiram Abiff. I shall now raise you in the same manner he was raised, under the sprig of cassia. [Master raises him by the Master Mason's grip.] By your being raised, our hope is signified, that in some measure you will repair his loss, by imitating his bright example.

Master now gives candidate the signs, token and pass-word in this degree, as follows:

First sign is that of surprise—Place the thumbs on the temples, the hands open and resting on the forehead so as to form a square: step back two paces, then forward two paces, then lower the hands till they touch the eyelids, and say BENCHORIM.

Second sign is one of admiration—Interlace the fingers, turn the palms upward above the head, let the hands fall on the wrist, (being still interlaced.) look upward and say, ACHARD, or HAKAR

Third sign is that of grief, and is given by two at the same time—Place the right hand on the heart, the left on the left hip, balance thrice with the knees—one says KY, the other replies, JEA. Instead of these words, some substitute the words CHAI, and JAH, (the Lord liveth.)

Token—Strike a light blow with the right hand over the heart, pass hands to the middle of the fore-arm, placing left hands on the elbow; this is repeated three times, one brother saying JAKINAI, and the other responding JUDAH.

The pass-word is JUDAH, and the sacred word JAKINAI.

Master now invests candidate with the apron, gloves and jewel of this degree, and thus addresses him:—I decorate you with a red ribbon, to be worn crossing the breast from the right shoulder to the left hip, to which is suspended a triangle fastened with green ribbon. I also present you with a white apron, lined with red, and bordered with green. The red is emblematical of that zeal which should characterize you as an I. of B., and the ,green, of the hope we entertain that you will supply the place of our lamented Hiram Abiff.

The first section of the closing lecture in this degree recapitulates the initiation; the second section is as follows:

Master—Are you an Intendant of the Building?

Senior Warden—I have made the five steps of exactness; I have penetrated the inmost part of the Temple; and I have seen the great light, in the middle of which were three mysterious letters, or characters, in Hebrew, without knowing what they meant.

Master—How came you to be received therein?

Senior Warden—By confessing my ignorance.

Master—Why were you received?

Senior Warden—To point out to me the darkness in which I was, and to procure me a true light to regulate my heart, and regulate my understanding.

Master—Where were you introduced?

Senior Warden—In a place full of wonder and beauty, where truth and wisdom reside.

Master—What was your duty?

Senior Warden—To superintend the work.

Master—Why were you made to walk backward and forward in the Lodge?

Senior Warden—To show me, that, in advancing to virtue, I should set humanity in opposition to the pride so natural to us.

Master—What did you see there in the Lodge?

Senior Warden—A triangle enclosing a circle, having on its circumference the letters J. A. I. N. and in its centre the letters J. J. J.

Master—What is signified by the circle in the triangle?

Senior Warden—The eternity of the powers of God, which hath neither beginning nor end.

Master—What is signified by the letters J. A. I. N.?

Senior Warden—They are the initials of the four Hebrew words, Jad, Ail, Jotsare, and Nogah, which are expressive of four attributes of the Deity; power, omnipresence, creation, and splendor.

Master—What is signified by the letters J. J. J.?

Senior Warden—Jah, Jokayn, and Jireh, [" The Lord, the Creator seeth."]

Master—What else did you see?

Senior Warden—A blazing star with five beams, in the centre of which appeared the letter J.

Master—What signify the five beams?

Senior Warden—The five equal lights of Masonry, the Bible, the square, the compasses, the key, and the triangle.

Master—What is signified by the letter J.?

Senior Warden—It is the initial of the ineffable name, as known by us.

Master—Are you in darkness?

Senior Warden—No, the blazing star is my guide.

Master—What is your age?

Senior Warden—27, or 5, 7 and 15.

Master—To what do those three numbers allude?

Senior Warden—To the five chiefs of the five Orders of Architecture, to seven cubits, which was the breadth of the golden candlestick with seven branches, and the fifteen Fellow Crafts, who conspired against the life of our Grand Master, Hiram Abiff.

In closing, the Master raps three, when Grand Marshal rises.

Master—Brother Grand Marshal, the last as well as the first care of I. of B.?

Marshal—To see that the Lodge is duly tyled, Thrice Potent.

Master—Attend to your duty, and inform the brethren that we are about to close this Lodge of I. B.

Master raps four, and Wardens rise.

Master—Brother Senior Warden, what is the hour?

Senior Warden—Seven at night.

•Master raps five, the brethren all rise.

Master—As it is seven at night, it is time to retire: Brother Junior Warden, give notice that I am going to close this Lodge of Intendant of the Building.

The signs are now given—first those of this degree, then the others in rotation back to Entered Apprentice.

Master raps five, Junior Warden raps seven, Senior Warden fifteen, and the brethren clap their hands five, seven and fifteen alternately, when the Master declares the Lodge closed.

MASTER'S ELECT OF NINE.

Some of the Societies call this degree "Illected Knights of Nine," but we have given its original name according to the French Rituals. It is founded on the award of punishment to the principal murderer of Hiram Abiff. After that murder was perpetrated, a great assembly of Masters was convened to take measures to apprehend the murderers. A stranger came and disclosed the fact that he had discovered a person concealed in a cave near Joppa, who answered the description of one of the supposed murderers. Solomon appointed nine Masters to proceed to the spot with the stranger as guide. On their way, Joabert, one of the nine, learned from the guide the location of the cavern, and he made his way there apart from the rest, where, by the light of a lamp, he discovered the murderer fast asleep, with a poinard at his feet. He took the poinard and stabbed him, first in the head, and then in the heart. The villain exclaimed, "Vengeance is taken!" and then expired. Joabert then cut off the murderer's head, and, taking it in his hand, and the bloody knife in the other, returned to Jerusalem with his companions. Solomon was at first offended at this summary vengeance, but at the intercession of the others he became reconciled.

The meeting is called a Chapter, and represents the audience chamber of King Solomon, hung with red and white hangings—the red representing flames. There is a group of nine lights in the east, and one in the west.

Master (representing King Solomon, and dressed in royal robes) sits in the east before a table covered with black, and is styled Most Potent.

There is only one Warden, who represents Stolkyn, and is called the Inspector, he sits in the west, with seven brethren around him.

Grand Marshal sits in the north.

The Inspector and brethren are dressed in black robes, and with their hats flapped. They wear white aprons sprinkled with blood red, and lined and bordered with black; on the flap of the apron a bloody arm, holding a dagger, and on the apron a bloody arm holding a bloody head by the hair. They also wear scarfs of wide black ribbon from the left shoulder to the right hip, with four rosettes near the extremity in front, four behind, and one at the bottom, to which is attached the Jewel of the Order, viz., a gold-handled dagger, with silver blade.

The brethren sit with knees crossed, and lean their heads on their right hands.

Most Potent Master raps seven, when the Grand Marshal rises.

Master—Brother Grand Marshal, are we all Masters Elect?

Marshal—We are, Most Potent.

Master—Your place in the Chapter?

Marshal—In the north.

Master—Your business there?

Marshal—To see that the Chapter is duly guarded.

Master—Please to inform the Sentinel that we are about to open a Chapter of Masters Elect, and charge him to keep guard accordingly.

Marshal goes to the door, informs the Sentinel, and returns to his post.

Master raps eight, and Inspector rises.

Master—Brother Stolkyn, are you a Master Elect?

Inspector—One cavern received me, one lamp gave me light, and one fountain refreshed me.

Master—What is the hour?

Inspector—Break of day.

Master raps eight and one, and the companions all rise.

Master—If it is break of day, it is time to open a Chapter of Masters Elect. Brother Stolkyn, you will inform the companions that we are about to open a Chapter of Masters Elect of Nine, for the dispatch of business, and I will thank them for their assistance.

Inspector repeats this order, when the brethren give the signs up to and including those of this degree, hereafter described.

Master raps eight and one, which is repeated by the Inspector and Marshal, and all the companions clap eight and one with their hands, when the Master declares the Chapter duly open.

If a candidate is to be admitted, he is prepared in an outer room by one of the companions, who is detailed as Master of Ceremonies, and who hoodwinks him, conducts him to the door of the Chapter, and raps eight and one.

Inspector raps the same from the inside, and demands—Who comes there?

Master of Ceremonies—A companion, who is desirous of going in search of the assassins of Hiram Abiff.

Inspector opens the door, and the candidate is led in and placed in the west behind the Inspector's seat.

Master to candidate—What do you desire of us?

Candidate—To be installed as a Master Elect, and avenge the death of our late Grand Master, Hiram Abiff.

Master—Have you the courage to revenge his death?

Candidate—I have.

Master—Then you shall have the opportunity.

Candidate—I am ready.

Master—You shall now be shown the place where one of the murderers lies concealed: a stranger has discovered it to me, and if you have the resolution, follow the stranger.

Candidate—I will follow.

Master of Ceremonies leads candidate out, and through several passages, or rough roads, and then into a room lighted by a single taper, seats him on a block, representing a stone, and says—I am now going to leave you: after I have gone you can remove the bandage from your eyes and drink some water from the spring to refresh yourself after so fatiguing a journey.

Candidate removes the bandage, and discovers a basin of water with a tumbler beside it. He is also astonished to see a human head lying on the floor, and a bloody knife, or poinard, beside it. The Master of Ceremonies returns and directs candidate to take up the knife in his right hand and the head in his left.

Candidate takes them and (under instruction) goes to the door of the Chapter and raps eight and one.

Master of Ceremonies (who has gone in, and raps eight and one from inside)—Who comes there—what do you want?

Candidate—An Intendant of the Building, who desires to enter this Chapter of Masters Elect of Nine.

Master of Ceremonies—By what right do you claim this privilege?

Candidate—I have performed a feat for the honor of the Craft, which I hope will entitle me to receive this degree.

Master of Ceremonies orders him to wait until the Most Potent is apprised of his wish, and his answer returned.

Master of Ceremonies informs the Inspector, Stolkyn, who informs the Master of what has occurred at the door.

Master orders candidate to be admitted, when he comes forward towards the altar with eight quick steps and one slow one, holding the head in one hand and brandishing the knife in the other. The ninth step brings him to the front of the altar, when he falls on his knees.

Master (speaking fiercely)—Wretch! what have you done? Do you not know that by this rash act, you have deprived me of the opportunity of making a public example of the vile assassin? Stolkyn, let him be immediately put to death.

The companions all fall on their knees, and one of them addresses the Master—Most Potent, we ask forgiveness for our worthy companion: his offence was but a mistaken zeal for the good of the Craft.

Master—He is forgiven; but let him beware for the future. On his next irregularity he will certainly suffer death.

The obligation in this degree is now given to the candidate in the usual form. While candidate is taking it, kneeling at the altar, the companions all stand over him with raised poinards, as if about to stab him. Meantime the bloody head is standing on the altar, facing him with ghastly grin. [See engraving, page 143.] The obligation is as follows :—

I do solemnly swear, in the presence of Almighty God, that I will revenge the assassination of our worthy Master, Hiram Abiff, not only on the murderers, but also on all who may betray the secrets of this degree; and furthermore, that I will keep and protect this Order with all my might, and the brethren, in general, with all my power , and furthermore, that I will obey the decrees of the Grand Council of Princes of Jerusalem ; and, if I violate this, my obligation, I consent to be struck with the dreadful poinard of vengeance, now presented to me, and to have my head cut off, and stuck on the highest pole, or pinnacle, in the eastern part of the world, as a monument of my villany! Amen! amen! amen! amen!

The signs, token, and words of this degree are now given to the candidate, as follows:

Signs—Strike towards the forehead as if stabbing with a poinard : the compan-

ion answers by putting his hand to his forehead as if feeling the wound. Strike at the breast as though plunging in a poinard, crying NEKUM, (vengeance:) companion answers by pressing his hand on his breast, and crying NECAR.

Token—Clench the fingers of the right hand, and elevate the thumb : the companion clenches the fingers of his right hand around the elevated thumb, and elevates his thumb. The eight clenched fingers together represent the eight companions of Joabert who went in search of the assassins, and the one elevated thumb represents Joabert himself.

Pass-words—Bugelkal, Naukam, Joabert, Abiram, and Akirop.

Sacred Words—Naukam, Necar, Bugelkal.

Mysterious Word—Jeva.

Candidate is now invested with the requisite clothing and jewel, when the

Master gives him a short history of the degree, as before explained.

The lecture is then given, which is a repetition of the opening, initiation, &c., when the Chapter is closed with ceremonies similar to the opening ones.

Master—Brother Stolkyn, what is the hour ?

Inspector—Evening, Most Potent.

Master raps eight and one, when the companions rise, and he says—If it is evening, it is time to close this Chapter of Masters Elect : Brother Stolkyn, you will inform the companions that we are about to close the Chapter.

Inspector gives notice that the Most Potent Master is about to close the Chapter.

Master raps eight and one, Inspector repeats, and companions clap eight and one with their hands, when the Chapter is declared duly closed.

MASTERS ELECT OF FIFTEEN.

This degree is founded on the capture of the two assassins of Hiram Abiff who had not been discovered at the arrest and punishment of the first one, described in the preceding degree. Their names were Jubela and Jubelo. Through one of his intendants, Solomon learned that two persons answering their description had come to the country of Cheth, and gone to work in the quarries of Bendaca. He thereupon wrote to Maacha, King of Cheth, that he should send for them, and requested his assistance in making the arrests. Fifteen Masters were selected for this duty, and they spent five days in the search, when Zerbal and Eliham discovered the two murderers cutting stone in the quarries. They were immediately seized, bound in chains, and brought to Jerusalem, where they were first imprisoned in the Tower of Achizar, and then executed for their crime, by having their bodies cut open, and their heads taken off, as described in the penalty of the obligation.

The Chapter in this degree represents the audience chamber of King Solomon, hung with red and white.

Thrice Illustrious Master, (representing King Solomon,) seated in the east.

Senior Warden, or Inspector, seated in the west.

Junior Warden, or Introductor, seated in the south.

In front of each of the above officers is a candlebra with five lights.

The brethren wear white aprons, on which is represented a square city (Jerusalem) showing three gates, and over each gate a human head impaled on a spike. The apron is lined and bordered with black. They wear scarfs of wide black ribbon, with three human heads, impaled on spikes, painted or embroidered on them where they cross the breast, and a golden poinard, with silver blade, hanging pendant, which is the jewel of the Order.

The Chapter is opened in precisely the same manner as in the preceding degrees, except that the Thrice Illustrious Master raps five, twice five, or three times five.

If a candidate is to be admitted, all the members except fifteen (without officers) retire outside. Candidate is prepared by a Master of Ceremonies, who places in his hand a human head, which he takes in his left hand by the hair, and a poinard in his right. He is then conducted to the door of the Chapter, when Master of Ceremonies raps three times five.

Junior Warden raps three times five from within, opens the door a crack and asks—Who comes there ?

Master of Ceremonies—A Master Elect, who is desirous of joining the other Masters to go in search of the remaining assassins of our Grand Master, Hiram Abiff.

Junior Warden—You will wait until our Thrice Illustrious Master is informed of his request, and his answer returned.

Junior Warden reports to his Senior, who informs the Master that a Master Elect craves admittance to join in the search for the murderers of Hiram Abiff.

Master—Let him be introduced in due form.

Junior Warden again raps three times five on the door, opens it, and introduces the candidate by instructing him to advance to the altar by fifteen triangular steps. On his arrival at the altar, he kneels, and companions surround him, interlacing their hands and holding them on their foreheads with palms outward.

One brother says—Thrice Illustrious, we ask pardon for our companion.

[The pardon here asked, and to be given, alludes to the rashness of Joabert in decapitating Jubelum, one of the assassins of the Grand Master, Hiram Abiff, as described and set forth in the preceding degree |

Master—Why do you ask pardon ?

Brother—Because he is not guilty.

Master—Is a pardon necessary for the guiltless ?

Brother—It is necessary, to qualify him for a Grand Master Elect.

Master—Is he well qualified ?

Brother—He is.

10

Master to candidate—My brother, the Grand Masters Elect here present, wish me to admit you to this degree: will you take the obligation appertaining to it?

Candidate—I will.

Master now administers the obligation, which is similar to the one in the previous degree, the penalty being to have the body opened perpendicularly and horizontally, and exposed to the air for eight hours, that the flies may prey on his entrails, also to have his head cut off and impaled on the highest pinnacle in the world; and that he (the candidate) will be at all times ready to inflict the same penalty on all who are guilty of disclosing the secrets of this degree.

The candidate is then instructed in the signs, words and token in this degree, as follows:

Signs—Place the point of a poinard under your chin, and draw it downward to the waist, as if in the act of ripping open the body, speaking the word ZERBUL. The brother will answer by giving the Entered Apprentice's sign as on page 7, and saying ELIHAM. Another way is to clench the fingers of the right hand, extend the thumb, place it on the abdomen, and move it upwards to the chin, as if ripping open the body with a knife. The brother answers as before.

Words—The pass-words are Eliham and Zerbal. Sacred words, Zerbal, Beniah, Benhakar, Bendaka, &c.

Candidate is now clothed as a companion of this degree, and salutes the Senior Warden as a Master Elect of Fifteen.

If there is no other business before the Chapter, it is then closed in same manner as in the preceding degree, except that the Master and other officers rap three times five, and the companions clap three times five with their hands, &c.

SUBLIME KNIGHTS ELECTED.

This degree was instituted by King Solomon to reward the Masters Elect of Fifteen for their prompt, zealous and successful efforts to apprehend the murderers of Hiram Abiff, and for their valuable services rendered in the erection of the Temple. He selected twelve from among these Masters Elect, on whom he conferred the degree, and gave them command over the work of the Twelve Tribes.

The Lodge, or Chapter, represents the ante-chamber of the Palace of King Solomon. It is hung with red and white curtains, and is lighted by twelve candles on four triangular branches.

The officers consist of Thrice Potent Master, representing King Solomon, sitting in the east: Grand Inspector in the west, and Master of Ceremonies.

The brethren wear white aprons, each with an inflamed heart embroidered or painted upon it, and lined and bordered with black. The ribbon, or Order, is similar to that in the preceding degree, except that in place of three heads, three hearts appear upon it. The jewel is the same.

In opening the Chapter, Thrice Potent Master raps ten, and Grand Inspector rises. Master makes the usual inquiries as to whether the Chapter is duly guarded, and the duties of the several officers, as in former degrees, which are answered by the Inspector.

Master raps eleven, and inquires of Grand Inspector—What is the hour?

Grand Inspector—It is twelve, Thrice Potent.

Master raps twelve, which is repeated by the officers, and the brethren clap twelve with their hands: Master says—If it is twelve it is time to labor by the greatest of lights. I pronounce this Grand Chapter open.

The brethren now give the signs of the different degrees, and then those of this degree, hereafter described.

If a candidate is to be admitted, he is prepared outside by the Master of Ceremonies, who brings him hoodwinked to the door, and gives twelve raps, which are answered by twelve by the Inspector, who demands, who comes there? &c.

Master of Ceremonies—A Master Elect of Fifteen desires to receive the degree of Sublime Knight.

Candidate gets admittance in the same manner as in the previous degree, and is led to the Grand Inspector in the west, who examines him in all former degrees.

Master—Companion Grand Inspector, what does this candidate desire ?

Inspector—To be admitted to the degree of Sublime Knight, as a reward of his former zeal and labor.

Master to candidate—My brother, you cannot receive this degree until we are assured that you were not an accomplice in the death of our Grand Master, Hiram Abiff. To prove this, I shall offer you a portion of his heart, which has been preserved since his assassination : you are to swallow it: every faithful Mason may do this without injury, but it cannot remain in the body of one who is perjured. Are you disposed to submit to the trial ?

Candidate—I am.

The candidate is now conducted to the altar by twelve upright regular steps, and kneels, when the Master presents to him on a trowel the symbolic piece of a heart, (a little cake,) which he swallows.

Master—This mystic oblation which, like you, we have received, forms a tie so strong that nothing can break it : woe to him who attempts to disunite us !

The obligation in the degree is then administered. It is similar to those of former degrees, the penalty being to have the hands nailed to the breast, &c.

The candidate is now instructed in the sign, token, and words, &c., viz. : Cross the arms on the stomach, the fingers clenched, and thumbs elevated, and raise the eyes upward. It alludes to the penalty of having the hands nailed, &c.

The token is exactly the same as that in Intimate Secretary. The pass - words are Stolkyn, Emerh, Emeth, and Amuriah. The sacred word is Adonia.

This ends the initiation.

The closing ceremonies are similar to those in previous degrees. Master raps ten and inquires about the duties of the officers : he then raps eleven and inquires of the Inspector—What is the hour ?

Inspector—Low six.

Master raps twelve, and brethren rise, the signs are given, &c.

Master again raps twelve, the officers twelve, and the brethren all clap twelve with their hands, when the Master declares the Chapter to be duly closed.

GRAND MASTER ARCHITECT.

This degree was established by King Solomon as a School of Architecture to perfect ingenious and deserving craftsmen in their calling, and animate them with a desire of arriving at distinction in the royal art. It was given to the Sublime Knights Elected.

The assembly is called a Chapter, and the room is decorated with white hangings, sprinkled with red flames. The five orders of architecture should be appropriately represented among the decorations. In the north should be placed a representation of the north star, with seven surrounding stars : it is emblematical of a guiding star of the Order.

Most Potent Master (representing King Solomon) is seated in the east.

Senior Warden (called Grand Inspector) in the west, and Grand Marshal in the south.

The brethren, or companions, wear stone colored aprons and scarfs; the apron has a star upon it, and in some cases a square and rule : the jewel is a gold medal, with the five orders of architecture, a star, and a case of mathematical instruments delineated on each side.

In the opening, Most Potent Master raps one, and Grand Marshal rises. Master inquires if the Chapter is duly guarded, &c., the same as in the former degrees.

Master raps two, when the Grand Inspector rises.

Master—What is the hour ?

Inspector—A star indicates the first instant, the first hour, and the first day in which the Grand Architect commenced the creation of the Universe.

Master raps one and two, when the companions all rise.

Master—Companions, it is the first instant, the first hour, the first day, the first year, when Solomon commenced the Temple ; the first day, the first hour, the first instant for opening this Chapter. It is time to commence our labors.

Master raps one and two, the other officers do the same, and the companions clap one and two with their hands, when the Master declares the Chapter duly opened for the dispatch of business.

When a companion is to receive this degree he is prepared outside by the Master of Ceremonies, who conducts him to the door of the Chapter and raps one and two, which is answered by the same from within. He is admitted through the door by the same ceremonies as in the former degrees, and conducted to the east, where he is thus addressed by the Most Potent Master:

Master—Brother, it has become necessary to form a School of Architecture for the instruction of the brethren employed in the Temple, as none but skillful architects can bring the same to perfection. In order to prevent some brethren from receiving the honors and rewards due only to brethren of talents, we have deemed it expedient to prove and test all those who present themselves as candidates for this degree. We therefore require you to make the tour of the Temple, for the purpose of examining the work, and to produce a plan drawn with exactness which you must present for inspection, that we may judge whether you are entitled to this degree.

Master of Ceremonies conducts candidate round the Chapter, and into several side rooms, (if there are any.) He finally halts in the west, by the Grand Inspector, where candidate draws certain plans, or is supposed to do so. Master of Ceremonies then informs the Master that candidate has completed the labor assigned to him.

Master—My brother, what are the fruits of your travels?

Candidate (instructed)—Most Potent, I have brought a plan of the works of the Temple, which I am ready to present for your inspection.

Master—Present it.

Master of Ceremonies conducts candidate to the Master, who receives and examines his plan, then hands it to some of the companions, who examine it approvingly, and hand it back to the Master.

Master—It is with pleasure we witness the skill you have manifested in fulfilling the conditions prescribed to you, but we require further proof before you can be admitted among us. We again require you to travel.

Master of Ceremonies again conducts candidate round the Chapter, stopping at the north, and explaining to him that the North Star, there represented, being a guide to mariners, so ought virtue to be a guide to every Grand Master Architect. Stopping again at the west, the candidate is instructed to approach the east by one and two steps, which brings him in front of the altar.

Master to candidate—What have you learned in your travels?

Candidate (instructed)—That virtue, as well as talents, should be possessed by every one admitted to this degree.

The obligation in this degree is then administered. It is similar to former obligations, as to secrecy, &c., the penalty being to have the hand cut in twain.

Most Potent Master then addresses candidate on his proficiency in Geometry, and in the Masonic art, and instructs him in the sign, word, and tokens, viz.:

Sign—Slide the right hand into the palm of the left, pause a moment, clench the fingers of the right hand, extend the thumb, and with it make the motion of tracing a plan in the palm of the left, directing your eyes to the brother, as if drawing from his dictation. This sign is varied in some Chapters, by using the fore-finger in place of the thumb.

Token—Join right hand to the brother's left, interlacing the fingers, place the left hand on your hip; the brother will do the same with his right hand.

Some give the following token, viz.: join right hands, interlacing the three last fingers, and fixing them so as to form a square; place the left hand on your brother's shoulder.

Pass-word—RABACIM or RAB-BANAIN.

Sacred word—ADONAI.

In closing, Most Potent Master raps one, when Grand Marshal rises, and the Master enquires the duties of the several officers, &c., which questions are answered in detail.

Master raps two, and Inspector rises.

Master—What is the hour?

Inspector—The Temple is completed, Most Potent.

Master raps one and two, and all the brethren rise, when he says—As we have finished the great work, our labors are ended, and we will close this Chapter.

The signs are now given as in previous degrees, when the officers rap one and two, the brethren clap one and two with their hands, and the Chapter is closed.

KNIGHT OF THE NINTH ARCH.

The history of this degree places its origin in the Vision of Enoch, which is thus given : A mountain seemed to him to rise in the heavens, and he was transferred to the top of it. He there saw a triangular plate of gold upon which were some characters which he was commanded never to pronounce. Presently he seemed to be lowered perpendicularly into the bowels of the earth through Nine Arches, and at the bottom of the Ninth, he saw the same triangular plate. He soon after built a temple under ground, similar to the Nine Arches seen in his vision, being assisted by Methuselah, his son. After completing this temple, he caused to be made a triangular plate of gold, and engraved upon it the ineffable characters which he had been commanded not to pronounce. This plate he enriched with precious stones, and placed it on a triangular pedestal of white marble, which he deposited in the Ninth Arch of his subterranean edifice. The access to this Temple of Enoch was by a trap door of stone, or key-stone, with an iron ring at the top, by which it could be raised. No one knew of the treasures deposited in the Ninth Arch, except Enoch himself. Enoch then built two great pillars on a high mountain near by : one of brass to withstand water, and the other of marble to withstand fire. On the marble pillar he engraved certain hieroglyphics, disclosing the concealment of the golden plate, &c., under ground ; on the pillar of brass he engraved the principles of Geometry, or Masonry. These events occurred before the flood, in the part of the world known afterwards as the Land of Canaan.

Some treasure having been discovered among ancient ruins by the workmen of King Solomon, he requested three Grand Master Architects (Gibulum, Joabert and Stolkyn) to make a further search. They went ; and while at work Gibulum stuck his pick-ax through an iron ring fastened to a stone. This proved to be a cubic stone, or trap, and on removing it a cavern was discovered. Gibulum offered to descend, and a rope was fastened round his body, and he was let down. He found this cavern to consist of Nine Arches, and at the bottom of the Ninth Arch he found a triangular plate of gold, with some mysterious characters engraved thereon. This was brought to King Solomon, who, with Hiram, King of Tyre, examined it closely. The inscription proved to be the mysterious word, the true pronunciation of which had been lost, and was until then unknown.

The meeting of the Knights is called a Chapter, and the room represents the audience chamber of King Solomon. It is hung with red and white curtains, and lighted by three candlebras of three lights each, viz. : one in the east, one in the west, and one in the south. A second apartment is also necessary to represent the cavern of Enoch.

Thrice Potent Grand Master (representing King Solomon) is seated under a canopy in the east. He is dressed in royal robes of yellow and blue, with a sceptre in his hand, and a crown upon his head.

Senior Warden (representing Hiram, King of Tyre) is clothed in royal robes of purple and yellow, with a crown on his head, and a sword in his hand.

Senior Grand Warden (or Grand Inspector, representing Gibulum) is seated in the west. He dresses in a blue robe, with sword in hand.

Junior Grand Warden (representing Stolkyn) is seated in the south.

Grand Treasurer (representing Joabert) is seated in the north, and wears a blue robe.

The brethren are clothed in black robes and caps, and each wears the apron, the order, and the jewel of this degree. The officers likewise all wear the order and the jewel.

The Order is a broad purple ribbon, extending from the right shoulder to the left hip, at the end of which is attached a golden triangle, with the mysterious word engraved thereon, enclosed in rays. The apron is of purple silk, bordered with white : on it a triangle.

In opening the Chapter, Thrice Potent Master raps seven, and Grand Inspector rises.

Master—Are we all Knights of the Ninth Arch ?

Inspector—We are, Thrice Potent.

Master then inquires the places and duties of the different officers, as in former degrees.

Master raps eight, and Junior Grand Warden rises.

Master—What is the hour?

Warden—The rising of the sun.

Master raps three times three, when the companions all rise, and he says—If it is the rising of the sun, it is time to commence our labors. Brother Stolkyn, you will please to give notice that we are about to open in this place a Chapter of Knights of the Ninth Arch, &c.

The signs are now given in former degrees, and then in this degree, as hereafter explained.

The two kings kneel at a pedestal in the centre of the Chapter, and raise each other by interlacing the fingers of the left hand, which is the token in this degree. The brethren kneel and raise each other in the same manner.

Thrice Potent Master raps three times three, the other officers each rap the same, and the companions clap three times three with their hands.

Master—I declare this Chapter open.

If a candidate is to be admitted, he is prepared in an outer room in company with two of the brethren, three being necessary for the ceremonies. They first go to the door in company with several other brothers, when the Master of Ceremonies raps three times three on the door.

Stolkyn raps three times three from within, partly opens the door, and inquires—Who comes there?

Master—Several Intendants of the Building, Elected Knights, and Grand Master Architects, who solicit the honor of being admitted into the secret vault under the Sanctum Sanctorum.

Junior Grand Warden—You will wait awhile until our Thrice Potent Master is informed of your request, and his answer returned.

The Warden (Stolkyn) goes and informs the Master, who gives him the answer, which he takes to the door, raps three times three, partly opens it, and says—My brethren, your request cannot now be granted.

Candidate is now conducted back to the preparation room, when presently nine brothers present themselves, and bring word as follows—It is the Thrice Potent Master's request that Grand Master Architects Joabert, Stolkyn, and Gibulum attend at once in the audience chamber.

Candidate and two companions are now introduced into the Chapter and taken before the Thrice Potent Master.

Master—My brethren, you know that in digging for a foundation for the Temple, we found the ruins of an ancient edifice. Among the ruins, we have already discovered much treasure which has been deposited in the secret vault. Are you willing to make farther researches among the ancient ruins, and report to us your discoveries?

Master of Ceremonies—We are.

Master—Go, and may success attend your labors.

Candidate and his two companions are conducted into a side room, where search is made among certain rubbish, when a ring is discovered in the floor, and a trap hoisted. One of the three, representing Stolkyn, addresses the candidate.

Stolkyn—This is evidently an entrance to a secret cavern. Are you willing to descend?

Candidate—Yes.

Stolkyn and Joabert tie a rope round his body, leaving two ends upward, and let him down, cautioning him that if he desires to ascend, to pull on his right; and if he wishes to descend lower, to pull on his left. In this way the candidate is lowered and raised twice, because he can see nothing. The third time they give him a light in his hand, and he descends and discovers the triangular plate of Enoch, described in the history of this degree. At this moment one of the persons above drops down something on the light, which extinguishes it, and candidate pulls to be drawn up. After he is drawn up, Joabert goes down on a knotted rope, and brings up the plate, when they all return to the Lodge and present the plate to the Master.

Master of Ceremonies—Thrice Potent, we have obeyed your commands, and herewith present you with the fruits of our labors, and solicit the honor of being made acquainted with the inscription on this cubic stone [meaning the trap with the ring in it] and this golden triangle.

Master (raising his hands)—Gibulum ishtov! [Gibulum is a good man—the grand word in this degree.]

Senior Warden raises his hands and makes the same exclamation.

Master (examining the plate)—My brethren, your request cannot now be granted. God has bestowed upon you a particular favor, in permitting you to discover the most precious jewel of Masonry. The promise which God made to some of the ancient patriarchs, that in fulness of time his name should be discovered, is now accomplished. As a reward for your zeal, constancy, and fidelity, I shall now constitute you Knights of the Ninth Arch, and I promise you an explanation of the mysterious characters on the golden plate, when it is fixed in the place designed for it, and I will then confer on you the most sublime and mysterious degree of Perfection.

Master directs the candidate and his companions to be conducted to the southwest, and from thence to approach the altar by three times three steps, and there take the obligation in this degree. Master of Ceremonies instructs candidate, when the three approach the altar, and the following obligation is administered:—

I, John Smith, do promise and vow, in the most solemn manner, and in the presence of the most holy and puissant, and most terrible, just and merciful God, that I will double my assiduity, zeal and love for my fellow brethren who have taken this degree of K. A.

I promise further never to assist at the initiation of any brother into this degree, nor to give my consent that he be initiated, unless he shall regularly have received all the foregoing degrees in a just and regular Lodge, and unless he shows a charitable disposition for Masonry, and also obtains a permission from under the hands and seals of the officers of a just and regular Lodge, according to ancient laws.

I furthermore promise never to give to any number less than three, and those to be well examined, this degree, unless when authorized for that purpose by a particular patent, and with a view of constituting a Chapter of K. A. Masons —which I will never consent to be holden within twenty-five leagues of one already regularly constituted.

I further promise carefully to observe and pay due obedience to all the laws, rules and regulations, established and appointed by this K. A. Chapter, as also to keep inviolable the secrets communicated in it.

I furthermore promise that I will not debauch any females related to a brother, knowing them to be such.

All this I promise under the penalties of my former obligations, and in case of failure, that my body may be exposed to the beasts of the forest as a prey; so God maintain me in my present obligation.

Thrice Potent Master now instructs candidate in the sign, token and words of this degree, as follows:

Sign—Kneel on the left knee, the right hand turned and placed on the back, the left hand raised above the head, (palm upwards,) the body leaning forward. It alludes to the penalty.

Token—The brothers raise each other from the position given in the sign by interlacing the fingers of the left hand. The one raising says, Tob, Banai, Amalabec. The one being raised says, Gibulum ishtov.

There are nine pass-words, one for each arch, viz.: 1st, Jov; 2d. Jeho; 3d, Juha; 4th, Havah; 5th, Elgibbor; 6th, Adonai; 7th, Joken; 8th, Eloah; 9th, Elzeboath.

Grand Word—Gibulum ishtov—signifying, Gibulum is a good man.

Candidate is now invested with the regalia of this degree, and is directed to salute the Senior Warden as a Knight of the Ninth Arch, which he does.

The Chapter is closed with a lecture, recapitulating the initiation, and by the Thrice Potent reciting the history of the degree. He adds, that the great flood of Noah, which took place in the year of the world 1656, destroyed most of the superb monuments of antiquity, including the marble pillar of Enoch. But the pillar of brass was preserved, by means of which the great institution of Masonry has been handed down to us. By this means the wisest man who ever lived, King Solomon, was enabled to erect the magnificent Temple which bore his name. He began the building in the fourth year of his reign, having selected for the site of it the most beautiful and healthy spot in all Jerusalem, and by governing the Craft with diligence and wisdom, he was enabled to present to a wondering world so perfect an edifice that its equal was never known, nor is it probable ever will be, in all future time.

Master then raps seven, and inquires the duties of the several officers, which is answered by Senior Warden.

Master raps eight and inquires of Junior Warden—What is the hour?

Junior Warden—The setting of the sun, Thrice Potent.

Master—If it is sunset, it is time to close our labors.

Master (rapping three times three, and companions all rising)—Brother Junior Warden, you will please to give notice that I am about to close this Chapter by three times three. [Notice given.] The brethren will attend to giving the signs.

The signs are now given, first those of this degree, and then all the others, backward.

Master and all the officers rap three times three in succession, the brethren clap three times three with their hands, when the Master declares the Chapter duly closed.

DEGREE OF PERFECTION;

OR, GRAND ELECT, PERFECT, AND
SUBLIME MASON.

The Lodge in this degree represents a subterranean vault, hung with red curtains, and the walls painted the same color. A part of Enoch's Pillar, found among the ruins, with pedestal broken, is placed in the west. In the east is Solomon's Pillar of Beauty, the Burning Bush, and a transparent triangle representing the Golden Triangle of Enoch found in the Ninth Arch, with the Hebrew letters JOD-HE-VAU-HE inscribed thereon. When not at work, the Lodge is illuminated by the Burning Bush, and when at work by twenty-four lights, viz. : three in the north, five in the south, seven in the west, and nine in the east.

The furniture of the Lodge consists of Holy Bible, Square, Compasses and Triangle, Altar of Incense, Altar of Sacrifice, Table of Shew Bread, Brazen Laver, Ark of the Covenant, Tables of the Law, Golden Candlesticks, two Brazen Columns, Golden Urn of Oil, Golden Vase, filled with water, Golden Goblet of wine, Gold Ring and Trowel, Silver Hod of ointment, and the Cubical Stone. Before each of the officers is a white triangular table.

The assembly is called a Grand Lodge of Perfection. It must consist of only twenty-seven working members. If a greater number join the Lodge, and are present at any meeting, the excess of twenty-seven take no part in the proceedings, but remain as spectators, or honorary members.

There are ten officers, as follows :

Thrice Potent Grand Master, representing King Solomon, sits in the east, and wears, as an official jewel, a crowned compass, with blazing sun in its centre.

Deputy Grand Master, representing Hiram, King of Tyre, sits on the right of the Thrice Potent, and is to preside during his absence. He wears, as an official jewel, a crowned compass, with a moon in the centre.

Senior Grand Warden, representing Adoniram, son of Abda, sits in the west, and wears a golden trowel for his jewel.

Junior Grand Warden sits in the south, and wears a golden sword for his jewel.

Grand Knight of the Seals sits at the left of the Senior Grand Warden in the west, with an ivory key for a jewel : his duty is to take care of the archives of the Lodge.

Grand Treasurer sits in the north, wearing a golden key for a jewel : duty, to keep the funds of the Lodge.

Grand Secretary is stationed in the south, wearing for his jewel a golden pen : duty, to keep a record of the proceedings.

Grand Orator sits in the south, between the Junior Warden and Secretary : he wears a golden scroll : his duty is to make discourses in illustration of the Order, instruct new brethren, and explain the Ineffable Degrees.

Grand Master of Ceremonies sits in the north, between the Treasurer and Captain of the Guards : his jewel, a golden staff : his duty, to prepare and conduct candidates.

Grand Captain of the Guards, representing Zerubbabel, is stationed in the north, between Master of Ceremonies and Knight of the Seals : his jewel, a golden spear : his duty to see that the Guards are at their proper stations, and to provide for the accommodation of members and visiting brethren.

In addition to the above is the Grand Tyler, stationed at the door : jewel, a golden flaming sword : his duty is to guard the entrance to the secret vault.

Likewise, in some Lodges, the Hospitable Brother, stationed in the north : jewel, a winged rod : his duty is to visit the sick brethren, and take charge of the charity funds of the Lodge.

The officers wear collars of broad white watered silk ribbon, with white and red rosettes at the bottom, from which the jewel is suspended.

Each of the brethren wears a sword : a triangular black apron bordered with gold lace and lined with white, in the centre of which is a golden delta with the Hebrew characters JOD-HE-VAU-HE thereon : a collar of flame colored ribbon, with white and red rosette at the bottom, from which hangs golden compasses, crowned, the points extended to ninety degrees : between the points a medal, with sun, blazing star, &c., on it.

In opening the Lodge, Thrice Potent Master raps three, Grand Marshal rises.

Master—Are we all Perfect and Sublime Masons ?

Marshal—We are, Thrice Potent.

Master raps five, Junior Warden rises.

Master—Brother Junior Warden, what is the hour ?

Junior Warden—High twelve.

Master—What do you understand by high twelve ?

Junior Warden—That the sun has gained its meridian height, and darts its rays with greatest force on this Lodge.

Master—It is then time that we should profit by its light.

Master raps seven, Senior Warden rises.

Master—My venerable Brother Senior Warden, what brings you here ?

Senior Warden—Love of Masonry, my obligation, and a desire for perfection.

Master—How are you to conduct yourself in this place ?

Senior Warden—With the most profound respect.

Master—Why is it that men of all conditions assembled in this place, are called brethren, and are all equal ?

Senior Warden—Because the ineffable name puts us in mind that there is one being superior to us all.

Master—Why is respect paid to the triangle ?

Senior Warden—Because it contains the name of the Grand Architect of the Universe.

Master raps nine, the brethren all rise.

Master—Brother Senior Warden, you will give notice that I am about to open a Lodge of Perfect Grand Elect and Sublime Masons, by the mysterious number 3, 5, 7 and 9.

Senior Warden makes proclamation that a Lodge of Perfect and Sublime Masons is about to be opened, &c.

The signs of all former degrees, up to this one, are now given.

Master raps three, when all the brethren give the first sign in this degree, as hereafter explained.

The second and third signs are given in like manner.

Master raps three, five, seven and nine ; Senior Warden the same ; Junior Warden the same ; and then all the brethren clap their hands the same, and the Master declares the Lodge open.

The brethren seat themselves in a triangular form round the altar.

If a candidate is to be admitted, he first gains admittance to the door of the ante-chamber by the nine pass-words of a Knight of the Ninth Arch : here he gives three distinct knocks, which are answered by three from within by the Master of Ceremonies, who partly opens the door and asks—Who comes there ?

Candidate—A Knight of the Ninth Arch, who wishes to be admitted into the sacred vault.

Master of Ceremonies—Give the pass.

Candidate—Shibboleth.

Master of Ceremonies—The pass is right—you may enter here.

Candidate (conducted by Master of Ceremonies) goes to the second door of the ante-chamber and raps three, five and seven, which are answered by similar raps from within. The door is partly opened, the pass, Elhanon, is given, when he passes to the door of the Lodge, and raps three, five, seven and nine.

Junior Warden—Thrice Potent, there is an alarm at the door of the sacred vault.

Master—See who knocks there.

Junior Warden goes to the door and raps three, five, seven and nine, partly opens the door, and inquires—Who comes there ?

Candidate—A Knight of the Ninth Arch, who is desirous of being admitted into the sacred vault and arriving at perfection.

Junior Warden—Give me the pass.

Candidate—Adonai.

Junior Warden—The pass is right : you will wait until our Thrice Potent Master is informed of your request, and his answer returned.

Junior Warden shuts the door, and goes and informs the Master of what has occurred.

Master—Let the Knight be introduced in ancient form.

Junior Warden opens the door, when the Master of Ceremonies conducts candidate to the west end of the Lodge, between the Wardens, and he makes the sign of admiration, as on page 135.

Master to candidate—My brother, what is your desire ?

Candidate—To be made a Grand Elect, Perfect and Sublime Mason.

Master—Before I can initiate you, you must satisfy us that you are well skilled in Masonry, otherwise you must be sent back until you are better qualified. Are you a Mason ?

Candidate—My brethren all know me as such.

Master—Give me the sign, token, and word.

Candidate gives those of Entered Apprentice, as on pages 7 and 11.

Master—Are you a Fellow Craft ?

Candidate—I have seen the letter G, and know the pass.

Master—Give me the sign, token and words.

Candidate gives signs, &c., of the Fellow Craft degree.

Master—Are you a Master Mason?

Candidate—I have seen the sprig of cassia, and know what it means. [Gives signs, &c., of the Master Mason's degree.]

Master—Are you a Secret Master?

Candidate—I have passed from the square to the compasses opened to seven degrees. [Gives the signs, &c., of a Secret Master.

Master—Are you a Perfect Master?

Candidate—I have seen the tomb of our respectable Master, Hiram Abiff, and have, in company with my brethren, shed tears at the same. [Gives sign, &c., of a Perfect Master.]

Master—Are you an Intimate Secretary?

Candidate—My curiosity is satisfied, but it nearly cost me my life. [Gives the signs, &c., of an Intimate Secretary.]

Master—Are you a Provost and Judge?

Candidate—I am, and render justice to all men, without distinction. [Gives the signs, &c., of a Provost and Judge.]

Master—Are you an Intendant of the Building?

Candidate—I have made the five steps of exactness, I penetrated the inmost part of the Temple, and have seen the great light in which was three mysterious characters, J. J. J. [Gives signs, &c., of an Intendant of the Building]

Master—Are you an Elected Knight?

Candidate—One cavern received me, one lamp gave me light, and one fountain refreshed me. [Gives signs, &c., of an Elected Knight.]

Master—Are you a Master Elect of Fifteen?

Candidate—My zeal and works have procured me that honor. [Gives signs, &c , of a Master Elect of Fifteen]

Master—Are you an Illustrious Knight?

Candidate—My name will inform you. [Gives signs, &c., of Illustrious Knight.]

Master—Are you a Grand Master Architect?

Candidate—I know the use of the mathematical instruments. [Gives the signs, &c., of that degree.]

Master—Are you a Knight of the Ninth Arch?

Candidate—I have penetrated the bowels of the earth through Nine Arches, have seen the brilliant triangle. [Gives signs. &c., of the Ninth Arch degree.]

Master—My brethren, I have carefully examined this Knight in the various degrees of Masonry, and find him perfect; do you consent that he shall be exalted to the sublime and mysterious degree of Perfection? If any brother present objects, let him state his objection.

A Brother (rising)—Thrice Potent, I have objections to him, which I will communicate, if the candidate retires.

Master orders candidate to retire into the ante-chamber, and he leaves the room with the Master of Ceremonies.

Presently the door of the Lodge is opened, and candidate is conducted back, and placed in the west.

Master to candidate—Before you can be exalted to this sublime degree, I must ask you certain questions relative to your past life, and I trust you will answer them sincerely and satisfactorily.

Master then asks candidate the following questions, which he answers in detail:—1st. Have you never wilfully revealed any of the Secrets of Masonry? 2d. Have you always been charitable towards your brethren? 3d. Have you never defrauded a brother? 4th. Are you in the habit of using the name of God profanely? 5th. Does your conscience accuse you of having committed any offence against your brethren, which ought to debar you from receiving this degree?

All these questions having been answered in the negative, the Master says—Brethren, do you consent that this candidate be admitted among us? If so, please to raise your right hands.

The brethren all raise their right hands.

Master—We accept you, my brother, as a Perfect and Sublime Mason. You will approach the altar and take the obligation.

Candidate (instructed by Master of Ceremonies) approaches the altar by three, five, seven and nine steps, and kneels on his left knee, when the Master administers the obligation—1st. Secrecy. 2d. To conceal the laws and regulations of this degree. 3d. To assist brethren in sickness with his counsel, purse, and arms. 4th. Not to assist in making a brother of this degree, unless he shall be of good moral character, and who has been an officer of some regular Lodge, and to receive him by virtue of a power granted by proper authority. 5th. To endeavor, on all occasions, to observe strictly duties to God and the community. 6th. That he will not be concerned in conferring this degree upon any Mason whose character and knowledge he disapproves, nor unless he has been elected and installed as an officer in some regular Lodge, Chapter, Encampment, or Council. 7th. That he will never fully pronounce, more than once in his life, the mysterious word of this degree. The penalty is to have the body cut open, and the bowels torn out and given to the vultures for food.

After administering the obligation, the Master makes a prayer, as in the text-book.

Master of Ceremonies now presents the Thrice Potent Master with a trowel, and a hod of ointment.

Master to candidate—My brother, I shall now proceed to anoint you with the holy oil wherewith Aaron, David, and the wise Solomon were anointed.

Master touches candidate with the trowel, on the head, the lips, and the heart, saying at the same time : Behold how good and how pleasant it is for brethren to dwell together in unity, &c.

Master then offers candidate bread and wine, and raises him from his kneeling posture : the brethren all take wine, &c.

Master now instructs candidate in the signs, tokens and pass-words of this degree, as follows :

First sign—Same as the due-guard of a Master Mason. [Page 30.]

Second sign—Bring your right hand to your left cheek, extending it as though to guard that side of the face ; your left is to support the right elbow ; apply the left hand in the same manner to the right cheek, supporting the left elbow with the right hand. It is pretended that Moses placed himself in these attitudes when he saw the burning bush.

Third sign—Give the sign of admiration, [page 135,] and then place three fingers of the right hand on the lips.

First token—Same as that of the Entered Apprentice. [Page 7.]

Second token—Same as the Master's grip. [Page 36.] Having given it, say, " Can you go farther ?" he will slip his hand above your wrist, to the middle of the arm, and so to the elbow ; he then puts his left hand to your shoulder, and presses thrice.

Third token—Seize each other's elbows with the left hand, and put the right hand on each other's neck, as if in the act of raising one up

First pass-word—SHIBBOLETH, repeated thrice.

Second pass-word—HELENIHAM.

Third pass-word — MAHAK-MAKAR-A-BAK. This is translated, God be praised, we have finished it.

First covered word—GIBULUM.

Second covered word—MAHABIN.

Third covered word—ADONAI.

Grand word—JEHOVAH. This word is given by repeating alternately, the names of the Hebrew letters used in the word Jehovah—JOD-HE-VAU-HE.

Master to candidate—You will now pronounce to me the mysterious word.

Candidate—I cannot but once in life.

Master—How will you then give it ?

Candidate—JOD-HE-VAU-HE. [Hebrew Jehovah.]

Master—I will now give you the true pronunciation of the name of the Deity, as revealed to Enoch, and he engraved the letters composing it on a triangular plate of gold, which was hidden for many ages in the bowels of the earth, and lost to mankind. The mysterious words which you received in the preceding degrees, are all so many corruptions of the true name (of God) which was engraved on the triangle of Enoch. In this engraving, the vowel points are so arranged as to give the pronunciation thus—YOW-HO. This word, when thus pronounced, is called the ineffable word, which cannot be altered as other words are, and the degrees which you have received, are called, on this account, Ineffable Degrees. This word you will recollect was not found until after the death of Hiram Abiff, consequently the word engraved by him on the ark, is not the true name of God.

Most Potent Master instructs candidate with the secret characters, and then invests him with the jewel, apron, &c., saying—I now salute you as a Grand Elect, Perfect and Sublime Mason, &c., [reading the charge from a text-book.]

In closing the Lodge, Thrice Potent Master raps three, when Grand Marshal rises, and Master inquires the duties of the various officers.

Master raps five, and says to Junior Warden—What is the hour ?

Junior Warden—It is midnight.

Master—If it is midnight, it is time to close our labors. [Raps seven, and Senior Warden rises.]

Master—Brother Senior Warden, how should Perfect and Sublime Masters part?

Senior Warden—They should part in peace, love and unity.

Master raps nine, when all the brethren rise, and the signs are given, beginning with those of this degree, and going backward through the other degrees.

All the officers rap three, five, seven and nine, and the brethren clap the same with their hands, when the Thrice Potent Master declares the Lodge duly closed.

Historical and Philosophical
DEGREES.

PRINCE OF JERUSALEM.

This degree is historical, and is founded on the rebuilding of the Temple, after the encouragement given by Darius, King of Persia, to Zerubbabel, a Prince of Judah, who journeyed to Babylon, as described in the degree of Knights of the Red Cross. Those who accompanied Zerubbabel on that journey were styled Knights of the East.

After the work of rebuilding had been commenced, Zerubbabel was much annoyed by the Samaritans, and finally forced to abandon the enterprise. He thereupon sent an embassy to Darius, the successor of Cyrus, who issued a decree prohibiting all persons, on pain of death, from interfering with the work, and the Temple was then completed.

Princes of Jerusalem have a right to inspect all Lodges or Councils of an inferior degree, and can revoke and annul all the work done in such Councils or Lodges, if the same shall be inconsistent with the regulations of Masonry. They must lead irreproachable lives, and if guilty of unmasonic conduct, they are punished at the discretion of the Grand Council.

The meeting is termed a Convention, or Grand Council. There are two apartments, one in the west, and the other in the east; and they should be connected by a hall. The one in the west represents the Court of Zerubbabel, at Jerusalem. It is hung with yellow drapery. The eastern apartment represents the Cabinet of Darius.

Most Equitable Sovereign Grand Master, representing Zerubbabel, sits on a throne in the western apartment, and wears a yellow robe and turban, and a red apron with yellow flap: on the apron is a picture of the Temple, a square, a buckler, a triangle and a hand: on the flap is a balance, and the letters D. Z. [Darius and Zerubbabel.] The jewel is a golden medal—on one side a hand holding a balance; on the other a two-edged sword with five stars around the edges and point, and the letters D. Z. above.

The other officers are clothed in yellow robes and caps, wear red gloves, and each carries a sword. They are—

Most Enlightened Senior and Junior Grand Wardens.

Valiant Grand Treasurer.

Valiant Grand Master of Ceremonies.

Valiant Grand Marshal.

Valiant Grand Tyler.

The brethren are Valiant Princes, and it takes five to open a Convention.

In opening, Master raps one, and says—Valiant Grand Master of Ceremonies, what is the first business of a Grand Council of Princes of Jerusalem?

Master of Ceremonies—To see that the Guards are at their proper stations.

Master—Attend to that duty, and in form the Guards that we are about to open a Council of Princes of Jerusalem.

Master of Ceremonies goes and stations the Guards, returns, and says—The Guards are set, Most Equitable.

Master (raps two, and Junior Warden rises)—Enlightened Junior Warden, what is our next business?

Junior Warden—To see that all present are Princes of Jerusalem.

Master—Attend to that duty.

Junior Warden (scrutinizing the brethren)—We are all Princes of Jerusalem, Most Equitable.

Master (raps three)—Most Enlightened Senior Warden, what is the hour?

Senior Warden—The rising of the sun.

Master—What remains to be done?

Senior Warden—Arrange the Princes in two columns, for the proper discharge of their duties.

Master—Attend to that duty.

The brethren now form in columns across the room from west to east—the Senior Warden on the left of the right column, and the Junior Warden on the right of the left column.

Master—Enlightened Senior and Junior Wardens, inform your respective columns that I am about to open this Convention of Princes of Jerusalem by three and two.

Senior and Junior Wardens repeat the orders of the Master.

Master—Attention, Valiant Princes, we will give the signs.

The signs are now given in other degrees, and then in this degree, see p. 158.

Master raps three and two, which is repeated by the two Wardens, when the Master declares the Grand Council duly opened and in order for business.

If a candidate is to be admitted to this degree, he is prepared outside by the Master of Ceremonies, hoodwinked, and led to the door of the Council chamber, where an alarm is given by rapping three and one.

The door is opened without ceremony, and the candidate is led to the east in front of the Master.

Master—What is your desire?

Candidate (instructed)—I come in behalf of the people of Israel to complain of the Samaritans, who refuse to pay the tribute imposed upon them for defraying the expense of the sacrifices offered to God in the Temple.

Master—I have no power over the Samaritans: they are subject to King Darius, who is at Babylon; it is to him that such complaints must be preferred; but as we are all interested in this thing, I will arm you, and cause you to be accompanied by four Knights, that you may more easily surmount any difficulty which may present itself in your journey to the Court of the King of Persia.

The bandage is now removed from the eyes of the candidate; he is armed with a sword and buckler, and decorated as a Knight of the East. The four Knights who accompany him are armed in a similar manner. They commence their journey, and are attacked by some armed ruffians, whom they repulse. They arrive at the door of the Cabinet of Darius. Meantime one of the Wardens has seated himself in the eastern apartment to personate Darius, and in front sits a brother as Minister of State. Candidate and the four Knights enter.

Candidate—Mighty King! the Samaritans refuse to pay the tribute imposed on them by Cyrus, King of Persia, for defraying the expenses of the sacrifices which are offered in the Temple which we are rebuilding: the people of Israel entreat that you will compel the Samaritans to perform their duty.

Darius—Your request is just and equitable; I order that the Samaritans shall immediately pay the tribute imposed on them. My Chief Minister shall deliver to you my decree for this purpose. Go in peace!

Candidate retires, and Minister of State follows, and delivers the decree to him.

In returning to the western apartment, candidate and his Knights protectors are again obstructed by lurking ruffians, but they fight their way until they are met by brothers with lighted torches, who conduct them safely to the presence of the Master.

Candidate (handing the decree)—I deliver to you the decree of Darius, King of Persia, which we have obtained after defeating our enemies, and encountering many dangers in our journey.

Master reads the decree, as follows:

We, Darius, King, &c., willing to favor and protect our people at Jerusalem, after the example of our illustrious predecessor, King Cyrus, do will and ordain, that the Samaritans, against whom complaints have been made, shall punctually pay the tribute money which they owe for the sacrifices of the Temple—otherwise they shall receive the punishment due to their disobedience. Given at Shushan, the palace, this 4th day of the 2d month, in the year 3534, and of our reign the third, under the seal of our faithful Darius. SANDRAM, Minister of State.

Master—The people of Jerusalem are under great obligations to you for the zeal and courage you have displayed in prosecuting so difficult a journey, and for the success which has attended your mission. As a reward for the service, we propose to confer upon you the mysteries of the degree of Prince of Jerusalem. Are you willing to take the obligation, which binds you to an exact observance of our laws, and a careful concealment of those mysteries?

Candidate—I am willing.

Master—You will then kneel before the altar for that purpose.

Candidate kneels, when the Master comes forward and administers the following obligation:

I, John Smith, do solemnly promise and swear, in the presence of Almighty God, the Great Architect of heaven and earth, and of these Valiant Princes of Jerusalem, that I will never reveal the mysteries of the degree of Prince of Jerusalem to any one of an inferior degree, or to any other person whatever. I promise and swear, as a Prince of Jerusalem, to do justice to my brethren, and not to rule them tyrannically, but in love. I promise and swear that I will never, by word or deed, attack the honor of any Prince of Jerusalem; and that I will not assist in conferring this degree except in a lawful Grand Council of Princes of Jerusalem. All this I promise and swear, under the penalty of being stripped naked, and having my heart pierced with a poinard. So help me God. Amen! amen! amen!

Master raises candidate, and then instructs him in the signs, tokens and words of this degree, as follows:

First Sign—Extend the right arm horizontally at the height of the shoulder. This is termed the sign of command.

First Token—Each places his left hand on his left hip, and the right hand on his brother's left shoulder.

Second Token—Join left hands, placing the thumb on the second joint of the little finger ; with the thumb strike five times on that joint.

Pass-word—TEBETH. The name of the Jewish month in which the Ambassadors entered Jerusalem.

Sacred Word—ADAR. The name of the month in which thanks were given to God for the completion of the Temple.

In some Councils the following sign is given, viz. : Present yourself before your brother with your sword advanced, and your left hand resting on your hip, as if to commence a combat. He will answer the sign by extending his arm at the height of the shoulder, the right foot forming a square with the toe of the left.

The March—Five steps on the diagonal of the square towards the throne.

Age—The age of a Prince of Jerusalem is 5 times 15.

Master to candidate—I now appoint and constitute you, with your four companions, Princes and Governors of Jerusalem, that you may render justice to all the people. I decorate you with a yellow sash, to which is attached a gold medal. The Balance on it is to admonish you to make equity and justice your guides. The Hand of Justice is a mark of your authority over the people. The Emblems of the Apron with which I now invest you, have reference to the works and virtues of Masons, and to your duty in the high office with which you are invested. As Princes of Jerusalem, you will assemble in two chambers of the Temple. Be just, merciful. and wise.

The Lecture is now given, and is a repetition of the initiation, the Master asking Senior Warden all the circumstances of his journey to Babylon, and interview with Darius, and the Warden answering the questions. It closes as follows :

Master—How are Princes of Jerusalem clothed?

Senior Warden—In cloth of gold.

Master—What are their decorations ?

Senior Warden—A yellow sash trimmed with gold from right to left ; to which was attached a golden medal, on which was engraved a balance, a sword, five stars, and the letters D. Z.

Master—What is signified by the five stars on the sash ?

Senior Warden—They are emblematic of the five Knights who journeyed from Jerusalem to Babylon.

Master—What is the age of a Prince of Jerusalem ?

Senior Warden—Five times fifteen.

In closing the Council the Master raps five, and says—Most Enlightened Junior and Senior Wardens, please to announce to your respective columns that I am about to close this Grand Council by five times fifteen.

Senior Warden (raps five)—Attention, Valiant Princes : it is the will of our Most Equitable Sovereign Grand Master that this Grand Council be now closed.

Junior Warden raps five and repeats the same order.

Master (rising)—Attention, Valiant Princes, we will now give the signs.

The signs are given backward.

Master raps five times fifteen, which is repeated by the two Wardens.

Master—Be just, merciful and wise ! I declare this Grand Council duly closed.

KNIGHTS OF THE EAST AND WEST.

This degree originated in Palestine, and was brought to the west by the Knights, eleven of whom made their vows of secrecy, friendship and discretion before a patriarch and Prince of Jerusalem. The meeting is called a Council.

The Council Chamber is hung with red drapery, sprinkled with gold stars. In the east is a throne, or canopy, elevated by seven steps, supported by four lions, four eagles, and between them an angel, or seraphim, with six wings : on one side is a transparency of the sun, and on the other side, one of the moon : below is a rainbow, and in front a basin of perfumed water and a skull and cross bones. Six elevated canopies of three steps each are placed in the north, and six in the south. Eleven of these are occupied by the eleven Venerable Ancients, and the twelfth, at the right of the Master, is left vacant. At the west are two canopies of five steps each for the Venerable Wardens.

A pedestal stands in front of the throne, on which lays a large Bible, with seven seals suspended therefrom.

Most Puissant Venerable Master sits on the throne in the east.

Grand Senior and Grand Junior Wardens sit on the two canopies in the west.

Twenty-four Knights (including officers) comprise the Council, and (excepting the Venerable Ancients seated on canopies) are called Respectable Ancients. If there are any more brethren present, they are called Respectable Knights; and must stand behind the Venerable Ancients.

All the brethren are clothed in white, with a zone of gold round the waist, long white beards, and golden crowns on their heads. The Knights, in their ordinary habits, wear a broad white ribbon from the right shoulder to the left hip, with the jewel suspended thereto. They also wear a cross of the Order, suspended by a black ribbon, round their necks.

There is a carpet on the floor called a draft—a heptagon in a circle—over the angles of which the letters B D S P H F: in the centre, a man clothed in a white robe, with a girdle of gold round his waist—his right hand extended, and surrounded with seven stars—he has a long white beard, his head surrounded with a glory, and a two-edged sword in his mouth—with seven candlesticks round him, and over them the following letters: H D P I P R C.

The Jewel is an heptagon of silver—at each angle a star of gold with one of the letters B D S P H G S thereon: in the centre a lamb on a book with seven seals. On reverse, same letters in the angles, and in the centre a two-edged sword between a balance.

The Apron is white, lined with red, bordered with yellow, or gold; on the flap is painted a two-edged sword, surrounded with the seven holy letters—or the apron may have the plan of the draft painted on it.

In opening the Council the Master lays his right hand on the Bible with seven seals.

Master—Venerable Knights Princes, what is your duty?

Senior Warden—To know if we are secure.

Master—See that we are so.

Senior Warden (goes to the door and returns)—Most Puissant, we are in perfect security.

Master (rapping seven)—Respectable Knights Princes, our Grand Council is now open, and I claim your attention to the business thereof.

Senior Warden—We promise obedience to all the commands of our Most Puissant Venerable Master.

The Knights all rise and salute the Master, when he returns the compliment, and requests them to be seated.

If a candidate is to be admitted, he is prepared by the Master of Ceremonies in an ante-chamber hung with red, and lighted with seven lights. He is clothed in a white robe, and is led, barefoot, to the door of the Council Chamber, where he gives seven raps.

Master (rapping seven)—The youngest Knight present will go to the door and demand who knocks.

A Knight steps forward, knocks seven times on the door, and asks—Who comes there?

Master of Ceremonies—It is a valiant brother and Most Excellent Prince of Jerusalem, who requests to be admitted to the Venerable and Most Puissant.

The Knight reports to the Master, who says—Let him be introduced.

Senior Warden goes and opens the door, and taking candidate by the hand, says—Come, my dear brother, I will show you mysteries worthy of contemplation. Give me the sign, token, and word of a Prince of Jerusalem.

Candidate gives sign, &c., [page 158,] and is then directed to kneel a short distance off in front of the Most Puissant Master, which he does.

Senior Warden—Brother, you no doubt have always borne in memory the obligations of your former degrees, and that you have, as far as in the power of human nature, lived agreeably to them?

Candidate—I have ever made it my study, and, I trust, my actions and life will prove it.

Senior Warden—Have you particularly regarded your obligations as a Sublime Knight of Perfection, Knight of the East, and Prince of Jerusalem? Do you recollect having injured a brother in any respect whatsoever? or have you seen or known of his being injured by others, without giving him timely notice, as far as was in your power? I pray you answer me with candor.

Candidate—I have in all respects done my duty, and acted with integrity to the best of my abilities.

Master—You will be pleased to recollect, my brother, that the questions which have now been put to you, are absolutely necessary for us to demand, in order that the purity of our Most Respectable Council may not be sullied; and it behooves you to be particular in your recollection, as the indispensable ties which we are going to lay you under, will, in case of your default, only increase your sins, and serve to hurl you sooner to destruction, should you have deviated from your duty: answer me, my dear brother.

Candidate—I never have.

Master—We are happy, my brother, that your declaration coincides with our opinion, and we are rejoiced to have it in our power to introduce you into our society. Increase our joy by complying with our rules, and declare if you are willing to be united to us by taking a most solemn obligation.

Candidate—I ardently wish to receive it, and to have the honor of being united to so respectable and virtuous a society.

Master orders the basin of perfumed water and a clean napkin to be brought to him, and directs candidate to wash his hands, which he does.

Master reads the first six verses of Psalm xxiv.

Candidate is raised and brought close to the foot of the throne, where he kneels on both knees, and placing his right hand on the Bible, his left hand between the hands of the Most Puissant Master, he takes the following obligation:

I, John Smith, do promise and solemnly swear and declare, in the awful presence of the only One Most Holy Puissant Almighty and Most Merciful Grand Architect of Heaven and Earth—who created the universe and myself through his infinite goodness, and conducts it with wisdom and justice—and in the presence of the Most Excellent and upright Princes and Knights of the East and West here present in convocation and council, on my sacred word of honor and under every tie, both moral and religious, that I will never reveal to any person whomsoever below me, or to whom the same may not belong, by being legally and lawfully initiated, the secrets of this degree which is now about to be communicated to me, under the penalty of not only being dishonored, but to consider my life as the immediate forfeiture, and that to be taken from me with all the tortures and pains to be inflicted in manner as I have consented to in my preceding degrees.

I further promise and solemnly swear, that I never will fight or combat with my brother Knights, but will, at all times, when he has justice on his side, be ready to draw my sword in his defence, or against such of his enemies who seek the destruction of his person, his honor, peace, or prosperity; that I never will revile a brother, or suffer others to reflect on his character in his absence, without informing him thereof, or noticing it myself, at my option; that I will remember, on all occasions, to observe my former obligations, and be just, upright, and benevolent to all my fellow creatures, as far as in my power.

I further solemnly promise and swear, that I will pay due obedience and submission to all the degrees of Masonry; and that I will do all in my power to support them in all justifiable measures for the good of the Craft, and advantage thereof, agreeably to the Grand Constitutions.

All this I solemnly swear and sincerely promise, upon my sacred word of honor, under the penalty of the severe wrath of the Almighty Creator of heaven and earth; and may He have mercy on my soul, on the great and awful day of judgment, agreeably to my conformity thereto. Amen. Amen. Amen.

Master takes a box of perfumed ointment and anoints candidate on his head, eyes, mouth, heart, the tip of his right ear, hand, and foot, and says—You are now, my dear brother, received a member of our society; you will recollect to live up to the precepts of it, and also remember that those parts of your body, which have the greatest power of assisting you in good or evil, have this day been made holy!

Candidate rises and is conducted to the west, where he is placed between the two Wardens, the draft, or carpet, lying before him.

Senior Warden—Brother, you will examine closely everything which our Most Puissant Venerable Master is about to show you.

Senior Warden (addressing the Council)—Is there a mortal here worthy to open the book with the seven seals?

The brethren all cast down their eyes and sigh.

Senior Warden—Venerable and respectable brethren, be not afflicted; here is a victim (pointing to candidate) whose courage will give you content.

Senior Warden to candidate—Do you know why our Ancients have long white beards?

Candidate—I do not know, but you do.

Senior Warden—They are those who came here, after passing through great tribulation, and having washed their robes in their own blood: will you purchase such robes at so great a price?

Candidate—Yes, I am willing.

The two Wardens conduct candidate up in front of the basin, bare both his arms, and each ties a string around one, as in the operation of blood-letting: then each Warden takes out a lancet and pierces the arm just deep enough to draw a drop of blood, which is wiped off on a napkin and shown to the brethren.

Senior Warden—See, my brethren, a man who has spilled his blood to acquire a knowledge of our mysteries, and shrunk not from the trial.

Master now opens the first seal of the great book, and takes from thence a bone quiver, filled with arrows, and a crown, gives them to one of the Ancients, and says—Depart, and continue the conquest.

He opens the second seal, and takes out a sword, and gives it to the next Ancient, and says—Go, and destroy peace among the profane and wicked brethren, that they may not appear in our Council.

He opens the third seal, and takes a balance, and gives it to the next Ancient, and says—Dispense rigid justice to the profane and wicked brethren.

He opens the fourth seal, and takes out a skull, and gives it to the next Ancient, and says—Go, and endeavor to convince the wicked that death is the reward of their guilt.

He opens the fifth seal, and takes out a cloth, stained with blood, and gives it to the next Ancient, and says—When is the time (or, the time will arrive,) that we shall revenge and punish the profane and wicked, who have destroyed so many of their brethren by false accusations.

He opens the sixth seal, and at that moment the sun is darkened and the moon stained with blood!

He opens the seventh seal, and takes out incense, which he gives to a brother; and also a vase, with seven trumpets, and gives one to each of seven of the Venerable Ancients.

The four remaining Venerable Ancients, in the four corners, whisk about inflated bladders of wind (the four winds.)

Master—Here is seen the fulfilment of a prophecy (Revelations vii. 3.) Strike not, nor punish the profane and wicked of our Order, until I have selected the true and worthy Masons!

The four winds are again agitated, and one of the Venerable Ancients with a trumpet blows a blast.

The two Wardens seize candidate's arms and take from him his apron and jewel of the previous degree.

The winds again move, and a second trumpet sounds, when the Junior Warden gives candidate the apron and jewel of this degree.

Agitation of the winds, and a third trumpet sounds, when the Senior Warden gives candidate a long white beard.

Bladders of wind whisked, and fourth trumpet sounds, when Junior Warden gives candidate a crown of gold.

Winds move, and fifth trumpet sounds, when Senior Warden gives candidate a girdle of gold.

Winds are agitated, when sixth trumpet sounds, and Junior Warden gives candidate the signs, tokens and words of this degree, as follows:

Sign—Look at your right shoulder; it will be answered by looking at the left shoulder. One says, ABADDON, the other, JUBULUM.

First token—Place your left hand in the right hand of your brother, who will cover it with his left; both at the same time look over their right shoulders.

Second token—Touch your brother's left shoulder with your left hand; he replies by touching your right shoulder with his right hand.

Sign for entering the Lodge—Place your right hand on the brother's forehead, (i. e. the Tyler's,) he will do the same.

Pass-word—JUBULUM, or according to some, PERIGNAN and GADAON.

Sacred word—ABADDON.

The winds now fly about very brisk, when the seventh trumpet sounds, and then all the trumpets sound together, when the Senior Warden conducts candidate to the vacant raised canopy on the right of the Master. [This last demonstration is intended to represent the end of the world, when all true Masons are to receive their reward by being conducted to a throne at the right hand of the Deity, having first been purified by washing their robes in their own blood.]

This ends the initiation, and a lecture is then given which explains the why and wherefore of the peculiar ceremonies in this degree—showing them all to be to the credit and glorification of Masonry. It is not particularly interesting.

In closing, the Master raps seven and says to Warden—What is the time?

Senior Warden—Time is no more!

Master (raps seven times)—Venerable Knights and Princes, as time is now no more, I declare this Council closed.

11

SOVEREIGN PRINCE

OF

ROSE-CROIX DE HARODIM,

AND

KNIGHT OF THE EAGLE AND

PELICAN.

This Order is called Rose-Croix from the rose on the cross of the Jewel being emblematical of the Son of God, who is compared to a rose by the evangelist. Harodim, because the first Chapter of the degree was held on a mountain of that name. Knight of the Eagle, because of the eagle on the jewel; and of the Pelican, which is emblematical of Christ, who shed his blood for mankind.

Three apartments are necessary for a Chapter in this degree. The first one represents Mount Calvary, and is hung with black: it is lighted by three candle-bras, each having eleven branches, and each branch holding a yellow wax candle—thirty-three lights in all. The candlebras are placed on three columns, or pillars, six feet high, in the west end of the room: on one is the word FAITH, on the second HOPE, and on the third CHARITY—the inscriptions being in letters of gold. At the east end is a hill, or bank, raised to represent Calvary; on it are three crosses, and on each cross is a skull and cross-bones. In front of this bank stands the altar, covered with black cloth: on it a cross, and two lighted candles of yellow wax: behind it a black curtain, extending to the ceiling, to intercept the view of the Mount. The Master's seat is on the step of the altar, as hereafter shown.

The second apartment should contain a transparency of Christ ascending to Heaven: over it a transparent triangle surrounded with rays. The Altar stands in front of the transparency, and is lighted by the transparency, as no naked lights are permitted in the room. Behind the transparencies should be an organ, or some solemn music.

The third apartment represents HELL. This is shown by transparencies of monsters and human beings suffering the torments of the damned, with devils stirring them up with pitchforks, &c., and flames encircling them. On each side of the entrance, human skeletons representing death, with arrows in their hands. The apartments are connected by one door.

The Knights are clothed in black, and wear swords. They have on over their clothes a white chasuble (similar to those worn by Catholic priests at mass) bordered with black, and on it a red cross two inches wide, and reaching from top to bottom.

The Master wears a brilliant star of seven points over his heart: it has a circle in its centre with the letter J on it, and around the edge the words Faith, Hope, Charity. The Senior Warden wears a triangle, and the Junior Warden wears the square and compasses.

The Aprons are white, lined and bordered with black: on the flap are three red roses placed triangularly, and a human skull and cross-bones: at the bottom, a globe surrounded by a serpent: on the pocket lid, the letter J. The brethren in the second chamber have their aprons lined and bordered with red: triple triangles and three squares within three circles, in each circle the letter J, on the flap: on one side compasses standing upright on a triangle, on the other the same standing on a square within a circle.

The jewel is a golden cross, suspended by a scarf of black ribbon, a black and a red rose just above it on the scarf: on the breast, a small cross of red ribbon.

Most Wise and Perfect Master is seated on a step of the altar in the principal apartment, having before him a small table, on which is a lighted yellow wax candle, a Bible, square and compasses, and a triangle. There are no chairs at all in the place, the brethren seating themselves on the floor.

Most Excellent and Perfect Senior Warden in the north, Junior Warden in the south, and Secretary, Treasurer, and Captain of the Guards, (all styled Most Excellent and Perfect,) comprise the remaining officers.

The brethren are styled Most Respectable and Perfect Knights.

In opening, the Master says—My Perfect Brothers, Knights Princes Masons, please to assist me to open this Chapter.

The two Wardens repeat this.

Master raps three and four, and the two Wardens rap the same.

Master—Most Excellent and Perfect Wardens, what is our care?

Senior Warden—To ascertain whether the Chapter is well covered, and if all the brethren present are true Knights.

Master—Convince yourselves, my perfect brethren, one from the south and one from the north.

The two Wardens examine all the brethren present in the sign, word and token of this degree, and report to the Master that all present are true Knights of Rose-Croix, and of the Eagle.

Master to Warden—What is the hour?

Senior Warden—It is the moment that the veil of the Temple was rent; when darkness and consternation covered the earth; when the stars disappeared, and the lamp of day was darkened; when the implements of Masonry were lost, and the cubic stone sweated blood and water; that was the moment when the great Masonic word was lost.

Master—Since Masonry has sustained so great a loss, let us endeavor, by new works. to recover the lost word, for which purpose we will open this Chapter of Rose-Croix.

Senior Warden—Brethren, the Sovereign Chapter of Rose-Croix is open; let us do our duty.

Junior Warden repeats the same, and the Knights kneel on their right knee at the altar and repeat the words, "Let us do our duty," seven times, making a pause before the seventh.

This ends the opening. and the business of the Chapter proceeds. If a candidate is to be admitted, he is obliged first to obtain permission to become a candidate, in the following manner: He presents his certificate that he is in good standing as a Prince of Jerusalem and a Knight of the East and West, and at the same time a written petition for admission to this degree. The certificate and petition he must bring personally to the door of the Chapter, and kneel there while they are read. He must then sign the petition, and remain on his knees until an answer to it is thrown out of the 'loor, when he rises and reads it. In the answer he will find a day appointed to receive him, and the name of the Knight who is to give him necessary instruction.

The Knight who is named in the answer, directs the candidate to procure three pairs of gloves, (one pair of which must be women's,) and two sticks of fine sealing wax for the seals. 2d. He is ordered to present to each of the brethren, one pair of men's, and one pair of women's gloves, and two sticks of sealing wax. 3d. He must make a donation of at least — dollars to the Superior Lodge, Chapter, or Council of the Sublime Degrees, which must be done before he is received, and may be appropriated either to defray the expenses of the Order, or be given to the poor. He must also present to the Chapter three white wax candles for the Master, and two to each of the Knights, at his reception, previous to his entering into the third apartment. 4th. He must solemnly engage on his honor, never to reveal the place where he was received, who received

him, nor those who were present at his reception. 5th. He solemnly promises to conform to all the ordinances of the Chapter, and keep himself uniformly clothed as far as he is able. 6th. He must promise to acknowledge his Master at all times and in all places; never to confer this degree without permission, and to answer for the probity and respectability of those whom he proposes. 7th. That he will be extremely cautious in granting this degree, that it may not be multiplied unnecessarily. If the candidate promises to perform these requisitions he may be admitted.

After these conditions are complied with, the Chapter is usually ready to receive him.

Master to Senior Warden—What is the cause of our assembling here?

Senior Warden—The propagation of the Order, and the perfection of a Knight of the East and West, who demands to be received among us.

Candidate is now balloted for, and if no black ball appears, he is at once placed in the Chamber of Reflection. This is an apartment painted black, a small table in the centre, on which is a Bible, and a skull and cross-bones; and the only light in the room is from within the skull.

Master of Ceremonies goes in to the candidate, dresses him as a Knight of the East and West, and puts on a sword and white gloves. He then says to him—All the temples are demolished; our tools are destroyed, with our columns; the sacred word is lost, notwithstanding all our precaution; and we are in ignorance of the means of recovering it, or of knowing each other. The Order, in general, is in the greatest consternation! Will you assist us in recovering the word?

Candidate—Most cheerfully.

Master of Ceremonies—Follow me.

Candidate is conducted to the door of the Chapter, where Master of Ceremonies raps three and four.

Senior Warden (from within)—What do you want?

Master of Ceremonies—It is a brother Knight of the East and West, who is wandering in the woods and mountains, and who, at the destruction of the second Temple, lost the word, and humbly solicits your assistance to recover it.

The door is opened and the candidate is introduced. All the brethren are seated on the floor, the right hand on their necks, their left covering their face, their heads down, elbows on their knees, and their jewels covered with black crape.

Master sits at the foot of the altar in the same position.

Senior Warden raps three and four, and introduces candidate to the Master as a Knight of the East and West, who was wandering in the woods, &c.

Master to candidate—My brother, confusion has come on our works, and it is no longer in our power to continue them; you must perceive from our looks, and the consternation which prevails among us, what confusion reigns on the earth. The veil of the Temple is rent, [at this moment the black curtain in front of Mount Calvary is withdrawn,] the light is obscured, and darkness spreads over the earth; the flaming star has disappeared, the cubic stone sweats blood and water, and the sacred word is lost; therefore it is impossible we can give it to you, nevertheless it is not our intention to remain inactive: we will endeavor to recover it. Are you disposed to follow us?

Candidate—Yes, I am.

Master—Brother Wardens, it is necessary that this worthy Knight, our brother, should travel for thirty-three years, to learn the beauties of the new law.

The two Wardens now lead candidate slowly round the room, and when he passes before the altar he must kneel, and when passing in the west he bends his right knee, they make him observe the columns and repeat the name of each as he passes them.

After passing several times round the room, the thirty-three years are supposed to have expired, and the Wardens stop before the Master.

Master to candidate—My brother, what have you learned on your journey?

Candidate (instructed)—I have learned three virtues by which to conduct myself in future, Faith, Hope, Charity; inform me if there are any others?

Master—No, my brother, they are the principles and the pillars of our new mystery. Approach near to us and make an engagement never to depart from that faith.

The brethren all rise.

Candidate now kneels on the step of the altar, places his hand on the Bible, and takes the following obligation:

I, John Smith, do most solemnly and sincerely promise and swear, under the penalty of all my former obligations, which I have taken in the preceding degrees, never to reveal, either directly or indirectly, the secrets or mysteries of Knight of the Eagle and Pelican, Sovereign Prince of Rose Croix, to any brother of an inferior degree, nor to any in the world besides, who is not justly and lawfully entitled to the same, under the penalty of being forever deprived of the true word, to be perpetually in darkness, my blood continually running from my body, to suffer without intermission the most cruel remorse of soul; that the bitterest gall, mixed with vinegar, be my constant drink; the sharpest thorns for my pillow; and that the death of the cross may complete my punishment, should I ever infringe or violate, in any manner or form, the laws and rules which have been, are now, or may be hereafter made known or prescribed to me; and I do furthermore swear, promise and engage on my sacred word of honor, to observe and obey all the decrees which may be transmitted to me by the Grand Inspectors General, in Supreme Council, of the thirty-third degree; that I never will reveal the place where I have been received, nor the ceremony used at my reception, to any person on earth but to a lawful Prince of Rose Croix; that I never will initiate any person into this degree but by a lawful patent obtained for that purpose, either from this Chapter, or from a Superior Council: so help me God, and keep me steadfast in this my solemn obligation. Amen.

Candidate kisses the Bible.

Master—Brethren, all is accomplished.

The brethren all place themselves on the floor and cover their faces with their hands, except the Wardens, who continue with the Master, and the candidate, whom they deprive of his apron and order.

The Master now invests candidate with the chasuble and says—This habit, my brother, teaches you the uniformity of our manners, and our belief, and will recall to your recollection the principal points of our mysteries. The black apron with which I invest you, is to mark our sincere repentance of those evils which was the cause of all our misfortunes, and it will also serve to show you those who are in search of the true word; the ribbon is the mark of our constant mourning, till we have found it. Pass to the west and assist us to search for it.

Wardens take candidate to the west.

Master knocks six and one, as a Knight, Wardens repeat it. All the brethren rise and place themselves under the sign of the good pastor, as on page 166.

Master—Brother Wardens, what is the motive of our assembling?

Senior Warden—The loss of the word, which, with your assistance, we hope to recover.

Master—What must we do to obtain it?
Senior Warden—To be fully convinced of the three virtues which are the basis of our columns and our principles.
Master—What are they?
Senior Warden—Faith, Hope, Charity.
Master—How shall we find those three columns?
Senior Warden—By traveling three days in the most profound obscurity.
Master—Let us travel, brethren, from east to north, and from west to south.
All the brethren travel in silence, bending their knees as they pass the altar in the east, and go seven times round. At the third time of going round the Master passes to the second apartment; at the fourth time, the Wardens; at the fifth time, all the officers, at the sixth time, all the brethren; at the seventh time, the Master of Ceremonies stops the candidate and says—You cannot enter unless you give me the word.
Candidate—I am in search of the word, by the help of the new law and the three columns of Masonry.
During this time the brethren in the second apartment take off their black decorations, and put on the red, and also uncover their jewels.
Candidate knocks on the door, and the Warden for answer, shuts the door in his face.
Master of Ceremonies—These marks of indignity are not sufficiently humiliating; you must pass through more rigorous proofs, before you can find it. [He then takes off the candidate the chasuble and black apron, and puts over him a black cloth covered with ashes and dust, and says]—I am going to conduct you into the darkest and most dismal place, from whence the word shall triumphantly come to the glory and advantage of Masonry; place your confidence in me.
Master of Ceremonies now takes candidate into the third apartment, and takes from him his covering, and makes him to go three times around, (showing him the representation of the torments of the damned,) when he is led to the door of the Chapter and the Master of the Ceremonies says—The horrors which you have just now seen, are but a faint representation of those you shall suffer, if you break through our laws, or infringe the obligation you have taken.
Master of Ceremonies raps three and four, and Senior Warden reports to Master that there is an alarm at the door.
Master—See who knocks.
Senior Warden—Who knocks there?
Master of Ceremonies—It is a Knight, who, after having passed through the most profound and difficult places, hopes to procure the real word as a recompense for his labor.
The Wardens report this to the Master.
Master—Introduce him to the west of the Chapter with his eyes open.
The Wardens bring in candidate, and then cover him again with his veil.
Master—From whence came you?
Candidate—From Judea.
Master—By what road have you passed?
Candidate—By Nazareth.
Master—Who conducted you?
Candidate—Raphael.
Master—What tribe are you of?
Candidate—Of the tribe of Judah.
Master—Take the initial letters of each of these words; what do they form?
Candidate—J, N, R, J.
Master—My brethren, what happiness! the word is recovered; give him the light.
The veil is taken off, and all the brethren, striking with their hands seven times, cry—Hosanna in the highest; on earth peace, good will towards men!
The music immediately plays the following anthem, which is devoutly sung by all the Knights:

Grateful notes and numbers bring,
While the "name of God" we sing
Holy, holy, holy Lord,
Be thy glorious name adored.
Men on earth and saints above
Sing the great Redeemer's love.
Lord, thy mercies never fail,
Hail, celestial goodness, hail!
While on earth ordained to stay,
Guide our footsteps in thy way:
Mortals raise your voices high,
Till they reach the echoing sky.

After the anthem is sung, Master says to candidate—Approach, my brother, I will communicate to you our perfect mysteries.
Wardens conduct candidate to Master, who continues—I congratulate you, my brother, on the recovery of the word, which entitles you to this degree of Perfect Masonry. I shall make no comment or eulogium on it. Its sublimity will, no doubt, be duly appreciated by you. The impression which, no doubt, it has made on your mind, will convince you that you were not deceived when you was informed that the ultimatum of Masonic perfection was to be acquired by this degree. It certainly will be a source of very considerable satisfaction to you, that your merit alone has entitled you to it. And I hope, my brother, that your

good conduct, your zeal, your virtue and discretion, may always render you deserving of the high honor which you have received, and I sincerely wish that your life may long be preserved, to enable you to continue an useful member, and an ornament to our Society.

Master now instructs candidate in the signs, token, and words of this degree, as follows:

First sign—termed the sign of the good Shepherd. Cross the arms on the breast, with hands extended and eyes raised to heaven.

Second sign—the sign of reconciliation. Raise the right hand, and with the fore finger point to heaven. It is answered by pointing to the earth with the fore finger. This sign and answer are given alternately.

Third sign—that of help. Cross the legs, the right behind the left. Answer: cross the legs, the left behind the right.

Token—Give the sign of the good Pastor; face each other; bow; place reciprocally the hands on the breast crossed; give the fraternal kiss, pronouncing at the same time the pass-word.

Pass-word—EMMANUEL.

Sacred word—INRI. This is given by pronouncing its letters alternately. They are initials of the words Jesus, Nazarenus, Rex, Judæorum. Jesus of Nazareth, King of the Jews.

Master to candidate—Go, my brother, and make yourself known to all the members of the Sovereign Chapter, and return again.

The candidate goes and whispers in the ears of the Knights the pass-word; he then returns, and kneels before the altar. All the brethren place their right hands on him.

The Sovereign Master now takes the ribbon, to which is suspended the true jewel uncovered, and says—By the power which I have received from the Sovereign Chapter of Rose-Croix de Harodim, I receive and constitute you Prince Knight of the Eagle and Pelican, Perfect Free Mason de Harodim, under the title of the Rose-Croix, that you may enjoy, now and for ever, all the privileges, prerogatives and titles attached to that sublime degree, as virtue and humanity are the foundations of it. I hope, my brother, never to see you dishonor the ribbon with which you have been invested, and which a perfect Mason should never quit but at his death.

The Lecture is now given, which merely describes the ceremonies of initiating a candidate in this degree.

In closing, the Master raps seven on the step of the altar.

Both Wardens rap seven, when all the Knights rise.

Master—Most Excellent Brother Senior Warden, what is the hour?

Senior Warden—The moment when the word was recovered; when the cubic stone was changed into a mystic rose; when the flaming star appeared in all its splendor; when our altars resumed their ordinary form; when the true light dispelled darkness, and the new law becomes visible in all our works.

Master now passes round a charity box for the brethren to contribute for brethren in necessity.

Master—Has any of the Respectable Knights present anything to offer for the good of the Order, or of this Chapter?

If nothing offers, Master says—Brother Wardens, give notice that this Chapter is now going to be closed.

Wardens each rap seven, and proclaim, respectively, that the Chapter is going to be closed.

The Master leaves his place, makes his obeisance, embraces all the Knights, and says—Profound peace.

All the brethren do the same.

Master (who resumes his place and raps three and four)—My brethren, this Sovereign Chapter of Rose-Croix is closed; let us do our duty.

All exclaim, Vivat.

Master—Let us go, my brethren, and make the reflection which our work requires; let us go, and return in peace.

GRAND PONTIFF.

This degree is founded on certain apocalyptic mysteries in the Revelations of St. John, relating to the New Jerusalem. The meeting is termed a Chapter, the room being hung with blue, sprinkled with gold stars. In the east is a transparency representing the Sun, and the New Jerusalem. Through this comes all the light which illuminates the Chapter. The draft, or carpet on the floor, represents a square city (celestial Jerusalem) with twelve gates, three on each side; and in the midst of the city a tree bearing twelve different kinds of fruit. The city appears to be elevated, or suspended in the clouds, and under it is represented the Old Jerusalem in ruins, and on the ruins is the hydra serpent with three heads, in chains. The New Jerusalem appears to be descending upon the old one, and crushing the hydra. On one side of the draft is represented a mountain,

Thrice Potent Master is seated on a throne in the east, under a canopy of blue and gold, and is clothed in white.

Faithful Warden, clothed in white, is seated in the west, with a golden staff in his hand.

These two are the only officers. The members are styled Faithful and True Brethren, and are clothed in white, each wearing a blue cap, or fillet, with twelve gold stars on it. They (as well as the officers) also wear the order, which is a broad crimson scarf, with twelve gold stars in front, and attached to which, hanging down at the side, is a square golden plate, with ALPHA engraved on one side and OMEGA on the other.

In opening the Chapter, Thrice Potent Master raps twelve in a slow and measured manner, and says to the Warden—Faithful brother, what is the hour?

Warden—The hour is foretold.

Master—Faithful brethren, the whole is Alpha, Omega and Emmanuel; let us work.

Warden raps twelve in same manner as the Master, and says—Faithful brethren, the Chapter is open.

When a candidate is admitted to this Order he must come decorated as a Knight of the East and West, and have on a blue satin cap, or fillet, with twelve gold stars in front. He is introduced into the Chapter without ceremony, and the Warden places him on the top of the mountain (on the draft) and says:

Warden—Brother, do you detest what is perfidious? do you promise that you will break all communications, correspondence and friendship with those who are so?

Candidate—I promise and swear.

Warden now backs down the mountain towards the New Jerusalem, and then takes a surveyor's chain and measures the four sides of it. He then advances to candidate again.

Warden—Brother, that city (pointing to Jerusalem) measures twelve thousand furlongs on each side.

Warden (leading candidate) again backs down the mountain, and places him before the draft facing the Master. Pausing a moment, he directs him to take three square steps towards the chained three-headed serpent, then one step on each side of the three heads—then causes him to kneel three times with his right knee, at the same time holding his right hand horizontally towards the Master.

Master—Resume your position, and receive the sign, token and words.

Warden now leads candidate back three steps, which brings him to the bottom of the draft, where he instructs him in the sign, tokens and word of the degree, as follows:

Sign—Elevate right hand horizontally, fingers extended: cross the three last fingers perpendicularly.

Token—Each places the palm of the right hand on his forehead: one says, Hallelujah! the other says, Praise the Lord! The first now says, Emmanuel; the second says, God bless you!

Pass-word—EMMANUEL.

Sacred Word—HALLELUJAH, or sometimes, ALLELUIA.

Candidate is now invested with the Order of the degree, which closes the ceremony.

Before closing the Chapter, the Lecture is given as follows:

Master—My faithful brother Warden, what are you?

Warden—I am a true Sublime Grand Pontiff.

Master—Where have you received this degree?

Warden—In a place where there is neither sun nor moon to light it.

Master—Explain this to me?

Warden—As the Grand Pontiff never wants any artificial light, the Faithful and True Brothers, the Sublime Grand Pontiffs, do not want riches or titles to be admitted into the Sublime Degrees, as they prove themselves worthy of admittance by their attachment to Masonry—the faithful discharge of their several obligations—their virtue, and true and sincere friendship for their brethren in general.

Master—What does the draft of this Lodge represent?

Warden—A square city of four equal sides, with three gates on each side; in the middle of which is a tree, which bears twelve different kinds of fruit. The city is suspended as on clouds, and seems to crush a three-headed serpent.

Master—Explain this to me.

Warden—The square city represents ancient Free Masonry, under the title of Grand Pontiff, which comes down from Heaven to replace the ancient Temple—represented by the ruins and the three-headed serpent underneath.

Master—How comes Masonry to have fallen into ruin, since we are bound to support it, and are attached to it by our obligations, which cannot be equivocal?

Warden—It was so decreed in old times, which we learn from the writings of St. John, whom we know was the first Mason who held a Lodge of Perfection.

Master—Where does St. John say this?

Warden—In his Revelation, where he speaks of Babylon and the celestial Jerusalem.

Master—What signifies the tree with the twelve different fruits, which stands in the centre of the square city?

Warden—The tree of life is placed there to make us understand where the sweets of life are to be found; and the twelve fruits signify that we meet in every month to instruct ourselves mutually, and sustain each other against the attacks of our enemies.

Master—What is the meaning of the satin fillet, with the twelve golden stars, which the candidate wore round his forehead?

Warden—It procures those who wear it an entrance into our Lodge, as it likewise procures the entrance of those who wear it into the celestial Jerusalem, as St. John himself informs us.

Master—What is the meaning of the twelve golden stars on the fillet of the candidate and on those of the brethren?

Warden—They represent the twelve angels who watched at the twelve gates of the celestial Jerusalem.

Master—What signifies the blue hangings, with the golden stars thereon?

Warden—The blue is the symbol of lenity, fidelity, and sweetness, which ought to be the share of every faithful and true brother; and the stars represent those Masons who have given proof of their attachment to the statutes and rules of the Order; which, in the end, will make them deserving of entering into the celestial Jerusalem.

Master—What age are you?

Warden—I reckon no more.

Master—What remains for you to acquire?

Warden—The sublime truths of the degree above this.

Master—What is your name?

Warden—Faithful and true brother.

In closing the Chapter, Thrice Potent Master inquires of Warden—What is the hour?

· Warden—The hour is accomplished.

Master—Alpha and Omega! Faithful and true brethren, let us rejoice.

Master now raps twelve, as in the opening, and says—It is time to close our labors.

Warden raps twelve in same manner, and notifies the brethren that the Thrice Potent Master is now about to close the Chapter.

The Master then says—I declare this Chapter closed.

GRAND MASTER

OF

ALL SYMBOLIC LODGES.

The Master of a Lodge in this degree represents Cyrus Artaxerxes, and holds his office for life. The ceremonies go back to the building of the second Temple. The Lodge is hung with blue and yellow drapery. A throne in the east is elevated nine steps, and is covered with a blue canopy : in front of the throne is a table, and on it lies a sword, a Bible, square and compasses, and a mallet. In the south is a candlestick with nine lights.

Grand Master is seated on the throne in the east, wearing royal robe, crown, two scarfs, or orders, one blue and the other yellow; and they cross each other on the breast.

Junior and Senior Wardens are both seated in the west, wearing blue and yellow scarfs, crossed in front and rear, and the jewel of the degree suspended from the yellow one. It is a golden triangular plate, with the word SECRET engraved on one side, and the letter R on the other.

The brethren dress as Princes of Jerusalem, and all of them wear blue and yellow scarfs.

In opening the Lodge, the Grand Master says—I desire to open this Lodge of Symbolic Grand Masters. [Descends to the lowest step of the throne in front of the table.]

Master inquires of the Senior Warden if the Lodge is duly tyled. Senior Warden ascertains that it is, and so reports.

Master raps one and two with the mallet on the table, and Junior and Senior Wardens both repeat the raps, which together make nine.

Master to Senior Warden—Where is your Master placed?

Senior Warden—In the east.

Master—Why in the east?

Senior Warden—Because the glorious sun rises in the east to illumine the world.

Master—As I sit in the east, I open this Lodge of Symbolic Grand Masters.

Senior Warden—I sit in the west to assist our Grand Master to open this Lodge.

Junior Warden says the same.

Each officer now raps one and two, and the brethren clap one and two with their hands, when the Lodge is declared to be duly opened.

When a candidate is to be admitted to this degree, he represents Zerubbabel, and enters the Lodge by himself without being introduced, having first decorated himself with the jewels and badges of the highest degrees he has taken. The Wardens take him by the hand, and place him in a blue elbow chair, opposite to the Grand Master, who demands from him all the words, from an Entered Apprentice up to this degree, and then interrogates him as follows:

Master—From whence came you?

Candidate—From the sacred vault at Jerusalem.

Master—What come you to do here?

Candidate—I am come to see and visit your works, and show you mine. that we may work together and rectify our morals, and, if possible, sanctify the profane—but only by permission of a Prince Adept, or Prince of the Royal Secret.

Master—What have you brought?

Candidate—Glory, grandeur, beauty.

Master—Why do you give the name of St. John to our Lodge?

Candidate—Formerly all the Lodges were under the name of Solomon's Lodge, as the founder of Masonry; but since the crusades we have agreed with the Knights Templars, or Hospitallers, to dedicate them to St. John, as he was the support of the Christians and the new laws.

Master—What do you ask more?

Candidate—Your will and pleasure as you may find me worthy, obedient, and virtuous.

The Wardens now lead candidate nine times round the Lodge, beginning at the south, and then by nine square steps he advances to the throne, and walks over two drawn swords, laid across. There must be a pot with burning charcoal close by the throne, that the candidate may feel the heat of the fire while taking the obligation.

On arriving at the table in front of the throne, the candidate lays his right hand on the Bible: the Master covers it with his right hand, and then administers the obligation as follows, the candidate repeating after him:

I, John Smith, do solemnly and sincerely swear and promise, under the penalties of all my former obligations, to protect the Craft and my brethren with all my might, and not to acknowledge any one for a true Mason who was not made in a regularly constituted and lawful Lodge. I furthermore do swear, that I will strictly observe and obey all the statutes and regulations of the Lodge; and that I never will disclose or discover the secrets of this degree, either directly or indirectly, except by virtue of a full power in writing, given me for that purpose by the Grand Inspector or his dep-

uty, and then to such only as have been Masters of a regular Lodge. All this I swear under the penalties of being forever despised and dishonored by the Craft in general. [Kisses the Bible.]

Master then gives candidate the signs, token, and words of this degree, viz.:

First sign—Form four squares, thus: with the fingers joined, and the thumb elevated, place your right hand on your heart—[this forms two squares.] Place the left hand on the lips, thumb elevated so as to form a third square; place the heels so as to form a square with the feet.

Second sign—Place yourself on your knees, elbows on the ground, the head inclined towards the left.

Third sign—Cross the hands on the breast, the right over the left, fingers extended, thumbs elevated, and the feet forming a square.

Token—Take reciprocally the right elbow with the right hand, the thumb on the outside, the fingers joined, and on the inside; press the elbow thus four times, slip the hands down to the wrists, raising the three last fingers, and press the index on the wrist.

Sacred word—RAZABASSI, or RAZA-HAZ BETZI-YAH.

Pass-words—JECHSON, JUBELLUM, ZA-NABOSAN. Some, however, give Jehovah as the sacred word, and Belshazzar as the pass-word.

The Lecture is now given. The first part of it is historical of the degree, and is usually omitted. It closes as follows:

Master to Senior Warden—What means the fire in our Lodge?

Senior Warden—Submission, purification of morals, and equality among the brethren.

Master—What signifies the air?

Senior Warden—The purity, virtue, and truth of this degree.

Master—What does the sign of the sun mean?

Senior Warden—It signifies that some of us are more enlightened than others in the mysteries of Masonry; and for that reason we are often called Knights of the Sun.

Master—How many signs have you in this degree of Grand Pontiff, which is Grand Master of all Lodges?

Senior Warden—1st, The sign of the earth, or Apprentice; 2d, of water—Fellow Craft; 3d, of terror—the Master; 4th, of fire; 5th, of air; 6th, of the point in view; 7th, of the sun; 8th, of astonishment; 9th, of honor; 10th, of stench, or strong smell; 11th, of admiration; 12th, of consternation.

In closing, the Grand Master says to Senior Warden—My brother, enter into the cave of SILOL—work with Grand ROFADAM—measure your steps to the sun, and then the great black eagle will cover you with his wings, to the end of what you desire, by the help of the Most Sublime Princes Grand Commanders.

Master now raps four and two, and makes the sign of the four squares ; the two Wardens rap the same, and make the same signs, and the brethren also make the signs and clap four and two with their hands, when the Lodge is declared closed.

CHIEF OF THE TABERNACLE.

This degree commemorates the Jewish Order of Priesthood—of Aaron and his two sons, Eleazar and Ithamar—and the Lodge is designated a Hierarchy.

The hall is hung with white hangings, sustained by red and black columns arranged at equal distances in pairs. The east is termed the Sanctuary, and is separated from the rest of the hall by a balustrade, and red curtains looped up on each side. Opposite to the curtains is a platform of seven steps on which is a throne, and in front of it an altar covered with red : on the altar lies a Bible and a poinard : above the throne is the Ark of Alliance, and above that the ineffable name in Hebrew, JOD-HE-VAU-HE (God, or Jehovah) with rays radiating therefrom. On the right of this is a transparency of the sun, and on the left of it is one of the moon. In front of the sun is placed the altar of sacrifices, and in front of the moon the altar of incense. These two side altars are on the platform a little further in front than the centre one. In the west there are two candlesticks with five branches each, in the form of a pyramid—in the east there is one candlestick with two branches. The officers are as follows :

Sovereign Grand Sacrificer, seated on the throne in the east, wearing a long dark robe, and over it a short yellow robe, without sleeves. He also wears a mitre of golden tissue, with a red delta in front, the ineffable name in Hebrew characters upon it : also a black scarf, from left shoulder to right hip, fringed with silver, with a red rosette at the bottom, from which is suspended a poinard.

The two Wardens are called Grand Priests, and are seated in front of the altar, on the platform, dressed the same as the Grand Sacrificer, except that they have no deltas in front on their mitres.

The brethren (Levites) are clothed in white robes, over which they wear the order of this degree, viz., a scarlet sash trimmed with gold fringe ; at the bottom, on right hip, a black rosette, from which hangs the jewel, which is a golden censor, or pot of incense. The apron is white, lined with scarlet, bordered with red, blue and purple ribbons : on it is pictured a golden chandelier with seven branches : on the flap of the apron is a violet-colored myrtle.

In opening, Grand Sacrificer raps six and one, and inquires—What is the hour ?

Senior Grand Priest—It is the moment when the children of Hiram come here to sacrifice.

Grand Sacrificer—Let us then begin our sacrifices.

Fires are now kindled on the altars of sacrifice and incense, and the business of the evening proceeds.

A candidate for this degree is introduced with his hat on, sandals on his feet, and clothed in white linen small clothes. He represents Hamar, and is taken into a dark apartment with an altar in the centre, over which a light is suspended. Upon the altar are three human skulls and a Bible, and there is a human skeleton standing in front of it. A fire, or sacrifice, is kindled on the altar, and when it is consumed, the candidate kneels and takes the obligation of the Levites, as follows :

I, John Smith, do promise and swear never to reveal the secrets of this degree to any person in the world, except he has acquired all the preceding degrees, and then, not unless within the body of a Sovereign Council of this degree of Chief of the Tabernacle, regularly holding its authority from some legally established Supreme Council of the thirty-third degree : nor will I be present, or aid, or assist at the communicating them, unless with the above-named authority, regularly obtained. And in case I should violate this my sacred obligation, I perjure myself : I consent that the earth should be opened before my eyes, and that I should be engulfed (swallowed up) even to my neck, and thus miserably perish. To the fulfilment of which, may God preserve me in my senses. Amen.

Grand Sacrificer—In token of your sincerity in taking this obligation, you will kiss the Bible.

Candidate kisses the Bible.

The candidate is now conducted into the eastern apartment, where the sign, token and words are given him by the Grand Sacrificer, as follows :

Sign—Advance the right foot, make the motion of taking a censor with the right hand.

Token—Seize mutually the left elbow with the right hand, bending the arm so as to form a kind of circle.

Sacred word—JEHOVAH.

Pass-word—URIEL. The answer to it is—The Tabernacle of Revealed Truth.

In closing, the Grand Sacrificer inquires—Is the sacrifice consummated?

Senior Grand Priest—It is, most Gracious Sovereign.

Grand Sacrificer then raps six slowly, and then one. The Priests rap the same, and the ceremies are thus closed.

PRINCE OF THE TABERNACLE.

This degree is intended to illustrate the directions given to Moses for building a Tabernacle in the promised land, as described in the twenty-fifth chapter of Exodus. There are two apartments adjoining each other. The first, termed the Vestibule, is where the brethren clothe themselves; and it is ornamented with various emblems of Free Masonry. The second is made perfectly circular by means of the hangings, which are usually blue and red. In the middle is a chandelier with seven branches, and each branch with seven lights—forty-nine lights in all. Also a round table, in the centre of which is a cluster of inflamed hearts, and some incense. One side is the altar. The Lodge is called a Hierarchy, and the officers are as follows:

Most Potent and Powerful Prince, representing Moses the lawgiver, stationed in the east. He is dressed in a surplice sprinkled with gold stars; wears a blue silk tunic, the collar decorated with golden rays, a sash of broad watered scarlet ribbon from right shoulder to left side, with a golden letter A suspended from it, which is the jewel in this degree.

There are three Wardens called Powerful Princes, stationed in the south, west and north, according to their respective ranks, as follows—Aaron, the Chief Priest, in the south; Bezaleel, the son of Uri, in the west; Aholiab, the son of Ahisamach, in the north.

In opening, the Most Potent inquires of the Chief Priest—Are we well tyled, and in perfect security?

Chief Priest—We are in safe security.

Most Potent—Are all present Princes of the Tabernacle?

Chief Priest—All are true and regular Princes.

Most Potent—What is the hour?

Chief Priest—It is the first hour of the first day of the seven, for building this Hierarchy; it is the first of the day of life, and the sweetness of the seven.

Most Potent—Since it is so, you will give notice that I am about to open this Sovereign Council of the Hierarchy.

Chief Priest—Brothers Bezaleel and Aholiab, you will notify the brethren that this Sovereign Council is about to be opened by six and one.

Wardens notify the brethren.

Most Potent raps six distinctly, and then one, Wardens repeat, one after the other, when the Most Potent says—I declare this Sovereign Council duly opened.

A candidate in this degree represents Eleazer, who succeeded Aaron in the duties of the Tabernacle. When about to be admitted, he is washed in water, and is led to the altar by six equal steps, and then one long step, where he kneels, and the Most Potent administers to him the following obligation :

I, John Smith, do promise and swear that I will never reveal to any person in the world whatever, the secrets of this Degree of Prince of the Tabernacle ; and that I will never confer them, nor aid, or assist in conferring them on any person or persons, by my presence, or otherwise, except under an authority regularly obtained from some Supreme Council of the thirty-third degree, which has been constitutionally established, giving full power so to do. That I will stand to, and abide by, all the laws, rules, and regulations which belong to this degree, or may regularly emanate from the Supreme Council of the thirty-third Degree, under which we are now acting ; and in case I should violate this sacred obligation, I consent to be stoned to death, (as St. Stephen was,) and that my body be left to rot above ground, deprived of burial. For the faithful performance of which, may the Almighty Architect of the Universe preserve me. Amen.

Most Potent—In token of your sincerity you will kiss the book.

Candidate kisses the book, and remains on his knees.

Most Potent now takes a hod of oil, and a trowel, and says—I anoint, Eleazer, thy right ear, thy right eye, and thy right thumb, with the holy oil, in token of thy being separated from the foibles of the world, and to set thee apart of well doers in this tabernacle of clay, to be raised at the great and awful day of judgment, as a shining monument of God's glory, in the house not made with hands, eternal in the heavens.

After the ceremony of initiation is over, the brethren seat themselves at the round table, where they are served with refreshments and wine; the refreshments are not placed on the table, but are handed to them as they order. After the eating, the Most Potent Prince takes a glass of wine, and says—The warm mid-day of our solemnities invite our inclinations to new libations: let us charge, and drink to the grandeur of the glorious destiny which associates us! [The brethren drink off the cup at one draught.]

The second toast is introduced in the same manner by the Chief Priest, who says—Powerful Brothers of the Hierarchal Lodge, I give you the health of all Free Masons, elected or to be elected, for the unity of the seven and of three.

The third toast is given by Most Potent, who says—Powerful Brothers, let us drink to the health of the President of the United States, and to all in authority: may the Sovereign Master of the Universe fill them and us with joy and prosperity.

In closing, the Most Potent gives the usual lecture, and then inquires the hour.

Chief Priest—It is the day of life and of tranquility.

Most Potent—Let us then retire.

The brethren now march round the circular room by six equal steps and one long step, and Most Potent then declares the Council closed.

DEGREE OF KNIGHT OF THE BRAZEN SERPENT.

This degree illustrates the Brazen Serpent set up by Moses, as described in the twenty-first chapter of Numbers. The Lodge is hung in red and blue drapery, and represents Moses's Tent: it is called the Court of Sinai: over head, the arch is sprinkled with stars. A throne is erected in the east, and over it is a transparency of the burning bush, in the centre of which Hebrew characters are seen which signify ONE WHO SHALL LIVE. In the centre of the Lodge there is a Mount, elevated by five steps, and in the form of a truncated cone. One bright light only is used to light the room.

Most Powerful Grand Master, representing Moses, is seated on the throne in the east.

Two Wardens, called Ministers, representing Aaron and Joshua, are stationed in the west and north.

Besides these there is a Grand Orator, or Pontiff—a Secretary, or Grand Inquirer—and an Examiner.

The officers and brethren wear a red scarf from the left shoulder to the right hip, upon which is painted or embroidered the words Virtue and Valor, where it crosses the breast. The jewel is a golden serpent entwined on a cross in the form of the letter T standing upon a triangle with the ineffable name in Hebrew engraved upon it. It is suspended by a white ribbon. The apron is white, sprinkled with black tears: on the flap a triangle with rays radiating from it: in the centre, the Hebrew letter H (pron. HE.)

In opening, the Master raps five, three and one, and inquires of the first Warden—What is the hour?

Warden—It is one past meridian.

Master—If it is one, it is time to attend to the wants of our brethren.

Master repeats his raps, and the Wardens do the same, when the Lodge is declared to be open.

If a candidate is to be admitted, he represents a traveler—a captive loaded with chains who is to be delivered by Moses. He is introduced into the Lodge by five slow, three hurried, and one solitary rap on the door—advances to the altar by nine serpentine steps, and the following obligation is administered:

I, John Smith, do solemnly promise and swear, in the presence of Almighty God, the Grand Architect of the Universe, that I will never reveal the secrets of this Degree of Knight of the Brazen Serpent; nor, by my presence, aid or assist in revealing them to any person or persons whatsoever, unless the candidate shall have taken all the preceding degrees in a regular manner, nor without a legal authority. I now swear allegiance and true faith. In case I should transgress this my solemn obligation, and thus perjure myself, I freely consent to have my heart eaten by the most venomous of serpents, and thus to perish most miserably; from which may the Almighty Creator of the Universe defend me! [Kisses the Bible.]

The Master instructs candidate in the signs, token and words of this degree, as follows:

Sign—Cross the arms on the breast, and incline the body as if to kneel on one knee. Entering Sign—Point to the earth as if showing a plant.

Token—Place yourself on the right of your companion, and take his left wrist in your right hand. He answers by taking your left wrist with his right hand.

Covered word—JOHN RALP.

Sacred word—MOSES.

Pass-word—INRI, [given by letters.]

In closing, the Master raps five, three and one, and inquires the hour. Warden answers, Four past meridian. Master then closes the Lodge with similar ceremonies to those in previous historical degrees.

PRINCE OF MERCY;

OR, SCOTTISH TRINITARIAN DEGREE.

This is founded on the triple Covenant which God made—first with Abraham, by circumcision; next with the Israelites in the wilderness, by the intermediation of Moses; third with all mankind by the death and suffering of Jesus Christ. From these three acts of mercy the name of this degree is derived.

The meeting is called a Chapter, and the place of meeting the Third Heaven. The hangings of the room are green, supported by nine columns, alternately white and red, upon each of which is an arm of a chandelier, sustaining nine lights, forming in all eighty-one lights. The canopy is green, white, and red; under which is a green colored throne. The Most Excellent Chief Prince uses an arrow, whose plume is on one side green, and on the other side red, the spear being white and the point gilded. By the altar is a statue which represents Truth, covered with the aforesaid three colors. This statue is the palladium of the Order.

The officers consist of Most Excellent Chief Prince, representing Moses, seated on the throne in the east, and dressed in a tri-colored tunic of green, white and red. Senior Warden, representing Aaron; Junior Warden, representing Eleazer. A fourth officer is called the Sacrificer, and a fifth, Guard of the Palladium:

The officers and brethren wear red aprons with sky-blue flaps, the aprons bordered with a white fringe, and a figure of the jewel of this degree embroidered thereon. Each wears a collar of broad tri-colored ribbon, from which is suspended the jewel, which is a golden equilateral triangle: in the centre of the triangle is a heart with the Hebrew letter H (he) upon it.

In opening the Chapter, Most Excellent Chief Prince raps three, five and seven.

A candidate being initiated into this degree represents Joshua, and simply approaches the altar by three equal steps, beginning with his left foot, and takes the following oath:

I, John Smith, do promise and swear, in the presence of the Grand Architect of the Universe, and this respectable assembly, and by the most sacred of obligations, that I never will reveal the secrets of this sublime degree of Prince of Mercy to any pe on or persons whatsoever in the world, except they have received all the degrees below this in a correct manner, and so thereby I shall know them to be regularly entitled to the same. I furthermore promise and swear never to entrust this degree to any person, nor assist at any reception, unless I or they shall have been or are authorized by a particular permission or warrant for that purpose, from some Supreme Council of the thirty-third degree, regularly and constitutionally established, to whose authority, laws, rules, and regulations, I now swear true faith and allegiance; and in that case I promise and swear, never to give my consent before I have been plainly informed of the life, manners and morals of the candidate. Should I violate or transgress this, my solemn obligation, I consent to be condemned, cast out, and despised by the whole universe. And may the Supreme Architect of heaven and earth, guide, guard, and protect me, to fulfil the same. Amen. Amen. Amen.

Chief Prince—In token of your sincerity in this obligation, kiss the Bible.

Candidate kisses the book.

Chief Prince now instructs candidate in the signs, token and words, as follows:

Sign of Entrance—Place the right hand above the eyes so as to form a triangle with the forehead.

Second sign—Form a triangle with the thumbs and the two fore fingers, and place them on the abdomen.

Sign of Help—Place the arms on the head, the hands open, the palms outward, and say—With me are the Children of Truth.

Token and Word—Take your companion's shoulders with your hands, press them slightly, saying—GOMEL.

Sacred words—JEHOVAH JAKIN, [Sovereign Master of all things.]

Common words—GHIBLIM, (Excellent Master,) and GABAON, (chamber of third heaven.)

Pass-word—GOMEL. In some Lodges it is MAGACACIA, and in others, ABI, and JAKINAL.

A Lecture is usually given in this degree, as follows:

Chief Prince to Senior Warden—Are you a Prince of Mercy?

Warden—I have seen the Great Light in Triple Alliance of the blood of Jesus Christ, of which you and I have the mark.

Chief Prince—What is the Triple Alliance?

Senior Warden—It is that which the Eternal made with Abraham by circumcision; that which he made with his people in the desert, by the intercession of Moses; and that which he made with mortals, by the death and suffering of our Saviour, Jesus Christ, his dearly beloved son.

Chief Prince—What is the age of a Prince of Mercy?

Senior Warden—Eighty-one years.

There is no particular formality in closing a Chapter in this degree.

SOVEREIGN COMMANDER OF THE TEMPLE.

The meeting in this degree is styled a Court. The room is hung with red drapery on black columns, from each of which projects a bracket, or branch, holding a light. In the centre is a chandelier with three rows of lights, viz.: twelve on the lower row, nine on the middle, and six on the upper row—twenty-seven in all. Twenty-seven lights are also placed on a round table in the centre, at which the Commanders are seated. The officers are as follows:

Most Potent Master Commander, seated on a throne in the east, the throne covered with red drapery, sprinkled with tears He wears a white robe; over it a red mantle lined with ermine, and on his head a pointed crown.

Two Wardens are seated in the west and styled Most Sovereign Commanders. Each wears the Order of this degree around his neck, which is a white ribbon edged with red, and having embroidered upon it, in red, four Teutonic crosses: from it hangs a golden triangle, (the jewel of this degree,) upon which is engraved the Tetragrammaton, or sacred word, in Hebrew.

The members (Sovereign Commanders) are seated at a round table in the centre of the Court. They, as well as the officers, wear white gloves, lined and bordered with red. Each wears a red sash, bordered with black, from the right shoulder to the left hip, from which is suspended a Teutonic golden cross. The apron is flesh-colored, lined and bordered with black: on the flap a cross encircled in a laurel wreath: on the apron a key.

In opening the Court, Most Potent Master raps twelve, repeats, and then raps three. Addressing the Senior Warden, he then inquires the hour.

Warden—It is ten.

The Master then declares the Court open for business. If a candidate is to be admitted, he is introduced and marched three times round the room, when he pauses in front of the altar, kneels, and takes the following obligation:

I, John Smith, in the presence of the one Almighty and only true God, the Grand Architect of the Universe, and of this Venerable Court of Sovereign Commanders of the Temple, do, of my own free will and accord, most solemnly and sincerely vow, promise, and swear, never to reveal the secrets of this degree which I am now receiving, to any person or persons below me, except in a Court lawfully holden, with a warrant or authority from some regularly established Supreme Council of the thirty-third Degree, empowering me, and them with me, to work in this Sublime Degree. I furthermore promise and swear, that I never will confer, nor assist in conferring this degree, upon any person who has not, in a legal and regular manner, taken all the foregoing degrees of Free Masonry. I furthermore promise and swear, that I will pay due regard and submission to the Supreme Council, under whose authority we are now acting; and that I will always govern myself by their laws, rules, and regulations, so far as the same shall come to my knowledge; and will do all in my power to support them, for the good of the Craft and the advantage of Free Masonry, agreeable to the Constitutions of the Order. To all this I solemnly swear, under the penalty of having the severe wrath of Almighty God inflicted on me; and may He have mercy on my soul in the day of judgment, agreeably to my performance of this sacred obligation. Amen. Amen. Amen.

Master—In token of your sincerity, you will kiss the Bible.

Candidate kisses the book.

Most Potent Master Commander then instructs candidate in the signs, token and words of this degree, as follows:

Sign, used only in the Court—Make a cross on the forehead of your brother with the thumb of your right hand. The answer consists in kissing the forehead on the place where the cross was made.

Ordinary sign—Place the two first fingers of the right hand on the mouth, the others closed and towards the examiner.

Token—Give three blows with the right hand upon the left shoulder of the brother—he will answer by taking your right hand and giving it three light peculiar shakes (not describable.)

Pass-word—SOLOMON.
Sacred word—I. N. R. I.
There is no lecture in this degree. In closing, the Master raps, as in opening, and inquires—What is the hour?
Senior Warden—It is four.
The Court is then closed.

KNIGHT OF THE SUN;

OR, PRINCE ADEPT.

This degree is called the Key of Historical and Philosophical Masonry. Its ceremonies and lectures give a history of the preceding degrees and explain the emblems. Its object is declared to be the inculcation of Truth.

The meeting is called a Council, and the room (called the Sanctuary) is illuminated by a single bright light, which is made by a glass globe placed in the south: the globe is filled with clear water and there are lights placed behind it enough to make it look like a brilliant sun. There are no hangings, but the walls are painted to represent mountains and forest trees. The officers are—

Thrice Puissant Grand Master, representing Father Adam, is stationed in the east. He wears a robe of pale yellow, the color of the morning, his hat on, and holding in his right hand a golden sceptre, on the top of which is a globe of gold. He represents the Sovereign Master of the World, and Father of all Men. He wears around his neck a golden chain, from which is suspended a golden sun, with a globe engraved thereon, which is the jewel of the degree.

There is but one Warden, who sits in the west, and represents Brother Truth. He wears the same ornaments as the Master: also the Order of the degree, which is a broad white watered ribbon with an Eye of gold embroidered thereon: it is worn as a collar.

There are seven other officers, viz.: Zaphriel, Zabriel, Camiel, Uriel, Michael, Zaphael, and Gabriel. These are the names of Cherubims, and they are dressed and decorated similar to Father Adam.

The remaining members are called Sylphs, and all assist in the ceremonies of the Council. They wear the jewel, suspended by a fiery red ribbon to the third button-hole of the coat.

In opening, the Master says to Warden—Brother Truth, what is the time on earth?

Warden—Mighty father, it is midnight among the profane, or cowans; but the sun is at its meridian here.

Master—My dear children, let us profit by its light, and it will conduct us in the path of virtue, and enable us to follow that law by which we cannot fail to come to the knowledge of Pure Truth.

Master makes a sign by putting his right hand on his left breast. The brethren respond by pointing upwards with the fore finger of their right hands, holding the hand above the head. This is to indicate that there is but one God, who is the personification of Truth.

Master—This Council is open: let us proceed with our duties.

If a candidate is to be introduced, he first presents himself in the ante-chamber, where there are a number of Sylphs, each with a bellows, blowing a large pot of fire. At first they take no notice of him, but presently the most ancient Sylph goes up to the candidate, covers his face with black crape, and tells him to go to the door of the Sanctuary and knock on it six times with his open hand.

Candidate goes and knocks.

Warden (opening the door a little)—What do you desire?

Candidate (instructed by Sylph)—I desire to go out of darkness to see the true light, and to know the true light in all its purity.

Warden—What do you desire more?

Candidate—To divest myself of original sin, and destroy the juvenile prejudices of error, which all men are liable to, namely, the desire of all worldly attachments and praise.

Warden closes the door, and goes and reports to the Master, who says—Introduce him to the true happiness.

Warden returns, opens the door, and taking candidate by the hand, conducts him to the middle of the Sanctuary, which is covered with black cloth.

Master to candidate—My son, seeing by your labor in the royal art, you are now come to the desire of knowledge of the pure and holy truth, we shall lay it open to you without any disguise or covering. But, before we do this, consult your heart, and see at this moment if you feel yourself disposed to obey her (namely, Truth,) in all things which she commands. If you are disposed, I am sure she is ready in your heart, and you must feel an emotion that was unknown to you before. This being the case, you must hope that she will not be long to manifest herself to you. But have a care not to defile the Sanctuary by a spirit of curiosity; and take care not to increase the number of the vulgar and profane, that have for so long a time ill-treated her, until Truth was obliged to depart the earth, and now can hardly trace any of her footsteps. But she always appears in her greatest glory, without disguise, to the true, good, and honest Free Masons; that is to say, to the zealous extirpators of superstition and lies. I hope, my dear brother, you will be one of her intimate favorites. The proofs that you have given, assure me of everything I have to expect of your zeal; for as nothing now can be more a secret among us, I shall order Brother Truth, that he will instruct you what you are to do in order to come to true happiness.

Candidate is now unveiled.

Warden to candidate—Brother, by my mouth holy Truth speaketh to you.

The Warden now instructs candidate in the principles of all former degrees, and in all the symbols and signs from Entered Apprentice upward. He explains the objects and ends of each degree, as fully set forth in the text-books.

Master—My dear son, what you have heard from the mouth of Truth is an abridgment of all the consequences of all the degrees you have gone through, in order to come to the knowledge of the holy truth, contracted in your last engagements. Do you persist in your demand of coming to the holy brother, and is that what you desire, with a clear heart?—answer me.

Candidate—I persist.

Master—Brother Truth, as the candidate persists, approach with him to the Sanctuary, in order that he may take a solemn obligation to follow our laws, principles, and morals, and to attach himself to us forever.

Candidate now kneels, when the Master takes both his hands between his own and administers the following obligation:

I, John Smith, promise in the face of God, and between the hands of my Sovereign, and in presence of all the brethren now present, never to take arms against my country, directly or indirectly, in any conspiracy against the Government thereof. I promise never to reveal any of the degrees of the Knight of the Sun, which is now on the point of being intrusted to me, to any person or persons whatsoever, who are not duly qualified to receive the same; and never to give my consent to any one to be admitted into our mysteries, only after the most scrupulous circumspection, and full knowledge of his life and conversation; and who has given at all times full proof of his zeal and fervent attachment for the Order, and a submission at all times to the tribunal of the Sovereign Princes of the Royal Secret. I promise never to confer the degree of the Knights of the Sun, without having a permission in writing from the Grand Council of Princes of the Royal Secret, or from the Grand Inspector or his deputy, known by their titles and authority. I promise also and swear, that I will not assist any, through any means, to form or raise a Lodge of the Sublime Orders, in this country, "without proper authority." I promise and swear to redouble my zeal for all my brethren, Knights, and Princes, that are present or absent; and if I fail in this my obligation, I consent for all my brethren, when they are convinced of my infidelity, to seize me, and thrust my tongue through with a red hot iron; to pluck out both my eyes, and to deprive me of smelling and hearing; to cut off both my hands, and to expose me in that condition in the field, to be devoured by the voracious animals; and if none can be found, I wish the lightning of Heaven might execute on me the same vengeance. O God, maintain me in right and equity. Amen. Amen. Amen.

The obligation is repeated three times in all, and the Master then raises candidate, and gives him a kiss on the forehead. He then decorates him with the collar and jewel of this degree, and gives him the sign, token and words, viz:

Sign—Place the right hand flat upon the heart, the thumb forming a square. The answer—raise the hand, and with the index, point to heaven. This is to show there is but one God, the source of all truth.

Token—Take in your hands those of your brother, and press them gently. Some Knights in addition to this, kiss the forehead of the brother, saying, ALPHA, to which he answers, OMEGA.

Sacred word—ADONAI. This word is answered by ALBRA, or ABBRAAK, (king without reproach.)

Pass-word—STIBIUM, (antimony.) To this pass-word some add HELIOS, MENE, and TETRAGRAMMATON.

After receiving the signs, token and words, the candidate goes round and gives them to all the brethren, after which he sits down among them.

The Warden (Truth) now rises and gives a lucid explanation of the emblems of Philosophical Masonry, and of those represented in the Moral Lodge.

The general lecture in this degree is next given, and then the closing lecture, but except on extra occasions, either of them are seldom gone through with. They explain the why and wherefore of the many implements used, and the curious ceremonies observed.

In closing, the Master says to Warden —Brother Truth, what progress have men made on the earth to come to true happiness?

Warden—Men have always fallen on the vulgar prejudices, which are nothing but falsehood; very few have struggled, and less have knocked at the door of this holy place, to attain the full light of real truth, which we all ought to acquire.

Master—My dear children, depart and go among men, endeavor to inspire them with the desire of knowing holy truth, the pure source of all perfection.

Master now puts his right hand on his left breast, when all the brethren raise the first fingers of their right hands, pointing upwards, as in opening.

Master raps seven, which is repeated by the Warden, and the Council is declared closed.

KNIGHT OF KADOSH.

This degree is intimately connected with the ancient Order of Knights Templars, as it commemorates their old ceremonies of initiation, and recounts the vicissitudes to which those Knights were subjected. It is quite a popular degree among the Masons of the United States. The meeting is called a Chapter, and the brethren are termed Grand Elected Knights.

Five apartments are necessary when initiating a candidate. The first is hung with black, lighted by a single lamp, of triangular form, suspended from the ceiling. The second apartment (called the Chamber of Reflection) represents a cavern, or grotto, with a mausoleum in the centre: it is connected with the first apartment by a passage, or hall-way. The third apartment is hung with red drapery: a throne is in the east, and a black veil is drawn in front of it: in front of the veil stands the altar, and on it lays two cross-swords, a dagger, a Bible, square and compasses: in front of the altar is the mysterious ladder, veiled in black. The fourth apartment should represent wild natural scenery, such as mountains, valleys, coasts, and a military encampment. The fifth apartment is also hung with red drapery: in the east is a throne, and over it a crowned double-headed eagle with wings extended, holding a two-edged sword in his talons: the cross of the Order is suspended by a black ribbon from the neck of the eagle: on its breast is an equilateral triangle, with the name of the Deity, in Hebrew, on it; and around the edge of the triangle is this inscription—NEC PRODITOR, INNOCENS FERET: the throne is ornamented with red Teutonic crosses, and behind it are three banners of the Order, viz.: one white, with a green cross, and the words "The Will of God;" a second green, with a red cross one side, and a double-headed black eagle on the other, surrounded by the motto "Victory or Death," embroidered in silver: the third is the ancient war banner of the Knights Templars, half black and half white. This last named banner is also used in the fourth apartment. The meeting is termed a Chapter, and the officers are as follows:

In the first apartment, called the Chamber of Judges, the Senior Warden presides: he is called the Grand Chancellor, and is assisted by two Judges, who sit on either side of him: besides the usual dress of a Knight of Kadosh, he has embroidered in gold on his left breast an emblem of Truth. The assembly in the third apartment is termed an Areopagus: Thrice Potent Grand Commander (representing King Frederick, of Prussia) is seated on the throne in the east, and presides here during the introduction of a candidate. The fifth apartment is called the Senate Chamber, and in transacting the ordinary business of the Chapter, the meeting is here only. The other apartments are solely used during the reception of candidates.

In the usual meetings, the Grand Commander sits in the east, the Grand Chancellor on his right, Grand Architect on his left; and besides these are present, a Master of Ceremonies, a Secretary, Treasurer, Captain of the Guards and Expert Brother.

The officers are Knights, each wearing a white woolen cloak, with a red cross on the left breast: white cap, with black and white feathers: a sword, and a dagger stuck in the left side of the sword belt. In some meetings they dress in black, and dispense with the white cloak. The Jewel in this degree is a red enameled Teutonic cross, which is suspended from a collar of red ribbon, or else attached to the button-hole of the coat on the left side. On the centre of the cross is a white pearl medallion with the letters J M on one side, and on the other a skull pierced with a dagger.

In opening the Chapter, Thrice Potent

12

Grand Commander says to Senior Warden (or Grand Chancellor)—Illustrious Knight, are you elected?

Warden—I am a true Elected Knight.

Commander—How came you so?

Warden—Fortune decided in my favor.

Commander—What proof can you give me of your reception?

Warden—A cavern was the witness of it.

Commander—What did you do in the cavern?

Warden—I executed a commission that had been entrusted to me.

Commander—Have you ever penetrated further?

Warden—I have, Most Potent.

Commander—How shall I believe you?

Warden—My name is Knight of Kadosh; you understand me?

Commander—What is the hour?

Warden—That of silence.

Commander—Give me, then, the sign to convince me of your knowledge.

Warden takes his sword in his left hand, and holds his right hand on the red cross on his left breast: the brethren all draw their swords and do the same. This is called the Saluting sign.

Commander (rapping one, very loud) —Elected Knights, the Chapter is open.

If a candidate is to be admitted, only five brothers can take part in the ceremony. It must first have been ascertained to a certainty that he is of good character, and has always been active and conscientious in his duties towards the Craft in general. Two of the brothers remain outside with the candidate until he is introduced. One of them goes to the door and knocks. One of the three brothers inside goes and opens the door and inquires—What do you want?

Outside brother—A servant Knight demands to be admitted to the degree of Grand Elected. as he has all the necessary qualifications.

Inside brother goes and reports this to the Commander.

Commander—Brother Knights, can we admit this Free Mason among us without risk of indiscretion from him?

Two Knights come forward, and one says—Most Potent, we are ready to swear and promise for him.

Commander then administers to them the following oath—each taking the other by the hand:

We promise and swear, by the living God, always supreme, to revenge the death of our ancestor; and which of us that should in any manner commit the most light indiscretion, touching the se-cret of our Order, shall suffer death, and shall have his body buried under the throne of this Illustrious Assembly. So God protect us in our design, and maintain us in equity and right. Amen.

The candidate is now introduced by the two Knights outside, and is left alone in the room with the Thrice Potent Grand Commander; but he sees him not, as the Commander is behind a black veil. The candidate prostrates his face to the ground, when the Commander addresses him on the principal points of Masonry, from its beginning, to the epoch of the assassination of Hiram Abiff; Solomon's design of punishing the traitors, in the most exemplary manner; the method he took in disposing the Masters who went in search of the three villains, in order to execute his vengeance; he repeats to him the zeal, constancy, and fervency of Joabert, Stokin, and Gibulum, who, after the most painful search, (by Solomon's order,) had the happiness of finding among the ruins of Enoch's temple in the Ninth Arch, the precious treasure of the Perfect Masons, &c. He continues to remind him of the firmness of the Grand Elect and Perfect Masons, at the time of the Temple's destruction, when they passed through the enemy, at all risks, till they obtained an entrance into the sacred vault, to find the pillar of beauty, that they might, by effacing the ineffable word, hinder its being exposed to the profane. He then reminds him of the seventy-two years' captivity, and the clemency of Cyrus, King of Persia, who, by the request of Zerubbabel, not only gave the Israelites their freedom, but ordered that all the treasure of the Temple, taken by Nebuchadnezzar, should be restored to them, in order to decorate the new Temple, which he ordered them to build to the infinite God, and created them Knights. Then he repeats the clemency of Darius to Zerubbabel, (at the head of the embassy from Jerusalem to Babylon,) with the complaints against the Samaritans, who refused to contribute to the sacrifices of the new Temple, according to the proclamation of his predecessor, Cyrus, in favor of the Knights of the East, when they received Darius' letter to all the governors of Samaria, &c.; how the ambassadors were received on their return to Jerusalem; and elected princes by the people. He then reminds him that, after this, the second Temple being destroyed, how the most zealous Masons united under Chiefs, and worked to the reformation of manners, and elevated in their hearts some spirit ual edifice, and rendered themselves worthy by their works. They were more particularly esteemed and distinguished in the time of Manchin, who was the most remarkable among them. A great many others embraced Christianity, and communicated their secrets to those Christians, whom they found had the good qualities of it, living in common, and forming themselves as one family; which shows how the brilliant Order of Masons sustained themselves until the sixth age, and how it fell into a state of lethargy after that; notwithstanding which, there have been always found some faithful Masons; which is clearly proved by the brilliant manner in which the Order of Masonry was received in the year 1118, when eleven Grand Elect and Perfect Masons, the most zealous, presented themselves to Garinous, Prince of Jerusalem, Patriarch and Knight Mason, and pronounced their promises between his hands. They taught him the succession of the time, and progress to the time that the princes went to conquer the Holy Land. The alliance and obligations that were formed between those princes, was, that they would spill the last drop of their blood, in order to establish in Jerusalem the worship of the Most High. He informs him that the peace which took place after these wars, hindered them from accomplishing their design, and therefore have continued in theory what they had sworn to do practically, never admitting in their Order only those who had given proofs of friendship, constancy and discretion. He then gives candidate a general history, in chronological detail, of the Masonic Order, its progress, its decline, and the manner how it was sustained, till the epoch of the Crusaders, and until the historical circumstances that have given occasion to the degree which the candidate expects; a degree that will give him a perfect knowledge of the precedent degrees, and the manner how Masonry has come to us.

After the address, candidate kneels, and lays his right hand on the Bible, and, with his left between the hands of the Commander, he takes the following obligation:

I, John Smith, hereby promise and swear, never to reveal the secrets of the Grand Elected Knights of Kadosh, or White and Black Eagle, to any person. I swear to take revenge on the traitors of Masonry; and never to receive in this degree, none but a brother who has come to the degrees of Prince of Jerusalem and Knight of the Sun, and then only by

an authority given to me by a Grand Commander or Deputy Inspector, under his hand and seal. I promise to be ready at all times to conquer the Holy Land, when I shall be summoned to appear; to pay due obedience at all times to the Princes of the Royal Secret; and if I fail in this my obligation, I desire that all the penalties of my former obligations may be inflicted on me. Amen.

Commander—In token of your sincerity, you will kiss the book.

Candidate kisses the Bible.

Commander—My dear brother, it is necessary for those to whom the secrets of the Elected Knights are confided, to be very circumspect, always attentive, and never to breathe a suspicion relative thereto, or to the mysteries and end of Masonry. The imprudence and indiscretion of many brothers have given knowledge to the world of many of our emblems, by which Masonry has greatly suffered, and will be repaired with difficulty. Their indiscretion has caused the loss and retreat of many puissant brothers, who would have been an ornament and support of our Lodge. Such indiscretion in this degree, my dear brother, would be without any recovery, as there are no more emblems; when every matter shall be discovered and disclosed to you, that will give room for some events of which you will see the consequences when you shall have heard all my instructions. The word which our brothers place at the end of their obligations, viz., Amen, signifies this is no more, that shall be no more; if this shall be again. This ought no longer to be a secret to you, who are going to have an explanation of the origin of Masonry, and what has occasioned the Society. Truth penetrates the cloud and the shade, which we can leave to come to the knowledge of what we were before in quality of Knights of Kadosh, White and Black Eagle, and what we are as Symbolic Masons, and what we can be by the destruction of our enemies. Let us pray.

Commander then kneels with candidate and reads from text-book the following prayer:

O most eternal, beneficial and all gracious, great Architect of the universe; we from the secret depths of our hearts offer thee a living sacrifice. We beseech thee to inspire our enemies with a just sense of the evil they have done us, and from their having a conviction of their wrongs, they might atone for their manifold injuries, which do not belong to us thy servants to redress ourselves, but by their eyes being opened we might be reconciled, and by a hearty union take possession of those blessed lands where the original Temple was first established, where we might be gathered into one band, there to celebrate thy holy praises once more on the holy mount, in whose bowels was deposited thy ever glorious, respectable, ever blessed, and awful name. Amen.

The black veil is now removed, when the Commander says to candidate—Bear in mind, my brother, that the slightest indiscretion will infallibly undermine us and throw us into an horrible abyss, where we should see buried the whole Order of Masonry, the remains of an illustrious and glorious Order. By its heroism in favor of the unfortunate, how great it has been in the time when its power, authority and riches were arrived, to the highest pitch, when the distinguished birth of those who were members of it, celebrated its glory. Our aim is to regain that enviable position; and while we would not intimidate those worthy brethren of the Craft who aspire to this degree, yet we fear to confer it with too much confidence on an ordinary friend lest his discretion should not be all we could desire. To you we are about to confide our mysteries; and if you have thus far made any remark that would keep you from pronouncing the obligation or vow we are obliged to take from you, before we can give you greater knowledge of the degree of Grand Elected Knight of Kadosh, consult yourself and see if you are disposed to penetrate farther, and fulfil exactly all the points of the obligation you are going to pronounce with me, in order to link you to us for ever

Commander pauses a while, and if the candidate wants to back out, at this stage, he is at liberty, and is so informed.

Candidate again kneels before the altar, and lays his right hand on the Bible, and his left between the hands of the Commander, who says—You swear and promise to me, on that you hold most dear and sacred, First, that you will practice the works of corporeal mercy, and live and die in your religion, never declaring to any man who received you, or assisted at your reception in this sublime degree.

Candidate—I promise and swear.

Commander—Say with me, Tsedakah, (righteousness.)

Candidate repeats Tsedakah.

Commander—Secondly, you promise and swear to have candor in all your ac-

tions, in consequence never to receive in this degree any brother who is not your most intimate friend, and then by the consent of two Grand Elected Inspectors, if to be met with, or by a patent given you for that purpose.

Candidate—I promise and swear.

Commander—Shorlaban, (or white ox, figuratively.)

Candidate repeats Shorlaban.

Commander—Thirdly, you promise and swear at all times to possess a sweetness of mind, as much as you are capable, to love and cherish your brothers as yourself, to help them in their necessities, to visit and assist them when they are sick, and never draw arms against them on any pretence whatsoever.

Candidate—I promise and swear.

Commander—Mathok, (sweetness.)

Candidate repeats Mathok.

Commander—Fourthly, you promise and swear to regulate your discourse by truth, and to keep with great circumspection and regard the degree of the White and Black Eagle or Kadosh.

Candidate—I promise and swear.

Commander—Say with me, Emunah.

Candidate repeats Emunah.

Commander—Fifthly, you promise and swear that you will travel for the advancement of heaven, and to follow at all times, and in all points, every matter that you are ordered and prescribed by the Illustrious Knights, and Grand Commander, to whose orders you swear submission and obedience, on all occasions, without any restrictions.

Candidate—I promise and swear.

Commander—Say with me, Hamal saggi, (great labor.)

Candidate repeats Hamal saggi.

Commander—Sixthly, you promise and swear to me, to have patience in adversity, and you swear never to receive a brother in this degree, on any pretext whatsoever, whose will is not free, as religious monks and all those who have made vows without restriction to their superiors.

Candidate—I promise and swear.

Commander—Say with me, Sabbal, burden, or patience.)

Candidate repeats Sabbal.

Commander—Seventhly, you promise, in the end, and swear to keep inviolably secret, what I am going to confide to you—to sacrifice the traitors of Masonry, and to look upon the Knights of Malta as our enemies—to renounce for ever to be in that Order, and regard them as the unjust usurpers of the rights, titles, and dignities, of the Knights Templars, in whose possession you hope to enter with the help of the Almighty.

Candidate—I promise and swear.

Commander—Then say with me, Gemulah, Binah, Tebunah, (retribution, intelligence, prudence.)

Candidate repeats the words, when the Commander relieves him, and says— By the seven conditions, and by the power that is transmitted to me, which I have acquired by my discretion, my untired travels, zeal, fervor, and constancy, I receive you Grand Inspector of all Lodges, Grand Elect Knight Templar, and take rank among the Knights of Kadosh, or White and Black Eagle, which we bear the name of; I desire you not to forget it. It is indispensable for you, my brother, to mount the Mysterious Ladder, which you see there; it will serve to instruct you in the mysteries of our Order, and it is absolutely necessary that you should have a true knowledge of it. The candidate then ascends the ladder. When he is on the seventh or highest step, and has pronounced the three last words, the ladder is lowered, and the candidate passes over it. He cannot retire the same way, because he has taken an obligation never to turn back contrary to the interests and views of the Order: hence the ladder is lowered and he passes over it. He then reads the words at the bottom of the ladder, Ne plus ultra.

Commander—The Mysterious Ladder of seven steps which you have just passed is emblematical of the seven points of your obligation, and which are connected with the history of this degree.

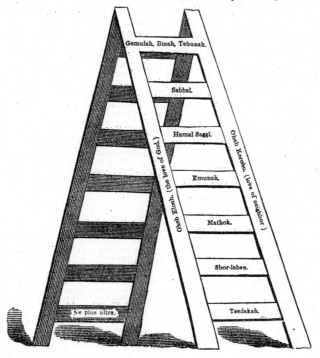

Commander now recites or reads to candidate a detailed history of the sufferings, burnings and final extirpation of the Knights Templars through the influence of the Catholic band of Knights of Malta, (not the Masonic Knights of that name.)

Commander gives one loud rap, and four Knights enter. He then gives to candidate the signs and token of the degree, as follows :

Sign—Place the right hand on the heart, the fingers separated; let the hand fall on the right thigh, bend the right knee, seize your poinard, raise it to the height of the shoulder as if to strike, and say NEKAM ADONAI. In some Chapters they merely let the hand fall from the heart to the right knee, which they grasp.

Order, or Saluting Sign—Hold your sword in the left hand, and place the right hand, with fingers separated, on the red cross which covers the heart.

Token—Place right foot to right foot, and knee to knee, present the right fist, the thumb elevated; companion seizes the fist, then presents his own, which you seize in like manner. Each now steps back a pace, and lifts his left arm as though to strike : one says NEKAMAH BEALIM, the other responds, PHARASLOL. Some Chapters use the token of Elect Nine. Others substitute for the words the question—Are you Kadosh ? and the response, Yes I am.

Commander now arms the candidate and decorates him with the attributes, and communicates the name he must take in future, which is uncommon to all others, and is Knight Kadosh, or Knight of the White and Black Eagle.

The Jewel is a red cross, as before described, but in the room of that now it is a black spread eagle with two heads, suspended to a broad order of fiery bloody color, worn from the left shoulder to right hip. The eagle, as if going to fly, with a naked sword in its claws.

This closes the initiation, and the Lecture in this degree is then given—Thrice Potent Grand Commander asking the questions, and Grand Chancellor, or Senior Warden, answering them.

Commander—Are you a Grand Elected Knight ?

Warden—I am.

Commander—Who received you in this degree ?

Warden—A worthy Deputy Grand Inspector, by consent of two others.

Commander—What was then done with you ?

Warden—He created me a Knight.

Commander—How can I believe you ?

Warden—My name, which I leave, will convince you.

Commander—What is your name ?

Warden—Kadosh, or Knight of the Black Eagle.

Commander—Was anything else done with you ?

Warden—The Deputy Inspector adorned me with the habit, ribbon, and jewel of the Order.

Commander—Where have you received the prize of your election ?

Warden—I have received it in a very deep grotto, in the silence of the night.

Commander—To what do you apply ?

Warden—I work with all my might and strength to raise an edifice worthy of my brothers.

Commander—What progress have you made ?

Warden—I have conquered the knowledge of the Mysterious Ladder.

Commander—Of what is that ladder composed ?

Warden—Two supporters and steps.

Commander—What are the names of the two supporters ?

Warden—Oheb Eloah, Oheb Kerobo.

Commander—What design have these two supporters ?

Warden—The first is the love of God, and the other the love of our neighbors.

Commander—What are the seven steps of the Mysterious Ladder ?

Warden—The virtues which I must practice, conformable to my obligations.

Commander—Name them to me.

Warden—Tsedakah, (or righteousness) practice or works of mercy. 2d. Shorlaban, (white ox, figuratively,) candor of our actions. 3d. Mathok, (sweetness,) sweetness of character, which all brethren must follow. 4th. Emunah, (truth in discourse.) 5th. Hamal saggi, (great labor,) advancement to the practice of Heaven. 6th. Sabbal, (a burden, or patience,) patience in adversity. 7th. Gemulah, Binah, Tebunah, (retribution, intelligence, prudence,) signifies that we must be prudent to keep secret every matter confided to us.

Commander—What are your ordinary pass-words ?

Warden—Manchin, name of the Grand Master most renowned among the Solitaries, known by the name of Kadosh.

Commander—What signifies that name?

Warden—Solitary, or separate.

Commander—What was the answer of the Solitaries, when they were asked to what they pretended ?

Warden—Abarekah, eth Adonai becol

heth, thamid tehillatho bepi, (see Psalm xxxiv. l,) which is, I will bless God at all times, and will praise him with my mouth.

Commander—Do they never say anything else ?

Warden—Yes, they say, also, Baahabah achullek him heani ; which is, I will assist the poor, and always sustain them with all my might and power.

Commander—How comes the cross surmounted with the eagle and the sword ?

Warden—That is, that I shall remember to employ my sword, in the fulness of time, under the banner of the black eagle, to support the Order.

Commander—Where did you work ?

Warden—In a place of security, to reestablish secretly the edifice ruined by the traitors.

Commander—What success do you expect from it ?

Warden—The right of virtue, the accord of brothers, the possessions of our forefathers, and everlasting happiness.

Commander—Have you shed tears ?

Warden—I have.

Commander—Have you ever worn the mourning ?

Warden—Yes, I wear it still.

Commander—Why do you wear it ?

Warden—Because virtue is despised, and as long as vice reigns innocence will be oppressed, and crimes will be left unpunished.

Commander—What is it that will punish vice and reward virtue ?

Warden—The Great Architect of the Universe alone.

Commander—How so ?

Warden—To favor our designs and desires. [Here every brother says three times, God favor our designs.]

Commander—Have you any other name than that of Kadosh, or Knight of the Black Eagle ?

Warden—I have still the name of Adam to teach me, that from the most low I must go up to the most high.

Commander—Give me the sign of knowledge against surprise.

Warden—Here it is. [Gives it in the following manner: he puts his right hand on the heart of a brother, in the same manner as with the poinard in the degree of Nine Elected—then gives the token of the Grand Elected, and then both strike the knee.]

Commander—How came you to carry your fingers extended on your heart ?

Warden—That my trust is in God.

Commander—How came you after that to extend your hand ?

Warden—To show to my brother that he is welcome to all in my power, and to encourage him to vengeance !

Commander—How came you to let your hand fall on your right knee ?

Warden—To show we must bend our knees to adore God.

In closing, Commander says—What is the hour ?

Warden—The break of day demonstrates.

Commander—If the break of day demonstrates, let us depart for revenge.

Grand Commander now puts his hand on his heart ; then lets it fall on his right knee, which is answered by all ; then the Grand Commander embraces each, and each the other all around, and then the Chapter is declared closed.

SUBLIME PRINCE OF THE ROYAL SECRET.

The meeting in this degree is termed a Sovereign Grand Consistory, and three apartments are necessary. They should be situated at least one story above the ground, and always on the top floor of the building. The first apartment is the guard room, and the second is the preparation room. The third apartment is occupied by members of the Consistory, is hung with black, sprinkled with tears, and has arranged in it death's heads, cross-bones, and skeletons. The throne is in the east, elevated by seven steps. On the throne is the chair of state, lined with black satin, flamed with red. Before the chair is a table covered with black satin, strewed with tears. On this cloth, in front, is a death's head and cross-bones ; over the death's head is the letter I ; and under the cross-bones is the letter M. On the table is placed a naked sword, a buckler, a sceptre, a balance, and a book containing the statutes of the Order. In the west is placed another table, covered with crimson, bordered with black, and strewed with tears; on the front of this cloth are the letters N K M K, in gold.

Sovereign Grand Commander, representing Frederick the Great, King of Prussia, is seated in a chair of State, on the throne. His dress is similar to that of a modern potentate, and he is armed with a sword and shield. On a table before him is a sceptre and a balance. The Lieutenant Commanders are dressed like the modern princes of Europe, and seated at the table in the west; their swords are crossed on the table. The Minister of State is placed at the Sovereign's right hand. The Grand Chancellor stands on the left hand of the Sovereign. Next to the Minister of State is placed the Grand Secretary. Next to the Grand Chancellor is placed the Grand Treasurer. Below the last named officers are placed on one side the Standard Bearer, the Grand Master Architect, and the Captain of the Guards. Below these officers are placed six members dressed in red, without aprons, wearing the jewel of the Order, suspended in front by a black ribbon.

The collar of the Order is black, edged with silver. On its point is embroidered in red a Teutonic-cross. On the middle of the cross is a double headed eagle in silver. The collar is lined with scarlet, on which is embroidered a black Teutonic cross. Around the waist is girded a black sash, embroidered with silver. A Teutonic cross is embroidered on the girdle to come in front. The jewel is a golden Teutonic cross. The collar, sash and jewel are worn by all the members.

The carpet representing the Camp is a nonagon, in which is inscribed a heptagon; in the heptagon is a pentagon; within this is an equilateral triangle, and in the triangle a circle. Between the heptagon and pentagon, upon the sides of the latter, are placed the standards of the five Standard Bearers, and the pavilions inscribed by the letters T E N G U. The emblems on the standard T are the Ark of the Covenant, an olive tree, and a lighted candlestick, on each side. The ground color of this standard is purple. On the ark is written the motto, Laus Deo. The standard E bears a golden lion, holding in his mouth a golden key, wearing around his neck a golden collar, on which is engraved 515. The ground is azure; the motto, Admajorem Dei glorium. On the standard N is an inflamed heart, in red, with two wings, surrounded by a laurel crown. The ground is white. The flag G bears a double headed eagle,

crowned, holding a sword in his right claw, and in his left a bloody heart. Ground is sea-green. The flag L has on it a black ox, (sable,) on a golden ground. On the sides of the nonagon are nine tents, and on its angles nine pendants, each belonging to its appropriate tent. The pendants are distinguished by numerals, and the tents by the letters I N O N X I L A S disposed from right to left. These tents signify the different grades of Masonry. Thus:

Tent S is Malachi—pendant, white, spotted with red; represents Knights of the East and West, and Princes of Jerusalem.

Tent A is Zerubbabel—pendant, light green; represents Knights of the East.

Tent L is Neamiah—pendant, red; represents Grand Elect, Perfect, and Sublime Masons.

Tent I is Hobben or Johaben—pendant, black and red; represents Sublime Elect, and Elect of Fifteen.

Tent X is Peleg—pendant, black; represents Elect of Nine. or Grand Master Architect.

Tent N is Joiada—pendant, red and black in lozenges; represents Provost and Judges.

Tent O is Aholiab—pendant, red and green; represents Intendant of the Buildings and Intimate Secretary.

Tent N is Joshua—pendant, green; represents Perfect Master.

Tent I is Ezra—pendant, blue; represents Master, Fellow Craft, and Entered Apprentice.

The equilateral triangle in the middle represents the centre of the army, and shows where the Knights of Malta are to be placed who have been admitted to our mysteries, and have proved themselves faithful guardians. They are to be joined with the Knights of Kadosh. The corps in the centre is to be commanded by five Princes, who command jointly or in rotation, according to their degrees, and receive their orders immediately from the Sovereign Grand Commander. These five Princes must place their standards in the five angles of the pentagon, as above described. Their names, as Standard Bearers, are as follows:

Standard T—Bezaleel.
Standard E—Aholiab.
Standard N—Mahuzen.
Standard G—Garimont.
Standard U—Amariah.

The heptagon points out the Encampment destined for the Princes of Libanus, Jerusalem, &c., and these are to receive their orders from the five Princes.

In opening the Consistory, the Sovereign Commander says—Salix.

Lieutenant Commanders all respond—Noni.

All together then say—Tengu.

Sovereign Commander gives the signs of this degree, and then of the other degrees, and all the members do the same.

Sovereign Commander—Let us imitate our Grand Master Jacques de Molay, Hiram Abiff, who to the last placed all his hopes in the Great Architect of the Universe; and pronounced the following words just as he passed from this transient life into eternal bliss :—Spes mea in Deo est, (My hope is in God.)

If a candidate is to be admitted, he must first be faithfully examined as a Knight of Kadosh. If the examination prove satisfactory, the Master of Ceremonies gives him the pass-word, which he repeats to the Lieutenant Commander at the door of the Consistory. The door is then opened, and Master of Ceremonies leads candidate up in front of the Sovereign Commander, who questions him as to his motives and desire to receive this degree, after which he administers the following obligation:

I, John Smith, do, of my own free will and accord, in the presence of the Grand Architect of the Universe, and in this Consistory of Sovereign Princes of the Royal Secret, or Knights of St. Andrew, faithful guardians of the faithful treasure; most solemnly vow and swear, under all the different penalties of my former obligations, that I will never directly or indirectly reveal or make known to any person or persons whatsoever, any or the least part of this Royal degree, unless to one duly qualified in the body of a regularly constituted Consistory of the same, or to him or them whom I shall find such after strict and due trial. I furthermore vow and swear, under the above penalties, to always abide and regulate myself agreeably to the statutes and regulations now before me; and when in a Consistory to behave and demean myself as one worthy of being honored with so high a degree, that no part of my conduct may in the least reflect discredit on the Royal Consistory, or disgrace on myself. So may God maintain me in equity and justice! Amen! Amen! Amen! Amen!

The signs and words in this degree are then given to candidate, as follows:

Sign—Place the right hand on the heart; extend it forward, the palm downwards; let it fall by the right side.

Sacred words—Those of the Carpet,

which are to be read backward around the circle from right to left, thus: One says Salix, and the other Noni; both then repeat (by letters) the word Tengu.

Pass-words—Phual Kol, Pharas Kol, Nekam Makah, both pronounce (by lettering) the word Shaddai.

The Sovereign Commander then delivers to candidate the charge:

My dear brother: The Saracens having taken possession of the Holy Land, those who were engaged in the Crusades not being able to expel them, agreed with Godfrey de Bouillon, the conductor and chief of the Crusaders, to veil the mysteries of religion under emblems by which they would be able to maintain the devotion of the soldier, and protect themselves from the incursion of those who were their enemies, after the example of the Scriptures, the style of which is figurative. Those zealous brethren chose Solomon's Temple for their model. This building has strong allusions to the Christian church. Since that period they (Masons) have been known by the name of Master Architect; and they have employed themselves in improving the law of that admirable Master. From hence it appears that the mysteries of the Craft are the mysteries of religion. Those brethren were careful not to entrust this important secret to any whose discretion they had not proved. For this reason they invented different degrees to try those who entered among them; and only gave them symbolic secrets, without explanation, to prevent treachery, and to make themselves known only to each other. For this purpose it was resolved to use different signs, words, and tokens, in every degree, by which they would be secured against cowans and Saracens The different degrees were fixed first to the number of seven by the example of the Grand Architect of the Universe, who built all things in six days and rested on the seventh. This is distinguished by the seven points of reception in the Master's degree. Enoch employed six days to construct the arches, and on the seventh, having deposited the secret treasure in the lowest arch, was translated to the abodes of the blessed. Solomon employed six years in constructing his Temple; and celebrated its dedication on the seventh, with all the solemnity worthy of the divinity himself. This sacred edifice we choose to make the basis of figurative Masonry. In the first degree are three symbols to be applied. First, the first of the creation, which was only chaos, is figured by the candidate's coming out of the black chamber, neither naked nor clothed, deprived, &c.; and his suffering the painful trial at his reception, &c. The candidate sees nothing before he is brought to light; and his powers of imagination relative to what he is to go through are suspended, which alludes to the figure of the creation of that vast luminous body confused among the other parts of creation before it was extracted from darkness and fixed by the Almighty FIAT. Secondly, the candidate approaches the footstool of the Master, and there renounces all cowans; he promises to subdue his passions, by which means he is united to virtue, and, by his regularity of life, demonstrates what he proposes. This is figured to him by the steps that he takes in approaching the altar; the symbolic meaning of which is the separation of the firmament from the earth and water on the second day of creation. [The charge proceeds by giving a figurative interpretation of the ceremonies, &c. of the first and second parts of the third degree.]

In the Master's degree is represented the assassination of Hiram by false brethren. This ought to put us in mind of the fate of Adam, occasioned by perverseness in his disobeying his great and awful Creator. The symbolic mystery of the death of Hiram Abiff represents to us that of the Messiah; for the three blows which were given to Hiram Abiff, at the three gates of the Temple, allude to the three points of condemnation against Christ, at the High Priest's Caiphas, Herod, and Pilate. It was from the last that he was led to that most violent and excruciating death. The said three blows with the square, guage, and gavel, are symbols of the blow on the cheek, the flagellation, and the crown of thorns. The brethren assembled around the tomb of Hiram, is a representation of the disciples lamenting the death of Christ on the Cross. The Master's word, which is said to be lost since the death of Hiram Abiff, is the same that Christ pronounced on the cross, and which the Jews did not comprehend, "Eli, Eli, lama sabacthani," "My God, my God, why hast thou forsaken me? have pity on and forgive my enemies"—Instead of which words were substituted, M. B. N. (Mac-be-nac,) which, in Arabian, signifies, "The son of the widow is dead." The false brethren represent Judas Iscariot, who sold Christ. The red collar worn by the Grand Elect Perfect and Sublime Masons, calls to remembrance the blood of Christ. The sprig of cassia is the figure of the cross, because of this wood was the cross made. The captivity of the Grand Elect and Sublime Masons, (i. e. by the Chaldeans,) shows us the persecution of the Christian religion under the Roman emperors, and its liberty under Constantine the Great. It also calls to our remembrance the persecution of the Templars, and the situation of Jacques de Molay, who, lying in irons nearly seven years, at the end of which our worthy Grand Master was burnt alive with his four companions, on the eleventh of March 1314, creating pity and tears in the people, who saw him die with firmness and heroic constancy, sealing his innocence with his blood.

My dear brother, in passing to the degree of Perfect Master, in which you shed tears at the tomb of Hiram Abiff, and in some other degrees, has not your heart been led to revenge? Has not the crime of Jubelum Akirop been represented in the most hideous light? Would it be unjust to compare the conduct of Philip the Fair to his, and the infamous accusers of the Templars to the two ruffians who were accomplices with Akirop? Do they not kindle in your heart an equal aversion? The different stages you have traveled, and the time you have taken in learning these historical events, no doubt will lead you to make the proper applications; and by the degree of Master Elect and Kadosh, you are properly disposed to fulfil all your engagements, and to bear an implacable hatred to the Knights of Malta, and to avenge the death of Jacques de Molay. Your extensive acquaintance with symbolic Masonry, which you have attained by your discretion, leaves you nothing more to desire here. You see, my dear brother, how, and by whom, Masonry has come to us. You are to endeavor by every just means to regain our rights, and to remember that we are joined by a society of men, whose courage, merit, and good conduct, hold out to us that rank that birth alone gave to our ancestors. You are now on the same level with them. Avoid every evil by keeping your obligations, and carefully conceal from the vulgar what you are, and wait that happy moment when we all shall be reunited under the same Sovereign in the mansions of eternal bliss. Let us imitate the example of our Grand Master, Jacques de Molay, who to the end put his hope in God, and at his last dying moments ended his life saying, Spes mea in Deo est!

In closing the Consistory, the Sovereign Commander inquires the hour, which is reported to be the fifth after sunset. He then says—Salix.

The Lieutenant Commanders and members respond as in the opening.

Sovereign Commander—Spes mea in Deo est! Let us depart.

SOVEREIGN GRAND INSPECTOR GENERAL.

This degree is conferred only on elected members of a Supreme Council, which is the governing body of Masons in any country. In the United States two Supreme Councils are allowed, which is an exception to the general rule. The number of working Inspector Generals cannot exceed nine, though there may be any number of honorary members.

A Supreme Council in this degree is hung with purple, with skeletons, skulls, cross-bones, &c. painted or embroidered thereon. The throne in the east is under a purple canopy, which is trimmed with gold. Over it, and beneath the canopy, is a transparency representing a Delta, in the centre of which is seen the ineffable name in Hebrew. Near the centre of the room is a quadrangular pedestal covered with scarlet cloth, on which rests an open Bible, with a naked sword across it. North of this pedestal stands a skeleton holding in its left hand the white banner of the Order, and in its right hand a poinard in the attitude of striking. Over the door of entrance, inside, is the motto of the Order, embroidered on a blue scarf, viz. : "Deus mcmque jus."

In the east there is a chandelier of five branches; in the south one of two branches; in the west one of three; and in the north a single bracket—making eleven lights in all.

Most Potent Sovereign Grand Commander, representing Frederick the Great, King of Prussia, is seated on the throne in the east. He is dressed in a crimson satin robe, trimmed with white, wears a crown, and holds a naked sword in his right hand.

There is but one Warden, seated in the west, and he is styled the Illustrious Lieutenant Grand Commander. He is dressed in a blue satin robe, wears a ducal crown, and he also holds a naked sword in his right hand.

The other officers are an Illustrious Treasurer of the Holy Empire—Secretary, Master of Ceremonies, and Captain of the Guards, all styled Illustrious.

The members are styled Illustrious Sovereign Grand Inspectors General; and all, including officers, wear the Order and Jewel of the degree, and in addition, a red Teutonic cross attached to the left side of the coat.

The Order (worn as a scarf) is a broad white watered silk ribbon, trimmed with gold, and with a white, red and green rosette (also trimmed with gold) at the bottom. Where it crosses the breast there is a golden Delta embroidered on it, surrounded with rays, and in its centre the figures 33 : on each side a golden dagger pointing towards the centre. The Jewel is a two-headed black eagle, crowned, with wings extended, and holding a sword in its talons : the beak, claws and dagger are of gold. It is worn suspended from the Order.

In opening, the Sovereign Commander raps four and one, two and one, then one, and then two, which raps are repeated by the Warden. He then gives the order that the Supreme Council shall now be opened for the dispatch of business. The Warden thereupon declares the Council open.

In admitting a candidate to this degree, no particular ceremony is performed. He must be balloted for after a vacancy among working members has occurred. He is introduced by the Master of Ceremonies, kneels at the altar and takes the following oath :

I, John Smith, do hereby swear and promise on my word of honor, on the faith of an honest man, in the presence of the Grand Architect of the Universe, and before this assembly, to guard and preserve the mysteries of this degree which has been conferred on me, not only from the profane, but from all of an inferior degree, under the penalties of all my former obligations ; and I consent, if I violate this obligation, to have my tongue torn out by the roots. May God keep me in this, or destroy me. Amen.

The candidate is then instructed in the signs and words of the degree.

First sign—Hold the hand to the mouth as if about to grasp the tongue. Second sign—Throw off the hand, opening it at the same instant.

Sacred words—Nekamah Baelim ; the brother answers, Begoal Kol. The brothers then embrace, at the same time saying Adonai.

Pass-words—For entry, Nekam ; the brother answers, Menachem. For retiring, Phual Kol ; the brother answers, Pharas Kol.

In closing, the Sovereign Commander

raps as in the opening, and inquires of the Warden—What is the hour?

Warden—The morning sun has appeared in the east, and illumines the Council.

Sovereign—It is then time to close our Council. Our Illustrious Lieutenant will please to notify the Grand Inspectors that we are about to adjourn. The Warden gives the notice, the signs, &c., are given, and the Council is then closed.

KNIGHT OF THE EAST,
OR SWORD.

This degree is seldom conferred, and is therefore left out of its proper order, which is introductory to that of Prince of Jerusalem. It is founded upon Zerubbabel's first journey to Persia, when he obtained permission and means from Cyrus, the King, (father of Darius,) to rebuild the Temple at Jerusalem. Those who accompanied him were called Knights of the East, or Knights of the Sword, and they were afterwards created Princes of Jerusalem.

There are two apartments used in this degree. The first is hung with green on the east, west, and north sides, so as to leave a space of six feet between the hangings and the wall. The space enclosed is an oblong square. It represents the apartment of Cyrus, King of Persia: the throne is in the east, two arm chairs in the west, and the seats for the members in the south. Behind the throne is a transparency, representing the dream of Cyrus, (mentioned hereafter,) and above, near the ceiling, is a triangular glory, and in it the ineffable name (Jehovah) in Hebrew. The glory rests on a luminous cloud, from which an eagle is issuing, with a label in its beak, and on it the words, "Give liberty to the captives." Below appear Nebuchadnezzar and Belshazzar, as captives loaded with chains. There should be an imitation wall around within this apartment, forming a long square. On each corner, and on each side of the wall, there should be towers, six in all. At the foot of the square, in the west, there should be a large tower, with two doors, one opening within the enclosure, and one outside in the space between the wall and the second apartment. There should be an arched bridge between this tower and the door of the second apartment, which is supposed to cross the river Euphrates.

The second apartment represents the Court of the Temple, at Jerusalem, and is hung with red. The carpet represents the furniture of the holy and most holy places. Above the ark, the Shekinah, (symbol of the presence of Jehovah,) is represented by a lamb reposing on a book sealed with seven seals. At the corner of the Temple is the column Boaz, broken. The carpet is covered with black, which is removed at the proper time for its being uncovered.

In the first apartment the presiding officer dresses in royal robes, and represents Cyrus, King of Persia, and is called Sovereign: Senior Warden represents Nebuzaradan, and is styled First General: Junior Warden (representing Mithridates) is called Second General. The other officers are a Chancellor, Grand Master of Ceremonies, Master of Dispatches, and Captain of the Guards. The brethren in this apartment are dressed in yellow or red robes, and wear turbans with suns embroidered in front. The Sovereign carries a sceptre. Wardens and brethren have naked swords in their hands, and wear green ribbon scarfs without any jewel. Apron, white, lined and bordered with green, without any emblems.

In the second apartment the presiding officer represents Ananias, and is styled Most Excellent Grand Master. He is seated in the east, wears a crown, and holds a gavel in his hand. The Senior Warden is seated in the west, and wears as a jewel a square within three triangles. The Junior Warden, in the south, wears a level within three triangles. In addition to these there is in this apartment a Grand Captain of the Guards, who dresses like the other brethren. The Master and officers wear their jewels suspended from the neck, by green ribbons, and the brethren from the bottom of green cordons. The jewel of the Master is a triple triangle enclosed in a circle. The other officers wear the usual jewel in a triple triangle, which is a gold medal with the five orders of architecture upon it, and covered by two steel cross-swords. The brethren wear the triple triangle, crossed by two swords, the hilts resting on the level. The jewels are of gold. Each brother has a trowel suspended from the string of his apron.

Council is opened in first apartment.

Sovereign—My brethren, assist me to open a Council of Knights of the Sword.

First General (or Warden)—Attention, Knights, you will assist our Sovereign in opening the Council.

Second General repeats this order.

Sovereign to First General—Brother

Senior, you will see that our Council chamber is well guarded, and that all present are true Knights.

First General goes and questions the Captain of the Guards—returns and says —Sovereign Master, we are well guarded from the eyes of the profane, and I observe that all present are true Knights of the Sword.

Sovereign—What is the time ?

First General—This day completes the seventy years of captivity.

Sovereign—Generals, Princes, and Knights, I have long since resolved to liberate the Jews who are in captivity : I am wearied with seeing them in chains; but before I liberate them I wish to consult you respecting a dream which I have had this night, and which requires an interpretation. I imagined I saw a ferocious lion about to throw himself on me and devour me—his appearance terrified me, and I hastily looked for some shelter from his fury ; but at that instant I saw my two predecessors, habited as slaves, beneath a glory, which Masons designate by the name of the Grand Architect of the Universe. I was made to understand two words which I saw issuing from a blazing star : they signified, Liberate the captives ; and I understood if I did not do this my crown would pass from me to strangers. I remained speechless and confused, and suddenly awoke. From that instant my tranquility fled. It remains for you, Princes, to assist me with your advice on this occasion.

While the Sovereign is speaking, the brethren cast their eyes downwards: when he is done they look at the First General, who draws his sword, and elevates the point, with his arm extended in front. The brethren draw their swords, placing them in the same position. The First General now points his sword downwards to signify his agreement with the Sovereign, then upwards again to signify liberty. The brethren all imitate him.

Sovereign—Let the Captivity be finished. Generals, Princes and Knights, this Council is open.

First and Second Generals each proclaim that the Council is open.

If a candidate is to be admitted, his hands are first bound with a chain of triangular links. He represents Zerubbabel as a captive. The Master of Ceremonies leads him to the door of the tower, where he is thus interrogated by the Guards :

Captain of Guards—What do you wish ?

Candidate—I wish, if possible, to speak with your Sovereign.

Captain of Guards—Who are you ?

Candidate—The first among my equals, by rank a Mason, and by misfortune a captive.

Captain of the Guards—What is your name ?

Candidate—Zerubbabel.

Captain of Guards—What is your age ?

Candidate—Seventy years.

Captain of Guards—What is the cause of this application ?

Candidate—The tears and misery of my brethren.

Captain of Guards—We will endeavor to make your sad request known to our Sovereign.

The Captain of the Guards knocks five and two at the door of the tower. This is repeated ; one by the Second General, two by the First General, and three by the Sovereign.

The Second General says—The Guard knocks at the door of the tower, in the manner of a Knight of the Sword.

First General—Sovereign Master, the Guard knocks at the tower.

Sovereign—Brother Senior, probably some one is to be introduced ; be prudent ; in my present embarrassed state the least advice is not to be disregarded.

The Second General goes to the door of the tower, knocks, and it is opened.

The Captain of the Guards lays aside his spear, comes before the Sovereign, crosses his arms, bows, and says—The first among Masons, his equals, aged seventy years, wishes to appear before you.

Sovereign—When he shall have been introduced into the tower of the palace, we will examine him.

The Guard bows, retires, and makes the candidate enter the tower, which is closed on him. The Sovereign questions candidate through the door, which is shut.

Sovereign—What is the cause of this application ?

Candidate—I come to implore the justice and benevolence of the Sovereign.

Sovereign—For what purpose ?

Candidate—That mercy may be shown to my brethren, who have been in captivity seventy years.

Sovereign—What is your name ?

Candidate—Zerubbabel ; I am the first among my equals ; by rank a Mason, by misfortune a captive.

Sovereign—What is that mercy which you demand of me ?

Candidate—That, under the protection of the Grand Architect of the Universe, the King will restore our liberty and allow us to return and rebuild the Temple of our God.

Sovereign—Since motives so just have conducted you hither, you are permitted to appear in our presence.

The Guards open the door of the tower, and cause the captive to prostrate himself in the west.

Sovereign—Zerubbabel, I have, like you, lamented the severity of your captivity. I promise to grant you liberty instantly, if you will communicate to me the secrets of Masonry, for which I have always entertained profound veneration.

Candidate—Sovereign Master, when Solomon communicated to us the first principles of Masonry, he informed us that equality was its foundation. Equality does not reign here; and your rank, your titles, and your court, are not admissible in the place where instruction is given in our mysteries. Besides, our exterior marks are unknown to you; my engagements are inviolable; I am unable to reveal our secrets, and if liberty is to be obtained at this price, I prefer captivity

Sovereign—I admire the discretion and the virtue of Zerubbabel; he deserves liberty as a reward for his firmness.

The brethren assent, by pointing their swords downwards, and then upwards.

Sovereign to Second General—Cause Zerubbabel to undergo the seventy trials, which I reduce to three, viz., 1st—That of the body; 2d. That of his courage; 3d. That of his mind; after which, perhaps, he may merit the favor which he demands.

The Second General causes him to go round the Lodge three times. The first time, a small shell is exploded; the second time, he is examined to ascertain whether he persists in his demand; the third time, he holds his hands at the top of his forehead. After this, the Second General knocks seven, and the First General says—What do you wish?

Second General—The candidate has submitted to his trials with firmness and constancy.

Sovereign—Zerubbabel, I grant to you the favor which you solicit, and consent that you shall be set at liberty.

Sovereign knocks seven, which is the signal at which the Generals divest Zerubbabel of his chains.

Sovereign—Return to your own country; I permit you to rebuild the Temple destroyed by my ancestors; its treasures shall be sent to you before the setting of the sun: you shall be acknowledged chief over your brethren. I ordain that all shall obey you in the country through which you shall pass; that they shall render you assistance as though it were to myself; I will only exact a tribute from you of three lambs, five sheep, and seven rams, which I will receive under the porch of the new Temple : if I demand this, it is rather in remembrance of the friendship which I have promised you, than as a reward. Come hither.

The Generals place candidate at the foot of the throne.

Sovereign—I arm you with this sword, as a mark of your superiority over your equals; I am persuaded you will employ it only in their defence, and I create you a Knight of the Sword.

In saying these last words, the Sovereign strikes him with his sword on the shoulders, and then raises him. He gives candidate the apron, and green cordon, which passes from left to right, and says —As a mark of my esteem, I decorate you with an apron and sash, which I have adopted in imitation of the workmen of your Temple. Though these decorations are not accompanied with any mysteries, yet I confer them on the princes of my court as marks of honor; henceforth you enjoy the same honor. I now commit you to the care of Nebuzaradan, (Master of Ceremonies,) who will give you guides to conduct you in safety to your brethren, in the place where to found the new Temple. Thus I decree !

The First General leads the candidate and places him in the tower, where he remains while the brethren silently pass into the second apartment. After they are in order, the candidate is led out and then conducted to the bridge. At its entrance he is opposed by guards, who rob him of his apron and sash, and endeavor to prevent his passage ; he attacks, drives them off, and arrives at the door of the second apartment, where the Master of Ceremonies knocks seven at the door. When the brethren hear the alarm, they detach the trowel from their aprons, and hold it in the left hand, and the sword in the right. The Second General (or Junior Warden as he is now called) knocks seven. This is repeated by the First General (or Senior Warden.)

Junior Warden—I hear a knocking at the door of the Lodge, in the manner of Knights of the Sword.

Senior Warden—Most Excellent Master, some one knocks at the door of the Lodge, after the manner of the Knights of the Sword.

Master—Brother Junior Warden, see who knocks.

Junior Warden goes, knocks, and opening the door, says—What do you wish ?

Candidate—I wish to see my brethren, that I may inform them of my deliverance from Babylon, and that of the unhappy remnant of the fraternity, which has been freed from captivity.

Junior Warden shuts the door and reports to the Master, who says—The news which the captive brings is true : seventy years are expired, and the day has arrived for rebuilding the Temple. Ask the captive his name, his age, and country, for fear of surprise.

Junior Warden knocks seven, opens the door, and says—What is your name ?

Candidate—Zerubbabel.

Junior Warden—What is your age ?

Candidate—Seventy years.

Junior Warden—Where is your country situated ?

Candidate—On this side of the river Staburzania, to the west of Assyria.

Junior Warden shuts the door, reports to Senior Warden, who reports to the Master, who says—His name is Zerubbabel, his country lies on this side of the river Staburzania, his age seventy years ; yes, my brethren, the captivity is ended ! The captive is truly the Prince of the sovereign tribe which is to rebuild the Temple. Let him be admitted among us and acknowledged as the one who is to direct and assist our labors.

Junior Warden knocks, opens the door, and conducts the candidate to the west.

Senior Warden—Most Excellent Master, behold Zerubbabel, who demands to be admitted into our fraternity !

Master—Zerubbabel, give us an exact relation of your deliverance.

Candidate—Cyrus gave me permission to approach the foot of his throne, he was touched with the miseries of the fraternity, he armed me with this sword, for the defence of my brethren, and honored me with the title of brother among his companions. He finally granted me my freedom, and committed me to the care of his faithful subjects, who conducted me on my journey, and assisted me in conquering our enemies at the passage of the river Staburzania, where, notwithstanding our victory, we lost the marks of distinction which had been given to us by the king, our deliverer.

Master—My brother, the loss which you have met with shows that the justice of our fraternity would not endure the triumph of pomp and grandeur. In decorating you with these honors, Cyrus was not guided by that spirit of equality which has always characterized you. By this loss, all the marks of distinction received from that prince have disappear-ed, but you have preserved those of true Masonry ; but before I can communicate to you those secrets, which, since our captivity have been preserved among the remnant of our fraternity, we must require of you assurances that you have not lost the sentiments, or the knowledge of Masonry, during your servitude.

Candidate—Examine me ; I am prepared to answer.

Master—What degree in Masonry have you received ?

Candidate—The degree of Most Excellent Master.

Master—Give me the sign.

Candidate gives the sign of Most Excellent Master, as on page 61.

Master—Give me the grip.

Grip given as on page 61.

Master—My brethren Knights, I believe Zerubbabel is worthy to participate in our new mysteries.

The brethren assent by elevating their swords.

Master—Most Powerful Senior Warden, cause the candidate to advance by three steps ; and at the third, let him kneel at the foot of the throne of the Grand and Sublime Architect, where he will make the engagements which we require.

Candidate advances by three steps to the altar, kneels, and takes the following obligation :

I, John Smith, do hereby premise, under the same obligations which I have contracted in the different degrees of Masonry, never to reveal the secrets of the Knights of the Sword, or Free Masons, to any one of an inferior degree, or to any one who is not a Mason, under the penalty of enduring a captivity so rigorous that my chains shall never be broken, and that my body be exposed to the beasts of the forest, and that a thunderbolt may dash me to atoms, as an example to others who are indiscreet. So mote it be.

The Master raises the candidate, and (while he and the brethren are sheathing their swords) says—My brethren, the destruction of the Temple subjected Masons to such severe calamities, we have feared lest their captivity and dispersion might have impaired their fidelity to their engagements ; for this reason, we have been obliged, while rebuilding the Temple, to remain in a secret and retired place, where we carefully preserve some ruins of the ancient Temple. We do not introduce any to that place, unless we know them to be true and worthy Masons, not alone by their signs, words, and grips, but also by their conduct; to such we communicate our new secrets with pleasure, but we require, as a pledge, that they should bring with them some remains or monuments of the ancient Temple; those which Cyrus has given to you are sufficient.

While these last words are pronounced, the captive is uncovered.

Master—Most Powerful Senior Warden, cause the candidate to recede three steps, that he may learn that we esteem perfect resignation as a Masonic virtue.

Candidate recedes towards the west.

Master—My brother, the object of our labors is to rebuild the Temple of the Grand Architect of the Universe; this sublime work has been reserved for Zerubbabel. The engagements into which you with us have entered under that name, require you to aid us in rebuilding the Temple in its splendor. The sword which Cyrus has given you, is to be used in defending your brethren, and punishing those who would profane the august Temple which we raise to the glory of the Holy One of Israel. It is on these conditions you participate in our secrets. The pass-word is LIBERTAS. Go give the brethren of this Lodge the signs, grips, and words, and return to me.

Candidate goes by the north, and returns by the south.

Master—My brother, after your deliverance Cyrus had you created a Masonic Knight, and I now present you with the trowel, the symbol of your new dignity, that hereafter you may labor with the trowel in one hand, and use the sword with the other, if the Temple should ever be destroyed, for it is in that manner we have proceeded to rebuild it.

Master gives the girdle and says—This scarf ought always to accompany you in all Lodges: you will have a mark of true Knighthood, which you acquired at the river Staburzania, by the victory obtained over those who opposed your passage! Master gives the green rosette, and says—Though we do not admit among our ceremonies any of the decorations given you by Cyrus, yet we are willing to preserve their remembrance by a rosette of that color which he had chosen, and we affix it to your cordon. [Gives the Jewel.] This Jewel is a badge of the Knights of the Sword; may justice and equity, represented by the sword, be your guides!

Master (giving the gloves)—We proceed to proclaim you a Knight of the Sword. My brethren, see that Zerubbabel shall hereafter rule the labors of Masonry!

They assent by saluting with swords

Candidate is then conducted to a chair designed for him, the Master saying—My brother, ascend the throne of the Sovereigns of our Lodges; preserve the triangular stone of this edifice, and rule the laborers as Solomon, Hiram of Tyre, and Joabert have done before you.

When the candidate is seated, the brethren sheath their swords, clap their hands three times, crying Zerubbabel each time.

The Lecture is now given.

In closing, the Master says to the Senior Warden—Are you a Knight of the Sword?

Senior Warden—Look! (places his hand on his sword.)

Master—Give me the sign.

Senior Warden gives the sign, as follows: Carry the right hand to the left shoulder, and move it downwards to the right hip with a serpentine motion; this represents the motion of waves. Draw your sword and bring it to the guard.

Master—Give me the words and the pass-word.

Senior Warden—Judah, Benjamin, and Libertas.

Master—Give the grip to the Junior Warden.

Given as on page 61.

Master—Where have you labored?

Senior Warden—At the rebuilding of the Temple.

Master—What hour is it?

Senior Warden—The hour of commencing that work.

Master—My brethren, since we have sufficient time to rebuild the Temple of the Lord, let us remember these things in silence. It is time to repose. Brothers Senior and Junior Wardens, announce in the south and in the north, that I am about to close this Lodge of Knights of the Sword.

Senior Warden makes proclamation that the Most Excellent Grand Master is about to close the Lodge.

Junior Warden does the same.

Master (rapping seven)—The Lodge is closed. Retire in peace.

Warders repeat this, and the Lodge is then closed.

THE END.

Lightning Source UK Ltd.
Milton Keynes UK
UKOW04f2017040716

277699UK00005B/74/P